GOD AND TIME

GOD AND TIME
Essays on the
Divine Nature

EDITED BY
Gregory E. Ganssle
and
David M. Woodruff

OXFORD
UNIVERSITY PRESS

2002

OXFORD
UNIVERSITY PRESS

Oxford   New York
Athens   Auckland   Bangkok   Bogotá   Buenos Aires   Cape Town
Chennai   Dar es Salaam   Delhi   Florence   Hong Kong   Istanbul   Karachi
Kolkata   Kuala Lumpur   Madrid   Melbourne   Mexico City   Mumbai   Nairobi
Paris   São Paulo   Shanghai   Singapore   Taipei   Tokyo   Toronto   Warsaw

and associated companies in
Berlin   Ibadan

Published by Oxford University Press, Inc.
198 Madison Avenue, New York, New York 10016

Oxford is a registered trademark of Oxford University Press

Library of Congress Cataloging-in-Publication Data
God and time: essays on the divine nature / edited by Gregory E. Ganssle and David M. Woodruff.
    p.   cm.
Includes bibliographical references and index.
ISBN 0-19-512965-2
1. God—Immutability.   2. Time—Religious aspects.   I. Ganssle, Gregory E., 1956–
II. Woodruff, David M., 1960–
BT153.I47 .G64 2001
212'.7—dc21   00-068152

9 8 7 6 5 4 3 2 1

Printed in the United States of America
on acid-free paper

For Jeanie and for Ann

Acknowledgments

We have many people to thank for helping us in this project. We benefited greatly from early encouragement from William Lane Craig and Michael Della Rocca. Daniel Howard-Snyder provided much encouragement, especially through organizing the Pacific Society of Christian Philosophers conference in April of 1999 at George Fox University at which several of these papers were presented and vigorously discussed. Our editor at Oxford University Press, Peter Ohlin, also has been extremely patient and helpful. The writers of these essays were patient and kind to read and consider yet another batch of comments. Most of all, we thank our wives, Jeanie Ganssle and Ann Woodruff for love, support, and friendship and for showing the most patience of all.

Contents

Contributors

DOUGLAS K. BLOUNT is Assistant Professor of Philosophy of Religion at Southwestern Baptist Theological Seminary.

WILLIAM LANE CRAIG is Research Professor of Philosophy at Talbot School of Theology.

GARRETT DEWEESE is Associate Professor of Philosophy at Talbot School of Theology.

GREGORY E. GANSSLE is Philosophy faculty at Rivendell Institute for Christian Thought and Learning.

WILLIAM HASKER is Emeritus Professor of Philosophy at Huntington College.

PAUL HELM is Emeritus Professor of Philosophy at King's College University of London.

BRIAN LEFTOW is Professor of Philosophy at Fordhan University.

ALAN G. PADGETT is Professor of Systematic Theology at Luther Seminary in St. Paul.

THOMAS D. SENOR is Associate Professor and Chair of the Philosophy Department at University of Arkansas.

QUENTIN SMITH is Professor of Philosophy at Western Michigan University.

EDWARD R. WIERENGA is Professor of Religion at University of Rochester.

DAVID M. WOODRUFF is Assistant Professor of Philosophy at Huntington College.

DEAN W. ZIMMERMAN is Associate Professor of Philosophy at Syracuse University.

GOD AND TIME

Introduction

GREGORY E. GANSSLE

God's Eternal Nature

Philosophical explorations into the nature of God have enjoyed a rehabilitation of reputation in recent years. Nearly every aspect of every divine attribute has been the focus of careful scrutiny. One aspect of the divine nature that has been in the center of much of this work is God's relation to time. From Augustine through Aquinas, the position held overwhelmingly by philosophers was that God is atemporal. God, on this view, is outside time. Most philosophers today disagree. While affirming that God is eternal, they understand his eternality as his being temporally everlasting. He exists at all times and through all times.[1]

The claim that God is atemporal is often taken to contain two parts. First, God exists but does not exist at any temporal location. Rather than holding that God is everlastingly eternal and, therefore, he exists at all times, these philosophers claim that God exists but he does not exist *at* any time at all. God is beyond time altogether. Second, it is thought that God does not experience temporal succession. If past and future events exist, then God's relation to each event in a temporal sequence is the same as his relation to any other event. God does not experience the birth of Caesar before he experiences the birth of Hitler. Both of these events are experienced by God in the "eternal now." It is often thought that there is duration in the life of God even if he is atemporal. This duration, however, is not *temporal* duration. In this view, God's being, although atemporal, is very different than that of an abstract object such as a number or a Platonic Form.[2] Although most thinkers who hold that God is atemporal hold both that God's existence is not temporally located and that he does not experience temporal succession, it is possible to hold the second without holding the first. In other words, some people think that God has temporal location but does not experience temporal succession.

3

The majority position, as we have said, is that God is everlasting. That is, God never began to exist and he will never go out of existence. God does, however, experience temporal succession. God experiences some events (e.g., the birth of Caesar) before he experiences other events (e.g., the birth of Hitler). Philosophers who hold this view also think that God's existence has temporal location. He exists at the present moment (and he has existed at each past moment and he will exist at each future moment).

Other philosophers think that neither of these alternatives is adequate. God's relation to time cannot be captured by either of the categories of temporal or atemporal. God, in their view, is in some third kind of relation to time. One "in-between" position is that God is best thought of as "omnitemporal."[3] God, on this view, is not in our time but he experiences temporal succession in his being. Our time is constituted by physical time (the kind of time measured in physics). God's time (metaphysical time) has no intrinsic metric and is constituted purely by the sequence of God's mental states. Whether the conception of an omnitemporal God is more like the conception of an atemporal God or more like the conception of a temporal God is an open question. Some will want to argue that this in-between view is better thought of as being a slight variation of one of the more widely held positions than as being a separate position in its own right.

There are several issues that help determine how best to think of God's relation to time. One issue includes other aspects of God's nature. What we want to say about God's power or knowledge or omnipresence is relevant to developing an adequate understanding of God's relation to time. Many issues besides what God himself is like will also enter our investigation of God's relation to time. Some of the most obvious include the nature of time, the nature of change, and the origin of the universe.

We bring these issues into our investigation in a number of ways. First, there may be an outright inconsistency between some of the things we hold about the nature of God or of time or the universe, on the one hand, and what we want to say about his relation to time, on the other. Such an inconsistency would provide a sufficient reason to modify our view of God's attributes (or our view of time) or to modify our understanding of his relation to time. The second consideration is that, short of an outright inconsistency, perhaps some of what we think is true about God or the world is *better explained* either by the view that God is in time or by the view that he is outside time. Of course it is likely that much of what we think is true about time or the universe is neutral regarding God's relation to time.

The Nature of Divine Knowledge

What issues concerning the divine nature are relevant to God's relation to time? The most prominent in the literature is the nature of God's knowledge. God is taken to be omniscient and infallible. He knows everything that can be known and he is never wrong. Anything God assents to is true. God's exhaustive knowledge raises the question of whether God can foreknow future free actions. This puzzle has a long and detailed history. In fact, the position that God is not temporal but is atemporal is often cited as the best solution to the apparent inconsistency between human freedom and divine foreknowledge. If God is atemporal, after all, he does not *fore*know anything. His knowledge of any event is not itself temporally located. If it is not temporally located, it is not located prior to the free choice in question. Boethius, Anselm, Aquinas, and many others have appealed to God's atemporality to solve this problem.

While the atemporalist's proposal seems to offer a good strategy, at least one significant problem remains. This problem is that of prophecy. Suppose God tells Moses, among other things, that you will mow your lawn next Saturday. Now we have a different situation entirely. While God's knowledge that you will mow your lawn is not temporally located, Moses' knowledge that you will mow your lawn *is* temporally located. Furthermore, since the information came from God, Moses cannot be mistaken about the future event.

The prophet problem is a problem, some will argue, only if God actually tells Moses what you will do. God, it seems, does not tell much to Moses or any other prophet. After all, why should God tell Moses? Moses certainly does not care about the state of your lawn. Since prophecy of this sort is pretty rare, we can be confident that God's knowledge does not rule out our freedom. Some have argued, however, that if it is even possible for God to tell Moses (or anyone else for that matter) what you will do, then we have a version of the same compatibility problem we would have if we held that God is in time and foreknows your lawn cutting. We can call this version of the problem the "possible prophet" problem. If the possible prophet problem is serious enough to show that God's atemporal knowledge of future acts (future, that is, from our present vantage point) is incompatible with those acts being free, then holding God to be atemporal does not solve the problem of foreknowledge.[4]

God's knowledge of future free acts, then, might not be secured by thinking of God as atemporal. Whether or not there is a way to answer the possible prophet problem is beyond the scope of this essay. There may be solutions to the problem of divine foreknowledge, but what has seemed like a strong reason to hold that God is atemporal is not as strong as many have thought. These considerations do not strengthen the case for God's temporality directly. Issues concerning God's knowledge of future free acts might turn out to be neutral with regard to God's relation to time.

If God's knowledge of the future was thought to be a support for an atemporal conception of God, God's knowledge of the *present* is widely thought to support a temporal one. It has been argued by many that if God is not temporal, he cannot know what is happening now.[5]

Why think that a timeless God cannot know what day it is today? There are two ways to get at this problem. First we can start with the fact that a timeless God cannot change. Any change in God would divide his life into the part before the change and the part after the change. Once we entertain before and after in God's life, we can no longer think of God as timeless.

If God knows that today is September 17, 1999, tomorrow, he will know something else. He will know that *yesterday* it was September 17, 1999, and that *today* is September 18, 1999. So God must know different things at different times. If the content of God's knowledge changes, he changes. If he changes, he is temporal and not timeless.

The quick answer to this concern is to deny that God knows something different at different times. First, it is obvious that someone who holds that God is atemporal does not think that God knows things *at* times at all. God's knowings are not temporally located even if what he knows is temporally located. It is not true, it will be insisted, that God knows something *today*. He knows things *about* today but he knows these things atemporally.

God knows that today is September 17 in that he knows that the day I refer to when I use the word "today" in writing this introduction is September 17. When we raise the question again tomorrow ("Can a timeless God know what day it is *today*?"), God knows that this second use of "today" refers to September 18. Temporal indexical terms such as "today," "tomorrow," and "now" refer to different temporal locations with different uses. In this way they are similar to terms such as "here," "you," and "me."

I remember sitting with a friend in a restaurant contemplating the item listed on the menu as "Your Favorite Pie." I asked the waitress, "So, what is Your Favorite Pie?" She replied, "It is not *my* favorite pie, it is *your* favorite pie." I replied, "It does not say, 'my favorite pie,' it says, 'Your favorite pie.'" The point is that the meaning of any sentence involving an indexical term depends upon the context of its use. Since indexical terms may refer to different items with different uses, we can make such sentences more clear by replacing the indexical term with a term whose reference is fixed.

So the sentence "I am now typing this sentence" can be clarified by replacing the indexical terms with other terms that make the indexicals explicit. For example, "I type this sentence at 12:46 P.M. (EDST) on September 17, 1999." Even better is "Ganssle types this sentence at 12:46 P.M. EDST on September 17, 1999." These sentences, it can be claimed, express the same proposition. In the same way, "I am writing here" can be clarified as "Ganssle writes on September 17, 1999, at 12:46 P.M. EDST in *Bruegger's Bagels* in Trumbull, Connecticut." God, of course, knows all of the propositions expressed by these non-indexical sentences. Furthermore, the content of his knowledge does not need to change day to day. The proposition expressed by a non-indexical sentence is true eternally (or everlastingly) if it is true at all. The proposition expressed by the sentence "Ganssle types this sentence at 12:46 P.M. (EDST) on September 17, 1999" will be true tomorrow and the next day and so on. God can know these things and be changeless. He can, therefore, be timeless.

There are many philosophers who reject this quick answer on the grounds that God can know all of the non-indexical propositions and still not know what is happening *now*. This kind of objection raises the second approach to the question of an atemporal God's knowledge of the present. This approach is not through change but through omniscience. I can know that you type a sentence at some date (call the date t_1) without knowing whether or not you are typing the sentence *now*. I might fail to know that t_1 is now. An atemporal God can know all propositions expressed by sentences of the form "event *e* occurs at t_n." Sentences of the form "event *e* occurs *now*," so the objection goes, express *different* propositions. In order for God to be omniscient, he must know all propositions. If some sentences are essentially indexical (if they do not express the same propositions as sentences of the form "event *e* occurs at t_n"), he cannot know them. If an atemporal God cannot know this kind of proposition, he is not omniscient.

There have been two basic kinds of responses to this line of argument. The first is to deny that there are such irreducible propositions. In knowing every proposition of the form "event *e* occurs at t_n," God knows every proposition about events. This response is, in effect, a defense of the quick answer given above. While this position has its adherents, it involves a controversial commitment to the B-theory of time. The B-theory of time (also known as the *tenseless* theory or the *stasis* theory) entails the claim that the most fundamental features of time are the relations before, after, and simultaneous with. Talk of tenses (past, present, and future) can be reduced to talk about these relations. The temporal now is not an objective feature of reality but is a feature of our experience of reality.

Those who think that there are propositions about events that cannot be reduced to propositions of the form "event *e* occurs at t_n," hold the A-theory of time (or *tensed* or *process* theory.) The A-theory claims that there is an objective temporal now. This is not a feature only of our subjective experience of reality; it is a piece of the furniture of the universe. Another way to explain this is that even if there were no temporal minds, the property of occurring now would be exemplified by some events and not others. There would be facts about what is happening now. The fundamental temporal properties are the tensed properties. So events objectively are past, present, or future. They are not past, present, or future only in virtue of their relation to other events.

As will be clear from the discussion in some of the essays in this volume, there are different versions of the A-theory and different versions of the B-theory. It is not for this introduction to canvass all of these versions or to weigh the evidence for or against any of them. Suffice it to say that the A-theory is held more commonly than the B-theory. If the claim that all propositions about events can be reduced to propositions of the form "event e occurs at t_n," entails a controversial theory of time, it will not be as successful a defense as many would like. This consideration, to be sure, does not mean that it might not be the correct response, but the burden of defending it is greater accordingly.

The second basic response is to embrace the conclusion of the argument and to hold that God is not propositionally omniscient even if he is factually omniscient. In other words, God knows every fact, but there are some propositions that can be known only by minds that are located indexically. God is not lacking any fact. His access to each fact, though, is not indexical. He knows the same fact I know when I think, "I am writing here today." The proposition through which he knows this fact, however, is different than the proposition through which I know it. God knows the fact through the non-indexical proposition "Ganssle writes in Bruegger's on September 17, 1999." Embracing this solution is, not surprisingly, not without its costs. First of all, we have to adjust how we describe God's omniscience. We cannot describe it in terms of God's knowing every proposition. It is not true, on this view, that God knows every proposition. God knows every fact.

One way to object to this view is to deny that propositions expressed by indexical and non-indexical sentences refer to or assert the same fact. To take this road is to hold that some *facts* are essentially indexical rather than just that some sentences or propositions are. I find it hard to think that this objection is plausible because of stories like the following. Suppose you assert to me (truly), "You are in the kitchen," and I assert to you (also truly), "I am in the kitchen." These sentences are not identical and, according to the view we are considering, they express different propositions. What makes both of these assertions true is one and the same fact: the fact consisting in a particular person (Ganssle) being in a particular place (the kitchen). My knowledge of this fact is mediated through a proposition that is expressed by sentences using the indexical "I," and your knowledge is mediated through propositions expressed by sentences using "you." If there is one fact that makes these different indexical sentences true, it seems that there can be one fact that makes the following two indexical sentences true: "Ganssle is now typing" and "Ganssle types on October 1, 1999." If these sentences are made true by the same fact, God can know all facts even if he does not know some facts in the same way we know them. Our knowledge of facts is conditioned by our indexical location. That is, we know them the way we do in virtue of our personal spatial and temporal coordinates.

A third response—which can be combined with the second—is possible, and that is to deny that God's knowledge is mediated by propositions at all. William Alston has argued that God knows what he knows without having any beliefs.[6] God's knowledge is constituted instead by direct awareness of the facts involved. This view entails that God's omniscience is not to be cashed out in terms of propositions. Furthermore, if God's knowledge of a fact consists in the presence of that fact to God's consciousness, it may be that this presence does not affect God intrinsically. If this is the case, God can be aware of different facts in their different temporal locations without himself changing.[7] Whether a strategy such as this one will succeed is an open question.

God, Time, and Creation

We have mentioned God changing with reference to the content of his knowledge of a changing world already. Other non-epistemic changes are thought by some philosophers to be required by God. These changes would also require God to be temporal. Providing an adequate answer to the argument about the changing content of God's knowledge is not enough. An atemporalist will still have to face the implications of these other arguments for the claim that God changes.

The Scriptures speak of God as answering prayer, performing actions, revealing his will to people, becoming man, and so on. It looks as though these are the sorts of things that require change on the part of the person who does them. Some have gone so far as to argue that God cannot be a person unless God changes. To argue that God cannot be a person unless he is temporal, however, lands one in what may be an unhappy commitment. Consider the following argument.

1. If God is personal, God is temporal. (Premise)
2. If God is temporal, time exists. (Premise)
3. God is necessarily a person. (Premise)
4. God is necessarily temporal. (1, 2)
5. Therefore, time exists necessarily. (3, 4)

If temporality is required for God to be a person, time is metaphysically necessary. This commitment is not uncontroversial. Many philosophers think that time is contingent. Others, no doubt, will embrace the conclusion without worry. Although we can imagine worlds that are timeless, these turn out not to be possible worlds. After all, we can also imagine worlds in which God does not exist. Would we conclude that it is metaphysically possible that God does not exist? Most theists hold that it is not possible for God not to exist. What my argument shows, perhaps, is that our ability to imagine is not always a reliable guide to modal reality.

Still, if we reflect on the nature of time itself, there is nothing that leads us to think that it is metaphysically necessary that time exists. Metaphysically necessary time would have to be something different from physical time, if our current cosmologies are anywhere near the truth of the matter. Time, as current physics grasps it, came into being at the big bang. Time as metaphysically necessary is something else indeed. As will be seen in the essays in this book, many philosophers readily grant the distinction between physical time and metaphysical time (whether or not they think metaphysical time exists necessarily).

If we do not hold that temporality is required for being a person, we may be able to uphold the contingency of time. God could be atemporal as long as there is no time but enter into time with its creation. On this view, there is no change in God until he creates the universe. After he creates the universe, God's knowledge and his actions change from moment to moment. If it is only contingent that God creates the physical universe, and if time (physical or otherwise) comes into being only with the creation of the universe, then time is contingent. If God is, as a result, in time, then his temporality is also contingent.

When God created the universe is pretty important for thinking about his relation to time. By "when he did it" I am not entering into questions about how to interpret the days in the first chapter of Genesis. What I am referring to is whether the universe had a beginning at all. It is strange to claim that God could create the universe even if the universe had no beginning. At least it is strange to our ears. People like Thomas Aquinas did not think it was strange. He realized that the universe could be everlasting and still be depending upon God for its existence.

If the universe had no beginning, that is, if it has an infinite past, then time is infinite. But could time be infinite? Arguments such as the Kalam Cosmological Argument aim to show that it is not possible that the past is infinite.[8] Suppose time came into existence with the universe, so that the universe has only a finite past. If God created both physical and metaphysical time, then God existed "before" time existed. God, then, had to be atemporal.

God's Relation to the World

There are various other considerations that have been put forward for thinking that God must be a person who changes (even if his personhood by itself does not require temporality). God, for example, acts in the world. He sustains the whole created universe. He also intervenes in the world. He spoke to Moses from the midst of the burning bush, and later he parted the Red Sea so the nation of Israel could cross safely. Later still, he became a human being in a particular time and place. If God spoke from the burning bush *before* he parted the Red Sea, then God's actions occur at different times. If his actions occur at different times, it looks as though he is temporal. It may be, though, that the effects of his actions are located successively in time but that his acting is not. In one eternal act he wills the speaking to Moses at one time and the parting of the sea at another. The sequence of the effects of God's eternal will does not imply that God's acts themselves are temporal.

Apart from performing action in the world, the Scriptures indicate that God interacts with human beings. He redeems his people, answers their prayers, and forgives their sins. He also comes to their aid and comforts and strengthens them. He is "a very present help in time of trouble." Can an atemporalist make sense of God interacting in these ways? It all depends, of course, on what the necessary conditions for interaction turn out to be. If it is not possible to answer a request (a prayer) unless the action is performed *after* the request, then the fact that God answers prayer will guarantee that he is temporal. Some thinkers have thought that an answer can only be initiated after a request. Others have argued that, although answers to requests normally come after the request, it is not necessary that they do so. In order to count as an answer, the action must occur *because of* the request. Not any *because of* relation will do, however. An answer is not normally thought of as being *caused by* the request, yet a cause-effect relation is a kind of *because of* relation. Answers are contingent, whereas effects of causes are in some sense necessary. The *because of* relation that is relevant to answering a request has to do with intention or purpose. If I make my son Nick a peanut butter sandwich in answer to his request, I make it in order to meet the need that he expressed. I have various reasons to meet that need, but it is not necessary that I make the sandwich. If I make the sandwich because he asked for it, I make it in response to his request. It is my intention to fulfill the request that makes my action an answer to his request.

When I make lunch for my children, the requests come before I make the sandwiches. If I knew ahead of time what they were going to ask for, I could make the sandwiches ahead of time. My action would still be an answer to their requests. I would perform the action because of and in order to fulfill the requests. It is because I do not know infallibly what my kids will ask for that I do not answer their requests ahead of time. Notice that it is not necessary for the request to come before the answer. If the relation between a request and an answer is not necessarily a temporal one, then it is possible that an atemporal God could answer prayer. He hears all our prayers in his one eternal conscious act, and in that same eternal conscious act, he wills the answers to our various requests.

Essays

The various essays in this book reveal that, in this introduction, we have touched only lightly on a few of the issues that are raised when pondering God's relation to time. In the first essay, "The Eternal Present," Brian Leftow investigates Boethius's concept of eternity to give a new and deeper understanding of what the life of an eternal God is like. He distinguishes *eternity* from *atemporality* on the basis of the claim that an atemporal thing both is timeless and has no duration. An *eternal* being, on the other hand, has a life characterized by an event. God is a living being, and it is the fullness of his life that demands that none of it slip away into the past. Rather, he has "perfect complete possession of all his life at once." This conception of eternity implies that God's life has certain properties that are what Leftow calls "typically temporal." Typically temporal properties (TTPs) are those that are generally such that whatever has them is temporal, and any temporal thing is temporal in virtue of having these properties. In order to be temporal, a being or thing must have the right sorts of TTPs. God's life has some TTPs but not others. As such it has duration, though not temporal duration. It does not pass away, nor does it have any part that passes away. God's life, however, is an event. It is an event with no temporal duration but with other modes of duration. It is a permanent event. God's life also has a present, Leftow argues. God's present is a non-temporal present. God's "now" is not a temporal now. The term "now," according to Leftow, picks out when the speaker tokens it. Not all whens are times. Eternity, Leftow argues, is also a when.

One of the strengths of Leftow's essay is that it shows that the eternalist position does not imply a poverty of the life of God. Rather, it is the richness of God's life that requires him to be eternal. This position goes far in removing the idea that those who think God not to be temporal think of him as something like an abstract object. Whatever God's relation to time is, he is a person. In fact his is the most fully realized life that is possible for a person.

In "Atemporal, Sempiternal, or Omnitemporal: God's Temporal Mode of Being," Garrett DeWeese argues that neither the standard view that God is temporal nor the classical view that God is atemporal captures the mode of God's life. God cannot be temporal because, DeWeese argues, all temporal things are contingent and God is not. God also cannot be atemporal because no atemporal thing can be a concrete entity. The reason no atemporal thing can be concrete is that an entity must be a possible relatum in a causal relation. No atemporal thing can be such a relatum. DeWeese supports this way of distinguishing concrete from abstract entities on the basis of the claim that causation is a temporal relation. DeWeese thinks that no satisfactory account of timeless causation has been or can be given. If causation is temporal and the ability to stand in causal relations is a mark of a concrete entity, only temporal things will be concrete. No traditional theist will hold that God is abstract. God stands in many causal relations with the created world. Therefore, traditional theists ought to think that God is not atemporal.

DeWeese holds that God is neither temporal nor atemporal. Rather, he is *omnitemporal*. To be omnitemporal is to be in metaphysical time (though not physical time) and to be a metaphysically necessary being. To be metaphysically temporal is to have one's temporal properties defined with respect to metaphysical time rather than physical time. For example, God's "now" is not determined by the physical now of any particular reference frame. God's now is the present of metaphysical time. Indeed God's present conscious experience is what grounds the now of metaphysical time. Metaphysical time is God's own time. Metaphysical time, as grounded in God's mental life, is as necessary as he is. While physical time is contingent, metaphysical time is not and, therefore, it does not infect God's being with contingency. An omnitemporal God, being both metaphysically necessary and able to stand in causal relations, avoids the pitfalls of both the temporal and atemporal notions of God's mode of being.

In "Divine Foreknowledge and the Arrow of Time: On the Impossibility of Retrocausation," Alan G. Padgett takes up one kind of argument to reconcile the foreknowledge of God with human freedom. This is the attempt to say that retrocausation is possible. If retrocausation were possible, a solution to the problem of reconciling divine foreknowledge and human freedom would be readily available. When I act freely, I perform an action that actualizes a state of affairs. My actualization of this state of affairs causes God to have certain beliefs about which states of affairs are actual and which are not. Furthermore, my action causes it to be the case that God has always had the belief in question.

Another way to look at this is to say that some of the beliefs that God had in the year 1000 are up to me. My action today causes him to have some of the beliefs that he had in the year 1000. If I choose to have Fruity Pebbles for breakfast, then God's belief has always been that I have Fruity Pebbles. If I, on the other hand, choose Lucky Charms, I cause God to have believed that I would have Lucky Charms. My action today can cause things to happen in the past.

Padgett argues that such retrocausation is impossible. It is impossible not only on one view of time, he claims; whether or not the world is timeless and, if time exists, whether the process or the stasis view of time is correct, retrocausation is impossible. It is fairly simple to show retrocausation to be impossible in the first two kinds of worlds. A timeless world cannot be one in which retrocausation occurs because retrocausation is inherently a temporal relation. There can be no temporal relations in timeless worlds. If time exists and the process theory is true, then retrocausation is impossible. It is impossible because only existing things have causal efficacy and only existing things can be acted upon.

In worlds that are temporal but in which the stasis theory of time is true, the argument is trickier. Padgett considers stasis worlds in which the distinction between backward and forward becomes relative to local or global considerations and those in which the direction of time is constituted by increase in entropy. He concludes that in neither of these worlds is retrocausation possible. If Padgett's analysis is correct, then anyone who proposes a solution to the foreknowledge and freedom debate that assumes the possibility of retrocausation will have to make explicit how such causation is possible. Padgett has shown that it is not likely that such an attempt will be successful.

In "God inside Time and before Creation," Dean Zimmerman turns to two puzzles that temporalists face. The first is the question of whether time necessarily requires intrinsic change. Here temporalists face a dilemma. Either the past is finite or it is infinite. If the past is infinite, then God has existed throughout an infinite number of finite intervals of time. Supposing that he created the universe a finite amount of time ago, then God existed throughout an infinite duration of time by himself. If time requires intrinsic change, then God was continually changing intrinsically throughout this infinite duration. Zimmerman claims that this position is not theologically well motivated.

If the past is finite, then either God himself has a finite past history, in that he existed throughout all time but his past is not infinite, or he was atemporal "before" the creation of the universe and became temporal as a result of his real relations to the changing reality. This dilemma, Zimmerman thinks, will motivate the temporalist to reconsider the doctrine that time requires intrinsic change.

The second question for temporalists is why God created when he did. If God endured an infinite duration of time before creating, it seems as though he has no good reason to create at one moment rather than at any other moment. It turns out, Zimmerman argues, that one can hold that God existed unchanging before creation and did not choose to create when he did arbitrarily. But the temporalist can hold this position only by rejecting substantivalism about times.

If substantivalism about times is true, either there was one partless extended time before creation or there were many. If there was more than one, then the question of why God chose to create when he did emerges again. If there is only one, we are left with the idea of an extended period of time that is partless. Zimmerman grants that some things (events or states of affairs) might be partless, but it is hard to see that a period of time could be partless.

The best answer is to give up on substantivalism about times. On a relationist view, before creation there could have been a temporal duration with no way of dividing it into periods whose lengths can be compared, so, Zimmerman states, "you cannot take some portion of the event and say that there must be either finitely many or infinitely many discrete parts of the event of comparable length in the whole period. And since the state is initial there is no beginning of time, no earlier 'first moment' distinct from this state."

The questions that a temporalist must face about time before creation, then, are not devastating to the view that God is temporal. God did not create when he did arbitrarily, and he did not have to exist through an infinite series of times changing intrinsically all the while.

In "Time Was Created by a Timeless Point: An Atheist Explanation of Spacetime," Quentin Smith rejects both the theistic and the standard atheistic explanation for the beginning of the universe. The theist holds that God caused the big bang. The standard atheistic story is that the big bang was uncaused. Smith holds that the big bang, and hence all of spacetime, *was* caused. It was caused by a simple timeless point. This hypothesis, Smith thinks, is to be preferred to the theistic hypothesis because it can be shown to be more probable. According to Bayes's theorem, the probability of a hypothesis is a function of both its prior probability (that is, its probability independent of the evidence to be weighed) and its posterior probability (that is, its probability on the evidence being considered).[9] Smith argues that, although the timeless simple point as the cause of the universe and God as the creator each has about the same prior probability, the simple point theory has a higher posterior probability than theism.

If the prior probabilities of each hypothesis are about the same, we must turn to the a posteriori probabilities in order to determine which hypothesis is more probable overall. Smith argues that the simple point hypothesis is more probable given the evidence of current cosmologies. The particular evidence that is relevant is that in its first instants the universe was in "a completely unstructured state, i.e., a state of utter chaos or maximal disorder." This state is exactly what we should expect on the hypothesis that the cause of the universe is "a timeless, partless, attributively simple, and totally lawless cause." The hypothesis that an omniscient, omnipotent, and wholly good person created the universe would lead us to expect something else altogether. We would predict that such a being would begin spacetime in "a very beautiful and magnificent way that exhibits an admirably high degree of naturally good order." The evidence, then, combined with the observation that most theistic explanations of the initial disorder seem to be ad hoc, leads us, Smith claims, to prefer strongly the simple point hypothesis to the theistic one. Smith's conclusion is that the most reasonable hypothesis is that the spacetime universe was caused to exist by a timeless simple point. Thus, there is an explanation for the existence of the universe but the explanation does not require God.

William Lane Craig, in "The Elimination of Absolute Time by the Special Theory of Relativity," examines the implications of both the special and the general theories of relativity for God's relation to time. He points out that it is commonly thought that relativity theory has decisively refuted the notion of absolute time. If this refutation had been accomplished, the process theory of time (A-theory) must be rejected. Einstein's rejection of absolute space and time, it turns out, was a result of a philosophical commitment to positivism that he inherited from Mach. As Craig writes, "The meaning of 'time' is made to depend upon the meaning of 'simultaneity,' which is defined locally in terms of occurrence at the same local clock reading." In other words, to be meaningful, "time" had to refer to something measurable by physics. Given this presupposition, if local clock readings turn out to be relative to inertial reference frame, then time itself will be held to be relative as well. The positivism on which Einstein built his theory has long since been discredited both in philosophy and in physics. Relativity per se does not eliminate absolute time.

Craig goes further and argues that if God is everlastingly temporal, his time implies that a Lorentz-Poincaré theory of relativity is correct. There is an absolute time. God's time is absolute time. Craig also shows that the common reasons for rejecting the Lorentz-Poincaré theory are not compelling.

In pursuing which measured time coincides with God's time, Craig explores the general theory of relativity. There are models in the general theory that posit a universal, cosmic time. This cosmic time, Craig claims, is God's metaphysical time. Much of Newton's thinking about time, including the distinction between physical time and metaphysical time and the existence of absolute time, has been vindicated. If God is temporal, absolute time exists. This theological position can be shown to be compatible with both the special and the general theories of relativity—that is, once the theories have been purged of archaic philosophical commitments.

Edward R. Wierenga, in "Timelessness out of Mind: On the Alleged Incoherence of Divine Timelessness," points out that two of the major objections to divine timelessness are the claims that a timeless God cannot be omniscient and that a timeless God cannot be a God who acts. Wierenga investigates a recent development of each of these objections by Richard Swinburne. Swinburne's formulation of each objection is based on certain metaphysical principles concerning time and events. The principle that is most important for the first argument against timelessness is that things do not possess properties at instants. Since Swinburne holds a timeless God is omniscient at an instant, timelessness turns out to be incoherent. Wierenga raises two objections to Swinburne's argument from his principle to the incoherence of timelessness but focuses on criticizing the principle itself. Any plausible construal of time or motion, he argues, shows that things *do* have properties at instants. Swinburne's principle ought to be rejected.

The second objection to timelessness is that a timeless God cannot perform actions. Swinburne argues for this claim based on the causal theory of time. From the causal theory of time, Swinburne concludes that backward causation and simultaneous causation are impossible. All that is left is causation through time in which the cause precedes the effect. If God is a cause, then he must precede in time his effects.

Therefore, he is temporal. Wierenga raises several objections to this move as well. One objection is against the idea that simultaneous causation is ruled out by the causal theory of time. Another is that Swinburne's account assumes that God's causing something will be a case of event causation rather than agent causation. Wierenga concludes that Swinburne has not shown timelessness to be incoherent.

In "Direct Awareness and God's Experience of a Temporal Now," I explore the implications of William Alston's claim that God knows what he knows without having any beliefs. Most discussions of God's knowledge assume that we ought to understand God's knowledge as being something like a propositional attitude, just as we understand human knowledge. Alston has challenged this construal of divine knowledge. God knows what he knows, Alston claims, in virtue of his direct awareness of facts. He does not have propositional attitudes at all. I argue that if God knows what he knows by direct awareness, then God must be atemporal. If God is temporal, he cannot have absolute immediate awareness of past or future facts. Absolute immediate awareness cannot span time. A knowing subject who is temporal can have direct intuitive awareness only of those facts that are temporally present.

My argument that direct intuitive awareness cannot span time focuses on God's experience of a temporal now. A temporal God will experience what is happening now in a manner that is different from his experience of the past or the future. As a result, God's cognitive experience of past or future facts must be mediated in some way. If some kind of mediation is present in God's cognition, it is not absolute immediate awareness. Therefore, a temporal God can have direct intuitive awareness only of present facts. In order to have direct intuitive awareness of all facts, regardless of their temporal locations, God must be atemporal.

William Hasker disagrees in "The Absence of a Timeless God." He argues that God's knowing by direct awareness does not imply timelessness. In fact, it requires that God be temporal. Timeless intuitive knowledge, he argues, is incoherent. For God to have timeless intuitive awareness of all facts, he would have to have awareness of some facts when they no longer (or do not yet) exist. Hasker argues that facts can be known only when they exist, so God cannot have timeless intuitive awareness of all facts.

Hasker considers what he calls a "medieval" solution to this argument. Perhaps facts do not exist only in time but also exist in eternity. Considerations similar to this one are found in Boethius and Anselm. God has direct awareness, then, of all facts and entities not when they exist in time but when they exist in eternity. Hasker rejects the medieval solution because the idea that physical things exist literally in eternity as well as in time is implausible.

Hasker raises one other objection to the timelessness of God. He argues that a timeless God could not know which moment is present. He can know all facts of the form "event e happens at time t_n," but he cannot know which event is occurring now. As a result of these objections, Hasker concludes that a timeless God is indeed absent. The God who exists is temporal.

Paul Helm, in "The Problem of Dialogue," takes up another aspect relevant to God's relation to time. This issue is God's relation to the world, specifically, his relation to human beings. The Scriptures affirm that God is in relationship with human beings. Being in relationship seems to imply the possibility of real give-and-take.

Several attributes of God seem to make real give-and-take impossible. Can a timeless God enter into dialogue? Furthermore, can a God who knows what you are going to do and say ahead of time engage you in a genuine dialogue? Helm examines two proposed solutions to the problem of divine-human dialogue: he ultimately rejects the solution proposed by William Alston and argues that Richard Swinburne's solution is sufficient to preserve genuine dialogue but comes at too high a cost. Helm claims that his own solution can preserve divine-human dialogue at a much lower cost than Swinburne's. Furthermore, Helm's solution, contrary to Alston's, can preserve genuine divine-human dialogue even if it turns out that God determines every event.

The last two essays, Thomas Senor's "Incarnation, Timelessness, and Leibniz's Law Problems" and Douglas Blount's "On the Incarnation of a Timeless God," cover the same topic. Can a timeless God become incarnate? Senor argues that timelessness is incompatible with the Incarnation. Senor defends his previously published arguments against two objections similar to Blount's. First, he defends his argument against the objection that it proves too much. Not only timelessness but many other divine attributes are shown, it is claimed, to be incompatible with the Incarnation. Second, Senor defends his claims against one of the ways that philosophers have attempted to explain the compatibility of timelessness and the Incarnation.

Senor argues that it simply is not the case that his argument will support the claims that properties such as omniscience are incompatible with the Incarnation. In order for these to be incompatible, it must be the case that Jesus, as a human being, could not have had the property in question. While it is not common or essential for human beings to be omniscient, it is not obviously impossible for a human being to have this attribute. Furthermore, there is nothing in the observable properties that Jesus had that requires him to have been omniscient. It was, on the contrary, observable that he was temporal.

Senor discusses the attempt to show that timelessness and the Incarnation are compatible. The most common approach is via the "qua-move." He explains three ways this move can be interpreted, and he finds each of them to be unsuccessful. The interpretation that is closest to Blount's two-natured view of the Incarnation is "S-qua-N is F" (or "*Jesus qua human being* is temporal but *Jesus qua Second Person of the Trinity* is timeless"). Senor claims that this move leads the one who holds it into the heresy of Nestorianism, in which "it is not the single person of the Redeemer who bears these properties but rather the divine nature bears the divine properties and the human nature bears the human properties."

Senor also discusses another move that is similar to the previous one. Rather than bringing the qua-move into the subject, perhaps we can push the qua into the properties. So rather than thinking of the *Redeemer qua Second Person of the Trinity* as omniscient but the *Redeemer qua human being* as limited in knowledge, perhaps we can think of the Redeemer as *omniscient qua God* but *limited in knowledge qua human being*. Senor argues that this move can be made, but only at a high cost. One cost is that of denying the Law of Excluded Middle. (It is not true that the Redeemer is either omniscient or not omniscient.) The other cost is to deny that there are any properties such as omniscience *simpliciter*. Senor calls this move "nominalism about the traditional divine properties."

Neither of these moves is very promising. Senor concludes that the doctrine of divine timelessness is incompatible with the Incarnation in a way that other divine attributes are not and, therefore, it should be rejected by Christian philosophers.

Blount defends the compatibility of timelessness and the Incarnation against arguments that Thomas Senor has raised in previously published works. (It ought to be noted that neither Senor nor Blount consulted the other's chapter in preparing his own.) If Senor's arguments are successful, Blount claims, they will provide equally strong reasons for rejecting many of the traditional attributes of God including divine omniscience, omnipotence, and omnipresence. No orthodox Christian philosopher will accept such conclusions. Something, then, must have gone wrong with the arguments. Blount identifies where he thinks Senor's arguments go wrong and he thus thinks that Senor's arguments against the compatibility of divine timelessness and the Incarnation fail.

Blount goes further than this defensive move by providing an explanation of how it is possible that a timeless God be incarnate. A "two-minds" view of the Incarnation, such as has been defended by Thomas Morris and is reflected in the Chalcedonian creed, provides the resources for understanding the compatibility of the divine nature and the human nature in one person. Blount shows that on this view of the Incarnation, a timeless God can indeed become man.

The essays in this volume demonstrate that the issues raised in working out a convincing position regarding God's relation to time are varied and complex. We are confident that these chapters will help push the discussion in new and exciting directions. There is, to be sure, much more work to be done. We submit these essays as an invitation to philosophers and theologians to join us in exploring God and time.

Notes

I was greatly helped in writing this introduction by Douglas Keith Blount's dissertation, "An Essay on Divine Presence," University of Notre Dame, 1997.

1. It is interesting that as recently as 1975, it was thought that the majority view was that God was not in time. See Nicholas Wolterstorff, "God Everlasting," in *God and the Good: Essays in Honor of Henry Stob*, ed. Clifton J. Orlebeke and Lewis B. Smedes (Grand Rapids: Eerdmans, 1975), rpt. in *Contemporary Philosophy of Religion*, ed. Stephen M. Cahn and David Shatz (New York: Oxford University Press, 1982), 77–98, esp. 77.

2. The most important contemporary discussion of this is by Eleonore Stump and Norman Kretzmann, "Eternity," *Journal of Philosophy* 78 (1981), 429–58. See also the response by Paul Fitzgerald, "Stump and Kretzmann on Time and Eternity," *Journal of Philosophy* 82 (1985), 260–69. Stump and Kretzmann's reply is found in "Atemporal Duration," *Journal of Philosophy* 84 (1987), 214–19.

3. See Garrett DeWeese, "Atemporal, Sempiternal, or Omnitemporal: God's Temporal Mode of Being," ch. 2 of this volume. For another "in-between" way of thinking of God's relation to time, see Alan G. Padgett, *God, Eternity, and the Nature of Time* (London: Macmillan, 1992, rpt. Eugene: Wipf and Stock, 2000), and Padgett, "God the Lord of Time: A Third Model of Eternity as Relative Timelessness," in *God and Time: Four Views*, ed. Gregory E. Ganssle (Downers Grove: InterVarsity Press, 2001).

4. For more on the prophet problem as well as the possible prophet problem, see Andrew Cortens, "Foreknowledge, Freedom, and the Prophet Problem," unpublished paper, and David Widerker, "A Problem for the Eternity Solution," *International Journal for the Philosophy of Religion* 29 (1991), 87–95. For an attempted solution, see Eleonore Stump and Norman Kretz- mann, "Prophecy, Past Truth, and Eternity," in *Philosophical Perspectives*, vol. 5: *Philosophy of Religion, 1991*, ed. James Tomberlin (Atascadero: Ridgeview, 1991), 395–424. Edward Wierenga responds to this article in "Prophecy, Freedom, and the Necessity of the Past," ibid., 425–45.

5. Arthur Prior, "The Formalities of Omniscience," in Prior, *Papers on Time and Tense* (New York: Oxford University Press, 1968), 26–44, and Norman Kretzmann, "Omniscience and Immutability," *Journal of Philosophy* 63 (1966), 409–21.

6. William P. Alston, "Does God Have Beliefs?" *Religious Studies* 22 (1987), 287–306, rpt. with variations in Alston, *Divine Nature and Human Language* (Ithaca: Cornell University Press, 1989), 178–93.

7. For more on direct awareness, see my "Atemporality and the Mode of Divine Knowl- edge," *International Journal for the Philosophy of Religion* 34 (1993), 171–80; "Leftow on Di- rect Awareness and Atemporality," *Sophia* 34, no. 2 (1995), 30–37; and "Direct Awareness and God's Experience of a Temporal Now," ch. 8 of this volume. William Hasker responds to some of my arguments in "The Absence of a Timeless God," ch. 9 of this volume. For a discussion of whether God's direct awareness determines his internal state, see ch. 2 of my dissertation, "Atemporality and the Mode of Divine Knowledge," Syracuse University, May 1995.

8. For more on the Kalam Cosmological Argument, see William Lane Craig, *The Kalam Cosmological Argument* (London: Macmillan, 1979), and William Lane Craig and Quentin Smith, *Theism, Atheism, and Big Bang Cosmology* (Oxford: Clarendon Press, 1993), sec. 1.

9. To be precise, $P(h/e.k) = P(h/k) \times P(e/h.k)/P(e/k)$, where h = the hypothesis in question, e = the evidence being considered, and k = background knowledge. We can read this as follows: The probability of the hypothesis on the evidence being considered along with any background knowledge we might have equals the probability of the hypothesis on the background knowl- edge (this is the prior probability of the hypothesis) multiplied by the probability of the evi- dence on the hypothesis and background knowledge divided by the probability of the evidence on the background knowledge alone.

Part One

GOD'S ETERNAL NATURE

1

The Eternal Present

BRIAN LEFTOW

Western theists agree that God is eternal. But they disagree over what eternality is. I hope here to clarify one view of eternality, that of Boethius, and show that some aspects of this view are coherent. On Boethius' view, God is not temporal. So I first give a minimal account of what it is to be temporal. This account lets me explain what sets Boethius' view of God's eternality apart from others. Boethius' view, I show, implies that though God's life is not temporal, there are events in it, and these events have what is typically a temporal property: they occur in a present. I argue that these are coherent claims.

Being Temporal

We can begin our minimal account of temporality with the notion of a date, an answer to the question "when does it happen?" An item can have a date just in case a sentence dating it can state a truth.[1] "Booth in 1865" is not even a sentence. It cannot state a truth.[2] So John Wilkes Booth himself is not the sort of thing that can have a date. "Booth shot Lincoln in 1865" is true: events have dates. "Booth was thinking in 1865" is true: processes have dates. "Booth was human in 1865" is true: states of affairs have dates. We sometimes transfer temporal predicates from states of affairs, processes, and events to objects involved in these.[3] If God was in our past, this was because God *existed* in our past. In fact, if "God was in our past" asserts anything, it is that God existed in our past; God's *existence* is what was primarily located in our past. But by transfer, we say that God was there too, even though "God in our past" is no more a sentence than "Booth in 1865."

21

I here take it without argument that events are the primary bearers of dates, the primary items which have "whens." Processes (I would argue) "reduce" to sequences of events.[4] States of affairs have dates in time (I would argue) just in case their obtaining—e.g., Booth's actually *being* human—is a temporal event.[5] An item's life or history thus consists simply of all the events in which the item figures—that is, all that ever happens to it—appropriately ordered and connected. And so it is lives or histories which are primarily temporal. To be a temporal being is to have a temporal life or history, one consisting of events which are temporal. Thus our question now becomes: what makes events temporal?

Typically Temporal Properties

All temporal events are involved in succession. Some occur and then do not occur—that is, are present and then are past. Some do not occur and then occur—that is, are future and then present.[6] Some have parts of which one of these things is true. Succession is the "and-then" relation between occurring and not occurring; any event which stands in an and-then relation or has parts which do is involved in succession. Just how an event is involved with succession depends on whether it has parts. A partless temporal event is involved in succession because it occurs and then does not, or vice versa. A temporal event with parts occurs part by part, some parts succeeding others, as a football game's second quarter succeeds its first. A temporal event's later parts continue it. Any temporal event which is not instantaneous continues, or persists, and does so just as long as it has a new part, one which has not already occurred.

Being present, being past, being future, and standing in and-then relations are typically temporal properties, or TTPs. That is, they are properties typical of temporal events which help make them temporal. A property is a TTP if a term predicating it is part of a definition of being temporal or figures appropriately in the right sort of non-defining sufficient condition for being temporal, one relevantly like "necessarily, whatever is past was temporal" rather than "necessarily, whatever is a pig is temporal." This is not a very helpful characterization of TTPs, obviously. But it is all I require. For it has one key feature. It leaves room for items other than temporal events to have TTPs. Properties which help define being F can also be had by items which are not F. If to be human is to be a featherless biped, then being bipedal helps make us human. But being bipedal also helps make birds birds, though nothing can be both human and avian. So too, if being temporal consisted in (say) being present or past or future, being temporal would contain being present, but this would not preclude non-temporal items' also being present. And if being present and then past is a non-defining sufficient condition of being temporal, this too does not preclude non-temporal items' being present.

With this notion of a TTP in hand, I can give my answer to the question "What makes events temporal?" It is: having the right TTPs. More precisely, my sole claim about what makes an event temporal is that one can in principle give an account of this in terms of having TTPs. It might seem regressive to explain events' being temporal in terms of typically *temporal* properties, for this might just seem to leave us asking what makes the properties themselves temporal. But as I use the term "TTP," it does not. I say that events are temporal if and only if they have the right set of properties, and I label the properties in this set "typically temporal" because they help to make some events temporal. For me, there need be no other sense in which these properties are temporal.

Theories of Eternality

Discussions of God's eternality often proceed as if there were just two options, that God is temporal and that he is not. But there is in fact a continuum of possible views of God's relation to time—as it were, of just how temporal God is—which ranges from a claim that God's life has all TTPs on one end to a claim that it has none on the other.

Maimonides may have held that God's life has no TTPs. For Maimonides held that God has no accidents whatever and that all temporal properties are accidents.[7] If events in God's life had TTPs, these would transfer to God, and so He would have what Maimonides would call temporal accidents.[8] Again, Schleiermacher's main thesis on God's eternality is that God is "absolutely timeless."[9] Schleiermacher explicitly denies of God only involvement in succession, but "absolutely" suggests that he would also deny any other TTPs to God, and so to his life.[10] Thus the no-TTP end of the spectrum may be inhabited. I am not sure the all-TTP end is. Being temporally after something is a TTP.[11] But if God is eternal, God's life is not temporally after anything—there was no such thing as a time before God existed. Temporally beginning and ending are also TTPs (for like reasons).[12] If God's life began or ended, it would not be eternal. Thus I suggest that all acceptable views of God's eternality must deny that God's life has some TTPs.

Boethian Eternity

On Boethius' account, God is neither temporal nor wholly atemporal. Unlike Maimonides, Boethius thinks that events in God's life have some TTPs. But Boethius holds that events in God's life do not have the right TTPs to count as temporal. Boethius wrote that "our now, as it were running, makes time. . . . God's now, permanent and not moving, . . . makes eternity."[13]

Talk of "now" moving suggests an image, that "the now" alights on ever-later events like a spotlight moving down a row of buildings, the events being present when the light hits, past when it passes on.[14] Behind the image is the fact that temporal events are future and then present and/or present and then past—i.e., that they are involved in succession. Again, for Boethius, an item is temporal if and only if "it does not grasp at once the whole space of its life . . . its future is not yet, and what has been done it does not now have."[15] An item is temporal iff it lives its life part by part, a part which was not yet succeeding a part which now is no longer: i.e., iff it is involved in succession. For Boethius, then, being involved in succession "makes" events temporal. If this is the whole of what makes events temporal, what is not involved in succession is not temporal. According to Boethius, God's "now" does not "move." The spotlight of the present stands still on events in God's life. They are present but never are past, or over. Nor have they parts which end, for these parts would just be smaller events in God's life. So events in God's life are not involved in succession. And so for Boethius, events in God's life are not temporal. Boethius instead calls them "eternal"; for him, temporal events pass away (time "passes"), eternal events do not. Events in God's life are permanently present. They are permanent features of reality. This is what makes them eternal, not temporal; God is eternal because such events make up his life.

For Boethius, God has a now, a present, yet God is not temporal. Seeing this, William Craig suggests that Boethius means his talk of God's now as mere metaphor.[16] But the context defeats this claim. The "God's now" passage comes from a treatment of how the Aristotelian categories apply to God. Boethius does not say of the category "when" (as he does of others) that it does not apply. Rather, he says that it applies, discusses the sample locution "God always exists" (*deus semper est*), and continues as just quoted. Now the Aristotelian categories are categories of literal predication. If Boethius thought when-terms applied to God only metaphorically, he would not say that the category of "when" applied to God. So Boethius means his sample locution to be a literal predication. The full passage runs this way:

> What is said of God, "always exists," signifies one thing, as if [*quasi*] He existed in every past time, exists in every present (however this may be), [and] will exist in every future time. According to philosophers, this can be said of the heaven and other immortal bodies. But it is not said of God in this way. God always exists because in Him "always" is of the present time, and there is this difference between the present of our things, which is now, and the present of divine things, that our now, as it were running, makes time and sempiternity, but God's now, permanent and not moving, . . . makes eternity.[17]

In Boethius' sample locution, "exists" is present-tensed, and so may carry a "when" element. If it does and Boethius means the tense literally, he must take "now" and "present" in this explanation as literally in the category of "when," else his sample use of "exists" will not show that "when" literally applies to God. "Always" is a clear answer to "when," and so clearly a when-term. Boethius makes a point of linking "always" to "present time." He cannot mean the use of "time" in the latter phrase literally, as he goes on to explain that God's now is non-temporal. So if Boethius thought "present" applied to God only metaphorically, then if he meant "always" as a literal when-term, he would not use "present time" to explain it. If "always exists" is a literal when-term when said of an eternal God, "always" or "exists" is. If either is, so is "present." So Boethius means "present" literally in this passage.

Thus for Boethius, though presentness is a property in the category of "when," it is not always or necessarily a property of temporal events. Temporal events have it, but it is not a temporal property *simpliciter*. Boethius nowhere explicitly deploys the concept of a typically temporal property. But he does have an account of what it is to be temporal: again, as he sees it, being temporal is being involved in succession. For Boethius, being involved in succession is being future and then present or present and then past or having parts of which one of these things is true.[18] So given my account of TTPs above, by figuring in Boethius' definition of being temporal, being present qualifies as a Boethian TTP. So on Boethius' account, events in God's life have a TTP. As being involved in succession is a TTP, on Boethius' account, events in

God's life also lack some TTPs—and to Boethius, lacking this particular TTP makes them non-temporal.

All acceptable views of God's eternality deny that God's life has some TTPs. I now suggest that most views also assert that it has some, i.e., that the Maimonidean end of the continuum I mentioned above is sparsely settled. Augustine, like Boethius, spoke of God as existing in an eternal present.[19] Augustine provided the large-scale framework for medieval theology, including its concept of eternality.[20] After Boethius, medieval Christian thinkers took Boethius' account of eternality as standard.[21] So given Christian medievals' dependence on and deference to the two of them, it seems unlikely that any Christian medievals defend complete divine atemporality.[22] So too, those who later deny in conscious dependence on a medieval heritage that God is temporal are unlikely to mean by this that God is wholly atemporal. Those today who deny divine temporality do not mean this either. For instance, Helm plumps for a "time-free" conception of God and rejects Stump and Kretzmann's talk of eternal duration and simultaneity. Yet he grants that a timeless God exists in a kind of present.[23] So Helm, too, ascribes to God at least one typically temporal property.[24]

It should be no surprise that most who deny that God is temporal nonetheless ascribe to him some TTPs. The Old Testament sources of Western monotheism consistently speak of "the living God."[25] If God is living, he has a life. Lives consist of events. There could not be an event with no TTPs: an event which is never present is just an event which never occurs, and being present is a TTP. But (again) many TTPs transfer from the events which primarily have them to objects those events involve. These include being present. So a God with a life must have a present, and so some TTPs.

Stump and Kretzmann first drew attention to Boethius' ascription of TTPs to a nontemporal God.[26] But the discussion their efforts sparked has not yet fully appreciated the nature of Boethius' view. So I now offer an account of two of its facets: the notion of a permanent or non-temporal event and that of a non-temporal present. The first is certainly problematic: it does not seem that there *can* be such a thing as a permanent event. Events are things that happen. The very notion of a happening seems to connote impermanence: don't happenings *begin* to happen? I now argue that there can indeed be permanent events, happenings which are present, yet never past or future, and have no past or future parts.

Events, Changes, Beginnings

Lombard holds that events are processes of change.[27] Processes begin, cease, and have parts which do so. Whatever begins, ceases, or has parts which do exists in time. So if events are processes of change, "non-temporal event" is a contradiction in terms. A weaker but related view would be that something happens only if there is a process of change from some prior state of affairs. But (I now argue) not all events need be processes of change, or need to begin.

My most basic point is that there are instantaneous events.[28] An instant is a period of zero duration. No process of change takes place during an instant, on pain of contradiction. For a process of change takes place during a period only if during that period some item first has an attribute F, then has its complement, not-F. But if something has F and not-F during an instant, then it has F and not-F at the same instant. So no event taking place wholly within one instant could be a process of change.[29] If there are instantaneous events, being an event does not entail being a process of change.

My case for instantaneous events begins thus: suppose that I walk from A to B without pausing. Consider some volume of space along the path I follow, which my body just exactly fills without changing the relative position of any of its parts while in that volume. I was there. If I never stopped walking from A to B, I was there for only an instant. This case suggests two things. One is that there are instants. There is a fact about how long I was in that place. So there was a temporal interval for which I was there. To put it a bit tendentiously, if something just fills a region of time, there is a region of time it just fills. The second point is that some events are instantaneous. My being in that place is a temporal part of a walking, an event. But surely events have only events as temporal parts. Surely motions have only movings as temporal parts, and movings are events. One objection to this might bring up Salmon's Russellian "at-at" theory of motion:

> When we ask how . . . an arrow . . . got from A to C, the answer is . . . by occupying the intervening positions at suitable times . . . the motion is described by the pairing of positions with times alone . . . the motion consists in being at a particular point at a particular time, and regarding each individual position at each particular moment, there is no distinction between being at rest at the point and being in motion at the point. The distinction between rest and motion arises only when we consider the positions of the body at a number of different moments. This means that aside from *being* at the appropriate places at the appropriate times, there is no *additional* process of *moving* from one to another. In this sense, there is no absurdity at all in supposing motion to be composed of immobilities.[30]

But Salmon's point is not that motions have non-motions as temporal parts. Salmon is instead giving an account of just how instant-thick temporal parts count as motions: they do so derivatively, due to the motions of which they are parts. This is why he can continue: "Once the motion has been described by a mathematical function that associates positions with times, it is then possible to differentiate the function and find its derivative, which . . . provides the instantaneous velocities for each moment of travel."[31] Only movings have instantaneous velocities. So even on an "at-at" theory of motion, motions have only movings—events—as temporal parts. More generally, it *happened* that I was at that place at that time. This was something temporary, caused (by prior motion) and a cause (of later motion).

Another objection: if asked what happened just then, we would say that I reached that place. So the event involved is not being there but reaching there. And reaching there is an event because it involves changes leading up to being there. My being there is not an event but a state, which terminates the events leading up to my being there.[32] Reply: the ending of a process which leads up to being there surely *sounds* like an event. What happened then? The movement to there ended. But it ended by my being there. "Reaching there" has two senses, one of process and one of success. I am reaching there (i.e., in the process of reaching there) until I succeed in reaching there. A succeeding is an event. Reaching there (success-sense) and being there are the same event. We *call* it reaching there if I moved there and this is the first instant I am there. If I then continue to be there, this is the same event (being there) continuing, but we no longer call it reaching there.

Let us consider some further instantaneous events. It is possible that time began. Since we have reason to believe in instants, we can also grant it possible that time had a first instant, its beginning.[33] If time had a first instant, time began at that instant. Time's beginning surely was a happening. Yet it was not a change from a prior state of affairs. There was no prior state of affairs. Nothing can be temporally before time, for whatever is temporally before something else is ipso facto part of time, and so not before all of time. So as it is possible that time begin, it is possible that an event not be a change. Nor would any other beginning occurring at time's first moment be a change from some prior state of things. And there might be many such beginnings. For instance, matter might begin to exist then. Even if matter's existing is a state of affairs, not an event, its beginning to obtain seems an event. Many other states' beginnings also seem to be events. So any such state which began to obtain at time's first instant would yield another non-change event. Thus as it is possible that time began, many sorts of non-change events are possible.

Again, on one reading of Big Bang cosmology, the universe came to exist ex nihilo, with the simple appearance of the Big Bang singularity. The universe's coming to exist was certainly an event. But it was not a change in the universe. First, in a change, an item goes from having an attribute F to having its complement, not-F. So in a change, the changing thing exists at the change's start and at its end.[34] But if the universe comes to exist ex nihilo, there is no subject for this event—nothing to which it happens—until it *has* happened.[35] Nothing was first not-F, then F, for when the universe did not exist, it had no attributes, not even that of non-existence. Further, if the universe's coming to exist was a change, it had both a start at which it was F and an end at which it was not-F. But if the universe came to exist in the Big Bang singularity, it came to exist in an instant: the singularity was at a single *point* of spacetime. So if the universe's coming to be had a start and an end, these can only have been at the same instant, that at which it came to exist. So for some F, the universe would have had to be both F and not-F at that instant. So on Big Bang cosmology, coming to exist is something which happens to the universe without being a change in it. The universe's coming to be might have involved a change in the way things are, if there was time and a state of things before the Big Bang. But "the way things are" is not the right kind of thing to be the subject of an event. Further, even if it were, the change in the way things are would just have been an event which occurred along with the non-change event which was the universe's coming to exist. Again, if there was matter before the Big Bang—if, say, there has been a cycle of universes, Big Bangs leading to Big Crunches leading to Big Bangs, etc.—then our universe's coming to be might have involved a change in that matter, but this change would merely have accompanied the non-change of our universe coming to be.

The universe's coming to exist is a dramatic case, but the logic of any coming to exist is relevantly similar. If I carve a statue, it does not come to exist ex nihilo. It comes to exist from the marble I carve. But the statue comes to exist only when I am done carving its marble, i.e., at the end of the last change in the marble.[36] The statue does not pass through intermediate stages, first barely existing, then half existing, then three-quarters existing. There are no such states. Had Michelangelo left *David* incomplete, then if we knew what he had had in mind, we might say of the result, "Here's poor old *David*, left half done." But we would not mean that *David* half existed. *David* half done is a statue. Someone with the right taste might even prefer it to the *David* we have. *David* half done is simply a statue which we know Michelangelo meant to modify.[37] At each stage of the carving, there exists (fully) an incomplete statue, and finally, at the end, there comes to exist, and exists, a complete statue.

Coming to exist is something that happens to *David*. True, we can also say that *David*'s coming to exist happens to the marble Michelangelo carves, but this is just loose speech. Strictly, what happens to the marble is that it is carved into the shape of *David*. Now just as the universe's coming to exist is not a change in the universe, *David*'s coming to exist is not a change in *David*. Here too, the item which comes to exist is not there till it *has* come to exist. And for no F was the complete *David* first not-F, then F, for when it did not exist, it had no attributes, though there were incomplete statues which did. All this has parallels for cases of ceasing to exist: ceasing to exist happens to *David*, must be instantaneous for the same reasons coming to exist must be, and is not a change in the item which ceases to exist because the item is not there to bear some supposed attribute of non-existence.

Beginnings and ceasings to exist are events, though not changes. Nor do they begin. If the only person waiting at a ticket window says, "The line begins with me," this is just a joke. Nothing begins with him until a second person starts to wait. (One person waiting is "the beginnings" of a line, but this just means that if a second person joins the first, the result will be a line.) For whatever begins, continues. Events begin only if they continue past their first instants. No event lasting only an instant continues. So no such event begins, though each (trivially) occurs at the first instant at which it occurs.[38] To be first is just to be unpreceded. An item is a beginning just in case it is unpreceded *and* something of the right sort succeeds it. A parallel claim holds for endings. If all this is right, instantaneous events neither begin nor end. They simply occur. Further, if any such event is a beginning, this is not among its intrinsic properties, at least if by "intrinsic property" we mean very roughly a property an event would have even if the universe ended at its spatiotemporal boundaries.[39] For if the universe ended at this event's spacetime boundaries, the event would not *be* a beginning, as no event would succeed it. So this event's being a beginning is just an extrinsic property which displays the intrinsic event-nature of what has it.

Again, supposing that there are instants, the occurring of any instant of time is an instantaneous event. So if my arguments have been sound, no such event contains a change, begins, ends, or is intrinsically a beginning. Let us ask, finally, whether an instant's occurring is itself a change. This question is distinct from that of whether it must supervene on some change (as is so if, as some argue, there can be no passage of time without some change taking place.)[40] And its answer is: no, it is not a change. The present instant has not previously existed. So its occurring is a coming to be, which is no change in it. Even if its occurring entails that the rest of time changes in some way, this other change only accompanies the non-change of the instant's occurring. It is not the occurring itself. And in fact, the rest of time does not change intrinsically at all with the occurring of a new instant. To pursue this question, I now say just a bit about what times and instants are.

One can treat times—temporal locations—as "substantival," or one can "reduce" them to other entities. Taken substantivally, times are parts of a substance, Time itself. They are primitive bits of the real furniture of the world. Occurring at a time is then bearing a relation, occupant-of, to one such bit. For some reductionists, times are not part of the world's real furniture, but instead "defined entities" or "logical constructions." For these, that is, talk of times is a complex paraphrase of talk about other items. To Prior, for instance, a time is a conjunction of all contingent truths we would want to say were true "at" the time in question, and to say that an event occurs at a particular time is really to say that a truth is part of a particular conjunction.[41] For other reductionists, there really are events, bearing (say) real relations of temporal overlap or distance, and a time is defined as (say) a set of events with certain overlap relations.[42] Whether this truly "eliminates" times depends on whether there are sets. If there are, it does not so much eliminate times as show how they depend on events. Again, when Forbes treats times as locations for possible events individuated at least by their temporal distances from actual events, he does not so much eliminate them as show how they depend on events.[43] Yet the thought behind such views is eliminative: they want to say that for an event to occur at a time is just really for it to occur at a particular temporal distance (zero or non-) from other events.

Instants are times of zero duration. It is possible to treat times substantivally but instants reductionistically—to say, that is, that while there is such a thing as Time, it has only parts of non-zero thickness. It is also possible to be a reductionist about times, yet within this be a realist about instants—to say, that is, that while times "reduce" to events and relations between them, events have parts of zero temporal thickness, or locations for possible events (or the relevant conjunctions of contingent truths) are ordered like the real numbers.

All this has served to set up an argument that the occurring of a new instant of time involves no intrinsic change in the rest of time and so no intrinsic charge *simpliciter*. I first give the argument as it applies to substantivalism with real instants (S+I). I then show how one must change it to apply it to other combinations of views.

Suppose S+I and that we "add" a new instant to (an open period of) Time. The result is not strictly speaking larger, but it does include something it did not previously include. If it does, we suppose, this makes the occurring of a new instant a change. But just what has changed? We can ignore the material universe: given substantivalism, the same Time could occur even if there were no material universe, and we seek a change that is *intrinsic* to the occurring of a new instant. So we seek a change in Time itself. Now one can "add" a new instant to a period of Time only if future Time does not exist; if it existed, there would be no "adding," but just the tenseless existence of all of Time. So the change, if there is one, can only occur to past or present Time. If the past no longer exists, it no longer changes either. Nor *has* it changed, if a thing must exist to bear the attribute of having changed.[44] Further, the ceasing to exist of all time prior to the new time was no change in either the old or the new time. The present moment (again) has not previously existed, so its occurring is a coming to be, which is no change in it. Where then is change? There is certainly something new happening, but (say I) that an event occurs does not entail that a change occurs.

Suppose on the other hand that the past does exist. Then the hoary paradox of increase leaps to view. One can suggest that the whole of Time, past plus present, has changed because it now includes something it did not, and so the occurring of this new instant is (again) a change in Time. But we can again ask: just what changes intrinsically? Intrinsically the past is exactly as it was. Not the present: that (again) comes to exist, which is not a change in anything. Not the sum of past plus present: this sum did not exist before the present moment did. It came to be with it, and its coming to be too was no change. One standard approach to this sort of paradox of increase is to hold that there are really two coincident objects where common sense sees but one, an object which does not change intrinsically and another which "grows" with the new addition. But whatever the merits of this view in other cases, we surely are not going to tolerate two coincident substantival Times. Events have one temporal date, not two.[45] Now when a new instant occurs, the past changes extrinsically, since something now succeeds it which did not before succeed it. But this change in the past is not the occurring, or part of it. The occurring does not happen to the past. It happens to the instant. And the past's extrinsic change is not intrinsic to the new instant's occurring, for it happens beyond the occurring's temporal boundaries.

Thus the argument as it applies to S+I. On substantivalism minus real instants (S–I), the "parcel" of new time added to Time has non-zero length. As it does, the parcel may contain processes of intrinsic change. But that it contains these would not entail that the new parcel of Time's coming to be is *itself* a process of intrinsic change. Against that latter claim, one can ask again: Just what in Time (as versus its contents) changes intrinsically? So it appears that whatever be the case about instants, on substantivalism, time's passing consists of events which are not intrinsic changes.

Reductionism with real instants (R+I) alters the dialectic facing S+I only by adding that the instants in question are universe-wide slices of events or depend for existence on these. On R+I, a new instant's occurring consists in or depends on new events' occurring in the universe. So R+I adds to S+I's picture of things two candidate items whose changes might be or might undergird changes which are new instants' occurring, the universe and its history. If we take the universe's history as something concrete—a sequence of events—then the claim that on R+I the four-dimensional universe-history changes if a new instant is added parallels the claim that on S+I Time changes if a new instant is added. So it faces the questions the latter claim did. "The universe's history" might also denote something abstract, some sort of aggregate of truths. If instants are conjunctions of truths, as in Prior,[46] perhaps an instant's occurring consists in a change in what truths there are.[47] But this "change" may consist simply in the adding of new truths. If it does, our earlier reasoning applies here too and with special force if history is a *set* of truths. Since sets have their members essentially, it is impossible that time's passage consists in a change in membership in the set of truths and necessary that "growth" in history consist simply in a new set coming to be, replacing an old, or the coming to be of a new set "alongside" the old, which changes the old only extrinsically. If the change is not an adding of truths, it consists in already existing items which were not true becoming true (and truths ceasing to be true). If such things occur, they are just a special sort of event happening to an abstract portion of the universe, and this "reduction" of instants becomes just a variation on the strategy of "reducing" instants to event in the universe. So let's now note what time's passage comes to if an instant's occurring is or supervenes on events happening to the universe, not its history. If the past is real, what happens will be the adding of a new zero-thickness event-slice to the universe, and things will be as with S+I. If only the present is real, what happens will be one zero-thickness event-slice replacing another, and so again simply an instantaneous coming to be. I take it, then, that there is a strong case that the occurring of a new instant of time is not itself a change. So if the passage of time consists of the occurring of instants, it consists of events which are not changes. And this is not surprising, for instants can only come to be instantaneously, not change. If the passage of time consists of the occurring of instants, it consists of comings to be.

I now try for the more interesting conclusion that no matter what is true about instants or substantivalism versus reductionism, time's passing consists of events which are not changes. To do so, I must consider the last combination of views, relationalism minus real instants (R–I).

On R–I, the new non-zero-length parcel of time either is just a large, complex event or is something else whose existence depends on this. Now if the new bit of time does not reduce to (i.e., is not identical with) its contents, but instead its existence supervenes on theirs, then arguably though the time's occurring supervenes on changes, its occurring is not itself a change. For a time to occur is for it to come to be. When *David* comes to be, recall, this supervenes on changes in something else, its marble, and still David's coming to be happens only to *David* and is not a change. The friend of R–I might say, "Since the new bit of time has non-zero length and is just a large, complex event, if this event includes a change, it is a change—and so its occurring is a change, since the occurring of an event is just the event itself." Suppose on the other hand that the time just *is* the complex event we would otherwise call its contents. Then this argument is available only to the reductionist who identifies times with the events occurring at them. And the reductionist identification is not plausible. For plausibly:

C. If time *t* just is the events which occur "at" it, then nothing else could have occurred at *t*.

But surely something else could have: at noon yesterday I ate an egg, but surely it would have been the very same time, noon yesterday, had I had tofu instead.[48] I now argue for (C).

There is nothing to a heap but its parts, conjoined. A spatial heap is just spatially extended objects existing spatially conjoined. A temporal heap is just temporally extended objects—events—existing temporally conjoined. So if there is nothing to *t* but events occurring "at" it temporally conjoined, *t* is a temporal heap. Heaps have all their parts essentially: add or remove even one, and you have a new heap. Consider a small heap, a board laid atop a stump.[49] Replace the stump with a soup can. Then replace the board with a hat. It seems clear that the resulting heap is not the heap you had at first. But then even the first replacement did not preserve the heap. If it had, then surely one more single-part replacement would not have destroyed it. Since there is no relevant difference between identity across time and identity across worlds in this case, we can infer that heaps have their parts essentially. Now perform the same sort of substitutions (mentally) on a "heap" consisting of events *e* and *e**. The same conclusion seems clear. Times are like heaps, if there is nothing to them but events in temporal conjunction. And this entails (C).

If the only version of R-I which might preserve the claim that time's passing consists of changes is true only if nothing could have occurred at any time save what actually did occur then, we can conclude that the passage of time does not consist of changes no matter what is true about instants or about substantivalism versus reductionism. But time (say I) does pass. Thus there are constantly events which are not changes.

Consider, finally, the continuing of a state of affairs. These do continue. If one paints a wall pink, there is a first day the wall was pink, a second day it was pink, and so on. Thus the wall's being pink, a state of affairs, seems to continue by having ever-new (albeit monotonous) temporal parts. If it does, the wall's continuings to be pink seem to count as (boring) events.[50] But what makes these events changes, if anything does, is just that they occur at ever-later times. So *if* they are changes—Lombard thinks not,[51] and I incline to agree—they are not intrinsically changes. For whether an event occurs later than anything depends wholly on whether that other thing precedes it. This is a matter outside the event's spacetime limits. Thus being later than anything is not an intrinsic property of the event. If it is not intrinsic to events to *be* later than other items, and only being later makes an event a change, the event is not intrinsically a change. But if events were by nature changes, surely being a change would be intrinsic to any event.

I take it, then, that being an event does not entail being a change or beginning to happen. Some arguments given here have parallels which show that being an event does not entail ceasing to happen either.

Events and Dates

I have rejected the attempt to capture the idea that events happen by saying that events are changes. Other theories of events try to capture this by saying that events have a date as part of their nature.[52] By a date, they tend to mean a location in some scheme for measuring time, or a point in time. But a date need not be either. A date is just whatever answers the question "When did it happen?" Thus whatever has a date happens—and thus the plausibility of such proposals.

The claim that an event's date is part of its nature faces a problem. For if its date is part of an event's nature, then that very event could not have happened at any other time. But if I delay an event, it seems, I bring it about that that very event happens later than it could have happened. So if its date is part of an event's nature, strictly speaking, one cannot delay (or hasten) an event. This is unintuitive. I think last night's concert could have started a bit later. It seems to me that I do not mean by this only that there could have been *a* slightly later concert last night. I mean that *that very* concert could have started later. Suppose that the difference in start-time is so small that no human could perceive it. If all else about the concert is just as it would have been, then the concert that started earlier and the slightly later concert there could have been are humanly indiscriminable. I feel no intuitive pull toward the claim that this indiscriminable difference matters to the events' identity.[53] So it seems to me that events' connection with their dates may be weaker, e.g., just that necessarily, if an item is an event, there is some fact about when it happens. In other words, it might not be part of an event's nature to have the precise date it has, but even if it is not, it is (I suggest) part of an event's nature to have some date or other.[54]

When something happens, there is also a fact about *what* happens (a burning, a spinning) and about what it happens to (a log, a top). Kim gives a simple, unitary account of events by saying that what happens is always that some particular has some property.[55] But this is not a natural account of some kinds of events. Actions are events. When I throw a ball, I acquire the property of being such that I throw a ball. I gain the property because I act. It is not the case that I act because I gain the property. Again, when the ball breaks a window, the window gains a property, being broken.[56] But it gains the property because something breaks it. It is not the case that something breaks it because it gains the property. If an event is some item at some date acting or being acted on, that seems a sufficiently illuminating account of what it is. There is at least some intuitive pull in Davidson's proposal to take events' place in the causal skein of things as part of their natures.[57]

Any genuine event is at least the kind of thing which can be a causal relatum, whether or not it happens to stand in causal relations. So I suggest that a happening or event is anything with a "when" that can be a cause or a being caused or be caused.[58] Events so construed seem to come in at least three varieties. Some are actions. Some are cases of being acted upon. And some are havings of properties the having of which makes an item a potential causal relatum.

This account builds in at least two plausible restrictions on what counts as an event. It disallows as events such states of affairs as 3's being prime, at least if (as we think) nothing brings it about that 3 is prime and being prime does not make 3 a potential causal relatum. It also requires that all properties the having of which constitutes an event be intrinsic, as only these make an item a potential causal relatum. For Socrates does not enter into causal relations in virtue of being or becoming admired by Plato, or in virtue of being shorter than Aristotle—though Socrates might be a causal relatum in virtue of his height, or his admirable wisdom. The account allows that the standing-there of a standing condition with potential causal relevance is a happening, albeit a boring one. I think this a merit.

Along the Event-Spectrum

With this account of events in hand, we can now ask whether being an event entails being temporal. As we have seen, this amounts to asking whether being an event entails having the right TTPs to count as temporal. There are many TTPs. As far as I can see, nothing in the bare concept of an event requires that an event have all of them. Being future is a TTP. But if time began, its beginning never had it. Being past is a TTP. But if time is to end, its ending will never have it. Being instantaneous is a TTP. Any enduring event lacks it. Being temporally enduring is a TTP.[59] Any instantaneous event lacks this. Having a beginning is a TTP. So is having an ending. Not only instantaneous but some enduring events lack these. This morning, I first prepared to work on this essay, then worked on it. Both were events. In one sense of "prepare," one is preparing to work only if one is not yet working. In this sense, either there was a last instant of my preparing but no first instant of my working, or there was a first instant of my working but no last instant of my preparing.

So there clearly can be events lacking some TTPs. Just as clearly, then, the TTPs are not an all-or-nothing package, each entailing the rest. So we can raise a question: might some events have some TTPs, but not the right ones to count as temporal?

Latin medieval philosophers thought so. Consider angels. They act and are acted on: Gabriel will hear a divine command and blow the Last Trumpet. There will be a point in his life when he hears the command and a point when he blows. So there are events in Gabriel's life. But medievals often held that events in angels' lives lack some TTPs. Aquinas, for one, held that angels' actions, etc., occur one after another, but have no dates in time.[60] If this is so, the whole answer to "When will Gabriel blow the Trumpet?" may be "After he hears God's command." Since Gabriel's blowing is an act and has a "when," it is an event. But on Aquinas's view, its "when" is not part of time, since every part of time is dateable in time.[61]

Bonaventure held that angelic lives have "before and after, but not newness and oldness."[62] Aquinas seems to read him as claiming that angelic lives (which are events) contain before-after relations but nonetheless exist in a single unpassing present, and so are never past or future and have no parts which are ever past (old) or future (new).[63] If Aquinas read Bonaventure aright, then Bonaventure was a Whiteheadian, in effect: Bonaventure's angelic lives sound very like single chronons in Whitehead's odd but quite coherent atomist account of time. If there are such events, they are not part of time. For all temporal events (I claim) are eventually past or future or have parts which are: time is not Whiteheadian. But Bonaventure's Whiteheadian angelic events (if that is what they are) do have a "when." They *are* events.

For many medievals, angelic lives or events in them lack some TTPs, and lacking these TTPs renders them non-temporal. So the medievals coined the term "aeviternal" for angelic lives.[64] Now we can make sense of the medieval claims about aeviternity just cited. They seem coherent.[65] This is some reason to think that events could be as the medievals thought, and so have some TTPs and yet lack TTPs necessary to counting as temporal. There cannot be such events if having the TTPs medievals ascribed to angels entails having the TTPs they denied to angels. But it is not clear that these entailments hold. Again, there cannot be such events if entailments so link TTPs that any event with a TTP must have the right ones to count as temporal. But again, those who would claim this must show that the entailments do hold: a tall order. I shortly argue that being present does not entail having the TTPs which would most clearly make an event temporal, and describe (what I claim is) an event which is present but lacks most TTPs we have met so far, thus being a fairly dubious candidate for the label "temporal."

All this brings us back to Boethius. God acts, e.g., in parting the Red Sea.[66] There is a point in his life when he does this. So there are events in God's life. But Boethius held (I submit) that events in God's life are even further from being temporal than later medievals thought events in angels' lives were. Thus he called events in God's life not temporal but eternal. And as with aeviternity, so with eternity: it is not self-evident that events must have all the TTPs temporal events have, or that events lacking various TTPs still deserve the title "temporal." Those who would dispute Boethius' claim that there can be non-temporal events at least have some arguing to do.

A Non-Temporal Present

Boethius asserts that God's life is not temporal and yet in God's life there is a now, a present. Some find this absurd. Craig, for one, writes that "to ascribe presentness to a timeless being in any literal sense is patently self-contradictory, for if a timeless being had presentness, it would exist now, at the present time."[67]

There are two quick answers to this. One is that some things may be present without existing now. There may be time-series discrete from ours, i.e., series no times in which occur before, after, or while any time in our own time-series occurs. If this *is* possible, as I think, then there may be a present in another time-series. Yet what is present in that time-series does not exist *now*, i.e., at the present of our series. Times in a time-series discrete from ours have no temporal relation to our times at all. The second is that it is at best question-begging to say that existing now entails existing at a time. "Now" is an indexical which picks out when the speaker tokens it. As my brief treatment of Aquinas and Bonaventure suggests, it is not obvious that every "when" is a time.

But quick answers are shallow. Craig's complaint stems from taking the Boethian claim "A non-temporal life has a present" as entailing "A life with no temporal properties has a temporal property, presentness." This *is* a contradiction. But I see no reason to think that Boethius asserted it. As I see it, Boethius held instead that being non-temporal is compatible with having some typically temporal properties, and being present is not intrinsically or necessarily a temporal property. For Boethius, being eternal does not consist in having no TTPs. It consists in having some TTPs, but not enough to count as temporal. Boethius began with a set of TTPs in mind, then deleted from his account of events in God's life those he thought incompatible with God's perfection. His concept of eternality was the result.

If this is what Boethius was up to, the charge that talk of an atemporal present entails contradictions is empty on its own. To make the charge of contradiction stick, one must show *why* being present entails being temporal, e.g., why it entails having TTPs Boethius denies God and why having these other TTPs makes events temporal. For Boethius, the basic difference between the temporal and the eternal present is that the temporal present passes, while the eternal does not: events eternal and present are permanent, not transient. So to make the charge of contradiction stick, one might try to show that being present *entails* being transient or impermanent. Put another way, one might try to show that being present entails being past or future at some date. But in fact, it does not.

The Permanence of Time

We use the term *"present"* in phrases like "the present day" and "the present lecture." In these, "present" connotes "the one going on now." There is no temporal limit on this construction. We can speak of the present year, the present millennium, the present geological epoch. We can also then speak of "the present Time," where "Time" denotes the entire temporal series whose parts include the present day, the present millennium, etc. "Our Time" would be just a lexical variation on this, since it too has the sense "the

Time going on now." One would use this phrase to distinguish our Time from other Times there may be, or *are* on some cosmological models.

So our Time, like days, millennia, and epochs, has the property of presentness. Time has this property just as days and millennia do, by having a part whose limit is an instant which is present directly, not in virtue of some part of itself. If this is what it is for Time to be present, Time is not also past or future. For Time would be past or future in the corresponding way only if no part of it were present. In a different sense, Time is present, past, *and* future. For Time has parts bearing each property. But we are not now talking about Time's parts. We are talking about the temporal status of Time as a whole. And as a whole, Time is present, just as today as a whole is present, and will be past as a whole at midnight.

But now note this: though Time's parts pass and are impermanent, Time as a whole is permanent, not transient. Time as a whole is present. But Time as a whole is never either past or future. For given that Time as a whole is present if any part of it is present, Time as a whole would be past or future only if no part of it were present, i.e., only if either all of it were past or all of it were future. But if a temporal item is past, it is earlier than something, and if a temporal item is future, it is later than something. And nothing can be earlier or later than all of Time. Earlier-later relations by definition obtain only between parts of Time. Time includes *all* times temporally related to our present moment.

An item which is present but never past or future is permanent.[68] Thus Time is permanent, though it consists of impermanent parts. Time's parts pass away. But it does not follow that Time itself does. For as each part passes, another takes its place. Further, it is not even clear that Time *can* pass away, if it includes all time.

Suppose first that a Time about to pass away has a last moment. Time as a whole passes away only if all of it is past. But now consider Time's last moment. When it arrives, it is present. Time as a whole is past only if this moment becomes past. But when would it be past? There is no later time, such that later, this earlier moment would be past. Even if there are Times other than ours, these would not be Times at which this last moment could be past. For $time_1$ is in $time_2$'s past only if $time_1$ is earlier than $time_2$. But if time-series are discrete, no moment in one is earlier than any moment in the other. So the last moment could be past only at itself—which would imply that one and the same moment is present and past at once, which is impossible. Thus a Time with a last moment cannot as a whole be past. Such a Time cannot be all past—be over, in one sense of the term— even if it reaches its last moment, and is over in another sense of the term. I now reject a countermove. One might suggest that while there can be no *time* at which all of time is past, still, were all of time past, it would be timelessly true that it is all past. But what is timelessly true is true not just "after time" but equally at all moments of time. This is clearly so for such standard examples of timeless truth as mathematics—and if God is timeless, it is true at all moments that he exists, timelessly. It is not timelessly true today that all of time is past.

Let us now consider a Time with no last moment. Such a time passes away only if all its moments are past. But again, when would they all be past? After each, there is always another moment. So whether Time has or lacks a last moment, Time cannot as a whole be past.

Let me now make two points about what the present argument does *not* imply. First, there is no similar case for Time's being unable to begin. For there is no contradiction in a first moment of Time's being at some time (itself) present without ever being or having been future. And second, the present argument does not entail that Time does not end or is not finite.[69] Its first part does not imply that Time has no end, or last moment. It merely displays a property a last moment would have. And its second part does not imply that Time is not finite. A Time with no last moment can have (say) a last full minute, after which there is an open interval shorter than a minute.

Thus being present does not entail being transient or impermanent, for Time is present and yet is neither. So too, being present does not entail being at some time past or future, for Time is now present but never was future or will be past. To make a case that "eternal present" generates a contradiction, then, one might instead argue that being present entails having *parts* which are transient or impermanent. But this is false. Being present entails this only if it entails having parts. And something is present which has no parts, namely, the present instant.

The critic might next retreat to a disjunction and assert that being present entails either being impermanent or having impermanent parts, or perhaps that being an event entails this. But this move can claim little intuitive support. Since the question at issue is whether being present entails being temporal, one could not support it by insisting that being present entails being temporal, and being temporal entails the disjunction. And it is not clear why else one would believe it.

An Isolated Present

It seems to me that an event could be present and permanent and have no transient parts. For it seems to me that there could be an event with no temporal extension and no temporal relations to any other item. Standard Big Bang models of the universe hold that the universe's history, retrodicted, converges to a single point at which matter has infinite density and physical laws break down—the Big Bang singularity. All agree that if this singularity did exist, it had no temporal extent; many hold that if it existed, this singularity was the first instant of time. Now if no physical laws obtained within the singularity, no law either required that the singularity erupt or prevented its remaining as it was, self-contained: it was physically possible that the singularity be all there ever would be to the universe. Had this been so, the singularity would have been an event with no temporal extension and no temporal relations to any other event. And if it had no temporal extent, it would have had no temporal relations to its own parts, for it would have had no temporal parts.

Perhaps the singularity would have been temporally simultaneous with itself, or with a time, t_0, the universe's first (i.e., unpreceded) and only instant. But even so, this event would have had no transient parts, since only events with temporal extension have them. It would have been as a whole present and never as a whole future or past. So it would have been permanent. For it would have occurred in an isolated instant of time—the only one in an instantaneous Time—and it would have occupied the whole of its Time.

Some might jib at calling something instantaneous "permanent." Craig, for instance, writes that "if time were composed of a single instant . . . a being existing at such a present would . . . be . . . temporal and fleeting."[70] In calling such a being fleeting, Craig suggests that it would be present for just that instant, then wink out and be past. But then the question would arise, *when* would it be past? Again, what is past must be so at *some time*. There is no such time in this example. If its instant is not in anything's past, to where would that being fleet, and if it has no future to become present, why would it fleet? An isolated instant is the first and last instant of its Time. But as we have seen, a last instant is never past.

If it still seems odd to call this item permanent, this may be because we think of permanence as lasting forever. But the item we are discussing *does* last forever, in its Time: it lasts as long as its Time does. What bothers us is that its forever seems short, and we think being permanent entails lasting a long time. But we think this only because in the Time we know, lasting through all of Time would include lasting a long time. If "present and never as a whole past or future" expresses a viable concept of permanence, it does so regardless of the length of the Time involved (or of whether there is a Time involved at all), for it simply has no implications about this.

Let us now try a thought experiment. I was willing to concede that the Big Bang singularity would have existed at a moment of time because the singularity contained mass-energy. It seems to me that mass-energy is intrinsically temporal—that if it exists, it exists in time. But mental events, conceived as such, do not seem to be or supervene on states of mass-energy; it does not seem analytically true that the occurring of a mental event requires the occurring of a physical event. So we can at least conceive of mental events which are not physical events. It is not so clear to me that such events must occupy times.

Imagine a universe temporally isolated from ours, i.e., one whose times are not earlier than, later than, or simultaneous with any time in our universe. Imagine that only one event ever occurs in this universe. Then this event has no temporal relations to any event which is not part of it, whether in its universe or ours. Suppose that in this isolated universe, a reductionist theory of time is true. On such views, as we have seen, times are not part of the world's primitive furniture. Instead, events occur, and whether they occupy times depends on their traits—on whether they are the sort of event which must or can lie at the base of a "logical construction" of a time. Imagine next that the sole event in our isolated universe is purely mental—that it is an event in the life of something not consisting of matter. Some mental events need not as such (i.e., if not involved with matter) have temporal parts. If in learning arithmetic I come to judge that $2 + 2 = 4$, for instance, it sounds downright odd to say that I judged that $2 + 2 = 4$ and then kept right on judging it, or that it took me a full two seconds to judge this or so on. Judging this (as distinct from stating or assenting to a token of a sentence expressing it) is not the sort of thing that takes time.

Very roughly, one judges this, in the sense I have in mind, just when one begins to assent (dispositionally) to it. Beginnings are either first instants or first stages. In the case at hand, the beginning cannot be a stage, for it is where the change from not assenting to assenting occurs. At any point after the first instant of assent, this change *has* occurred. It is not still occurring. It is not a time-taking change, with stages. Some might object that assenting involves tokening a sentence, and tokening takes time. But there are unexpressed assents. Seeing is believing: we typically accept or assent to all sorts of claims about the world in merely having visual experience. My wife enters my study. I recognize her and smile. I do not think to myself, "here's my wife." I simply see that it is she and respond. Yet I can afterward explain, truly, that I smiled because I believed that my wife had entered the room. Again, if assenting involves tokening, the question arises as to just when in the course of tokening I have assented. One view would be that I have not assented that $2 + 2 = 4$ till I finish tokening a sentence expressing this. But surely I assertively token "$2 + 2 = 4$" *because I assent*. If I do, the assent must be there to initiate my tokening. If I did not have the full claim that $2 + 2 = 4$ somehow before my mind, I would not begin tokening "$2 + 2 = 4$." And if I had the content but had not yet assented, then again, I would not begin to token that sentence. Now if it is not true that one has not assented till the sentence is complete, but the assent does not antedate the sentence or occur as soon as one begins tokening it, then presumably the assent occurs some time during the tokening. But just when? One could avoid this question by holding that the boundary between non-assent and assent is vague, with stages. One could then claim that I begin to move from not assenting to assenting in beginning to token the sentence, I do not make it to fully formed assent till the sentence-token is (almost?) complete, and there is no definite instant of first assenting. But we have terms for the states between not assenting and assenting: I doubt but do not fully disbelieve, I suspect, I have a hunch, I incline to believe, etc. It is not plausible that I go through this range of mental states in the course of forming the token. It is still less so that I would start tokening a sentence expressing (when complete) assent that $2 + 2 = 4$ because I (say) doubt but do not fully disbelieve that $2 + 2 = 4$.[71] Suppose, then, that the only event in our isolated universe is a judging that $2 + 2 = 4$. If this does not take time and its occurring does not supervene on anything which must exist in time, why would it exist at a time? Recall that being a beginning or a change from a prior state are *extrinsic* properties. If they are, the intrinsic character of an event of judging does not entail them: There can be such an event not preceded by a state of not judging or followed by a dispositional assent. Yet it would be an event. It would occur. There would be a "now" for the mind doing the judging; it could also judge that it is now judging that $2 + 2 = 4$. So this, I submit, could be a non-temporal event, occurring in a non-temporal present, as permanent as the isolated Big Bang singularity—or as the life of Boethius' God.

Once more, some may jib at calling this event permanent, once again thinking that being permanent entails lasting a long time. But Boethius would reply that permanence need not entail *lasting* at all. For Boethius, God's being eternal is its being the case that all events in God's life are present, but never past or future. As Boethius sees it, the permanence of being everlasting in time is just a pale imitation of this sort of permanence.[72] If God is Boethian-eternal, no event in God's life is ever over, or has parts which are ever over. But this is not to say that events in God's life persist forever. They do not persist at all. For an event to persist is for it to have ever-new parts continue it as its earlier parts end. So only events whose parts end persist. Events in God's life simply *occur*. They do not continue to occur. No part of them is impermanent, while temporal events achieve the only sort of permanence open to them only by surmounting their parts' impermanence. Temporal events are permanent if *some part of them* is always there. Eternal events are permanent because the whole of them is always there. Boethius can claim that his doctrine of eternity ascribes a superior sort of permanence to God because on his account, events in God's life are (as it were) too permanent to need to persist.

Further, there is reason not to judge that forever is short in the case of the event I have described. Some might argue as follows:

> If the event is in time, its Time lasts only an instant. Thus its Time has no metric, nor does its existence. In this Time, there are no temporal units for its instant to be zero *of*—though it remains an instant on mereological grounds, being indivisible. "Short" is a metric concept. Thus it does not apply in this Time.

This argument is not finally persuasive. We can at least conceive of an extended Time with no metric—one such that there is no fact about how many unit distances of any sort lie between two points in it. And we can make sense of there being points in this Time, and understand the claim that the points are much shorter than the Time as a whole. One needs no metric to make sense of zero duration's being short. We know that zero of any possible distance-unit is the minimum number of that unit, just by understanding the concept of zero, and the conceptual tie between minimum number and being short is similarly plain. We know that had this event's Time continued, an instant would have been its shortest possible part.

The real reason to at least withhold judgment on whether forever is short in this case is that the event I have described, and its present, may not be temporal at all. Neither is part of a longer Time, or has any extended time within it, or has temporal relations to any Time, or any temporal relations within itself. So nothing discernible here makes this event or its present temporal.[73] As far as we can tell, they may not be. But taking no time at all makes an event temporally short only if it is the kind of thing that takes time, long or short: only if it is temporal. The life of Boethius' God also takes no time, but it is not the sort of thing that is temporally short or long. Calling Boethius' God's life short because it takes no time to occur is like calling a bodiless God short because he has no height.

At the least, I have now described an event which is present but lacks many other TTPs noted above, and found no reason to call it temporal. To accept the Big Bang scenario above, one must accept that there could be a zero-time event which is not a boundary of some longer event, and an instant of time which is not a boundary of or logically constructed from some extended stretch of time. One need not do so to accept my second case, for it does not suppose that the mental event described is temporal, and if the event is not, it is not instantaneous, and its present is not an instant of time. I claim, then, that neither "God exists in an eternal present" nor "God exists in an eternal now" appear to entail a contradiction, for it is not clear that being present entails having any property that rules out being permanent. These claims, then, are prima facie coherent. And this is prima facie reason to take them as possibly true.

When God Exists

I have argued that it is possible that God's life consists of permanent events. In closing I want to discuss one other facet of Boethius' view. Boethius held that the Aristotelian category "when" applies to God. For Boethius, then, there is a fact about when God exists. And this makes sense; his sample when-locution "God always exists" does sound like an answer to "When does God exist?" For Boethius, we recall, "God always exists because in Him 'always' is of the present time . . . the present of divine things . . . God's now, permanent and not moving, . . . makes eternity."[74] For Boethius, "God always exists" asserts that God exists in the eternal now. Evidently, Boethius thinks that "in the eternal now" answers "When does God exist?"[75] A date is an answer to "when?" Thus for Boethius, "in the eternal now" gives a date for God's existence: eternity is a date, logically speaking. I now argue that if that God is timeless, eternity *is* a date.

An Argument for the Date-Claim

It seems to me that a term x functions literally as a date-term if a sentence is true which has the form "proposition p tenselessly-is true at x, and due to this, at t, p was already true." Now consider the claim that

1. It was true from all eternity that $(p)(q)((p\& (p \to q)) \to q)$.

Statement (1) is true. Its force is that at any time, *modus ponens* was already valid. Lucas captures this thought by the convention of dating all logical truths as true from a date $-\infty$.[76] So (1) implies that

(2) it tenselessly-is true from all eternity that $(p) (q) ((p \& (p \to q)) \to q)$, (t) (at t, it was already true that $(p) (q) ((p \& (p \to q)) \to q)$

If (1) is true and implies (2), (2) is true, and so "from all eternity" is a date-term. We have no qualms granting instantiations of (2) for any time after time's first instant, if there was one. But consider even a supposed first instant. We would not want to say that it *became* true at that instant that $(p) (q)((p \& (p \to q)) \to q)$. For this would have been true even if time never existed. If so, it seems that we should say that at that instant, it was already true that $(p) (q)((p \& (p \to q)) \to q)$. If we should say this at the first instant, then of course we should say it at every later instant.

The first-instant "already true" has roughly the force of "true, and would have been true even if time had not existed." At each later instant, a further note is added, that it *was* true earlier. But while "already true" does not entail at the first instant all that it entails at later instants, its meaning may well be the same. For all t, a proposition is already true at t just in case it is true at t and would have been true had time never reached t. At the first instant, being already true implies being true even if time had not existed. At later instants, it does not imply this. At any instant after the first, being already true implies that the proposition was true at an earlier time. At the first instant, it does not.

"From all eternity," then, functions literally as a date-term in (1) and (2). Now had time not begun, it would have been the case that $(p) (q)((p \& (p \to q)) \to q)$, but not at any time—and so timelessly. That $(p) (q)((p \& (p \to q)) \to q)$, then, is a timeless truth at least if time does not begin: and "from all eternity" allows for this. But suppose that time had not begun. Then that $(p)(q)((p \& (p \to q)) \to q)$ would have been timelessly true, but in one respect *not* true "from all eternity." For there would have been no later time from which (as it were) to look back to eternity, as "from all eternity" suggests. Instead, it would simply have been true *at eternity* that $(p)(q)((p \& (p \to q)) \to q)$. Eternity would have been the date of this truth, logically speaking: "at eternity" inherits the dating function of "from all eternity" if the dates involved collapse into sheer timelessness. So if time had not begun, eternity would have been the date of all timeless truths. But the contingent fact that time exists cannot make a term change its logical category. If there is a possible circumstance in which "at eternity" is a date-term, it is a date-term *simpliciter*. So logically speaking, eternity is a date.

Eternity is the date of what "was true before the beginning of time."[77] This does not place eternity in some fictive infinite past, as Lucas imagines.[78] No past date, however long ago, could be before time's beginning: that is, could be a date which would have occurred had time never begun. A better analogue is the present of a discrete temporal system. Say that at some time in some other time series,

R. Rurik rules Ruritania.

Suppose that our time began. What then should we say about (R)'s status as our time begins? (R)'s truth is surely not in our time's past. If it is, (R)'s time is not discrete from ours, and in any case, at its first moment, our time *has* no past. Nor *is* (R) true at that time, nor will (R) become true: if (R)'s series is discrete from ours, (R)'s truth has no temporal relation to our time. At our time-series' first moment, (R)'s truth is a given, but with no temporal relations to our time, and would have been given had our time never begun. That is, (R) is true without any ordinary tense applying to it, and so (R) is "already true" as our time begins in the sense in which timeless truths are.

Note, though, in that other time-series, (R) expresses (at some time) a *present* fact. (R) is true at a present with no temporal relations to ours. And it makes no difference to our ability to speak of (R) and (R)'s date whether (R)'s present has temporal relations to anything else. Thus (R) provides an analogue in particular for the claim that eternity as Boethius conceives it is a date. If "when (R) occurs" can give a date, so can "at the eternal now." "At eternity" functions as a date-term.

As Boethius suggests, eternity is when a timeless God exists. It does not follow that "God exists" is not true at every other date. What does follow is that it is not facts located at any time t which make it true at t that God exists. If Boethius is right, the semantics of claims about God is "Ockhamist." Ockham held that if there are now truths about the future free actions of human beings, what makes these truths true now are the actions themselves, in our futures.[79] Implicit in this is the more general claim that truths at one date need not have truthmakers at that date, but can be made true by truthmakers located at other dates. Boethius, I suggest, agrees. And this does not mean that he assigns some Pickwickian interpretation to the claim that it is now true that God exists. A timeless God is as objectively there as a temporal God would be. He is just there more permanently than a temporal God could be, and so does not count as temporal. Because he does not, one cannot say that God exists *while* you read this. But one can say that God exists *and* you read this. So too, on a Platonist philosophy of mathematics, one cannot say that $2 + 2 = 4$ *while* you read this, but one can say that $2 + 2 = 4$ *and* you read this—and that the truthmakers for mathematical truths are objectively there, though not temporal. Nor a fortiori does eternity's being when God exists entail that God cannot act now. God does indeed act now. What this means, for Boethius, is that there occur now events which God directly causes, and God's contribution to their occurring has no temporal relation to these effects at all.

Eternity, then, is a date, logically speaking. And this is what one would expect if events can be both eternal and genuinely present.

Notes

1. Here and throughout this essay, "can" and other modal terms express "broadly logical" modalities. For some explication of these, see Alvin Plantinga, *The Nature of Necessity* (New York.: Oxford University Press, 1974), ch. 1.

2. Someone might object: suppose one tokens it in answer to the compound question "Who shot Lincoln and when?" But the question gives the token a context which in effect adds components to "Booth in 1865." Given the context, by saying the words "Booth in 1865," one tokens the sentence "Booth shot Lincoln in 1865."

3. "——is temporal" itself is one such predicate.

4. For argument to the contrary, see Helen Steward, *The Ontology of Mind* (New York: Oxford University Press, 1997), 94–99.

5. Any item's existing is a state of affairs. Some such states of affairs have dates in time. If they do so just in case their obtaining is a temporal event, the obtaining of (say) *this building's existing* is an event, whence it seems to follow that this building's existing is an event. This claim is counterintuitive: asked, "What was going on on campus yesterday?" nobody would reply, "The buildings were existing." I justify this counterintuitive claim below. See, especially, note 57.

6. Here are three contentious metaphysical claims that attract me:

    i.   Only what is present exists ("presentism").
    ii. Only existing things have properties.
    iii. There are no unexemplifiable properties.

If (i) is true, items which we want to call past and future do not exist. If (ii) is true, these items have no properties. But only past items would have a property of pastness, and only future items a property of futurity. So if (i) and (ii) are not just true but necessary, as befits metaphysical theses, pastness and futurity are not possibly exemplified—and so if (iii) is true, there are no such properties.

For present purposes I need not commit myself for or against pastness and futurity. The text suggests one way to paraphrase talk of them away, if need be. If one does eliminate pastness and futurity, a further simplification suggests itself: why talk of presentness, a distinctively temporal property, along with existence and a primitive distinctively temporal relation, and-then, when one can talk instead simply of existence, which is not distinctively temporal, and the primitive distinctively temporal relation, and-then? I also find this move tempting, though it would require me to give some non-property account of tense.

Obviously, if I embraced (i)–(iii) and then added this last move, I would have to alter this essay's machinery radically. But I think the claims I want to make would survive intact, and so I stay with talk of presentness, etc., to avoid complications.

7. Moses Maimonides, *The Guide for the Perplexed*, tr. M. Friedländer, 2d ed. (New York: Dover, 1956), pt. 1, ch. 57, pp. 80–81.

8. Aquinas holds that God has no accidents (*Summa theologiae* 1a.3.6; henceforth ST) and that God exists in an eternal present (*ST* 1a.10.2c et ad 1). Hence he holds that not all TTPs are always accidents (*ST* 1a.10.2 ad 3).

9. F. Schleiermacher, *The Christian Faith*, tr. H. R. Mackintosh and J. S. Stewart (Philadelphia: Fortress Press, 1928), 203.

10. Schleiermacher's general deference to Kant suggests the same. For Kant, all temporal properties are phenomenal, functions of the ways things appear to us, and so only things which appear to us have them (or, in other of his moods: can be known to have them). For Kant and Schleiermacher, God does not appear to us. There is a complication: Schleiermacher endorses Augustine's and Boethius' accounts of eternality (ibid., 205), which impute the TTP of presentness to God. But I incline to discount this. I think Schleiermacher just did not notice that talk of presentness in this context violates Kantian strictures, or else took it (wrongly) as a metaphor.

11. Some may think "temporally" otiose. But 2 is after 1 in the natural-number series, and this "after" is not temporal. Using "temporally" lets me not ask whether "after" is used literally in "2 is after 1."

12. Again, some may think "temporally" otiose. But the positive integer series begins with 1, and the negative integer series ends with −1. Using "temporally" lets me not ask whether these claims use "begins" and "ends" literally.

13. Boethius, *De trinitate*, in *Boethius: The Theological Tractates*, ed. H. F. Stewart and E. K. Rand (New York: G. P. Putnam's Sons, 1926; (henceforth *DT*), 4.71–74, p. 22, All translations mine.

14. So C. D. Broad, *Scientific Thought* (London: Routledge and Kegan Paul, 1923), 59.

15. Boethius, *Philosophiae consolationis*, in Stewart and Rand, *Boethius* (henceforth *PC*) 5.6.22–24, p. 422.

16. William Craig, "On the Alleged Metaphysical Superiority of Timelessness," *Sophia* 37 (1998), 2.

17. DT.4, 64–74, p. 20.

18. Boethius contrasts everlasting temporal lives with properly eternal lives (*PC* 5.6.31–38, p. 424): as he sees it, the difference between them is that eternal lives are lived all at once (36–38). The implicit contrast is that temporal lives, everlasting or not, are lived part by part. Now the whole of an everlasting temporal life is never future and then present: a life which occurs at each moment of time is never as a whole future. Nor is it ever present and then past: a life which occurs at each moment of time is never as a whole past. As *wholes*, then, everlasting temporal lives are as apart from succession as eternal lives. But as they are lived part by part, they have parts which are future and then present or present and then past. And this, says Boethius, is what makes them temporal. So Boethius' point here is that a life can count as temporal *just* by having parts involved in succession.

19. Augustine, *Confessions* 11.13.16.

20. Partly through his heavy influence on the content of Lombard's *Sentences*.

21. See, e.g., Aquinas, *ST* 1a.10.1.

22. There may have been countervailing authorities. Ps.-Dionysius *may* hold to complete atemporality. His text is just not precise enough to let one say with confidence, but as he was as radical a negative theologian as Maimonides, this is not an unreasonable way to read him. Few if any, though, would assign Ps.-Dionysius anywhere near the importance of Augustine for medieval theology. Now medieval authors do often defer to "authorities" verbally but defend views the "authorities" reject (leading to Alan of Lille's famous plaint that authority has a wax nose, i.e., one molded to suit the viewer). But those whom I have found doing this on the nature of eternity were temporalists, e.g., Scotus and Ockham.

23. Paul Helm, *Eternal God* (New York: Oxford University Press, 1988), 27–36; for "present," see 28.

24. On my view, being temporal is being such as to possibly be involved in succession. So being temporal contains being present, and so being present comes out a TTP.

25. See, e.g., 1 Samuel 17:26, Psalms 84:2, Hosea 1:10.

26. Eleonore Stump and Norman Kretzmann, "Eternity," *Journal of Philosophy* 78 (1981), 429–58.

27. Lawrence Lombard, *Events* (London: Routledge and Kegan Paul, 1986), 131–32, 166. By calling them processes I imply only that they have beginnings and ends separated by some interval of time.

28. Contra ibid., 140.

29. Items can be changing during instants in a different sense. An item is in motion at an instant, for instance, if it is so disposed that it would be elsewhere during the next interval, however short, immediately following that instant. Again, an instantaneous event may be the *terminus* of a change, and so be "a change" in the different sense "that to which a process of change moves."

30. Wesley Salmon, *Space, Time, and Motion*, 2d ed. (Minneapolis: University of Minnesota Press, 1980), 41.

31. Ibid.

32. So Lombard, *Events*, 141–42, and Helen Steward, *The Ontology of Mind* (New York: Oxford University Press, 1997), 74.

33. It in any case *seems* possible that time began in this sense, which counts in favor of at least the possibility of instants.

34. It need not exist through a process of change. A bicycle can be disassembled and have its parts scattered. While scattered, the bicycle does not exist (or so one would think). Suppose now that one reassembles it, but some of its paint has chipped while the parts were scattered. Then the bicycle, when it comes back into existence, has changed from the state it was in at the end of its prior period of existence. But it did not exist during a process of change; it was never chang*ing*.

35. So Aquinas, *ST* 1a. 45.2 ad 2.

36. At least, in one sense of "come to exist." In another sense, the statue is coming to exist throughout the carving.

37. This strikes me as just intuitively obvious. If I had to argue it, I would try to show that artefacts are relevantly like heaps, and so are items for which mereological essentialism holds: every part they have is necessary to their identity. If this is true, then only an item with precisely the parts of Michelangelo's final *David* is Michelangelo's *David*.

38. By parallel reasoning, no single-instant event ends.

39. One reason for the "very roughly" emerges below.

40. For discussion of this, see W. Newton-Smith, *The Structure of Time* (New York: Routledge and Kegan Paul, 1980), 13–47.

41. A. N. Prior, *Past, Present, and Future* (New York: Oxford University Press, 1967), 79–82, 88–92; Prior, *Papers on Time and Tense* (New York: Oxford University Press, 1968), 122–26. This is likely not the end of the "reduction"; Prior is skeptical of propositions (so Prior, *Objects of Thought* [New York: Oxford University Press, 1971], passim).

42. So Bertrand Russell, *Our Knowledge of the External World* New York: W. W. Norton, 1929) 94–95.

43. So Graeme Forbes, "Time, Events, and Modality," in *The Philosophy of Time*, ed. Robin Le Poidevin and Murray MacBeath (New York: Oxford University Press, 1993), 80–95.

44. Nor has it ceased to exist, if a thing must exist to bear *this* attribute. If the past stretched from t to t_n, then it has become true that stretch of time $t - t_n$ used to exist. But this is true due to a fact about the present, that it now was preceded by $t - t_n$. That $t - t_n$ preceded it does not

represent a change in the present: the present never was preceded by any other stretch. And on substantivalism, the becoming true of this proposition is not a change in Time, since Time does not consist of propositions.

45. Leaving special relativity out of the picture.

46. Or perhaps in some Prior-style view which *is* ultimately committed to propositions.

47. If instants are not conjunctions of truths but depend on them, e.g., because their existence supervenes on the conjunctions', the moves to make parallel those in the text below about reductionists whose instant occurring supervenes on events.

48. One reply here: It would not have been the very same time, but would have been *another* noon yesterday. It would have had the same position in time (i.e. relations to all other times) the actual noon did, but been a different individual. I find this reply implausible. A time just *is* a position in a temporal series, as a spatial point just is a position in space. There is nothing else to it: same time position, same time. A second reply would go "it would not have been the same time or the same time-series. A time just is a position in a time-series—actual noon, a position in the actual time-series. Actual noon has essentially its relations to all other actual times, as you say. But still, had you eaten tofu, it would not have been actual noon, nor would any other actual time have ever occurred. It would have been a different time-series altogether, though one containing almost the same events as actually occurred." Is it plausible, though, that what time occurs now depends on what happens later?

49. The example is Chisholm's, and the argument which follows is indebted to him.

50. If a state's beginning and its continuing to obtain are events, then its obtaining at any time is an event, since at that time it either begins or continues to obtain, or (if states can recur) begins a new episode of its obtaining. Now "in existence" certainly *sounds* like a state. If existing is a state a thing is in, then, it follows that a thing's existing at a time is an event. I incline to accept this. But if existing is a state, it is a state of individuals, and so many would object here, thus blocking the argument. See, e.g., C. J. F. Williams, *What Is Existence* (New York: Oxford University Press, 1981).

51. Lombard, *Events*, 84–85.

52. So Jaegwon Kim, "Events as Property-Exemplifications," in *Action Theory*, ed. Douglas Walton and Myles Brand (Dordrecht: Reidel, 1980), 159–77. Lombard also asserts this (*Events*, 212–16).

53. Lombard's argument that dates are essential (*Events*, 205–216) is that a certain sort of transworld switching of *two* events is impossible. Even if this is so, it should not affect our intuitions about whether *one* event can switch times.

54. Still, it would be reasonable to reply, "You really do not have such fine-honed intuitions about event-identity. What you really believe is that some event qualitatively just like last night's concert could have started later. Nothing you really believe bears on whether the later concert would have been the very event the earlier concert was." So I do not see my argument here as strong.

55. Kim, "Events."

56. Either the window continues to exist as a broken and so scattered object, or strictly speaking it is the window's fragments that gain a related property, being the remains of a window, as soon as they come to be.

57. Donald Davidson, "The Individuation of Events," in Davidson, *Actions and Events* (New York: Oxford University Press, 1980), 163–80.

58. Only events, facts and substances are plausible candidate causal relata. (For cases for "fact-causation," see, e.g., Jonathan Bennett, *Events and Their Names* [Indianapolis: Hackett, 1988], and D. H. Mellor, *The Facts of Causation* [New York: Routledge, 1995]. For discussion of agent causation, see Timothy O'Connor, ed., *Agents, Causes, and Events* [New York: Oxford University Press, 1995].) Facts and substances have no "when."

59. Stump and Kretzmann ("Eternity") want to allow for non-temporal duration. I will not discuss this here.

60. *ST* 1a.10.5c et ad 1; 1a.53.3.

61. One line of argument that angelic events cannot be dated held that being dated requires being physically related to the "universal clock," the motion of the outermost heaven of Aristotle's cosmology, a condition all immaterial beings fail: so, e.g., *ST* 1a.61.2 ad 2.

62. Bonaventure, *In II Sent.*, d. 2, pt. 1, 1, 3.

63. *ST* 1a.10.5c. Thomas rejects the view as contradictory. For a differing reading, see Richard Cross, "Four-Dimensionalism and Identity across Time: Henry of Ghent vs. Bonaventure," *Journal of the History of Philosophy* 37 (1997), 398–99. Thomas's own view is that angels' existences are *totum simul* (1a.10.5 ad 2, 3)—have a permanent present like God's—but are not eternal because their actions involve succession. Perhaps his own view influences his reading of Bonaventure's.

64. They could not settle for "non-temporal," for as they saw it, events could lack various combinations of TTPs, and so there were more ways than one to be non-temporal.

65. In the case of Bonaventure read *modo* Whitehead, this takes some showing. Dean Zimmerman and I provide it in "Extending the Present" (forthcoming).

66. God's parting the Red Sea and the Red Sea's parting are distinct events. One's subject is the Red Sea, the other's, God. So if the Red Sea parted at *t*, this does not settle the question of when God parted it, i.e., did the action which resulted in the sea's parting. It might be that God's parting it does not occur at *t*.

67. Craig, "Alleged Superiority," 1.

68. While I hit on this claim independently, I have since found it in Quentin Smith, "A New Typology of Temporal and Atemporal Permanence," *Noûs* 23 (1989), 323. Smith's account of eternity is close to what I claim was on Boethius' mind.

69. These are not the same properties. It is conceivable that time be non-finite but end, i.e., have a last moment: the series of negative integers is non-finite but has a last member. And as shown below, it is conceivable that time be finite but never end.

70. Craig, "Alleged Superiority," 3.

71. For a more careful discussion of this kind of mental event, see my *Time and Eternity*, 285–90.

72. *PC* 5.6. 40–56, p. 424.

73. Zimmerman, in his contribution to this volume, suggests that conscious states involving phenomenal quality experiences cannot be instantaneous. If no conscious state could lack temporal duration, this event's being mental would render it either temporal or unconscious—and nobody would suggest that God's mental life could consist wholly of unconscious states. Zimmerman's claim deserves more discussion than I can give it here. I will say just this: even if the claim is correct—which is questionable—it would imply something about *all* conscious states only if all conscious states involve phenomenal quality experiences. But this seems false even in the human case. There is nothing it is like phenomenally or sensorily for me to become aware that 2 + 2 = 4, though contingently my becoming so aware may have sensory or phenomenal company. Further, it is plausible that only beings with senses experience phenomenal qualities and that purely intellectual mental states have no such contents. It is also at least legitimate to hold that God has no senses and that the cognitive component of his mental life is purely intellectual. So I am not sure that Zimmerman's argument poses a problem for the claim that a Boethian-eternal God's mental life is relevantly like a mental event without temporal duration.

Still, I hold that temporality is finally a modal property, that of being possibly earlier or later than something. So for all I have said, the present in my example *could* be temporal. Nothing we know about it rules out its being possibly later or earlier than something. But equally, nothing rules out its not being possibly so, and so being atemporal.

74. *DT* 4.69–74, p. 20.

75. Objection: maybe the answer he means it to give is just "There is no 'when.'" Reply: this amounts to rejecting the question. So if this were what Boethius meant, he would not have held that the category "when" applies to God.

76. J. R. Lucas, *The Future* (Oxford: Blackwell, 1989), 114.

77. And equally of what will be true after the end of time, if any.

78. Though it does sit well with Hasker's and Zagzebski's notion that eternal facts have the "hardness" of past facts.

79. See Ockham, *Treatise on Predestination, Foreknowledge, and Future Contingents*.

2

Atemporal, Sempiternal, or Omnitemporal

God's Temporal Mode of Being

GARRETT DeWEESE

In the literature of philosophical theology, several different terms are used to elucidate the metaphysics of "eternity" as God's temporal mode of being. My aim in this essay is to offer definitions of four crucial terms: temporal, atemporal, sempiternal, and omnitemporal. Certain metaphysical implications which flow from the definitions offer philosophical theologians clear alternatives from which to choose in explicating God's eternity. First, I suggest that the definition of atemporality has clearly detrimental implications for traditional conceptions of God's being. Next, I argue that if God's eternity is conceived as sempiternal, then it follows that God is logically contingent, a rather unwelcome result. Finally, I claim that omnitemporality, while not without some difficulties, may offer the best conceptual framework for understanding God's relation to the temporal universe and to us.[1]

A Preliminary Distinction

We cannot assume that the same concept is intended by different uses of the same term. For my purposes it will be important to distinguish two kinds of "time."

Physical time is the time most familiar to us as we go about our daily lives; it is also the time that figures in physical theories. Physical time refers to time in any temporal world containing physical objects. "Measured time" is physical time in those worlds where laws of nature allow for the mensuration of time with some physical clock. Whitrow explains, "greater accuracy in the measurement of time can be obtained by means of atomic and molecular clocks. Implicit in these developments is the hypothesis that all atoms of a given element behave in exactly the same way, irrespective of place and epoch. The ultimate scale of time is therefore a theoretical concomitant of our concept of universal laws of nature."[2]

The mensuration of time in a given world would depend on a clock appropriate to the laws of nature of that particular world,[3] but since not all physical worlds have the sort of regular laws which allow for a metric of time, not all physical time is measured time. It is demonstrable that the measurement of time by a particular clock in the actual universe is affected by acceleration and gravity.[4] So physical time in the actual world (and in any possible worlds with laws and forces relevantly like those in our world) is relative to a local reference frame. So it would be proper to speak of "local time" to underscore the fact that any mensuration of physical time will necessarily depend upon local reference frames, and that observations of the same temporal processes will not necessarily be equivalent from one local reference frame to another. Since the existence of any physical world is contingent, so too is the existence of physical time.

Metaphysical time, roughly, is the succession of moments or events through which concrete objects persist, but since concrete objects need not be material objects, metaphysical time is not identical to physical time.[5] The flow and direction of metaphysical time grounds the ordering relations of physical time.[6] Thus even if a temporal physical world lacked regular laws, and hence lacked a temporal metric, that world would undergo a succession of moments (flow) with a determinate order (direction) which is grounded in metaphysical time.

If God experiences succession in his being, then metaphysical time is "divine time." Whether or not such time has a metric is a question that I shall leave open, but it is not necessary that the metric of time derived from any temporal world be applicable to metaphysical time.[7]

While I cannot argue for it here, I believe it can be shown that it follows from the nature of causation together with the causal theory of time that the topology of metaphysical time is linear and unidirectional.[8] Further, if two temporal series are related, then the same topology applies to both. Hence, since metaphysical time is related to every possible physical time, the topology of physical time is also linear and unidirectional.

Temporality

We naturally understand by "temporal" the mode of existence of an object that is in time. But what is meant by "in time"? Generally, I think we understand by this expression that the entity in question exists in the past or the present or the future, or exists earlier than or simultaneous with or later than some other entity which is also in time. Using the terminology which has become standard since McTaggart,[9] we can say that a temporal entity either possesses a monadic A-property (of pastness, presentness, or futurity), or it stands in a dyadic B-relation (of earlier than, simultaneous with, or later than). Thus we have:

(1) T is a *temporal entity* iff$_{df}$ T possesses an A-property or stands in a B-relation to some other entity.

Several important consequences follow from this definition. First, a temporal entity is located in a (metaphysical or physical) temporal series in virtue of its A-properties or B-relations. That is, it has temporal location. To exist "in time" then is to exist "at a time."[10]

A second important consequence is that (metaphysically or physically) temporal entities are concrete. Why? The reason has to do with the relation between concrete entities and causation. It is well known that the abstract/concrete distinction is notoriously difficult to draw; yet it will suffice for present purposes to give what is generally accepted to be a sufficient condition for concreteness: a concrete entity is one which is possibly the direct terminus of a causal relation. On the plausible interpretation of the conservation laws as causal laws,[11] every point of spacetime is directly caused by an earlier point of spacetime. Thus every spacetime point is concrete even if unoccupied by a material object.[12]

Now, every spacetime point has A-properties or stands in B-relations. Hence every spacetime point is a temporal entity. Similar reasoning shows that spacetime regions, as well as events and event-boundaries, are likewise possible termini of a causal relation. (And indeed, if we consider an example of a putative uncaused event, such as the emission of an alpha particle by a radioactive isotope, there is no reason to hold a priori that such an event could not be the possible terminus of a causal relation.) So it follows from these considerations that every temporal entity is also concrete.

A third consequence of (1) is that every physical temporal entity is contingent. An entity can have temporal location if and only if time exists, and there is no reason to believe the existence of physical time is logically necessary. To the contrary, it can be argued that physical time is contingent. States of affairs consist in an entity's having a property or standing in a relation. Since temporal entities have A-properties or stand in B-relations, they constitute temporal states of affairs. But we can conceive of a possible world with no temporal states of affairs, a (physically) timeless world.[13] If a possible world had, say, only three spatial dimensions and no temporal dimension, the world would be timeless, be changeless, and contain no temporal entities. Now if conceivability is prima facie evidence of logical possibility, then the existence of physical time is not logically necessary, and temporal entities are contingent.[14] Is this claim compatible with the claim that God is temporal? Yes, since if God is temporal, God's time would be metaphysical rather than physical.

Fourth, (1) has as a corollary that since a temporal entity is one that has temporal location, and a temporal location may be a point in time, a durationless instant, it follows that a temporal entity need not be an enduring entity. It may seem strange to hold that an entity can be said to exist if its existence has no duration. But it seems to me that this is correct. Consider the event of my *starting* this essay. Given that I have started, the event of my starting must have existed. Clearly that was an event located in time (it is past—an A-property; it is earlier than midnight—a B-relation), but equally clearly my *starting* did not endure through a span of time. The event of starting was an instantaneous event. Similarly, *beginning* a class, *winning* a race, *ending* a lecture, and *losing* a game are all instantaneous events. Even though the same terms may often refer to a process, the process begins or ends at a point in time. And these events are located in time; they have A-properties or stand in B-relations. Thus there would seem to be no reason not to regard them as temporal entities.

Brian Leftow, however, disagrees: "A being is *intrinsically* timeless iff it does not 'contain' time, i.e., does not endure through time. If there are events without duration, they are intrinsically timeless even if they are located in time."[15] But by my definition (1), being located in time is what constitutes an entity as temporal. However, Leftow regards an argument similar to the one I gave above as insufficient to show that instantaneous events are temporal and not timeless entities. So I shall offer another based on a spatial analogy. By definition, a point in geometry has no extension, but it has location. The point exists in space. It would seem at least very odd to argue that the point was "spaceless" even though located in space; rather we would want to say it was a spatial point. And it would be most surprising if what was plausible in the spatial case was not analogous with what was plausible in the temporal case. So it is plausible to accept that a point in time is a temporal point, not "timeless." But this leads to a clarification of what it is to be timeless or atemporal.

Atemporality

It seems straightforward to define atemporal as the negation of (1):

(2) A is an *atemporal entity* iff$_{df}$ A has no A-properties and stands in no B-relations.

Atemporal entities thus do not exist at any time.[16] How then do they exist, if indeed they do?

First, it can be argued that atemporal entities must be abstract. We saw above that temporal entities are concrete; how can it be shown that atemporal entities are not concrete? On a causal theory of time, temporal relations are causal relations.[17] So if an entity is possibly the terminus of a causal relation, it possibly stands in a B-relation.[18] But by (2), atemporal entities stand in no B-relations, and therefore atemporal entities cannot be concrete. If something must be either concrete or abstract, a reasonable supposition, atemporal entities must be abstract.

Second, there are good reasons to think that any atemporal entities which exist must exist necessarily.[19] The contingency of physically temporal entities is linked to the contingency of physical time in which they are located. So it seems reasonable to suppose that anything not located in physical time would not be infected by time's contingency. The shortest way to show the reasonableness of this is not to attempt to prove the necessity of an existential proposition, but to produce candidates for the category "necessary abstract atemporal entity."

Platonic forms or universals, and mathematical and logical entities, are standardly offered as examples of atemporal entities. I cannot devote the time or space here to defending realism about universals. So we will consider mathematical entities and assume that whatever we conclude of them we could also say of logical entities. William Kneale, for example, argues that numbers are atemporal:

An assertion such as "There is a prime number between five and ten" can never be countered sensibly by the remark, "You are out of date: things have altered recently." And this is the reason why the entities discussed in mathematics can properly be said to have a timeless existence. To say only that they have a sempiternal or omnitemporal existence (i.e. an existence at all times) would be unsatisfactory because this way of talking might suggest that it is at least conceivable that they should at some time cease to exist, and that is an absurdity we want to exclude.[20]

However, many philosophers do indeed want to say that numbers exist eternally but not atemporally. Stephen Davis, for one, says that the number seven is eternal but not atemporal:

> But if the number seven is not just eternal but timeless, then . . . the following statements cannot be meaningfully made:
>
> The number seven existed on 27 July 1883.
> The number seven was greater than the number six during the whole of the Punic Wars.
> The number seven existed yesterday and will exist tomorrow.
>
> But the number seven is not a timeless being; all three of these sentences, in my opinion, are not only meaningful but true.[21]

I believe that Kneale is right and Davis is wrong about this. If numbers were temporal entities, then as has been shown they would be concrete entities and would be possible termini of causal relations. But it is very odd to speak of causal relations with numbers; what could possibly be meant by saying that something caused (or was caused by) *seven?* Further, temporal entities are contingent. Although individual instantiations of numbers may indeed be contingent, the numbers themselves, together with their fundamental logical and mathematical relations, would seem to remain necessarily unchanged.[22] So since we have good reason to believe that numbers are not contingent but are necessary entities, they must be atemporal.

How then should we account for Davis's examples? I believe the simplest answer is to maintain that all three examples are ill-formed statements which seem to express truth not because numbers have temporal location but precisely because they do not. Statements made about atemporal entities are made at a time, and a truth value may be assigned at that time, but this does not entail that the subject of the statement itself be located in time. A proposition about timeless entities that is tenselessly true is true *now*, but this does not entail that the subject of the statement itself be located at the present.

These considerations regarding numbers lead to the following. Mathematical statements are necessarily true if true, and necessarily false if false. The only way a mathematical statement could fail to have a truth value would be if the numbers involved in mathematical statements failed to exist. But since it has been shown that numbers necessarily exist, mathematical truths are necessarily true, hence abstract and atemporal. I believe similar reasoning could be applied to logical truths, since the foregoing argument tacitly rests on a logicist analysis of mathematics.

A third statement we can make about atemporal entities is that, in addition to being abstract and logically necessary, it is logically impossible that they change. This follows directly from (2). For x to change is for x to have a property P at t_1 that x does not have at t_2. But for this to be true, x must occupy a location in a B-series (i.e., stand in a B-relation) such that the state of affairs x's-having-P-at-t_1 is earlier than the state of affairs x's-not-having-P-at-t_2. But by (2) atemporal entities do not stand in B-relations. Therefore atemporal entities must be changeless.

Given that atemporal entities are necessary, changeless things, it is clear why many philosophical theologians have wanted to say that God is atemporal. An atemporal God would be immutable, immaterial, and necessary. All seem to be attributes of God that a traditional theist would want to maintain. The tradition goes back at least as far as Augustine and includes Boethius, Anselm, and Aquinas. Contemporary philosophers of religion who argue for God's timelessness or atemporality include Paul Helm, Eleonore Stump, Norman Kretzmann, and Brian Leftow. But surely none of these would want to say that God was an abstract entity! So if my argument is correct, there is good reason to suspect that God is not atemporal.

The atemporal view of God's temporal mode of being is not without further difficulties. Critics of the atemporal view include Duns Scotus and Ockham in the Middle Ages, and recently, Anthony Kenny, Richard Swinburne, Nelson Pike, Stephen Davis, William Hasker, William Lane Craig, and Alan Padgett. (Interestingly, the great Continental rationalists all held to an atemporal view of God's existence, while the British empiricists took the opposing line. I leave to the reader to work out whether there is more to this correlation than historical accident.)

The reasons given for opposing the atemporality of God generally have to do with whether or not the notion of an atemporal personal being is even coherent. Cogent arguments have recently been given by both friends (Leftow) and opponents (Hasker) of atemporality for believing that the notion is indeed coherent. Stump and Kretzmann, of course, offered their much-discussed concept of ET-simultaneity to explain how an atemporal person could be related to the temporal world. But not all philosophers buy the Stump-Kretzmann argument. Opponents of atemporality claim that God's providential interactions with creation, his interactions with people, including answering prayer, and indeed his very nature as a person, as opposed to an abstract object, demand that he is in some sense not outside of time.[23] These philosophers have had to propose some other temporal mode of God's being which nevertheless maintains his essential attributes. They have typically used words such as "everlasting," "sempiternal," "relatively timeless," or "omnitemporal" to describe God's being. The final two sections of this essay will be devoted to defining and drawing the necessary distinctions between two of these terms. Although my focus is on philosophical theology, the definitions and distinctions are as general as those given above of temporality and atemporality.

Sempiternality

The concept of a sempiternal entity may be derived from the etymology of the term: an entity that exists at all times. But this, of course, is ambiguous. What is generally meant is an entity which, once it has begun to exist, cannot, as a matter of nomological necessity, cease to exist at any subsequent moment. As a definition,

(3) S is a *sempiternal entity* iff$_{df}$ if S exists, then (i) S possesses an A-property or stands in a B-relation, and (ii) S is nomologically necessary.

It might appear that (3) contradicts what was said above regarding the contingency of temporal entities. But this is not so. S is still contingent; only if S comes into existence is S nomologically necessary. If time were to cease, so would S, for there would be no time in which S could be located. In other words, what (3) attempts to capture is the concept of an entity that, once it has begun to exist in time, will necessarily exist as long as the physical time in which it is located exists. To distinguish the concept of sempiternality from temporality, we may make use of the notion of possible futures. It seems reasonable to believe (*pace* determinists) that the future can go any one of a number of possible ways. The future is, to borrow the felicitous phrase of Borges, "a garden of forked paths." If we picture time something like a tree structure, then what we have is a universe in which the past is singular and real, the future is a branching tree of possibilities, and the present is the edge of growing reality as future possibilities collapse into the one reality.[24] Each different branch represents a possible future (or possible world) which gets "cut off" as time advances.

Now, any particular entity which is physically temporal will exist in some of those possible futures, and not exist in others. However, a sempiternal entity, once it begins to exist, will continue to exist at all times subsequent to its coming into being, but only in those possible futures in which the laws that render the sempiternal entity nomologically necessary continue to obtain. For example, suppose one family of branches of possible futures represents those futures in which the universe, being subcritical, collapses on itself in a big crunch. Some of these possible futures are such that no rebound universe results, so the spacetime points of that crunched world would no longer exist. But other possible futures are such that some crunched worlds would result in rebound universes, and it is possible that in some of these rebound universes, different laws will obtain. In these possible futures, therefore, some sempiternal entities, which existed in the past history of these futures, will no longer exist. Thus sempiternal entities, being only nomologically necessary, do not exist in all possible futures as a matter of metaphysical necessity.[25]

What sorts of entities might be sempiternal? The most likely candidates are contingent physical entities such as Planck's constant, the charge of an electron, the net sum of mass/energy in the universe (given that conservation laws are true natural laws),[26] and perhaps also fundamental particles such as protons (if they do not decay) and possibly quarks or strings. There are possible worlds in which these things never exist, or have different expressions. Further, they have not all existed from the beginning of time, assuming some version of big bang cosmology is correct. But it seems to be nomologically necessary that once they began to exist in the actual world, they necessarily exist as long as time—the physical time of their respective worlds—exists. Indeed (statements of) the laws themselves would seem to be sempiternal.

Sempiternal entities share the property of contingency with temporal entities, and the property of changelessness with atemporal entities. Some sempiternal entities clearly are concrete things (fundamental particles); and while some would seem to be abstract things (Planck's constant, statements of physical laws), it is the numerical value or the mathematical expression which is abstract, not the entity itself.

Omnitemporality

The final temporal mode of existence to be discussed is omnitemporality. Often one finds "omnitemporal" in the literature used as equivalent to sempiternal, but one can also find it used as equivalent to atemporal. I propose to use "omnitemporal" for an entity which is metaphysically temporal and exists necessarily.

If we understand this entity as metaphysically (as opposed to physically) temporal, and if "existing at all times" introduces a metaphysical modality, then the entity exists of metaphysical necessity.[27] But it follows from the topology of dynamic time that the "now" of metaphysical time coincides with the "now" of any possible physical time,[28] so an omnitemporal entity will be temporally present at every present moment of any possible physical time. As a definition, we have:

(4) O is an *omnitemporal entity* iff$_{df}$ (i) O is necessarily metaphysically temporal, and (ii) O necessarily exists.

What this definition of omnitemporality tries to capture is what is intuitively contained in the notion of "everlasting" as the temporal mode of divine existence. For a traditional theist, sempiternality will not do, since sempiternal things only exist contingently, while the theist wants to insist that God exists necessarily. And further, many objections to the notion that God is temporal are grounded in understanding God's time as physical time, thereby making God, in some sense, dependent upon the physical time of this universe. So if the objections to atemporality as the mode of divine existence are found to be compelling, then another mode must be found which includes necessary existence and metaphysical time. Omnitemporality as defined by (4) does this.

First, to say that an entity is metaphysically temporal is to say that it is a temporal entity, but that the temporal properties and relations which belong to it are defined with reference to metaphysical and not physical time. What constitutes metaphysical temporality is the same relation that constitutes any other temporality: causation. My suggestion is that the causal succession of mental states in God's conscious life grounds the flow and direction of metaphysical time.[29] And given that God is creator and sustainer of the contingent order, his causal sustenance of every world will ground the time of that world.

As it is possible that there not be an intrinsic metric to metaphysical time, it is possible that no quantitative temporal relations—e.g., temporal distance—hold for O. What this means is that, although moments of a temporal world can be placed in a one-to-one correspondence with moments of metaphysical time, one could give no sense to the statement that a certain duration of metaphysical time lasted a certain number of seconds (days, years, etc.).[30]

But what about the possibility of timeless worlds? It follows from (4) that metaphysical time is necessary, so can there be any timeless worlds? I suggest that there are two possible ways to think of timeless worlds. First, one could argue that atemporal worlds were simply abstract objects which exist timelessly, just as numbers do. This would have the consequence, as seen above, that timeless worlds were necessary. But this is a consequence that not all would be willing to accept.

Second, then, one could argue that a timeless world is one which is intrinsically timeless but extrinsically temporal. That is, if W_A is an atemporal world, and M is the metaphysical temporal series of O, then W_A will have temporal location in M but will not have temporal duration in M. So a timeless world would be intrinsically timeless but extrinsically temporal, in that it would possess an A-property or stand in a B-relation to an entity in M. By showing that a timeless world is extrinsically temporal, we avoid the claim that timeless worlds are necessary.

But perhaps an eclectic solution is best. If W_A were a non-actual possible timeless world, it would be an abstract entity and exist necessarily. But if W_A were an actual timeless world, it would be extrinsically temporal by virtue of having location in the metaphysical temporal order, and would be contingent (as indeed all concrete objects other than God are).

The claim that O is temporally present at every present moment of any possible physical time may now be stated more carefully. For any temporal world W and any physical time t that lies in the present at metaphysical time m, t is an instantaneous state of affairs, t is actual as of time t, and no state of affairs in W that is earlier than or later than t is actual as of time m.[31] Now, since simultaneity is a transitive and reflexive relation, any time or event which is simultaneous with time m will also lie in the present at time t. Consequently, to be present at physical time t is to be present at metaphysical time m and vice versa. So it is correct to say of O that "O is (temporally) present," while it would not be correct to say that of an atemporal entity such as, say, the number seven.

If omnitemporality is to meet the objections that have been raised against atemporality, then God as an omnitemporal being must be able to sustain temporal relations. As an omnitemporal being, God would be "above" physical time but still temporally present and thus able to enter into relations with temporal entities. As I see it, this means not only that the temporal entity must in some sense be present to God, but also, contra such atemporalists as Leftow, Stump, and Kretzmann, that God must have the A-property of presentness, in the sense just given. This is because I do not see that any account offered so far of atemporal causation is satisfactory, and I doubt that a satisfactory account can be formulated. And if my arguments above are correct, an atemporal entity is abstract and so could not enter into causal relations.

Omnitemporality, as God's temporal mode of being, offers conceptual resources for understanding many theological claims. As omnitemporal, God would experience succession in his mental states, thus being much more analogous to what we mean by "person." As omnitemporal, God could experience change in his relational properties, so that an individual would at one time be an object of God's wrath and at a later time, after redemption, would be an adopted child of God.[32] God's providence is also more easily understood if God is omnitemporal, as is the efficacy of petitionary prayer. And if one desires to maintain a form of libertarian free will, an omnitemporal God coheres well with Ockhamist or Molinist solutions to the dilemma of foreknowledge and free will. Finally, in Trinitarian theology, the individual persons of the Trinity would exist in dynamic relationship before the creation of the temporal world, thus grounding the dynamic emphasis of the *perichoresis*, the mutual indwelling, or interpenetration, of the Trinity. And an omnitemporal God certainly makes understanding of the temporality of the Incarnation much easier.

Conclusion

I believe the definitions and clarifications given above for temporality, atemporality, and sempiternality are defensible and consistent with common usage. And the definition of omnitemporality makes precise what is claimed by saying both that God is temporal and that he exists necessarily. It seems to me that it is just such a sense that omnitemporality must bear if it is to be a viable alternative to the atemporal view, with its long and respectable pedigree. At the end of the day, though, I want to acknowledge that all arguments about God's temporal mode of being, mine included, must be offered in a spirit of humility, of faith seeking understanding.

Notes

I want to thank Michael Tooley and Greg Ganssle for invaluable comments on earlier versions of this essay.

1. In this essay I assume without argument that ours is a dynamic world in which temporal becoming is a genuine fact, and that the present and the past are real but the future is not. For a defense of a causal theory of dynamic time, in which the past and the present are real but the future is not, see Michael Tooley, *Time, Tense, and Causation* (Oxford: Oxford University Press, 1997); hereafter *TT&C*. Richard Swinburne defends a causal theory of time in *The Christian God* (Oxford: Clarendon Press, 1994), 72–95. See also Hans Reichenbach, *The Direction of Time*, ed. Maria Reichenbach (Berkeley: University of California Press, 1956), 24.

2. G. J. Whitrow, *The Natural Philosophy of Time*, 2d ed. (Oxford: Clarendon Press, 1980), 43.

3. While the numbers assigned to temporal measurements depend upon the physical clocks used in the measurement, the existence of quantitative temporal intervals is necessary as truth-makers for statements of the laws of nature in that particular world. See Tooley, *TT&C*, 274–82.

4. The first direct experimental confirmation of the time dilation predicted in Einstein's theory of relativity was in 1941, and it has been reconfirmed numerous times since. Paul Davies, *About Time* (New York: Simon and Schuster, 1995), 55–58, 81–83.

5. This is not intended as a definition of metaphysical time but rather as a rough characterization which will serve our purposes at this point. Now, a concrete object is one which is possibly the terminus of a causal relation. Barring a dogmatic commitment to naturalism, it is surely possible that there is at least one immaterial concrete object—God—which possibly exists apart from any physical world.

6. If the medieval philosophical theologians were correct in positing a distinct kind of time in which angels exist, metaphysical time would ground the ordering relations of angelic time also. See, for example, Thomas Aquinas, *Summa theologiae* 1a.53.3.

7. The distinction between physical and metaphysical time is drawn by Alan Padgett in "God and Time: Toward a New Doctrine of Divine Timeless Eternity," *Religious Studies* 26 (1989), 209–15, and in Padgett, *God, Eternity, and the Nature of Time* (New York: St. Martin's, 1992; repr. Eugene: Wipf and Stock, 2000). William Lane Craig comments, "The distinction between ontological [i.e., metaphysical] time and measured (or empirical) time seems to me to be an extremely important insight, which is a salutary counterbalance to the universally repeated and extravagant assertions that STR has forced us to abandon the classical views of time and space. This erroneous inference is rooted precisely in the failure to draw the sorts of distinctions which Padgett has emphasized." Craig, "God and Real Time," *Religious Studies* 26 (1990), 339.

8. For arguments, see, for example, Brain Leftow, *Time and Eternity* (Ithaca: Cornell University Press, 1991), 21–33, hereafter *T&E*; J. R. Lucas, *A Treatise on Space and Time* (London: Methuen, 1973), 35–42; and Richard Swinburne, *Space and Time* (London: Macmillan, 1968), ch. 10.

9. J.M.E. McTaggart, *The Nature of Existence* (Cambridge: Cambridge University Press, 1927), vol. 2, ch. 33, rpt. as "The Unreality of Time," in *The Philosophy of Time*, ed. Robin Le Poidevin and Murray MacBeath (Oxford: Oxford University Press, 1993), 23–34.

10. Strictly speaking there is a difference between a time and an instant: an instant is a metaphysical "slice" of time, without duration, but with temporal location. A time is the complete collection of all events and entities which exist at an instant in a given world. But for the purposes of this paper the distinction is not relevant; I shall use the two terms interchangeably.

11. See Tooley, *TT&C*, 341–44, for the argument.

12. This, of course, assumes that space is substantial, arguably a corollary of a causal theory of dynamic time. See Tooley, *TT&C,* 258–64. If the reader rejects the thesis of substantial space, then the weaker claim is that actual spacetime entities occupying spacetime regions are possibly the termini of causal relations, which still yields the desired conclusion regarding the concreteness of temporal entities.

13. Kant, of course, maintained in the "Transcendental Aesthetic" of his first *Critique* that time is the "form of inner sense," a "necessary representation that underlies all intuitions." He claims that while we can imagine eventless time, we can never conceive of the absence of time. In this I think Kant was just wrong. The possibility of (physical) timeless worlds is discussed further in the section "Omnitemporality" below.

14. A timeless world W thus conceived would be *physically* timeless. If metaphysical time exists, W should be conceived as occupying an instant of metaphysical time, and although W *contained* no causal relations, the entire world would be the terminus of God's causal activity in that metaphysical instant. W thus would be intrinsically timeless but extrinsically temporal. And if God is temporal, he would be relatively timeless in W but still intrinsically (metaphysically) temporal.

15. Leftow, *T&E*, 31. Leftow's reasons for taking this position are, I think, related to his own definitions of timelessness and eternity. Leftow desires to maintain that God is timeless, that is, he exists in an eternal (or atemporal) reference frame. But he also wants to allow that temporal entities may be present in eternity. Thus he defines an entity K as temporal "iff K can have a location in a B-series," and as timeless (atemporal) "iff K can exist now but cannot be located in a B-series." He continues: "If these definitions hold no nasty surprises, they let us say that a temporal thing can occur within an atemporal reference frame without compromising the absolute distinction between temporal and timeless things or reference frames. . . . They also let us say that events A-occur in both eternity and time, but B-occur only in time. Yet temporal events that A-occur in eternity also B-occur in time, and so occur in eternity as ordered in timeless analogues of their B-relations" (241). Admittedly, this passage is not entirely clear, especially out of the context of the intricate argument of the book. But I will make two observations about Leftow's argument. First, while Leftow desires to be neutral throughout as regards tensed or tenseless theories of time, there seem to be several places where his argument must assume a tenseless view or else it will not work. And that is consistent with my second observation. Leftow accepts—too easily, in my opinion—the Minkowski spacetime manifold of special relativity as a true metaphysical description of the universe. Thus he cannot allow any absolute reference frame; he sees all reference frames—temporal and timeless alike—as relative. If, however, we reject the tacit acceptance of a tenseless view of time, and reject also the Einsteinian interpretation of special relativity, then there is no reason to adopt Leftow's more restrictive definitions. See Tooley, *TT&C*, ch. 11; Quentin Smith, *Language and Time* (Oxford: Oxford University Press, 1993), ch. 7; and William Lane Craig, *Divine Foreknowledge and Human Freedom* (Leiden: Brill, 1991), appendix 1.

16. Compare Pike's definition of "timeless" as an entity which lacks temporal location and temporal extension. Nelson Pike, *God and Timelessness* (London: Routledge and Kegan Paul, 1970), 7.

17. Any theory of time, whether dynamic or static, must give an account of three features of time: flow, direction, and topology. If time is dynamic, then a causal theory offers the most satisfactory account of all three features, and especially of direction, "time's arrow." Explanations of time's arrow grounded in time-asymmetric physical processes (e.g., entropic processes) or in "indelible traces" left in the world can both be reduced to causal relations.

18. This assumes that causation is a temporal relation. At this point the atemporalist will object that this begs the question, that God's causal relation to the world is atemporal. But no satisfactory account of atemporal causation is available. Paul Helm attempts such an account in "Eternal Creation," *Tyndale Bulletin* 45 (1994), 326–30, but admits that in his account "'causation' is used in an analogical or stretched sense." The burden is on the atemporalist to provide a plausible account of atemporal causation which does not beg the question against a dynamic theory of time. Indeed, I have argued elsewhere that any theory of a timeless God who is related to the temporal series is committed to the B-theory of time. See my "Timeless God, Tenseless Time," *Philosophia Christi,* ser. 2, vol. 2, no. 1 (Spring 2000).

19. The modality is metaphysical, not logical, necessity.

20. William Kneale, "Time and Eternity in Theology," *Proceedings of the Aristotelian Society* 61 (1960–61), 98.

21. Stephen T: Davis, *Logic and the Nature of God* (Grand Rapids: Eerdmans, 1983), 17.

22. See George Bealer, *Quality and Concept* (Oxford: Oxford University Press, 1982), 123.

23. For a survey of historical and contemporary arguments on both sides of the question, see my "God and the Nature of Time," Ph.D. diss., University of Colorado, 1998), chs. 5–8.

24. This notion of time has been advocated by Storrs McCall, *A Model of the Universe: Space-Time, Probability, and Decision* (Oxford: Clarendon Press, 1994). McCall's realism about possible futures seems to have grown over the years since he first adumbrated his concept of branching futures in "Objective Time Flow," *Philosophy of Science* 43 (1976), 337–62.

25. While this might satisfy some process theologians, most in the Judeo-Christian tradition would want to say something stronger of God.

26. That these entities are represented by numbers does not count against their contingency, since the numbers express a relation or a determinate value in certain units. I do not mean to imply that the numerical value of physical constants is immutable. Certainly different units of measurement yield different values. Further, Field has argued that it is a mistake to regard scientific theories as entailing the existence of numbers. See Hartry Field, *Science without Numbers: A Defense of Nominalism* (Princeton: Princeton University Press, 1980). Field may or may not be correct in this. The point at issue, though, stated more precisely, is that the mathematical expression of the constant is fixed.

27. Philosophical theologians debate whether the proper modality to ascribe to God's existence is logical or metaphysical. I believe that the latter is correct. See Richard G. Swinburne, *The Christian God* (Oxford: Clarendon Press, 1994), 144–49, for a defense.

28. Greg Ganssle has suggested to me that an objection to this claim is the relativity of simultaneity entailed by the standard Einsteinian interpretation of special relativity, which would have the consequence of "a strange fracturing of God's consciousness" which follows from the loss of the transitivity of simultaneity on the Einsteinian interpretation. This seems to be a problem for any view of God's temporality if simultaneity is relative.

The heart of the problem is Einstein's operationalist definition of time, described by Lawrence Sklar, "Time, Reality, and Relativity," in *Reduction, Time, and Relativity,* ed. R. Healey (Cambridge: Cambridge University Press, 1981). This leads to a failure to keep separate the concepts of metaphysical time, which grounds all causal successions, and the measurement of physical time, which will be affected by relevant physical laws.

However, alternative mathematical formulations of special relativity are available which are empirically equivalent to the standard interpretation and maintain absolute simultaneity. Certain of these formulations are arguably superior to the standard interpretation for reasons independent of the question of the relativity of simultaneity. See John Winnie, "Special Relativity without One-Way Velocity Assumptions," *Philosophy of Science* 37 (1970), 223–38, as well as references cited at the end of n. 15 above.

29. It is an interesting question of philosophical theology whether God's mental life consists essentially in a causal succession of mental states. If this were so, it would not be a limitation on God, since he is the cause of his own being, including his own mentality. Further, it would aid our understanding of the dynamic relations among the persons of the Trinity prior to creation (cf. the doctrine of *perichoresis*, or the "interpenetration" of the persons of the Trinity). If, then, causal succession of mental states is an essential property of God's mental life, then metaphysical time would have the same necessity as God himself.

30. Swinburne concludes, "There would be no difference between a divine act of self-awareness which lasted one millisecond and one which lasted a million years" (Swinburne, *The Christian God,* 140). Compare Psalm 90:4 and 2 Peter 3:8: "With the Lord a day is like a thousand years, and a thousand years are like a day."

31. This analysis is stated in tenseless terms so as to avoid possible ambiguities between metaphysical and physical temporal indexicals. The rationale for tenseless analysis of tensed statements ex is found in Tooley, *TT&C,* 190–95.

32. See, for example, Nicholas Wolterstorff, "God and Time," *Philosophia Christi,* ser. 2, vol. 2, no. 1 (Spring 2000), 5–10.

Part Two

GOD, TIME, AND CREATION

3

Divine Foreknowledge and the Arrow of Time

On the Impossibility of Retrocausation

ALAN G. PADGETT

Recent discussion of divine foreknowledge has raised again the old issue of whether or not it is possible to bring about the past, that is, to cause the past to be what it was.[1] In this essay I argue that such backward causation against time, or retrocausation, is impossible and thus cannot help us out of the problem of divine foreknowledge and human freedom. However, this should close the door to only one of many ways of solving this dilemma.[2]

To begin, what does it mean to say that some event is impossible or necessary? A good heuristic device, stemming from Leibniz's philosophy, is to speak of "possible worlds." Clearly, the world might have been different, even considering the whole history of the world past, present, and future. The story of the world, all of it, might be different. Let us understand a "possible world-story" to be a coherent and compossible set of descriptions of what the world might have been like.[3] Every event or object we stipulate as being in that particular story brings with it any essential and necessary properties into the world-story in question. Further, to qualify as a *world*-story, for every object or event mentioned in the story, a full description occurs in that world-story. Finally, all necessary truths we assume to be affirmed in every world-story, though we lack time and knowledge to stipulate every part of the story.[4]

How best to say that something "happens" or "exists" in a world-story is a delicate matter. To say that some event "happens" in a world-story, as in any story, is to say that the description of that event is affirmed in that world-story. An object is real in a story when its existence or reality is affirmed in that story. A necessary event, then, is one whose description is affirmed in all possible world-stories which we could (given prior stipulations and constraints) coherently tell. An impossible event is one whose description is never coherently affirmed in any story. I will argue that retrocausation is never properly affirmed in any world-story because it is incoherent or incompatible with other, prior parts of the story of each possible world.

What, then, is backward causation? By retrocausation I understand a complex event in which one event causes another event which is prior to it in time. Thus a present event might cause a past event to be what it was, or a future event might cause a present event to be what it is. Retrocausation involves making the past what it was, not "changing" the past (changing the past is incoherent).[5] I exclude, from the beginning, all non-causal relationships between things from consideration as examples of retrocausation. For example, I would allow for the retrosatisfaction of truth conditions for future-tensed propositions. In other words, I allow that what happens in the future is what makes future-tensed propositions true or false. This is because the satisfaction of truth conditions is a logical, not a causal, relationship; it is not an example of retrocausation. We can agree to treat future-tensed propositions as true or false in the abstract language-game of logic, even if no one can know their truth-value until what they describe takes place (or not). Backward causation against the arrow of time I understand to be a causal force that occurs between real objects and events, not a relationship between ideas or propositions.

What is it, then, for one thing to cause another? Theories of causation abound in the literature.[6] I shall adopt one for the purpose of this essay; however, I claim that any adequate theory of causation will come, *mutatis mutandis*, to the same conclusions I reach here.

In brief outline, let us agree for the purpose of this argument that one event or thing causes another against a background of certain relevant states of affairs. Among these states are:

1. the initial conditions at a time
2. the causal powers of the objects involved
3. the relevant relationships between the objects involved
4. the nature of the objects involved

An "object" is a continuant or "substance": God, people, and trees are examples of objects in this sense. Objects in concrete relationship create events in spacetime.[7] Given these objects, relationships, and states, event A causes event B if the occurrence of A brings about or makes to be the case the occurrence of B in the context of that state of affairs.[8] Because such causation is based upon the nature of the objects involved, I am interested here only in natural causation in this sense, viz. effects brought about by the natural powers of existing, real objects.

Sometimes philosophers speak of causation in terms of laws of nature. But the laws of nature are merely our description of the law-like regularities of physical objects. So talk about laws of nature reduces to talk about the nature and causal powers of objects. Thus, the account I give of causation includes so-called laws of nature. For example, it is a law of nature that nothing can be accelerated beyond the speed of light. But clearly, this law is our description, a quite general one, of the nature of physical objects and their causal powers. The "laws of nature" are a particular kind of description of the nature and causal powers of physical objects.[9]

One refinement is still needed for this summary outline of causation. Sometimes we find that many events work together to cause some effect. In this case, A will have to be considered a complex event, a mereological sum of events. Retrocausation would then take place when A, or some part of A, is temporally after its effect, B. To take an example from Dummett, if I pray that my son would be among the survivors of a shipwreck in the past, but which I have just heard about, if my prayer is efficacious, then it will be part of the cause of my son being among the survivors. This would be an example of retrocausation, even though my prayer is only a part of a large complex event which causes my son to have been among the survivors.

This sketch of the idea of causation leaves open the issue of time in the concept of retrocausation. The philosophy of time is, if anything, even more complicated than causation.[10] With respect to the reality of the temporal process from past to future (or just "process" for short) philosophers basically fall into two camps. There are those who follow the process theory (or A-theory, or tensed theory) and those who reject that view in favor of what I call the stasis theory (or B-theory, or tenseless theory).[11] According to process theories (which come in several types), temporal passage is an objective part of the world. Stasis theorists deny this proposition, holding that past, present, and future are subjective or mind-dependent properties of events. Remember, the "time" we are talking about here involves the passage from past to present to future, not the anisotropy of time nor the measure of time.

Possible world-stories fall into three large classes with respect to the reality of process in that world-story. First, there are those which are altogether timeless, where time itself does not come into the story. Second, there are those temporal world-stories in which the process theory of time is true. Third, there are stasis worlds in which past, present, and future are subjective and are not affirmed as part of the "real" or external world. These are all the possibilities there are regarding worlds and time. I shall argue that retrocausation, it turns out, is impossible in all three of these world-stories, and therefore is impossible in all world-stories we could coherently tell.

First of all, do these three options exhaust all possibilities? Yes, they do. For time must be part of a world or not. If it does not occur, then we have the first class of world-stories. If it does occur, then either process is part of that world-story or it is not. If it is, then we have the second class of world-stories. If it is not, then we have the third class. So all possible world-stories are included in these three classes.

We begin by considering the case of the first class of worlds. In such stories, events (if there are any) are completely timeless. The concept of retrocausation, however, entails a temporal separation between events. So retrocausation is impossible in the first class of worlds, by definition.

Our next consideration is the class of world-stories in which the passage of time is of ontological importance for the objective world, that is, world-stories that affirm the process theory of time. Our discussion of this class will turn on a rational intuition or noetic insight I offer for your consideration: the causal impassibility and impotence of the unreal. If something lacks reality, how can it be changed in any way, in a causal sense? If something lacks reality, how can it affect real things? On the process theory of time, the past is unreal. For this reason, it can no longer be affected by nor affect the present. I cannot now make the past be what it was, because those events are gone and cannot be changed: they no longer exist. Likewise, the future is not real and can have no effect on the present. For only what is real can directly cause anything to happen.[12] Now the past, of course, does affect the present, but only through a causal chain, that is, only through *indirect* causes.

Imagine the history of every object in the world-story, divided by the smallest episode in each object's life. The smallest episodes will be the ones (however short) in which no change takes place in that object. According to the process view, only present episodes of objects are fully real. The present episode of any object we will understand to be in a process of becoming. The former episode is falling away into the past, and thus into non-reality. The future episode of the object is coming into being, passing from non-reality to reality. Only the present episodes of all objects are fully real. The present instant (NOW) will thus be an abstract, conceptual, durationless pointer which picks out all those real episodes for every existing thing in the universe which are simultaneous with all other real episodes. Only present episodes are fully real; and only what is real or actual can directly bring something about (i.e., apart from a causal chain of events).

The standard objection at this point is that the process theory would not allow us to bring anything about. For if I cannot affect nor effect the future, then the future will never get here. For the very next moment is, after all, future relative to the present. If I cannot bring about the future, then all causation must be simultaneous if it is to happen at all (the objection goes). But that conclusion lands us in an infinite regress of simultaneous causes rather than a temporal progression of causes.

The answer to this problem from a process perspective is to *think of the present in two ways*: the present episode of all real objects, and the NOW understood as an abstract and conceptual point. The NOW points to all real episodes, without reducing all real episodes to a durationless instant. Think of this abstraction as a kind of red laser pointer, which highlights the present episode in all real things, without reducing those episodes to its own abstract, durationless instant. So the present episode of some real object is in the process of becoming. It is not a mere instant of time. As the history of an object advances, it passes from one episode to the next one: what is now present becomes past (unreal), and what was only potential (future) becomes actual (present). Such an understanding of becoming does allow for temporal passage. But what counts as future (and therefore as merely potential rather than fully real) changes with the passage of time. Thus *the future never becomes real as future*, but only in the process of becoming. In the process of becoming, what was (merely) future becomes actual (present).[13] So the process theory of time is coherent with our intuition about the causal impassibility and impotence of the unreal.

Given the intuition that what is not real cannot directly causally affect us, nor can it be affected, it turns out that any possible world-story which affirms the process theory of time cannot consistently affirm any description of retrocausation. For any such description would imply a contradiction when joined with our insight about the causal impotence and impassibility of the unreal. Any stories which we would like to tell about retrocausation will not be affirmed in any possible world-story with prior commitments to both our basic intuition and the process theory of time.[14]

Perhaps the proponent of retrocausation will want to reply that our intuition about the causal impotence and impassibility of the unreal may be true but is not logically necessary. However, before taking this move she ought to reflect on the following point. Part of what we mean when we say something is real is that it can, at least in principle, causally interrelate with other things. So part of what we mean when we affirm that something is unreal simply is that it is causally impotent and impassible. Our intuition, then, upon a little reflection, turns out to be an analytic truth. It is therefore affirmed in all possible world-stories.

This leaves us with the third class of worlds, those that affirm the stasis theory of time. In this class of world-stories, duration does occur ("time" in one sense of the word), but temporal process is either denied altogether, or relegated to an illusion, or understood in some way to be merely subjective. On such theories, the passage from future to present does not change the reality or unreality of any object or event. Any experience of the A-series (as McTaggart called process) simply will not be affirmed in such stories; or it will be seen as a kind of secondary quality, caused by the primary qualities of before, after, and simultaneity. What is objectively real, on the stasis theory, is the B-series of ordered events in a before-after series.[15]

Even within the third class of world-stories, however, retrocausation is not universally affirmed. There are some subclasses of worlds in which retrocausation is impossible. One well-known world is the so-called Gödel universe, based upon certain solutions to the equations of general relativity discovered by Kurt Gödel.[16] In the Gödel world-story, the matter in the universe is in rotation, and the universe possesses a spatial homogeneity—but not isotropy. This model of the universe allows for closed time-like curves for world-lines of objects, and thus for "time travel."[17] While the majority of the matter in this universe travels "forward" in time, some world-lines are possible which are closed, time-like loops. Indeed, for any two points P and Q on the world-lines of massive material objects, where P is before Q on that line, it is possible in the Gödel universe to travel in such a way as to move "forward" in (local) time, and still travel from Q "back" to P.

The problem with worlds like this, where one can travel backward and forward in "time," is that the distinction between before and after seems rather arbitrary. True, for any given mass it will be possible to designate a local, proper time for that object and its world-line. But the universe as a whole does not seem to have any objective, universal way of deciding which direction is "past" and which is "future." The mathematics will work in either direction! Granted that the Gödel universe is temporally orientable, in closed time loops any instance of forward causation is also just as truly called a case of backward causation. P comes "before" Q in one perspective, and just as validly P comes "after" Q in another perspective.

Perhaps, one might respond, this is just the way things are. Temporal order is a matter of perspective and convention. If this is so, then of course what *looks like* retrocausation is possible. For the "retro" part of backward causation will not be true universally, and also not true for God (I assume for this paper that God is also temporal in some sense). What is measured as retrocausation in one frame of reference will be normal, forward causation in another frame of reference. But of course in this case what we do not have is genuine retrocausation, that is, backward causation against an objective arrow of time.

Reflection on the Gödel universe leads us to some conceptual necessities for any world-stories which affirm retrocausation. Two things must be affirmed in any world-story in order to make a claim of retrocausation significant: (a) time must be anisotropic, and (b) the purported case of retrocausation must be in a topologically "open" world-line, one which not only in fact but even in principle cannot be closed. For strictly speaking any "forward" causal connection in a closed time-line could be just as well called a case of retrocausation. The idea of backward causation includes the notion that one is going backward against something, after all, and not just arbitrarily choosing a temporal starting point and direction (or "arrow"). Thus not every world-story in the third class (i.e., stasis worlds) can coherently affirm a genuine and significant case of *backward* causation.

According to some philosophers, time and causation are merely human points of view. Many of these philosophers have been idealists, but not all. Gödel himself may be included among them.[18] In some world-stories, therefore, "backward" and "forward" are just a matter of perspective, and thus there is no ontologically real arrow of time. In such worlds, genuine retrocausation does not occur because the ordering of events as before and after is merely conventional. In order for the "backward" part of the concept to be meaningful for the problem of omniscience (i.e., for God), the arrow of time needs to be ontologically real. This provides us with a third criterion, viz. (c) temporal order and causal asymmetry must be ontologically genuine. Let us call the world-stories which affirm all three of these criteria STAT worlds (stasis theory with an objective arrow of time).

In order for there to be any theologically meaningful use for the idea of "backward causation," these three criteria must be affirmed. It is indeed logically possible that event A might cause event B, and B would *seem* to be earlier in time to some human (but not to an omniscient, omnipresent God). The problem is that such an event would not be ontologically genuine retrocausation, only apparent retrocausation. In such cases, God could easily know what looked like "future" to us but was not really future, not future to God.[19]

We turn our attention now to that set of worlds where the stasis theory of time is affirmed, along with our three criteria for theologically meaningful retrocausation (i.e., STAT world-stories). If the A-series of past, present, and future is not an objective part of the world, according to STAT world-stories, what accounts for the ordering of events in an objective B-series at all? That is, what accounts for the temporal anisotropy of time in these worlds? This is a key question for those who would assert the coherence of retrocausation. As Mellor wrote, "If only the *A* series existed, that would be the direction of time. But as it doesn't, the difference between *earlier* and *later* must be sought elsewhere."[20] According to Mellor, what gives temporal order to events is their causal order: "The direction of time is the direction of causation."[21] One event occurs before another, in time, because the first event is a cause of the second or the second event is simultaneous with some effect of the first. When one affirms, then, that A is before B in time, in those world-stories which affirm a causal explanation for temporal anisotropy, one means that A is causally prior to B or A is simultaneous with some event that is causally prior to B. However, when that is what one *means* by temporal precedence, then clearly the affirmation of a description of retrocausation is analytically false, that is, it implies a contradiction. When the arrow of time simply means the direction of causation, backward causation against the arrow of time is conceptually incoherent.

A more traditional stasis theory about what temporal order consists in, for STAT world-stories, is the view of Grünbaum.[22] According to this theory, the difference between earlier and later in time has to do with the increase of entropy. Roughly, the ability of a system to do "work" is a measure of entropy.[23] Increase in entropy entails the dissipation of energy from part of the system to the whole and a decrease in the whole system's ability to do work, that is, a decrease in available energy. An increase in entropy involves necessarily a dissipation of energy from some part of the system to the system as a whole.

If we affirm a physical theory of the order of time in a STAT world-story, then event A is before event B if and only if entropy (or some other physical process) has increased between A and B. This implies that event A is part of an episode of a system with lower entropy than another episode of that system which includes event B. But now we have to ask, how is it possible on this theory for B to cause A? To cause A, some object (or objects) of which B is an expression will have to bring about A. And these objects will have to expend energy, that is, do some "work." Remember we are considering cases of natural causation, brought about by real objects. B can only cause A when the objects-in-relation we call B bring about A. But that means that these objects will have to increase entropy in order to change from B to A. This in turn implies, however, that B must (on this theory) be temporally prior to A. And this contradicts our original supposition, viz. that A was before B in time. So any work that objects in the future might exert to cause the past to be what it was will increase entropy between the future and the past. But this is contrary to the theory of temporal order under consideration. This means that on the theory of temporal order advocated by Grünbaum, once again, retrocausation is impossible.

The two cases we have analyzed are similar at several points. In fact, any physical theory of temporal order for STAT worlds will have this same problem with retrocausation. But on a stasis theory of time, if some physical, causal process does not account for temporal order, what does? Is it just a brute fact of the universe? That does seem a little hard to swallow. At this point the defender of the possibility of retrocausation may object. Why does she have to develop some theory of temporal order at all? That is, why does the defender have to affirm some view of what it is for something to be later than another in time? The answer to this objection is twofold. First, a defender of retrocausation should tell us what is meant by "retro," that is, what is meant by temporal precedence. The possibility of retrocausation is by no means obvious, and those who assert its possibility need to argue for it. The defender of the possibility of retrocausation owes us an analysis of what exactly she is asserting to be possible. The second reason is inductive. I have supplied an analysis of retrocausation in a very large number of possible world-stories, being as comprehensive as I can be, and found retrocausation to be incoherent in each world-story (that is, incompatible with other truths affirmed in each story). So I conclude that retrocausation is incompatible ("externally incoherent") unless and until defenders of retrocausation can give me some reason to believe otherwise.

I am aware that certain models or interpretations of modern physics imply or include the idea of retrocausation. But if my conceptual analysis is correct, such models and solutions will (logically must) turn out to be empirically false, or else not examples of retrocausation. More precisely, the world-lines allowed in these models will not in fact be retrocausation, or the events connected by, e.g., a tachyon beam will be merely measured as being "past" within some inertial system and its associated metric, and not ontologically or genuinely past. In any case, as William Lane Craig has argued, there are other ways in which modern physics can be interpreted, in which backward causation does not occur.[24]

I offer, then, a rebuttal rather than a refutation of the possibility of retrocausation. The idea of retrocausation, when it is spelled out, is either incoherent or incompatible with other truths. I have admitted that *apparent* backward causation is logically possible, but merely apparent retrocausation does not help divine foreknowledge. This is because God will need to know what is future to God, in order to use backward causation to know the future. Otherwise, God simply uses ordinary causation to know what is present or past to the divine mind (even if that event appears to be future to humans on earth). What is future to an omniscient and omnipresent God is really future, not just apparently future to us. In conclusion, then, unless a coherent and compatible theory of temporal order is given by defenders of retrocausation, philosophers and theologians should avoid solutions to the problem of divine foreknowledge and human freedom which imply retrocausation.

Notes

I am grateful to the Society of Christian Philosophers (Midwest and Pacific meetings) and the Minnesota Philosophical Society for the opportunity to read and discuss earlier versions of this essay. I am also thankful to George Mavrodes and William Lane Craig, as well as Greg Ganssle, for their helpful criticism of an earlier draft.

1. See representative essays by Michael Dummett, "Bringing about the Past," *Philosophical Review* 73 (1964), 338–59, rpt. in Dummett, *Truth and Other Enigmas* (London: Duckworth, 1978); Alfred J. Freddoso, "Accidental Necessity and Power over the Past," *Pacific Philosophical Quarterly* 63 (1982), 54–68; George Mavrodes, "Is the Past Unpreventable?" *Faith and Philosophy* 1 (1984), 131–14; Thomas Talbott, "On Divine Foreknowledge and Bringing about the Past," *Philosophy and Phenomenological Research* 46 (1986), 455–69; and Bruce Reichenbach, "Hasker on Omniscience," *Faith and Philosophy* 4 (1987), 86–92.

2. For a good review of the issues and alternatives, see Linda Zagzebski, *The Dilemma of Freedom and Foreknowledge* (New York: Oxford University Press, 1991), and John Martin Fisher, ed., *God, Foreknowledge, and Freedom* (Stanford: Stanford University Press, 1989).

3. I avoid the usual language of a "possible world" simply to call attention to the fact that possible worlds are sets of descriptions, not of objects. This insight avoids many of the problems associated with recent possible worlds ontology. In other words, I advocate a "fictionalist" account of possible worlds. See further D. M. Armstrong, *A Combinatorial Theory of Possibility* (Cambridge: Cambridge University Press, 1989).

4. Thus Stalnaker: "I am making up this world—it is a pure product of my intentions—but there are already things true in it which I shall never know." Robert Stalnaker, "A Theory of Conditionals," in *Causation and Conditionals,* ed. E. Sosa (New York: Oxford University Press, 1975), 178.

5. See Bob Brier, *Precognition and the Philosophy of Science* (New York: Humanities Press, 1974), 27f.; David Lewis, "The Paradoxes of Time Travel," *American Philosophical Quarterly* 13 (1976), 145–52.

6. A good recent volume (with bibliography) is Daniel Hausman, *Causal Asymmetries* (Cambridge: Cambridge University Press, 1998).

7. On the primacy of objects in causation, see Andrew Newman, "The Causal Relation and Its Terms," *Mind* 97 (1988), 529–50.

8. "Event" here is a term of convenience. I understand an event to be a change in an object, or in the relationship between objects.

9. Thus I follow those who see "laws of nature" as constructs, e.g., D. M. Armstrong, *What Is a Law of Nature?* (Cambridge: Cambridge University Press, 1983); Nancy Cartwright, *How the Laws of Physics Lie* (Oxford: Oxford University Press, 1983); and Cartwright, *Nature's Capacities and Their Measurement* (Oxford: Oxford University Press, 1989).

10. For much of what follows, see A. G. Padgett, *God, Eternity, and the Nature of Time* (London: Macmillan, 1992; Eugene: Wipf and Stock, 2000).

11. I introduced the terms "process" and "stasis" in my doctoral dissertation ten years ago (see Padgett, *God, Eternity, and the Nature of Time*, 3–6). I prefer these terms to A and B, since as letters they convey no meaning relative to the theories they represent. I also dislike the more common terms "tense" and "tenseless" because analytic philosophers already confuse grammar with ontology all too often! Also, the term "stasis" is a technical word with no meaning in ordinary language—it cannot have the negative connotations that "block universe" and "static theory" do. So I continue to use these names for the two theories.

12. An indirect cause is one that operates through a causal chain.

13. I refute McTaggart's argument that the system of tenses in the process theory is contradictory in Padgett, *God, Eternity, and the Nature of Time*, ch. 5.

14. This is the conclusion reached by William Lane Craig in his review of the literature on this topic, *Divine Foreknowledge and Human Freedom* (Leiden: Brill, 1991), 113–57. Craig concludes, "There is no unequivocal evidence supporting either the presence or even possibility of backward causation, and there is good reason to reject its real possibility on the basis of the nature of time" (156).

15. See, i.a., Adolf Grünbaum, *Philosophical Problems of Space and Time*, 2d ed. (Dordrecht: Reidel, 1973), and D. H. Mellor, *Real Time* (Cambridge: Cambridge University Press, 1981). His view on this point is unchanged in Mellor, *Real Time* II (London: Routledge, 1998).

16. Gödel's three papers from 1949–52 on this topic are helpfully collected in Gödel, *Collected Works*, vol. 2, ed. S. Feferman et al. (New York: Oxford University Press, 1990).

17. See Howard Stein, "On the Paradoxical Time-Structures of Gödel," *Philosophy of Science* 37 (1970), 589–601; David Malamant, "'Time Travel' in the Gödel Universe," *PSA 1984*, vol. 2, ed. P. D. Asquith and Philip Kitcher (East Lansing: Philosophy of Science Association, 1985), 91–100; and Malamant, "Minimal Acceleration Requirements of 'Time Travel' in Gödel Space-Time," *Journal of Mathematical Physics* 26 (1985), 774–77.

18. See, e.g., Palle Yourgrau, *The Disappearance of Time* (Cambridge: Cambridge University Press, 1991).

19. This fact was recognized soon after the publication of Einstein's famous paper on the special theory of relativity; see Leslie Walker, "Time, Eternity, and God," *Hibbert Journal* 18 (1919), 36–48.

20. Mellor, *Real Time*, 149, his italics.

21. Ibid., 150.

22. Grünbaum, *Philosophical Problems*.

23. Technically, entropy is the measure of the amount of energy it would take to return the system to its initial state.

24. I thank Leon Horsten for raising this question. For a brief overview of the philosophical interpretations and proposed "solutions" in contemporary physics which employ retrocausation, see Craig, *Divine Foreknowledge and Human Freedom*.

4

God inside Time and before Creation

DEAN W. ZIMMERMAN

Two Questions about Time

Many theists reject the notion that God's eternity consists in his timelessness—i.e., in his lacking temporal extension and failing to possess properties *at* any times. Some of these "divine temporalists" hold that, for philosophical reasons, it is impossible to accept both the timelessness of God and the view that God knows what happens at different times and brings about events in time.[1] Many reject divine timelessness as a dubious import from Platonism with no biblical or theological warrant.[2] And some question the very intelligibility of the doctrine.[3]

There are many serious questions a divine temporalist must answer. One of the most frequently discussed is whether a temporal God could know ahead of time what I will freely do, or how any indeterministic system will behave. I shall leave the most theologically pressing questions to others, however.[4] Here I address two closely related, more purely metaphysical questions facing divine temporalists: (1) Does time necessarily involve change? (2) Did God have a sufficient reason for creating when he did? The latter raises the further question whether a divine temporalist can say that, in some sense, time had a beginning.

In what follows, I ignore the relativity of simultaneity, treating *earlier than* and *later than* as simple two-place transitive relations requiring no indexing to reference frame. Some of the arguments will have to do with time's passage before creation, when I suppose there were no spatial frames of reference; so ignoring relativity cannot hurt in that context. Another excuse for treating simultaneity as non-relative here is the fact that most contemporary divine temporalists hold an "A-theory" of time—that is, a theory of time according to which there is an objectively distinguished present.

A-theorists are forced to treat the "simultaneity" of special relativity as something other than *real* simultaneity, that relation that holds between events if and only if it is ever true that both are *present*. In particular, *presentist* A-theorists—those who think that the difference between what is present and everything else is that, well, there *is* nothing else—cannot very well maintain that what is happening *now* is relative to reference frame without also holding that what *exists* is relative to reference frame. And one would be hard pressed to make any sense out of that.[5]

Defining "Intrinsic Change"

There is a sense in which it is a trivial truth that time involves change. This is because there is a trivial kind of change: the species of mere Cambridge change that Sydney Shoemaker calls "McTaggart change."[6] It seems clearly necessary that, as long as time is passing, everything that exists is getting older—however much things may remain intrinsically and spatially unchanged. Most philosophers who have claimed that time necessarily involves change have meant something more interesting than this. Somehow we must dismiss as irrelevant to the thesis that time involves change all "changes" involving the gain or loss of temporally extrinsic properties, like *being exactly thirty-four years old*, and (for tidiness) spatially extrinsic ones, too, like *being three miles from a burning barn*. There is a growing literature on the question how best to characterize intrinsic properties.[7] Elsewhere, I have proposed the following procedure for defining the intrinsic.[8] Begin with two merely prima facie marks of temporal and spatial intrinsicness:

> (D1) P is potentially temporally intrinsic $=_{df}$ there is no property Q such that either: (a) necessarily, if something has P then something either did or will have Q; or (b) necessarily, if something has P then either it was not the case that something had Q or it will not be the case that something has Q.[9]
>
> (D2) P is potentially spatially intrinsic $=_{df}$ there is no property Q such that either: (a) necessarily, if something has P then there is something outside its boundaries that has Q; or (b) necessarily, if something has P then it is not the case that there is something outside its boundaries that has Q.

These criteria jointly constitute mere *potential* intrinsicness only because of problems posed by disjunctive properties, like *being red or three feet from a pig* and *being round or the only thing that exists*.[10] Such properties (if indeed they are properties and not, as some believe, mere "concepts" to which no real universals correspond) are *potentially* spatially and temporally intrinsic; but they can be possessed by something "in virtue of" its possession of a property that fails to satisfy one or both of these definitions.

There are a couple of ways in which one could try to shore up this hole. One might, for example, presuppose some kind of "logical atomism"; there is a basic stock of nondisjunctive, nonconjunctive, simple properties. Certain of these (perhaps all of them?) pass tests of intrinsicness; any property reached through property-building operations of conjunction, disjunction, and negation working only from the stock of simple intrinsics is itself intrinsic. Anything built in part out of a simple property that fails these tests, or out of a relation, is itself extrinsic. I would be reluctant to take this route myself, in case there are any families of complex properties each of which involves at least one of the others but none of which is "built" entirely out of simple properties. Perhaps the ethical and the modal constitute two such families of properties. And the possibility of infinite complexity is also worrisome; do we really want to rule out, on a priori grounds, the possibility of properties that do not admit of analysis into any set of simple properties?

An alternative is to appeal to a rather rich notion of parthood for properties—a notion which others have attempted to explicate in a variety of ways.[11] If there is such a property as *being either [red and three feet from a pig] or [red and not three feet from a pig]*, surely it includes *being three feet from a pig* as a part in way that *being red* does not; and this despite the fact that, necessarily, something has the one if and only if it has the other. Similarly for *being both [either red or three feet from a pig] and [either red or not three feet from a pig]*; this, too, has a part that *being red* lacks, despite their necessary coextensiveness. These gerrymandered properties have *being three feet from a pig* among their "Boolean parts"—where a Boolean part of a property is one that can be reached by successive eliminations of disjuncts, conjuncts, and the ontological analogue of the negation operator.[12] But *being red* itself does not have such a part. This suggests the following test for "complete intrinsicness," a category which rules out the above two gerrymandered properties in virtue of their containing parts that are not potentially intrinsic.

(D3) P is a completely intrinsic property $=_{df}$ every property that is a Boolean part of P is potentially temporally intrinsic and potentially spatially intrinsic.

The category can then be expanded to arrive at a more general account of intrinsicness that allows *some* of the gerrymandered properties to qualify as intrinsic as well.

(D4) P is an intrinsic property $=_{df}$ P is necessarily equivalent to a completely intrinsic property.

Theism and the Thesis That Time Involves Change

I think it is fair to say that most philosophers who claim that time necessarily involves change mean that, for time to be passing, some things somewhere must be changing intrinsically. So let us assume the following thesis about time and see what consequences follow for the relationship between God and the temporal order.

(A) Necessarily, for all times t and t^*, t is earlier than t^* if and only if either (1) there is a temporally non-trivial property or relation P such that something ceased to have or began to have it after t but before t^*, or (2) something came into being or passed away after t but before t^*.[13]

Aristotle, Aquinas, and Leibniz all seem to be committed to something like (A), while maintaining different views about God's eternity and the beginning of time.[14] It is true that Leibniz sometimes writes as if the mere *possibility* of something's having gained or lost a property is sufficient to open up a temporal gap.[15] However, he does believe that if there were a moment before which nothing in fact differed in any of its properties or relations, then there was no temporal interval before that moment even though there was the logical possibility of earlier inconsistent states. So even if he is not committed to (A1), Leibniz is committed to the weaker consequence of (A1) which is my main concern:

> (A1*) If a time *t* is such that (1) there is *no* temporally non-trivial property or relation P such that something ceased to have or began to have it before *t*, and (2) *nothing* came into being or passed away before *t*, then *t* is the first instant of time.

Abstractly, there are four possibilities: (1) God is timeless and time had a beginning; (2) God is timeless and time had no beginning; (3) God is temporal and time had a beginning; and (4) God is temporal and time had no beginning. Aquinas holds the first view.[16] Aristotle must have held either (2) or (4). But it is, naturally, hard to find anyone who accepts (3), the view which would seem to do the least justice to the doctrine of divine eternity. Since I am exploring divine temporalism, only (3) and (4) will be considered. What happens when each of these views is conjoined with (A), the doctrine of no time without change?

On the face of it, (4) would seem the more natural choice between the two. On this view, God's eternity consists in there being no (finite) interval of time such that God does not exist before that time, nor a (finite) interval such that God does not exist after that time. (It is important to speak of intervals and not instants in this statement of temporal eternity; for if time began with a continuous open interval of instants, of finite length, every instant would be preceded by instants at which God existed, but he would only have a finite past history.) But, given (A1), God's infinite past existence has been characterized by constant change. If both God and other things existed during an interval, then the change may not have involved God directly. But if there were periods during which only God existed, then God himself must have been undergoing constant intrinsic change during those times. Some have held that the creation is co-eternal with God, but dependent upon him—like a footprint in the sand formed by the pressure of a foot planted there for all eternity.[17] But those who would accept (4) and (A) while affirming that the creation is not infinitely old must suppose that God existed by himself for an infinite length of time, changing constantly.

This supposition is hard to make plausible. It might be thought that, in Christian theology anyway, the internal communion among the persons of the Trinity could be appealed to as the source of dynamic, changing relationships within the Godhead. But God's omniscience and the immutability of his character (not to be confused with the stronger doctrine of God's absolute immutability) make any sort of purely internal divine change nearly unintelligible.[18] If God knows everything at once with utter clarity, does it make sense to suppose that he thinks first about one thing and then another—or that he thinks harder about some particularly knotty problem? God need not take time, for instance, to deliberate about what sort of world to create.[19] On a Trinitarian view, the Father loves the Son, the Son loves the Father and is submitted to his will, and so on. But surely God's steadfast character precludes, say, the degree of Christ's love for the Father waxing and waning. And this view must come to grips with Augustine's puzzle about why God should have created the universe at precisely the time he chose rather than earlier or later—a question to be explored at length below.[20]

A Creation of Finite Age and a Temporal Deity

A theist who accepts (A) and is committed to a creation of finite age thus finds herself pushed in the direction of the remaining alternative (3). But does this view not have the unacceptable consequence that God has only existed for a finite period? How could any substantial doctrine of divine eternity be compatible with such a view?

If one did not know better, one might almost think that Leibniz held (3).[21] He certainly held that time began with the creation of the world.[22] And there are passages that *suggest* the view that God exists in time: Leibniz frequently talks of God's *having decided* to create one among the infinity of possible worlds; and he often describes God as acting in time and, indeed, *enduring* through time.[23] Explicit references to the doctrine of divine timelessness, as understood by other philosophers, are, if not outright denials of the doctrine, at least quite negative: he quotes with approval a passage from Laurentius Valla's *Dialogue on Free Will*, in which Valla questions whether Boethius himself understood what he meant by an "eternity superior to time;"[24] and he criticizes Hobbes's claim that God's foreknowledge consists in his timeless awareness of all events at once, for "one has no reason to resort to the question how the future is present to God" to explain God's foreknowledge.[25] But the passages that suggest a temporal God cannot admit of a straightforward reading, given (a) his conception of time as ideal and (b) his commitment to God's unchanging knowledge of all past, present, and future states of the monads. Really, there are just monads that count as "in time" in virtue of each one having a series of (in some sense) incompatible "perceptions" of everything else, a series that matches up with those of all the others, so that the set of perceptions corresponding to each perception in any monad's series is an equivalence class. These correspondences are the foundation for the merely phenomenal attributions of simultaneity we all make. And since God does not himself have a series of incompatible perceptions, he does not even qualify as "in time" in the (merely phenomenal) sense that monads do. Still, something Leibniz says in his correspondence with Samuel Clarke suggests the best thing a person who held (3) could say about God's eternity.

Clarke identifies God's immensity and eternity with his filling up infinite space and lasting through infinite past and future time—time which would pass even if God alone existed. (Clarke need not worry about having to posit an infinite series of intrinsic changes in God preceding creation, since he rejects (A).) Leibniz responds to Clarke with his own account of divine immensity and eternity, an account which, on the face of it, might seem to be compatible with God's temporality and a finite past:

> 'Tis true, the immensity and eternity of God would subsist, though there were no creatures; but those attributes would have no dependence either on times or places. If there were no creatures, there would be neither time nor place, and consequently no actual

space. The immensity of God is independent upon space, as his eternity is independent upon time. *These attributes signify only*, [with regard to these two orders of things] *that God would be present and co-existent with all the things that should exist*. And therefore I don't admit what's here alleged, that if God existed alone, there would be time and space as there is now: whereas then, in my opinion, they would be only in the ideas of God as mere possibilities.[26]

Here, Leibniz *seems* to be saying that God's eternity amounts to this: he would exist atemporally if there were no time; but if anything were to exist at a time, then God would exist at that time as well.

Due to Leibniz's idealism about time, and the way in which God is supposed to be aware of all states of all monads, it would be wrong to say that he thought God's coexisting with things at times implied that God was in time. But could Leibniz's account of eternity be used by someone who thought God's coexistence with temporal things *did* require his being in time? Should the Christian or other traditional theist be satisfied with an account according to which God has *in fact* only a finite past history? I am not sure how to answer this question; theists from different theological traditions would no doubt approach it in quite different ways. What is clear, however, is that there is little else one could say to save divine eternity from within this perspective. God could *not have* been timeless *before* the beginning of time, and *then* have begun to exist in time once a changing world was created.[27]

Thus acceptance of (A) in conjunction with the view that God exists in time and that the creation has a finite past leaves the theist with a rather unhappy dilemma: either God existed in a state of constant intrinsic change for an infinite stretch of time before he created the world, or God has a finite past history.

Perhaps Time Does Not Necessarily Involve Change

If (A) is false, as Clarke and Newton believed, then this is a false dilemma: it is perfectly possible that, before he created the world, God alone existed throughout an infinite (or perhaps in some sense "neither infinite nor finite"—an alternative considered below) period of time during which no changes occurred—an infinite stretch of what Prior called "dead time."[28] But *could* (A) be false? One might try to argue directly against the possibility of a period of dead time preceding creation in the following way: at the last moment of dead time it would be true that all succeeding moments would be "live" ones. But this could not have been true before the last moment, and so represents a change occurring *during* dead time. But dead time is supposed to be time in which no change occurs. Thus the hypothesis of dead time leads to a contradiction.

This argument is far from conclusive. First of all, it would only work as an argument against *absolutely* dead time—what we might call "stone-cold dead time," in which nothing changes intrinsically or *extrinsically*. So it is not an argument that directly supports (A). Furthermore, it is by no means obvious that in order for a period of stone-cold dead time to end, there must be a final moment of the period of dead time.

If there were a final moment, then (on the assumption that time is continuous or at least everywhere dense) there could be no first moment of live time. But why not suppose it to be the other way around: no last moment of dead time, and a first moment of live time? Indeed, the most plausible rule I know of for deciding whether a state has a last moment of being or a first moment of non-being is the one Norman Kretzmann attributes to Peter of Spain—and his rule favors this latter assignment of first and last moments.[29] But if there is no last moment of dead time, then the above *reductio* will not go through.

As Prior points out, this response to the argument requires "that we do not (like Locke) suppose time to have an intrinsic 'metric.'"[30] For if a certain set of instants in stone-cold dead time intrinsically constituted a day's worth of time, then instants following them would be a day closer to live time. So again there would be some changes in what was supposed to be utterly changeless dead time. The supposition that time lacks an "intrinsic metric" is examined more closely below, where it is seen to suggest an answer to another puzzling question confronting the temporalist.

Augustine's Question: Why Did God Create When He Did?

It seems coherent, then, to deny that time requires change and to suppose that God existed for an infinite stretch of dead time before creating. But there remains Augustine's question: why did God wait precisely as long as he did? In the controversy between Leibniz and Clarke, Clarke readily admits that God could have created earlier. But then Leibniz can argue as follows: "Since God does nothing without reason, and no reason can be given why he did not create the world sooner; it will follow, either that he has created nothing at all, or that he created the world before any assignable time, that is, that the world is eternal."[31] (Leibniz's own position, alternative 3, escapes this sort of argument by denying that the world could have been created earlier than it was.) Clarke is forced to assert simply that "God may have very good reasons for creating this world, at that particular time he did," although he has no suggestions about what these reasons might be.[32]

Picking up where Clarke left off, Brian Leftow has recently suggested that God might have been waiting until he had maximized his pleasure in anticipating the act of creation, setting to work only when further delay would no longer increase the enjoyment he found in looking forward to making the world.[33] Of course, holders of Clarke's view could solve the problem more simply by rejecting the principle of sufficient reason and its corollary pertaining to God's choices. If God were confronted by a set of mutually incompatible states of affairs none of which was intrinsically better than any other, but any one of which was better than none, then it would be an imperfection in God if he could not arbitrarily select one among these states of affairs and bring it about. The indecisiveness of Buridan's ass is not a virtue but a defect. The set of possible times at which creation could commence presented God with just such an array of alternatives, and although there is no sufficient reason for his choosing the time he did, it was better (one might suppose) that he pick one arbitrarily than that he either not create at all or create a world coeternal with himself.[34]

Maimonides on God's Existence before Creation

I think there is another alternative worth exploring for the temporalist; one which would allow that God existed *before* the creation and before any changes occurred, while denying that it makes sense to suppose creation could have begun earlier or later than it did. Moses Maimonides claims that the changeless eternal interval during which God existed before change began is not exactly like the intervals of *true* time which pass when things are changing.

> In the beginning God alone existed, and nothing else. . . . Even time itself is among the things created; for time depends on motion, i.e., on an accident in things which move, and the things upon whose motion time depends are themselves created beings, which have passed from non-existence into existence. We say that God *existed* before the creation of the Universe, although the verb *existed* appears to imply the notion of time; we also believe that He existed an infinite space of time before the Universe was created; but in these cases we do not mean time in its true sense. We only use the term to signify something analogous or similar to time.[35]

True time is (following Aristotle's formula) the measure of motion. It is, says Maimonides, "a thing created; it comes into existence in the same manner as other accidents."[36] Thus it makes no sense to ask why God created the universe at this particular instant of true time. If God creates changing things, and does not create a sempiternal changing universe, then he has no alternative but to begin true time when he does—namely, at the first moment of true time.

But can the same question be raised with respect to the infinite interval of "something analogous or similar to time" which passed before God created true time? Could God have ended this period of "pseudo-time" earlier or later than he did? My guess is that Maimonides would have said no. Unfortunately, he in fact says nothing more about the pseudo-time before creation.

"Pseudo-Time" as Metrically Amorphous

The preceding supposition that dead time lacks an intrinsic metric suggests a way of filling in some details about the nature of Maimonides' changeless pseudo-time—the dead time before creation during which only God existed. The essential idea to be explored is that the assertion that more (or less) pseudo-time could have elapsed is empty of factual content—"more (less) pseudo-time elapsed" does not really describe an alternative state of affairs, just as some philosophers have thought that "Everything doubled in size overnight" does not describe an alternative to everything's remaining the same size. Thus God's decision to end pseudo-time did not require that he make an arbitrary choice among alternatives.

Those philosophers who believe that time (or space or spacetime) has no intrinsic metric (or is "intrinsically metrically amorphous") typically assume that standard measure theory is correct in treating temporal intervals as consisting of a non-denumerable set of durationless instants.[37] Thus temporal intervals resemble geometrical lines which consist of non-denumerable sets of unextended points. Both lines and temporal intervals admit continuous orderings of their members, and are such that every line segment or temporal interval (of either finite or infinite length) includes the same number of unextended elements.

Now determination of a metric for pseudo-time consists in the assignment of numerical coordinates to instants, and the adoption of a "metric rule"—i.e., a way of finding out the distance between instants on the basis of their coordinates.[38] If we are assigning coordinates with an eye to determining distance relations, we will want to stipulate at least that "the coordinate numbers satisfy the same betweenness relations as the points to which they are assigned."[39] So if instant B falls between A and C, the number assigned to B will fall between those assigned to A and C.

What further constraints are there upon our choice of metric? Every instant is intrinsically alike, and is also the same number of instants away from any other instant (including the first instant of live time); so one might think that nothing else constrains our choice of a metric rule given an arbitrary assignment of coordinates. But if it is purely a matter of convention which metric rule we pick, then there is no fact of the matter concerning how long God waited before creating. Although such a result would also make it false that God existed for an infinite period before creation, we could retain an essential ingredient of this claim by maintaining that God existed before change began and that every interval of that period is such that God existed before it.

There are two popular ways of trying to show that choice of a metric rule is conventional: the first is essentially epistemological and can be found in Poincaré and Reichenbach;[40] the second appeals to the structure of space and time and has been championed by Adolf Grünbaum (who finds evidence of it earlier in Riemann).[41] Whatever one might think of their arguments for the metrical amorphousness of the periods of time with which we are familiar, there are special reasons to think that the dead time before creation would lack a metric.

The simplest sort of metric rule we could adopt to go with our coordinatization of pseudo-time would tell us that the distance between any two instants is equal to the difference between their coordinates. Such a rule will suffice to divide up pseudo-time into congruence classes—sets of intervals having the same measure according to our metric rule and coordinate system. It might be thought that we could choose the wrong metric rule to go with our assignment of coordinates. But how could we tell if we got it wrong? Since the interval admits no changes, no set of continuous instants can be intrinsically different from any other. Our rule will never assign an interval a smaller measure than that of any interval it wholly includes. So nothing intrinsic to the sets of instants themselves can show our rule to be wrong. But could it not be that, if clocks or other devices for measuring time had existed during this pseudo-time, they would have distinguished different congruence classes than those set apart by our arbitrary coordinates and simple rule? For instance, could it not be true that two intervals A and B which come out congruent on our simple rule are such that, if there had been a certain clock running during both of them, its hands would have moved twice as far during A as they did during B? Could it not be that *any* of our standard devices for measuring time would show similar discrepancies? But then would this fact not show that our arbitrary coordinates and metric rule were wrong?

Here Poincaré and Reichenbach would say no, it would not. One could just as well say that our rule was right, but that there were "universal forces" at work in the two intervals which would cause any clock to move half as fast during B.[42] But it is *impossible in principle* to tell which of these alternatives is the case—so they are not real alternatives at all. There is no factual difference between the supposition that our simple metric rule picks out congruent intervals during which universal forces would have been at work, distorting the deliverances of all measuring devices, and the seemingly incompatible supposition that the clocks introduced would have been running at a steady pace determining a more complex metric rule. So we could *not* choose a wrong metric rule to go with our arbitrary coordinate assignment. But if any rule will do, there can be no determinate fact of the matter about how long an interval of dead time lasts. So the supposition that God could have allowed a longer or shorter interval of dead time before creating does not represent a real possibility.

Many will, with good reason I think, resist this sort of argument for conventionalism.[43] It may be "impossible in principle" to tell the difference between a metric rule that is really faulty and one that is correct but appears faulty because of the presence of universal forces messing up all the clocks. But Richard Swinburne has pointed out a deeper, non-verificationist reason to doubt that a metric rule for pseudo-time could get things wrong: if there were no laws of nature in force during that time (a plausible enough assumption for one who thinks that laws of nature are contingent and depend upon God's activity, or that they depend upon the kind of world God happens to create), then nothing could ground counterfactuals concerning what various kinds of clocks would or would not do throughout a given interval of pseudo-time. In the absence of all truths about such matters as how many times an object like the earth would have circled an object like the sun during a certain interval, there could be no truths about how many years (days, etc.) passed during the interval.[44] So even though the general verificationist arguments for the metrical amorphousness of time may well fall through, the theist still has a special reason to think that pseudo-time in particular is metrically amorphous.[45]

Why Did God Create at This Instant, Rather than Some Earlier or Later Instant?

One problem remains, however, for the project of salvaging the principle of sufficient reason: throughout the discussion so far, I have been assuming that the interval of pseudo-time is an extensive continuum made up of instants; but then one can still ask why God chose one particular instant, rather than some earlier or later instant, to be the last moment of pseudo-time; or, if pseudo-time is an open interval of instants, why he did not choose some earlier open subset of the interval to mark the end of pseudo-time.[46] To salvage the principle of sufficient reason here, some real ingenuity is called for. I shall work my way toward a solution, beginning with a consideration of the once popular view that time does not consist of instants, that every event and every period of time is of some finite duration. Someone who adopts the view I will finally suggest would not even need to appeal to the metrical amorphousness of pseudo-time in order to save the principle of sufficient reason.

Whitehead is famous for advocating a "no instants" view of time, but it can be found much earlier, for instance in Malebranche: "For ultimately duration has no instants as bodies have no atoms; and just as the smallest part of matter can be infinitely divided, infinitely smaller and smaller parts of duration can be given, as is easy to demonstrate."[47] As Whitehead, Russell, and others have shown, we can make do without instants and still preserve all the metrical truths about relations among them by substituting an "abstractive set" of durations in place of each instant—a set that, so to speak, "hones in on" that instant alone.[48] But, since the infinitely divisible (but "pointless") temporal continuum we are positing still consists of earlier and later parts, we can still ask: Why did God stop it at the end of *this part*, rather than *some earlier part?*

There are only two ways I can think of to save the principle of sufficient reason at this point: one must suppose *either* (a) that every part of this continuous period of changeless time is essential to the whole (and that there were not other periods, of other lengths, available for God to choose), *or* (b) that the period in question does not really have parts after all. In either case, stopping pseudo-time at the end of some earlier subinterval would not be an option, and so the principle of sufficient reason would be saved. But how plausible is either supposition? I shall argue that the former must confront serious objections, but that the latter can at least be coherently maintained. However, before giving arguments for either claim, I must catalogue the range of philosophical theories one might have about the nature of "times" and describe the theological misgivings the divine temporalist will probably feel about one of them.

Theism and the Varieties of Substantivalism and Relationalism about Times

On a "substantivalist" account, times are treated as something distinct from the events happening "at" them; on the most plausible version of such a theory, "spacetime" is an entity distinct from the things and events located in it, and "times" are infinitesimal slices of this four-dimensional manifold. "Relational" accounts, on the other hand, come in two basic flavors: (i) those that identify times with sets of simultaneous events (where events are taken to be particular things, usually spatially located and non-repeatable), and (ii) those that identify times with some more abstract, proposition-like entity—a complete, momentary state-of-the-whole-world. I shall assume this pretty well exhausts the options for metaphysical theories about the nature of times. One frequently voiced objection to the thesis that God is in time is that it makes the deity subordinate to a created thing, namely, *time itself*. Some think that Augustine is making this sort of point when he affirms that God is "the eternal Creator of all time, and that no time and no created thing is co-eternal" with God.[49] Such worries would have considerable force for a theist committed to substantivalism about times. The argument for divine temporalism above might seem to be pushing the substantivalist toward the view that time and individual times are *contingent things* that nonetheless *must* coexist with God since he must exist in time. And this will seem problematic to those theists who want to deny that God had to create any contingent thing at all.[50]

Many prominent A-theorists are relationalists of type (ii): they take great pains to show that "times" need not be construed as some kind of contingent thing, and that whatever work they are needed for can be done by conjunctions of tensed propositions or states of affairs—and so, on this account of the nature of times, there is no *extra* problem about the relationship between God and times over and above problems about the relationship between God and such "abstract objects" as propositions or states of affairs more generally.[51] This sort of divine temporalist responds to the theological worry, then, by simply denying that God's being in time is to be analyzed as any kind of relation to contingent creatures called "times." It is necessarily true, of everything, that it is the subject of tensed propositions. But that does not imply that there are contingently existing things called "times" with which God had to coexist.

The temporalist might try another response. One might hold that, if there are things in time, then there must exist contingent things called "times" and God must be related to them. But this could be conjoined with the thesis that God need not have been in time, since he need not have created things in time. Given that he chose to create times, he cannot help but coexist with them (temporally); but that need not be thought to limit him in any way—or so one might argue. Type (i) relationalists will deny that times are necessarily existing abstracta. On their view, times are contingent things, sets or mereological sums of simultaneously existing events. Although this would make times contingent things (at least the times that include contingent events—and this will presumably be all of them, or nearly all); it need not force the divine temporalist to say that God had to coexist with some contingent things that are in any significant sense independent of him. If every event is dependent for its occurrence upon divine activity (perhaps activity going on earlier, perhaps right then), then every time is dependent for its existence upon God.

Rejecting the Question "Why End Dead Time at Just This Point?"

Now I am ready to tackle the two ways in which one might try to save the principle of sufficient reason from the latest assault. Supposition (a), that pre-creation dead time has parts but that each is essential to the whole, cannot be maintained on either relationalist construal of times. Consider relationalism (i): times are really just sets of simultaneous events. The only events going on during pre-creation dead time are those involving God; and since, *ex hypothesi*, no changes are going on in God, the period contains just one long event—a temporally extended, probably infinitely complex, act of thinking with God as the subject. This event is a single act, and so is not divisible into a first half, second half, etc. It is still temporally extended, however; but then, if we are rejecting substantivalism about times and constructing them out of sets of events, the defender of the first supposition is in trouble. Since, according to (a), the interval contains parts, there must be many sets of events counting as "times" which include this single divine event as sole member, and these times must be temporally ordered. Yet each contains the same partless event, and nothing more. So there is really only the one time before creation after all. The same sort of problem arises for the species of relationalism that takes times to be proposition-like states of the whole world. There is just the one state, involving God and his single act. I cannot see any way to introduce distinctions within this period that will provide the materials out of which distinct times can be constructed—at least no way that is not tantamount to returning to a kind of substantivalism about times. If God alone exists unchanging, there are no changing states of affairs or events upon which a constructivist approach to times can gain a purchase. Some other things would have to be introduced to "mark" distinct parts of this event; but, given temporalism about the deity, they are tantamount to a type of thing with which God must coexist, and we are back to the theological objection to divine temporalism—that it implies that God had to coexist with something else.

Alternative (b) runs afoul of an initially quite plausible principle: nothing can be temporally extended unless it either has some parts earlier than other parts, or at least coexists with something that has parts earlier than other parts. Many events that take time are divisible into shorter events that occupy proper parts of the interval throughout which the whole event lasts. Now perhaps there are simple events—i.e., events that are not divisible into shorter events—that last for more than an instant. But must there not be, in the interval during which such an event occurs, *something* that is divisible into parts that come before other parts?

The temporalist says that God has always been "in time" in at least the sense that there have always been tensed truths about God—for instance, it has *always* been true that God is presently omniscient, benevolent, etc. The temporalist is unlikely to be happy construing times substantively as some kind of extra thing that *had* to coexist with God. But the point that is important for present purposes is this: *if* one adopts a substantival view of times, and tries to posit an extended but partless event involving God and occurring during dead time, either there is just one of these substantival times at which the pre-creation event occurs, or there is more than one. If more than one, the question "Why not create sooner?" returns with as much force as ever; if only one, as (b) suggests, then God exists for but an instant before he creates.

One might try to insist that this first substantival "time" is itself extended but partless. Although I am not sure quite what to make of this suggestion, it seems to me to verge on the incoherent. Perhaps an *event* may last a while but be partless, or a *state-of-affairs* obtain for a while without this fact consisting in there being a number of distinct states-of-affairs obtaining for shorter periods during the interval; indeed, I find both suppositions quite plausible, as will appear. Yet how could a thing introduced as a *mere time period* be extended yet partless? Periods of time must have different parts for each "place" in them at which an event could occur; a "period" without subperiods has only one "place" for events to occur; if it is impossible for non-simultaneous events to occur in a given period, then the "period" is but an instant.

The relational construals of times—as sets of events, or proposition-like states of the whole world—are less objectionable from a theistic perspective. But there are problems in applying them to the dead time before creation. I am supposing that, whatever intrinsic state God is in during this period, it does not change. So, throughout the period, there is only one event available to be in a set of simultaneous events—alternatively, only one proposition-like state of the world. On either story about events, then, there is only one time in dead time. But then is not this period only an instant in length, so that God's past turns out, unacceptably, to be finite?

Solving the Problem by Treating Periods as More
Fundamental than Instants

Not necessarily. The things with which the relationalist identifies "times" must, of course, be able to play the role of "instants" in both ordinary and scientific contexts. So, if we have a theory of motion with variables ranging over moments of time, the relationalist's "times" must satisfy the postulates of our theory; they must, for example, form a compact series if our theory says they should. But there is no reason to suppose that the category of things relationalists posit as satisfying the role of "instants" in ordinary contexts *must* satisfy all aspects of that role (including durationlessness) in *every* context. Our theories (scientific and otherwise) have much to say about post-creation times, but all we want to say about the pre-creation period of time is that it is extended but includes no changes. During that period, there is only one item belonging to the category of things that will, after that point, qualify as instants (i.e., either sets of events, or obtaining proposition-like world-states); but it may be that the pre-creation "time," although it belongs to the same category according to *one* way of dividing things up, differs from subsequent "times" in important ways. I shall consider how this might be, first on a simple version of the sort of relationalism that takes times to be sets of events, and then on a Priorian world-state account.

The type (i) relationalist typically builds "instants" of time out of sets of (possibly temporally extended) events in something like the way Russell proposed in *Our Knowledge of the External World*:

> Let us take a group of events of which any two overlap, so that there is some time, however short, when they all exist. If there is any other event which is simultaneous with all of these, let us add it to the group; let us go on until we have constructed a group such that no event outside the group is simultaneous with all of them, but all the events inside the group are simultaneous with each other. Let us define this whole group as an instant of time.[52]

(By "simultaneous" Russell clearly means "temporally overlapping.") Russell then goes on to show what postulates about events are needed to ensure that instants, so defined, form a compact series (achieving true continuity requires more than Russell provides in these lectures).[53] But all these postulates could be satisfied by the events of our world even if they included a first member that had duration but no parts. True, a set of events constructed so as to qualify as "the time of the first event" would count as an "instant," according to the theory; but there is nothing in Russell's postulates that implies that the event in question is in fact *brief*.

Matters are similar with the type (ii) relationalist. Prior's "times," world-states implying everything that is true at a given moment, are something like maximal consistent conjunctions of tensed propositions. Again, to affirm that such times constitute a compact series requires certain tense-logical postulates; a continuous series, still more.[54] And positing an initial world-state requires another postulate.[55] But one can make all these suppositions while denying that the initial world-state is literally instantaneous.

But does this move not take us back to the objectionable thesis that the past is finite in length, and so God's life is finite in length? No. There may be an initial state in the series of times, a state that ended a finite number of years ago, without the whole of past time qualifying as finite in any sense that puts limitations on how long God has existed. Richard Swinburne has a nice argument for the conclusion that there would be no difference "between a divine conscious act that was God's only conscious act and was qualitatively identical throughout which was of finite length, and one which was of infinite length."[56] I shall skip the details, but the idea should be clear enough. In this pre-creation, pre-laws-of-nature period, there is temporal duration but no way of dividing it up into periods with lengths that can be compared—so you cannot take some portion of the event and say that there must be either finitely many or infinitely many discrete parts of the event of comparable length in the whole period. And since the state is initial there is no beginning to time, no earlier "first moment" distinct from this state.

One might raise the following sort of theological objection to this view: if we are free to say that the period in question is of any length at all, then we can say it is *infinitesimal*. But in that case, we can say with just as much truth that God's history is *not* in fact limitless, that the period during which God has existed is finite—only infinitesimally longer, in fact, than the history of his creation.[57] And surely we want this to come out as definitely false, completely inappropriate as a way of describing the length of time during which God has existed. At this point one might respond with an appeal to the alleged impossibility of instantaneous conscious states. Here is one of C. L. Hamblin's objections to "the contention that phenomenal time is subdivisible into instants":

> Instants can have no content: it takes too many of them to make up a durable experience. The red book on my table can turn green for half a second or half a century but it cannot turn green durationlessly and instantaneously at the stroke of twelve, remaining red at all times earlier and later. To put the objection another way: the temporal continuum is richer than we need for the description of the world, in that it permits the description of phenomenally impossible states of affairs such as that my book should be red at all rational points of the time-scale and green at all irrational ones.[58]

And so one might argue that an experience of red or any other conscious state that lasts for but an instant is "phenomenally impossible." But in that case, God's single conscious act preceding creation, whatever else it might be, is definitely *not* instantaneous. Could it be non-instantaneous but still infinitesimal? I doubt that we need worry too much about how this ostensible possibility is to be ruled out: Hamblin's reason to doubt the possibility of instantaneous conscious states probably applies just as well to the possibility of merely infinitesimal conscious states. Standard analysis has no place for infinitesimal durations; what is being suggested is that the proper mathematization of a continuum of conscious events requires the additional complexity posited by non-standard analysis. But could the additional complexity—the positing of conscious events of infinitesimal duration—correspond to any mental reality, divine or otherwise? If not, and if absolutely instantaneous consciousness is impossible, then, although God's pre-creation state may not properly be said to be either finite or infinite, it is also definitely *not* instantaneous or infinitesimal—it lasts for a period, although there is no fact of the matter about the length of the period.

It looks, then, as though the divine temporalist has plenty of options as she faces questions about the time before creation. She need not suppose that God did anything arbitrary in deciding to create when he did (although I do not see that there would be a huge cost involved in supposing this); nor need she suppose that God was undergoing some kind of eternal, internal change before creating. Nor need she be committed to "times" as some kind of independent, contingent things, necessarily coeternal with the everlasting God.

Conclusions

The morals to be drawn from this reconnaissance mission into several possible temporalist doctrines of creation, are these: (1) it is hard to be a divine temporalist and accept the philosophical thesis that there is no time without change; and (2) one can maintain both that God existed unchanging before creation, and that he did not choose to create when he did arbitrarily, but only by eschewing substantivalism about times—a move for which the divine temporalist has independent motivation.

Notes

Much of the material in this essay was presented in 1991 at a conference of the Society of Christian Philosophers, at Valparaiso University. I received helpful comments from Norman Kretzmann and Eleonore Stump on that occasion. Richard Swinburne kindly provided suggestions and then-unpublished work of his that helped fill in some large holes in the final sections. Robin Collins helped me to see a serious lacuna in my argument. Brian Leftow was extremely generous in providing references and criticisms; I am quite sure I have yet to satisfactorily address some of his objections. Many participants in the 1999 Pacific Regional Meeting of the Society of Christian Philosophers and the 1999 edition of Metaphysical Mayhem provided trenchant criticisms and useful suggestions, including (at the SCP) William Lane Craig, Peter Forrest, and Ned Markosian, and (at MMIV) David Chalmers, William Hasker, Hud Hudson, David Lewis, Trenton Merricks, Quentin Smith, and David Sosa. My colleagues Tamar Gendler, John Hawthorne, Philip Peterson, Ted Sider, and Brian Weatherson gave me the hardest time of all; due to their objections, the entire first half of the essay is missing!

1. Norman Kretzmann gives an argument for the incompatibility of God's immutability (and thus of his timelessness as well, since the latter implies immutability) with knowledge of propositions involving temporal indexicals; see "Omniscience and Immutability," *Journal of Philosophy* 63 (1966), 409–21. Nicholas Wolterstorff offers a similar argument explicitly aimed against divine timelessness; see Wolterstorff, "God Everlasting," in *God and the Good: Essays in Honor of Henry Stob*, ed. Clifton J. Orlebeke and Lewis B. Smedes (Grand Rapids: Eerdmans, 1975), rpt. in *Contemporary Philosophy of Religion*, ed. Steven M. Cahn and David Shatz (New York: Oxford University Press, 1982), 77–98. Stephen T. Davis and Richard Swinburne give arguments for the temporality of God on the basis of his bringing about events in time: see Davis, *Logic and the Nature of God* (Grand Rapids: Eerdmans, 1983), 11–13, and Swinburne, *The Coherence of Theism* (Oxford: Clarendon Press, 1977), 214–15. The most recent arguments along these lines may be found in Alan Padgett, *God, Eternity, and the Nature of Time* (New York: St. Martin's, 1992; repr. Eugene: Wipf & Stock, 2000); and Swinburne, "God and Time," in *Reasoned Faith*, ed. Eleonore Stump (Ithaca and London: Cornell University Press, 1993), 204–22. Edward Wierenga raises some serious objections to Swinburne's argu-

ment in "Timelessness out of Mind: On the Alleged Incoherence of Divine Timelessness," ch. 7 of this volume.

2. See Oscar Cullman, *Christ and Time*, tr. Floyd Filson (London: SCM Press, 1951); William Kneale, "Time and Eternity in Theology," *Proceedings of the Aristotelian Society* 61 (1960–61), 87–108; Bruce Reichenbach, "God Limits His Power," in *Predestination and Free Will*, ed. David Basinger and Randall Basinger (Downers Grove: InterVarsity Press, 1986), 112–15; Richard Rice, "Biblical Support for a New Perspective," in Clark Pinnock et al., *The Openness of God* (Downers Grove: InterVarsity Press, 1994), 11–58; and John Sanders, "Historical Considerations," in ibid., 59–100.

3. Samuel Clarke claims that "there are many Learned Men, of far better Understanding and Judgment [than the Schoolmen], who have rejected and opposed [divine timelessness]." And in a footnote he quotes approvingly from two such men, Gassendi and Archbishop Tillotson, the latter of whom says of the doctrine that the eternity of God is *duratio tota simul*, "let them that can, conceive." See Clarke, *A Discourse Concerning the Being and Attributes of God, in The Works*, vol. 2 (New York and London: Garland, [1738] 1978), 540–41.

4. Many divine temporalists have been working out what they should say about traditional doctrines of providence, foreknowledge, immutability, etc. In the vanguard are the contributors to *The Openness of God*: Clark Pinnock, Richard Rice, John Sanders, William Hasker, and David Basinger. See, for instance, Sanders, *The God Who Risks* (Downers Grove: InterVarsity Press, 1998), and Basinger, *The Case for Freewill Theism* (Downers Grove: InterVarsity Press, 1998).

5. For defenses of the A-theory in the face of relativity, cf. A.N. Prior, "Some Free Thinking about Time," in *Metaphysics: The Big Questions,* ed. Peter van Inwagen and Dean W. Zimmerman (Oxford: Blackwell, 1998), 104–17; Quentin Smith, *Language and Time* (New York: Oxford University Press, 1993), ch. 7; Michael Tooley, *Time, Tense, and Causation* (Oxford: Clarendon Press, 1997), ch. 11; and esp. Franklin Mason, "Presentism and the Special Theory," forthcoming.

6. Actually, Sydney Shoemaker calls this sort of change "McTaggartian change"; but if we don't have to pronounce "Cambridgean," then we shouldn't have to pronounce "McTaggartian" either. See Shoemaker's "Time without Change," in Shoemaker, *Identity, Cause, and Mind* (Cambridge: Cambridge University Press, 1984).

7. See, e.g., Roderick M. Chisholm, *Person and Object* (La Salle: Open Court, 1976), 127; Jaegwon Kim, "Psychophysical Supervenience," *Philosophical Studies* 41 (1982), 51–70, rpt. in Kim, *Supervenience and Mind* (Cambridge: Cambridge University Press, 1993), 175–93 (cf. esp. 184); and David Lewis, "Extrinsic Properties," Philosophical Studies 44 (1983), 197–200.

8. This theory of the intrinsic was first set forth as appendix A of my paper "Immanent Causation," in *Philosophical Perspectives*, vol. 11, *Mind, Causation, and World*, ed. James Tomberlin (Oxford: Blackwell, 1997), 433–71. Rae Langton and David Lewis take a similar approach in their "Defining 'Intrinsic,'" *Philosophy and Phenomenological Research* 58 (1998), 333–45. Our work was independent.

9. Notice that (b) rules out such properties as being the first event or the last event. Matthew Davidson has objected that there may be properties about which it is necessarily always true that they both will be exemplified by something and that they have been exemplified by something. Call such properties "universal time-impliers," since, if there were such, every property would be necessarily such that, if something has it, then something will have a time-implier and something did have a time-implier. If there are universal time-impliers, then nothing will count as a potentially temporally intrinsic property according to (D1). Why might one think there are universal time-impliers? I am not sure what reasons Davidson had in mind, but here is a set of views that would require them. If one thought that every possible world is a temporal one, that time cannot possibly end or begin, and that there could be no moment at which absolutely

nothing exists, then properties everything has necessarily, or essential properties of necessary beings, would all be universal time-impliers. To dispel this worry, one may simply modify the definiens of (D1) so that it begins: "there is no property Q that is not a universal time-implier and that is also such that either: (a). . . ."

10. A proposal in the spirit of this one is considered by David Lewis, in "Extrinsic Properties," and rejected for its failure to cope with disjunctions of this sort.

11. There is David H. Sanford's method of distinguishing various kinds of disjunctive, conjunctive, and independent predicates in terms of their boundaries; and Roderick M. Chisholm's intentional procedure, dividing properties along lines marking our ability to conceive of them independently. Cf. Sanford, "A Grue Thought in a Bleen Shade: 'Grue' as a Disjunctive Predicate," in *Grue! The New Riddle of Induction*, ed. Douglas Stalker (Chicago and La Salle: Open Court, 1994), 173–92; and Chisholm, "Properties and States of Affairs Intentionally Considered," in Chisholm, *On Metaphysics* (Minneapolis: University of Minnesota Press, 1989), 141–49. It is my hope that, on any sensible approach to the problem of determining whether one property is a negation of another, or a conjunction or disjunction of two others, the definitions below which make use of the notion of "Boolean part" will remain adequate.

12. Note that properties formed in non-Boolean ways, such as by attaching the modal property-building operator "necessarily exemplifying . . ." or the intentional operator "believing something to exemplify . . ." to a property, are treated as non-composite by this test of intrinsicness.

13. (A1) implies that time is non-circular and dense.

14. Cp. Aristotle, *Physics* 4.11; Aquinas, *Summa theologiae* 1.46; and Leibniz, *The Leibniz-Clarke Correspondence*, ed. H. G. Alexander (New York: Barnes and Noble, 1984), Leibniz's third paper, par. 4. Sometimes Leibniz writes as if the mere *possibility* of something's having gained or lost a property is sufficient to open up a temporal gap (see, e.g., "Reply to the thoughts on the system of preestablished harmony contained in the second edition of Mr. Bayle's Critical Dictionary, Article Rorarius," in Leibniz, *Philosophical Papers and Letters*, ed. Leroy E. Loemker, 2d ed. [Dordrecht: Reidel, 1969], 583).

15. See, e.g., ibid.

16. See *Summa theologia*, 1.46.1, 2.

17. The analogy is put into the mouths of "the Platonists" by Augustine, *City of God*, bk. 10, ch. 31.

18. Brian Leftow has an ingenious proposal for a kind of constant change in God prior to creation that would explain why God created when he did; see Leftow, "Why Didn't God Create the World Sooner?" *Religious Studies* 27 (1991), 157–72. Leftow's suggestion will be considered below.

19. Aquinas reminds us of this, and concludes that the first moment of creation was the first moment of time—God did not need a moment alone beforehand to think about what he would do. See *Summa theologicae*, 1.46.2, 3 and reply.

20. See Augustine, *Confessions*, 11.30, and Augustine, *City of God*, bk. 11, chs. 5, 6. Compare Leibniz's argument with Clarke, *The Leibniz-Clarke Correspondence*, Leibniz's fourth paper, par. 15. Recently, Brian Leftow has suggested that "God can delay creating to enjoy anticipating a universe and/or desiring to create one" ("Why Didn't God Create the World Sooner?" 163).

21. Indeed, *this* one did think Leibniz held (3), when, as a graduate student, he wrote the first draft of this paper. I thank Jeremy Pierce, Nicholas Jolley, and John Hawthorne for helping me get clearer about this.

22. *The Leibniz-Clarke Correspondence*, Leibniz's fifth paper, par.55.

23. E.g., Leibniz, *Theodicy* (La Salle: Open Court, 1985), 355, and Leibniz, "Refutation of Spinoza," in *Leibniz: Selections*, ed. Philip P. Wiener (New York: Charles Scribner's Sons, 1951), 489.

24. Leibniz, *Theodicy*, par. 406.

25. Leibniz, "Reflexions on the Work that Mr. Hobbes Published in English on 'Freedom, Necessity, and Chance,'" ibid., par. 398. Also, in his discussions of the problem of foreknowledge and free will, he grants that there must be a sufficient ground in the present of the truth of future free actions in order for God to foreknow them (ibid., par. 34–47, 360).

26. *The Leibniz-Clarke Correspondence*, Leibniz's fifth paper, par. 106; my italics.

27. William Craig ("Tensed vs. Tenseless Theory of Time," 222) talks as though God could be in time once he begins to sustain a universe, but exist timelessly "*sans* creation"—which means not exactly *before* time, although it sometimes sounds like it.

28. Arthur N. Prior coins this term in "The Logic of Ending Time," in Prior, *Papers on Time and Tense* (Oxford: Clarendon Press, 1968), 98–115. The brief arguments that follow are thumbnail sketches of ones Prior examines more carefully in this paper.

29. Peter's views are described and given a rationale by Norman Kretzmann, "Incipit/Desinit," in *Motion and Time, Space and Matter*, ed. Peter K. Machamer and Robert G. Turnbull (Columbus: Ohio State University Press, 1976), 112–13.

30. Prior, "The Logic of Ending Time," 115.

31. *The Leibniz-Clarke Correspondence*, Leibniz's fourth paper, par. 15.

32. *The Leibniz-Clarke Correspondence*, Clarke's fourth reply, par. 15.

33. Leftow, "Why Didn't God Create the World Sooner?" 163–71.

34. Cf. Thomas Senor, "Divine Temporality and Creation *ex nihilo*," *Faith and Philosophy* 10 (1993), 86–92.

35. Moses Maimonides, *The Guide for the Perplexed*, tr. M. Friedländer, 2d ed. (New York: Dover, 1956), pt. 2, ch. 13, p. 171.

36. Ibid.

37. I have in mind primarily Adolf Grünbaum and Wesley C. Salmon. See Grünbaum, *Philosophical Problems of Space and Time*, 2d ed. (Dordrecht: Reidel, 1973), and Salmon, *Space, Time, and Motion*, 2d ed. (Minneapolis: University of Minnesota Press, 1980).

38. Cf. Salmon, *Space, Time, and Motion*, 59–62.

39. Ibid., 60.

40. Compare Henri Poincaré, *Science and Hypothesis* (New York: Dover, 1952), and Hans Reichenbach, *The Philosophy of Space and Time*, tr. Maria Reichenbach and John Freund (New York: Dover, 1958).

41. See Grünbaum, *Philosophical Problems of Space and Time*, and B. Riemann, "On the Hypotheses Which Lie at the Foundations of Geometry," in *A Source Book in Mathematics*, ed. David E. Smith (New York: Dover, 1959).

42. For the distinction between "universal" and "differential" forces, see Reichenbach, *The Philosophy of Space and Time*, ch. 1.

43. For cogent summaries and criticisms of analogous arguments for conventionalism with respect to spatial measurements, see Graham Nerlich, *The Shape of Space* (Cambridge: Cambridge University Press, 1976).

44. For elaboration of this thesis, see Swinburne, "God and Time," 208–11.

45. If a period of dead time in which God exists alone would be metrically amorphous, then the divine temporalist has a handy solution to another theological objection. The claim that nothing could exist without being in time—i.e., that as a matter of logical necessity anything that exists is the subject of tensed propositions—does not imply that God's life is *necessarily* divisible into temporal periods like hours and days; it is true that, before creation, God *then* existed, but it need not have been true then that the moment of creation was approaching at some rate or that distinguishable periods of God's life were passing by. This point is made by Swinburne, ibid., 218–20.

46. I thank Robin Collins for posing this question.

47. Nicolas Malebranche, *The Search after Truth*, bk. 1, ch. 8, sec. 2, pp. 38–39.

48. Compare A. N. Whitehead, *The Organization of Thought, Educational and Scientific* (London: Williams and Norgate, 1917), chs. 7 and 8; Whitehead, *The Concept of Nature* (Cambridge: Cambridge University Press, 1920), chs. 3 and 4; Bertrand Russell, *Our Knowledge of the External World* (London: Allen and Unwin, 1926), 124–27; Russell, "On Order in Time," in Russell, *Logic and Knowledge*, ed. Robert C. Marsh (New York: Capricorn, 1971), 347–63; and C. Anthony Anderson, "Russell on Order in Time," in *Rereading Russell: Essays on Bertrand Russell's Metaphysics and Epistemology*, ed. C. Wade Savage and C. Anthony Anderson (Minneapolis: University of Minnesota Press, 1989), 249–63.

49. *Confessions*, tr. R. S. Pine-Coffin (Hammondsworth: Penguin, 1964), bk. 11, ch. 30, p. 279.

50. Cf. Leftow, *Time and Eternity*, 273–79.

51. See A. N. Prior, *Past, Present, and Future* (Oxford: Clarendon Press, 1967), ch. 5 ("The Logic of Successive World-States"); R. M. Chisholm, "Objects and Persons: Revisions and Replies," in *Essays on the Philosophy of Roderick M. Chisholm*, ed. Ernest Sosa (Amsterdam: Rodopi, 1979), 317–88, esp. 346–59; and, for discussion of Chisholm's construction of times, see Dean Zimmerman, "Chisholm and the Essences of Events," in *The Philosophy of Roderick M. Chisholm*, ed. Lewis Hahn (La Salle: Open Court, 1997), 73–100. (I should note that, although Prior identifies his "times" with maximal, consistent world-states or propositions, he would not himself have regarded this as an identification of times with "abstract entities"—for he did not think that quantification over sentential variables required ontological commitment to propositions. See Prior, "Oratio Obliqua," *Proceedings of the Aristotelian Society*, supp. vol. 38 [1963], 115–26).

52. (London: Allen and Unwin, 1926), 124.

53. Russell, *Our Knowledge*, 125–27. For more detailed treatments, see Russell, "On Order in Time"; Anderson, "Russell on Order in Time"; and Richard Jozsa, "An Approach to the Modeling of the Physical Continuum," *British Journal for the Philosophy of Science* 37 (1986), 395–404.

54. Prior takes these issues up in several places; see, e.g., Prior, *Past, Present, and Future*, 71–72.

55. See ibid., 72–73, and Prior, *Papers on Time and Tense*, ch. 10.

56. Swinburne, "God and Time," 219.

57. I thank Peter Forrest for this objection.

58. C. L. Hamblin, "Instants and Intervals," *Studium Generale* 24 (1971), 127–34; the passage cited is on 128.

5

Time Was Created by a Timeless Point

An Atheist Explanation of Spacetime

QUENTIN SMITH

Consider the most obvious question of all
about the initial state of the universe: Why is
there an initial state at all? Why, for example,
is there something rather than nothing?
     —Lawrence Sklar, *Physics and Chance*

Explanatory Atheism and Theism

Why does time exist? In the context of the "spacetime theories" of the special or general theory of relativity, this question should be more appropriately phrased as "Why does spacetime exist?" I will narrow the question further and adopt the results of contemporary general relativistic cosmology, namely, that spacetime began to exist about fifteen billion years ago. Accordingly, my question will be "Why did spacetime begin to exist?"

There are two familiar, contemporary responses to this question. The theist says that the question has an answer and that this answer is that God caused spacetime to begin to exist. The standard response of the atheist is to say that there is no answer to this question; spacetime's beginning to exist is a brute fact or has no explanation. This standard atheist response seems to give theism a prima facie theoretical superiority to atheism; theists offer a detailed explanatory hypothesis about why spacetime begins to exists, and standard atheists are content to leave spacetime's beginning to exist unexplained.

I reject standard or traditional atheism and side with theism on this issue. A theory that includes an explanatory hypothesis about some observational evidence *e*, such as spacetime's beginning to exist, is *ceteris paribus* epistemically preferable to any theory of the observational evidence *e* that does not include such an explanatory hypothesis. No atheist has ever provided a proof that the existence of spacetime is a brute fact and, consequently, standard atheism remains, in this respect, an unjustified hypothesis.

My agreement with theism runs deeper: I agree that there is a *cause* of spacetime's beginning to exist. Further, I agree with many theists that a *simple being* caused spacetime, where "simple" means here "has no parts." (Note that "simplicity" is used in many different senses and that I later use it in a different sense, a sense where "simplicity" expresses a property of hypotheses, not of concrete particulars.) I also agree with some theists, such as Brian Leftow, that the cause of spacetime exists *timelessly*.[1] And I agree with theists that the cause of spacetime is *essentially uncaused* and exists *a se* (i.e., is not dependent upon any concrete object). And I agree with Plantinga and most other contemporary analytic theists that the cause of spacetime has a *metaphysically necessary* existence.[2] I also share the view of these theists that this metaphysically necessary being *contingently* causes spacetime to exist (such that this necessary being exists in some merely possible worlds where it does not cause spacetime). I further agree with theists that the act of causation is a case of *singularist causation* that relates a necessary being to a contingent being, spacetime. Moreover, I agree with theists that the cause of spacetime is *transcendent*, at least in the sense explicated in this passage from Plantinga: "Perhaps we can also give an explanation of what it is for a being to be *transcendent:* such a being transcends the created universe; and a being transcends the created universe if it is not identical with any being *in* that universe (if it is not created) and if it depends on nothing at all for its existence."[3] Note that a being is transcendent, by this definition, only if it *transcends the created universe*, such that a being can possess the property of being transcendent only in the possible worlds where there is a created universe. Thus, the property of being transcendent is possessed contingently by the necessary being that causes spacetime, but it can be possessed by a being that does not cause spacetime, such as an abstract object, assuming abstract objects do not depend on God for their existence.

However, I argue that the timeless, uncaused, simple, independent, necessary and transcendent being that causes spacetime's beginning to exist is not God but a spatially zero-dimensional point. This point contingently has the property of being the big bang singularity from which our maximal spacetime ("the Friedmann universe") exploded and began to expand. This point is also the big bang singularity postulated by quantum gravity cosmologies, as I shall show below. (The idea that quantum gravity cosmology eliminates the big bang singularity is a popular myth, as we shall see.) Since the point is posited by both classical general relativistic cosmology and by the new quantum gravity cosmology, there are two *independent* empirical avenues to its existence. General relativistic cosmology and quantum cosmology cannot both be true, but since the point's existence is posited by both cosmologies, the hypothesis that the point exists has empirical warrant regardless of which cosmology is true.

The timeless point that, in the actual world, has the property of being the big bang singularity is "timeless" in the sense that it exists outside of the time of general relativity and quantum gravity cosmology. In this essay, I use "time" to mean the time postulated by general relativity and quantum gravity cosmology and "timeless" to mean existing outside of the time postulated by these theories.[4] Note that this allows many theists to agree with my thesis that "God is timeless," for they could agree that "God exists in time" in some sense, even though God does not exist in the temporal dimension of the four-dimensional spacetime of general relativity or quantum cosmology.

My arguments and theses in this essay depart from my previous discussions of big bang cosmology, for there I treated the big bang singularity as a *temporal* being, as metaphysically *contingent*, as *dependent* upon spacetime (and thus *lacking aseity*), as *contingently* uncaused, and as *immanent* (rather than transcendent) in the sense that I identified it with the initial temporal boundary of spacetime that exists for an instant at $t = 0$.[5] I asserted that since the singularity is uncaused, spacetime's beginning to exist is uncaused. One crucial difference is that I here treat the singularity as a *timeless point* rather than as a *spatiotemporal* point that exists at the first instant $t = 0$. This way of treating the singularity is more physically justified than the spatiotemporal treatment, since a spacetime point in general relativity requires a metric and (as all agree) the singularity has no metric (the metric is "undefined on the singularity"). Time cannot be extended backward to the singularity at a hypothetical first instant $t = 0$; rather, there is no first instant $t = 0$ and each interval is half-open in the earlier direction.[6] Second, I here treat the singular point as a metaphysically necessary and independent being, rather than as a metaphysically contingent being that depends for its existence on the existence of spacetime. This suggests that my present arguments against theism are not merely "negative" atheistic arguments (e.g., "the existence of spacetime is not caused by God"), but rather are positive arguments that God has a "competitor," so to speak, that shares many of God's properties (being metaphysically necessary, being essentially uncaused, being timeless, simple, existing *a se*, causing spacetime to begin to exist, being transcendent, being the uncaused cause of all contingent beings and thus as being "the ultimate ground of being"). My positive argument is that this competitor—the timeless point—fares better than God in a theory of the most likely causal explanation of why spacetime begins to exist.[7]

This point is a concrete object if only for the reason that it has causal powers; unlike John Leslie, I follow the received view that "x has causal powers" entails "x is concrete." The concreteness of this point makes the following conditional true: if this essentially uncaused and metaphysically necessary point is the being that causes spacetime, then there does not exist the deity of perfect being theology (a metaphysically necessary, omnipotent, omniscient, disembodied, free, and perfectly good person *who causes every concrete being other than himself in each possible world in which there are concrete beings other than himself*).

These clarifications of my notions of the point and God enable me to answer a pertinent question raised by David Woodruff (private communication) about whether God could cause the point to exist and also cause the point to have the properties that would result in there being a spacetime in which intelligent life develops. I would say that perhaps it is formally logically possible that there is some *other* point that is such a God-caused point, but that the different point I am talking about has the essential property of being uncaused. Woodruff also raises the question: is there is a possible world in which there is no spacetime and in which both God and the timeless point exist? My definition of perfect being theology implies the answer is negative: the concrete, timeless point is essentially uncaused, and God causes every concrete being other than himself in each possible world in which he exists.

I shall make the case that the proposition *the above-described point is the cause of spacetime's beginning* has a significantly higher probability of being true than the proposition *the god of perfect being theology is the cause of spacetime's beginning*. From the viewpoint of metaphysics or philosophical cosmology, the negative conclusion that the god of perfect being theology does not exist, which merely tells us what does not exist, is less important than the positive thesis that spacetime's beginning has a cause, namely, a point that has the various properties I have mentioned. If we wish to call this atheistic theory a type of atheism that differs from "traditional atheism," we may call it "explanatory atheism."

Since my argument is probabilistic, I need to assess the comparative prior and posterior probabilities of the two relevant hypotheses, namely,

(h_1) There exists a metaphysically necessary, essentially uncaused, timeless, and independent (*"a se"*) point that, if spacetime begins to exist, is the transcendent cause of spacetime's beginning to exist.

(h_2) There exists the god of perfect being theology who, if spacetime begins to exist, is the transcendent cause of spacetime's beginning to exist.

It is a familiar idea that it can be more or less epistemically probable whether or not a hypothesis is metaphysically necessary, even though in other senses of "probability" a metaphysically necessary hypothesis h by definition has the probability one, $p(h) = 1$.[8] In this essay I use "probability" only to mean epistemic probability, which I shall identify with a type of personalist probability.

I first examine the issue of whether h_1 or h_2 has greater prior probability; in the later parts of this essay, I determine which has greater posterior probability conditional upon the observational evidence e about spacetime's beginning to exist. This entails that "my argument that the point hypothesis is more probable than the theistic hypothesis" requires a restricted interpretation. I am not arguing that the point hypothesis is more probable than the theistic hypothesis conditional on all the relevant observational evidence, but only on a part of this evidence, the evidence e about spacetime's beginning to exist. Roughly speaking, I am arguing that *given contemporary cosmogonies (confirmed theories of the beginning of spacetime)*, the probability of theism is lower than the probability of the point hypothesis. Despite this limited scope, my argument (if successful) nonetheless refutes perfect being theology, for this theology *implies* that there is no atheistic hypothesis conditional upon the observational evidence e of spacetime's beginning to exist that is more probable than the theistic hypothesis conditional upon the observational evidence e of spacetime's beginning to exist. Even more strongly, the observational evidence e turns out (as we shall see) to falsify a prediction implied by the theistic hypothesis (in conjunction with the auxiliary proposition that spacetime begins) and thereby falsifies theism.

There is a limitation upon the domain of my argument. The theistic hypothesis and the point hypothesis are not the only two hypotheses about possible causes or explanations of spacetime, and consequently my conclusion in this essay is limited to showing that *the point hypothesis (h_1) is significantly more probable than the theistic hypothesis (h_2)* (regardless of how probable the point hypothesis is relative to other explanatory hypotheses, be they religious hypotheses about Brahman, Tao, Hegel's Absolute Spirit, the Godhead of God postulated by Meister Eckhardt, or various atheistic hypotheses).[9]

In What Sense Are Both Theism and Explanatory Atheism "Possibly" True?

Some may say that first in the order of things is to ask if the hypotheses of a metaphysically necessary point and a metaphysically necessary God have even a *possibil-*

ity of being true. If we adopt the plausible assumption of theists such as Plantinga, Craig, and Leftow that S5 is the system for metaphysical modalities, then by the "possibility of being true" we cannot mean metaphysical possibility, for at most only one of these hypotheses can be metaphysically possible. If the point hypothesis is metaphysically possible, there is some metaphysically possible world W in which this hypothesis is actually true. But if the point hypothesis (which implies the point exists of metaphysical necessity) is actually true in W, then the point exists in every metaphysically possible world, and thus is metaphysically necessary. In this case, the theistic hypothesis would be metaphysically impossible (for reasons given in the previous section).

How shall we decide which of these two hypotheses is metaphysically possible (if one of them is metaphysically possible)? The standard or widely accepted procedure to decide such issues has been to rely on one's so-called modal intuitions. But Hintikka has correctly noted that in the absence of an epistemological theory of modal "intuitions," appeals to modal "intuitions" have an unknown epistemic value, if any, and that until and unless such an epistemological theory is developed, these so-called intuitions should be called "hunches."[10] If we treat these individually variable hunches about the metaphysical necessity or impossibility of theism as having epistemic weight by virtue of the fact that the hunches *seem self-justifying* to the person who has the hunch, then what Paul Moser calls "substantive relativism about justification" would apply to these hunches: "the view that whatever one takes to be justified is actually justified . . . [which entails] an 'anything goes' attitude toward justification and evaluative assessment."[11] I think substantive relativism about justification is self-referentially incoherent: one could take to be justified that whatever one takes to be justified is not actually justified. It would then follow, given substantive relativism about justification, that whatever one takes to be justified is both actually justified and not actually justified.

We can avoid a mutually question-begging debate, an epistemically valueless trading of hunches, and a self-contradictory substantive relativism about justification *if we interpret "possible" as meaning formal logical possibility*, which is governed by S5. If the point hypothesis is true in some formally logically possible world W, then it is actually true in some formally logically possible world W1. This means it is a formal logical possibility that the point exists of metaphysical necessity, which the theist can accept without giving up at the outset her belief that God exists of metaphysical necessity. The theist can consistently conclude, if the arguments go in her favor, that the formally logically possible world W1 in which the point is metaphysically necessary is a metaphysically impossible world. (Metaphysically possible worlds are a proper subclass of formally logically possible worlds.) Likewise, the explanatory atheist can conclude, if the arguments go in her favor, that God exists of metaphysical necessity in some formally logically possible worlds that are not metaphysically possible. Thus the theist and atheist can begin with the same premise: there is at least one formally logically possible world W2 in which God, but not the point, is metaphysically necessary and, second, there is at least one formally logically possible world W1 in which the point, but not God, is metaphysically necessary. What they both are trying to find out by means of logical argumentation, and without mutually question-begging hunches, is whether W1 or W2 is metaphysically possible.

Formal logical possibility includes propositional logic and predicate logic with identity. It includes not only first order predicate logic with identity, but also second order predicate logic with identity, third order predicate logic with identity, and predicate logic of order omega.[12] Mathematics is definable in terms of set theory, and set theory is definable in terms of predicate logic of order omega; thus mathematical and set-theoretical truths are formally logically necessary truths.

It may be objected that we have all learned on our mother's knee that first order predicate logic with identity is about "narrowly logical necessities," that mathematics and set theory are about "broadly logical necessities," and that "broadly logically necessary" means metaphysically necessary.[13] I grant that we learned that this is *Plantinga's* philosophy of logic, but I would note the following theses. (a) Mathematics is definable in terms of set theory. (b) If first order predicate logic with identity is narrow logic, then, by strict analogy, second and higher order predicate logics with identity are narrow logics (Plantinga offers no reason to deny this inference; in fact, he does not discuss the subject). (c) One of the two axioms of second order predicate logic with identity is the axiom of extensionality,[14] which is also a basic axiom of set theory. (d) This and other axioms of higher order logics enable set theory to be defined in terms of predicate logic of order omega. (e) Since mathematics is definable in terms of set theory, and the latter in terms of predicate logic of order omega, mathematics and set theory are not about metaphysical necessities but about transfinite predicate logic necessities, i.e., narrowly or formally logical necessities. For this reason, I will include set theory, and thus mathematics, in the formally logically possible worlds in which the theistic and point hypotheses are possibly true. (I will use "formal logical possibility" since "narrow logical possibility" is Plantinga's technical phrase and my *formally logically necessary/metaphysically necessary* distinction is different from the distinction marked by his widely adopted uses of the phrases "narrowly logically necessary" and "broadly logically necessary," which seems to me to represent an arbitrary, or rather, mistaken, distinction.)

Theism, Explanatory Atheism, and the Concept of Probability

What is the probability that the theistic and point hypotheses are not merely logically possible, but also metaphysically possible (and thus necessary)? The probability we are talking about is an epistemic probability, not a statistical or "actual frequency" probability, for by definition the statistical or "actual frequency" probability of the theistic or point hypothesis is zero or one (assuming the dubious thesis that the notion of statistical probability can coherently be applied to these hypotheses). Henceforth, by "probability" I mean epistemic probability, which I identify with personalist probability.

The point hypothesis (h_1) cannot be known to be probably *metaphysically possible* (and thus probably *metaphysically actual and necessary*) if it has a zero degree of prior epistemic probability. The hypothesis h_1 (or equivalently, the hypothesis that h_1 is *metaphysically possible*) has a zero degree of posterior probability *if its prior probability is zero*. If the point hypothesis's prior probability is zero, then the point hypothesis's posterior probability is zero, regardless of how much evidence there is for general relativistic or quantum cosmology. This follows from Bayes's theorem: $p(h)$ is the prior probability of a hypothesis h, and $p(h/e)$ is its posterior probability, its probability given the evidence e. If $p(h) = 0$, then $p(h/e) = 0$. In Bayes's theorem, $p(h/e) = p(h) \times p(e/h)$, divided by $p(e)$. If $p(h) = 0$, then the numerator of the equation is zero. In other words, if $p(h) = 0$ and zero is multiplied by the probability n of e/h, we get zero since $0 \times n = 0$, for any number n. If we divide this by the probability n of e, we get $0/n$, which is 0, since zero divided by any number n equals 0. This shows that it is essential to our argument to show that the prior probability of our timeless point hypothesis is a positive, non-zero number (and the same for the theistic hypothesis [h_2]).

If the hypothesis of a metaphysically necessary point or deity has a formally logically possible truth but a prior probability that is a positive, non-zero *infinitesimal* number (in the sense of Abraham Robinson's theory of non-standard real numbers)[15] or a *negligible standard real number*, the posterior probability will remain infinitesimal or negligible regardless of how much evidence e there is for the hypothesis. How can we justifiably obtain *non-negligible prior probabilities*?

The solution to the problem involves, in part, adopting Shimony's "tempered condition" for prior personalist probabilities.[16] This condition implies that the prior probability $p(h)$ be sufficiently high to allow the possibility that h be preferred to all rival "seriously proposed hypotheses" as the result of the envisaged observations relevant to formulating the observation statement e. I think (contra Shimony) that this tempered condition can be more than a stipulated axiom required for the theory of personalist probability to be a useful theory. I think it can be justified (at least in our explanatory project) by defining the set S of "serious hypotheses" as the small, finite set of hypotheses (i) that have a very high degree of *nonarbitrariness* (in the sense defined in a later part of this essay on non-arbitrariness) and that (ii) exclude the hypotheses that are *less parsimonious* than a parsimonious hypothesis of the first degree.[17] Generalizing upon Schlesinger's mathematical characterization of degrees of parsimony, we can say that any hypothesis that is *parsimonious to the second degree or higher* is formulated by virtue of adding explanatorily idle conditions to a parsimonious hypothesis of the first degree. A hypothesis is parsimonious to the first degree if and only if it includes the least number of explanatory conditions required to explain the data e. Thus we exclude from our set S of hypotheses about spacetime's beginning (a) arbitrary hypotheses such as that 8,617 disembodied finite minds jointly formed a total cause of spacetime's existence and (b) nonparsimonious hypotheses such as that a three-centimeter line (rather than a point) caused spacetime, which is a hypothesis obtained by adding the explanatorily useless condition to the point hypothesis that this point plus the additional points on a three-centimeter line formed the total cause of spacetime. With these two conditions, nonarbitrariness and first degree parsimonious, determining our set S of (formally logically) possible explanatory hypotheses, we can ensure that the point hypothesis and the theistic hypothesis each have a prior probability that is both non-negligible and is sufficiently high to allow the possibility that the hypothesis be preferred (once the evidence is obtained) to all rival hypotheses in the set S. (In partial analogy to Parfit's theory,[18] we can include the standard atheistic theory that spacetime has no explanation in our set S of possible explanatory hypotheses. We may call it the "null explanatory hypothesis," reminding us that "for no reason" counts as an answer to "Why did spacetime begin to exist?") Accordingly, we can say that the set S includes only hypotheses that are parsimonious and non-arbitrary possible answers to the question "Why did spacetime begin to exist?"

The same considerations apply to the probability of the evidence e. In Bayes's theorem, e is more fully expressed as e/k, that is, the evidence e conditional upon "background knowledge" k. In our case, k is the proper class of logical truths. However, Bayes's theorem implies that both theism and explanatory atheism are false if $p(e/k) = 0$, for in this case the probability of theism (or explanatory atheism) given the evidence e and the background logical truths k would equal a mathematically undefined expression, namely $n/0$, where n is the numerator and zero the denominator. This is an unacceptable result, since it is mathematically meaningless to divide by zero. I think the solution of the problem is the application of the criteria of non-arbitrariness and first degree parsimony to give us a finite class of possible evidence propositions e'. As we will see later, one of the two most non-arbitrary ways for spacetime to begin to exist is a maximum (maximal order) or a minimum (minimum order), which gives the evidence e I shall discuss later in this essay a significant prior probability.

By "probability" I mean the *degree of belief of a logically possible, perfectly rational finite mind*. If a hypothesis is 80 percent probable, that means a possible, perfectly rational, finite mind would believe the hypothesis to the degree 80 percent if that mind understood that hypothesis and all the relevant considerations that would be considered by a mind that is perfectly rational and finite. Just as scientists constructing theories are attempting to "approximate the truth," so humans are implicitly attempting to approximate the judgments of a (logically possible) perfectly rational, finite mind when we are more or less confident in some hypothesis, i.e., when we believe it to some degree.[19]

Personalist probability (with which I have identified epistemic probability) is a kind of objective, mind-independent probability, since it is defined counterfactually as what a perfectly rational finite mind would believe to a certain degree, if there were such a mind and belief. This does not *require* the factual existence of such a mind (this is the sense in which it is mind-independent). The truthmakers of the relevant counterfactuals are possible worlds in which the perfectly rational, finite mind and its beliefs exist. This is how I shall understand personalist probability. Clearly, philosophers of a nominalist, physicalist, extensionalist, and verificationist bent would prefer to say that the expression "degrees of belief" has meaning (semantic content) only insofar as it refers to belief-tokens of mental organisms in the actual world. Since I have argued elsewhere that nominalism, physicalism, extensionalism, and verificationism are false, it seems to me there are grounds for rejecting these theories.[20]

The Background Truths upon Which the Prior Probabilities of Theism and Explanatory Atheism Are Conditional

Since the theistic and timeless point hypotheses involve explaining why spacetime exists, the "prior probabilities" of these hypotheses are a priori probabilities; they are probabilities determined prior to taking into account any a posteriori evidence that consists of the existence of spacetime or anything else that exists and is knowable only posteriori. The prior probability $p(h)$ is definable in terms of a conditional probability $p(h/k)$, where the background truths k relative to which the probability $p(h)$ is conditional are a proper class (not a set)[21] of a priori truths, the truths comprising *formal logic*, as I explained previously. The fact that some mathematical truths (truths of predicate logic of order omega), say, can be learned by actually existent intelligent organisms in an a posteriori manner is consistent with saying that such truths are known a priori by a perfectly rational finite mind in some possible world.[22] For our purpose of determining a priori personalist probabilities, we are only interested in what is known a priori by such a mind. If we say that "$p(h)$ is an unconditional probability" this shall mean that it is not conditional upon any *merely* a posteriori evidence e or upon anything else but formal logic; thus, $p(h) = p(h/k)$.

The class k of truths of formal logic does not include all a priori truths. Some a priori necessary truths, such as *I am here now*[23] and *If something is red, it is colored,*[24] are not truths of formal logic. Although many metaphysically necessary truths are knowable only a posteriori, some are knowable a priori, and the examples about indexicals and colors are examples of a priori metaphysical necessities.[25]

The most important implication of my definition of the background class of truths k is that if something is a metaphysical necessity, but is not a truth of formal logic, it does not belong to k. The exclusion of merely metaphysical necessities from k enables us to avoid begging the question in favor of explanatory atheism or perfect being theology. I am not denying that some metaphysical necessities, such as the a priori truth *If anything is red all over at* t, *it is not green all over at* t, are self-evident to all normal humans. The problem is that most of the alleged metaphysical necessities that pertain to our explanatory project, such as *necessarily, no disembodied mind can exist* or *necessarily, no point can exist except as a part of a spacetime manifold,* evoke different "hunches" in different people, and there is no epistemological theory (that has yet been formulated) that enables us to decide which of these "hunches" has epistemic rather than merely psychological significance.[26]

When Plantinga says that the atheists' and theists' probability judgments are individually relative to different background beliefs, specifically to classes k_1 and k_2 of rationally acceptable metaphysical theses, this statement is premised upon his inclusion of (alleged) metaphysical necessities in his background classes and his use of individually relative "metaphysical intuitions" as the method of access to these alleged necessities.[27] We avoid this substantive relativism about justification by using only formal logical truths in k. By the time of his three books on warrant, Plantinga's epistemological position seems closer to the methodology of the present essay, and he now seems to reject substantive relativism about justification or warrant.[28] His new non-relativistic position enables him to say that it is warranted to be a theist and not warranted to be an atheist, rather than merely that theism is warranted for a theist and atheism is warranted for an atheist.

Whether or not the *alleged* metaphysical necessities h_1 and h_2, the point hypothesis and the theistic hypothesis, *are* metaphysical necessities is not determined by one's "hunches," but is determined by (1) assessing their comparative prior probabilities conditional upon the background class k of formal logical truths and (2) assessing their comparative posterior probabilities conditional upon the observational evidence e.

Since the criteria used in these assessments belong to inductive logic, the assessment is logical, not an appeal to "hunches."

The Criteria for Assessing the Prior Probabilities of Theism and Explanatory Atheism

Apart from delimiting the background knowledge k, there is another issue that needs to be addressed. *What criteria* does a perfectly rational, finite mind use for assessing the comparative prior probabilities $p(h_1/k)$ and $p(h_2/k)$, where h_1 and h_2 are the point and theistic hypotheses respectively? (These will also be the criteria that we—actual human organisms—use to approximate the assessments of this possible mind in our actual degrees of belief.)

Criteria for determining a priori personalist probabilities, conditional only upon the background knowledge k, are the hypotheses' degree of *conservativeness, symmetry, simplicity*, and *non-arbitrariness*, criteria that are also used in the empirical sciences to decide a priori among *observationally equivalent* hypotheses. I reject verificationism, conventionalism, positivism, Millian-Quinian empiricism, and other anti–a priorist or anti-realist epistemological or metaphysical theories, and hold that conservativeness, symmetry, simplicity, and non-arbitrariness are a priori criteria that can determine which of two *observationally equivalent* hypotheses is more likely to be true. Our present task is to determine the *prior* probabilities of the timeless point hypothesis and the theistic hypothesis, conditional upon k. Whether or not these two hypotheses are observationally equivalent is addressed at the end of this essay on the comparative posterior probabilities of these hypotheses.

Explanatory power, predictive success, predictive comprehensiveness, and *predictive novelty* are criteria for assessing the probabilities of hypotheses relative to the observational evidence, and thus are not employed in the first (prior probability) stage of our inquiry. I shall now begin evaluating the prior probability of the point hypothesis and the theist hypothesis conditional upon k by assessing which of the two is more conservative, symmetrical, simple, and non-arbitrary.

The Comparative Prior Conservativeness of the Theistic and Point Hypotheses

The point hypothesis and theistic hypothesis we are examining are:

(h_1) There exists a metaphysically necessary, essentially uncaused, timeless, and independent ("*a se*") point that, if spacetime begins to exists, is the transcendent cause of spacetime's beginning to exist.

(h_2) There exists the god of perfect being theology that, if spacetime begins to exist, is the transcendent cause of spacetime's beginning to exist.

Whether the point hypothesis or the theistic hypothesis has greater prior probability is partly determined by which is more conservative relative to k, which is the extent to which each is similar to what is already known, namely, the proper class k of all truths of formal logic that are knowable by a perfectly rational, finite mind. Roughly speaking, if the entity, God, postulated by the theistic hypothesis is radically different than the abstract objects of formal logic, then the postulation that God exists is a radical, non-conservative departure from what is already known to exist. But if the entity, the point, is much more similar than God to what is already known to exist, the formally logical abstract entities, then the point hypothesis is more conservative than the theistic hypothesis and thus, if all else is equal, is a priori more likely to be true. This can be spelled out more precisely and in more detail.

The hypothesis h is more conservative than h' if and only if h conserves more of what is already known than h' and h introduces fewer novel properties than does h'. In our special case of the theistic and point hypotheses and the background logical truths in k, we can use a more precise definition. The point hypothesis is more conservative than the theistic hypothesis if and only if the point hypothesis conserves more of the properties *essentially* possessed by *all* of the abstract objects pertinent to formal logic, and ascribes fewer novel essential properties, than does the theistic hypothesis. By a "property" that is novel or conserved, I do not mean whatever can be expressed by a linguistic predicate, but a *kind* that is intrinsic to reality or a *universal* that is determinative of such a kind. I would say "natural kind," but given that I am talking about supernatural properties, non-natural properties (of abstract objects), and natural properties, a more general term is needed. "Real kind" is the appropriate phrase here, which contrasts with "artificial kind."

Both the point hypothesis and the theistic hypothesis conserve at least four properties in the sense that they ascribe four properties to the point, or God, such that these four properties are essentially possessed by all the abstract objects of formal logic:

(C1) being timeless (existing outside of the time postulated by general relativity)

(C2) aseity (existing non-dependently on the existence of spacetime or any other concrete beings, if there are such existents)

(C3) being transcendent if spacetime exists

(C4) metaphysical necessity, i.e., existing in all the metaphysically possible worlds

The point hypothesis ascribes only two novel properties:

(N1) being an unextended spatial point

(N2) being able to cause spacetime to begin to exist

Note that the property of *being a point* is conserved, since there are abstract points, e.g., the points in the abstract topological space postulated by point-set topology. The point hypothesis introduces the novel idea (novel relative to the existentially quantified truths in k) that there is a point that is concrete rather than abstract. Something is concrete if and only if it is (a) mental and/or has (b) extended or unextended spatiality or temporality and (c) is able to cause something and/or is able to be causally affected by something. The concrete, timeless point that is postulated by (h_1) has, like all the concrete spatial points and mass points that belong to our universe, a zero-dimensional spatiality, and thus it is *concrete* by virtue of instantiating (N1).

Having property (N2) also implies it is concrete. Unlike the spatial and mass points of our universe, the timeless point has no metrical properties, but having metrical properties is not a necessary condition of being concrete. (I am here assuming substantivalism about spacetime for ease of exposition and because I think it is true; my argument could be reformulated with only minor modifications in terms of relationalism [reductionism] about spacetime.)

The property (N2) is a dispositional property, like the divine property of omnipotence, and it determines the kind of entity the timeless point is. The properties our hypotheses ascribe can be "occurrent" or "dispositional."

The theistic hypothesis ascribes six novel properties, not merely two:

(N3) being a person

(N4) being omniscient

(N5) being omnipotent

(N6) having libertarian free will

(N7) being perfectly morally good

(N8) being a spirit (= having a mind that requires only itself to engage in mental activity, and does not require a brain or some other physical body)

Since the point hypothesis is more conservative than the theistic hypothesis, relative to the abstract objects in the proper class k, it follows that *if all other things are equal*, the point hypothesis has a higher prior probability than the theistic hypothesis.

The argument from conservativeness is one way of interpreting some of David Woodruff's plausible remarks about the theistic and point hypotheses, although Woodruff does not agree with all my theses. Woodruff does not mention the criterion of conservativeness, but I believe his following statements (with which I concur) can be interpreted in terms of this criterion. Woodruff writes:

> In assessing degrees of [a priori] probability for contingent things (or the degree of probability that a thing is truly necessary) we would no doubt include simplicity as one factor, but again it seems to me that this would only be one thing and not even the first or most important thing in the assessment. The first thing we would assess here would be its likelihood given what else we think necessarily exists. . . . Suppose that if either exists (the point or God), that they are necessary. Then ask given what we would accept as necessarily existing apart from these things, say numbers or sets, properties, relations and so forth, which one of these (if either) is more likely to exist. Well, the theist thinks that God is personal (and concrete . . .) and that is radically different from the rest of the necessary things. Whereas, the point is not personal (and I think not concrete) and thus far more similar to the rest of the necessarily existing things. To me this suggests that the prior probability of the point, given what we normally accept as necessarily existing, is higher than the prior probability of God.[29]

I am not sure how much weight we should put on my claim that the point is concrete and Woodruff's claim that it is not, since we may just define "concrete" differently; Woodruff and I are both talking about a point that is hypothesized to cause spacetime, and if Woodruff allows non-concrete objects to be causes, perhaps this is a mere ter-minological difference. The main issue, I think, concerns Woodruff's true statement that *God is personal* and *the point is not personal* and that this makes the point "far more similar to the rest of the necessarily existing things." Woodruff is a theist, but I think his plausible remarks here indicate that the sort of considerations I have adduced about conservativeness can be accepted as intersubjectively justified by both theists and atheists. It seems likely that Woodruff or some others who think theism is true will be looking at the "other things" in the "if all other things are equal" modifier that es-sentially belongs to the relationship between a hypothesis's conservativeness and the extent to which this conservativeness affects the hypothesis's prior probability of being true.

This brings us to the question *"Are* all other things equal?" Maybe the theistic hy-pothesis is more symmetrical, simpler, and more non-arbitrary than the point hypoth-esis, such that these "other things" make theism more a priori probable than the point hypothesis, despite the fact that theism is much less conservative than the point hypothesis.

The Comparative Prior Symmetry of the Theistic and Point Hypotheses

Symmetry is a criterion relevant to a hypothesis's a priori probability. I shall take my point of departure from Van Fraassen's *Laws and Symmetry* since this work contains the most philosophically sophisticated discussion of symmetry.[30] However, we will (in due course) need to offer a different, more comprehensive, and stronger definition of symmetry than the one Van Fraassen and others use.

The theistic hypothesis contains more a priori symmetry (i.e., symmetry with k) than does the point hypothesis, and thus (considered *only* in respect to the symmetry criterion) has a greater prior probability than the point hypothesis. But what is this cri-terion? As a first approximation, I shall quote Van Fraassen's example: "The para-digm of symmetry is the mirror image. I and my image are a symmetric pair."[31] The theistic hypothesis exhibits symmetry with k by virtue of postulating an omniscient being. Omniscience can be mapped onto the elements of k by an injective function that preserves exact similarities with respect to truth. To see this, consider the defini-tion of symmetry that Van Fraassen and others use. Symmetries are injective func-tions that map each element in a domain onto some element in the codomain, such that the relevant essential properties possessed by the element in the domain are also possessed by the element in the codomain to which the element in the domain is related.[32]

The theistic hypothesis ascribes the property of omniscience, which entails that the hypothesized person knows (at least) each formally logical truth. Let our domain be the proper class of God's *intentional acts* (in Brentano's sense) that are God's "know-ings" of the formally logical truths in the proper class k, such that for each such truth p, there is a distinct knowing that p. Let our respect be *truth* and let the symmetry func-tional relation associate each *divinely known p* with each *theorem p*, such that all the elements in the domain (each divinely known p) are exactly similar to the elements in the codomain (each theorem p in k) in respect of the property *being true*. Each divinely known p has the essential property of being true, and each theorem p in k has the essential property of being true.

Note that this functional relation is *bijective*, giving us a stronger symmetry than Van Fraassen's merely *injective* function (Van Fraassen calls these injective functions "one-to-one functions,"[33] but in the precise language of set theory "*the graph* of an injective mapping is said to be *one-to-one*."[34]) A *function* relates each element in the domain to some element in the codomain. A *bijective* function relates each element in the domain to a unique element in the codomain, such that no two elements in the domain can be related to the same element in the codomain and there is no element in the codomain that is not related to an element in the domain. An *injective* function relates each element in the domain to some member(s) in the codomain, such that all the elements in the domain can be related to the same element in the codomain. Further, there is a third functional relation that is more symmetrical than an injective relation and less symmetrical than a bijective relation, namely, a *surjective* functional relation, whereby at least one element in the codomain is uniquely related to some element in the domain.

Thus, the theistic hypothesis, by virtue of including omniscience in its set of ascribed properties, contains a domain that is maximally (bijectively) symmetrical with k.[35] How does the set of properties ascribed by the point hypothesis compare with theism in regard to the criterion of symmetry?

The point hypothesis's conserved properties (being timeless, etc.) are also conserved by the theistic hypothesis, so its distinctive degree of symmetry will be exhibited in its set of novel properties, namely, the properties of being a spatially zero-dimensional point and being able to cause spacetime's beginning. The property of being a spatially zero-dimensional point is the only distinctive property that bears a symmetry relation. The domain is the property of *being a spatially zero-dimensional point*, and the respect is *being pointlike*, i.e., being a concrete or abstract point. The domain, consisting only of the property of being spatially zero-dimensional point-like, is exactly similar only to the abstract *points* in the codomain k in respect of point-likeness, giving us merely an injective symmetry, the lowest degree of symmetry. The atheistic hypothesis (h_1) fares poorly with respect to the criterion of symmetry.

The theistic hypothesis is considerably less conservative (with respect to k) than the point hypothesis by virtue of postulating a person, but is considerably more symmetrical (to k) by ascribing omniscience to this person. This is a conclusion with which both atheists and theists can agree.

There is no reason to think that, *ceteris paribus*, (h_1)'s greater conservativeness raises the prior probability of (h_1) to *the same degree of prior probability as* (h_2)'s greater symmetry raises the prior probability of (h_2). But there is also no reason to suppose that considerations of conservativeness and symmetry make one hypothesis have an *enormously higher prior probability, ceteris paribus*, than the other hypothesis. There is no defeater for the rational belief that their comparative prior probabilities, considering only conservativeness and symmetry, are approximately equal.

Will our two remaining criteria, simplicity and non-arbitrariness, give one of the two hypotheses a significantly higher prior probability conditional upon k?

The Comparative Prior Simplicity of the Theistic and Point Hypotheses

According to Eliot Sober, simplicity is informativeness.[36] According to dozens of other philosophers, simplicity is something else, such as explanatory power, or predictive comprehensiveness, or predictive novelty, or non-ad-hocness, etc. Physicists often say that simplicity is a hypothesis's beauty or its naturalness, but make no attempt to explain what the phrase "beautiful hypothesis" or "natural hypothesis" could possibly mean. In response to the philosophers' theories of simplicity, I agree that such properties as informativeness, explanatory power, predictive comprehensiveness, predictive novelty, and non-ad-hocness are theoretical virtues that can make one hypothesis more probable than another if all else is equal, but these virtues are conditional upon observational evidence e and cannot help us in determining the probability of our two hypotheses (h_1) and (h_2) conditional only upon k. "Simplicity," which perhaps wins the prize for being the most equivocally used word in the philosophical and scientific literature, is used in the present part of this essay to express a virtue of hypotheses (in more familiar language, a "theoretical virtue") distinct from the abovementioned ones, namely, a virtue that makes one hypothesis more a priori probable, *ceteris paribus*, than another hypothesis, conditional only upon k.

Since my discussion is restricted to the comparative probabilities of the point hypothesis and theism, I will define the kind of simplicity that is pertinent to such hypotheses. I will define "simplicity" in terms of properties rather than parts since neither the timeless point nor God is a whole composed of parts and thus the two hypotheses are equally "simple" in the compositional sense of implying that God and the point have no parts. The relevant comparison concerns properties or attributes, not parts, and thus we may call our simplicity "attributive simplicity" as distinct from "compositional simplicity."

The hypothesis h ascribes an *attributively simpler* set of essential n-adic properties to x than does h' if and only if the set S containing all and only the non-trivially essential properties ascribed by h contains *fewer logically independent kinds of properties* than the corresponding set S' of properties ascribed by h'. The two kinds of properties F and G are logically independent if and only if, for any possible existent x, "x exemplifies F" does not logically imply "x exemplifies G" and "x exemplifies G" does not logically imply "x exemplifies F."

Kinds of properties are being mental, being physical, being animate, being abstract, etc. Kinds of properties can have subkinds that are also kinds of properties; for example, being animate has several subkinds, such as being a plant and being an animal. By contrast, being the number one, being the number two, and being the number three are properties of the same kind, namely, being a positive whole number. Trivial essences, such as being-self identical and being something, are possessed by everything (where "thing" is understood broadly to range over concrete objects and abstract objects) and thus are not relevant to the comparative degrees of simplicity of our two hypotheses.

The set S1 of logically independent kinds of non-trivially essential properties ascribed by h_1 is:

S1: {being a spatial point, being metaphysically necessary, timelessness, aseity (i.e., existing independently of any other concrete object, if there are other concrete objects), being able to cause spacetime, being transcendent if there is a created spacetime}.

Why is the property of *being metaphysically necessary* logically independent of the property of *aseity*? Because it is logically consistent for the point to exist in every metaphysically possible world and to be dependent on some concrete object in each of these worlds, and, second, it is logically consistent for the point to exist nondependently on any other concrete object and yet to exist in only some metaphysically possible worlds.

There are many truths about what non-trivial essential properties the point does not possess; it is true that the point does *not exemplify* the properties of being animate, having a metric, being a part of a spacetime manifold, having parts, being caused, being mental, etc., but this point possesses only six logically independent kinds of non-trivially essential properties. If someone argues that *being essentially uncaused, being temporally unextended*, and *being partless* are also logically independent kinds of non-trivially essential properties, then she may add them to the atheist set S1 and to the theist set S2, which will not affect the comparative simplicity of theistic and point hypotheses. Of course, one may object to this; for example, does not *being a zero-dimensional spatial point* entail the property of *being partless*, such that these two properties are not logically independent? And does not *aseity* entail being *uncaused*, and does not being *timeless* entail being *temporally unextended*?

The set S2 of logically independent kinds of non-trivially essential properties ascribed by h_2 is:

S2: {being personal, being omniscient, being omnipotent (and thus being able to cause spacetime), having libertarian free will, being perfectly good, being a spirit, being metaphysically necessary, aseity, timelessness, being transcendent if there is a created spacetime}.

Neither being omniscient nor *being a spirit* (i.e., being an unembodied mind) logically implies being personal. Some logically possible beings, such as *Brahman* (specifically, the impersonal, omniscient spirit postulated by the Hindu philosopher Shankara) or *sunyata* ("emptiness"), the impersonal, omniscient spirit postulated by the Mahayana Buddhist Asvaghosha, are examples of such logically possible beings. Furthermore, omnipotence does not logically imply aseity, since there is some logically possible being that cannot exist without creating other concrete objects (some Leibniz scholars interpret his god in this way), such that this being cannot exist unless other concrete objects exist.

Many theists hold that the divine attributes are not logically independent from one another. But they mean by this that they are not *broadly logically* or *metaphysically* independent from one another, and my definition of attributive simplicity uses "logically independent" to mean *formally logically* independent, as I have indicated. (I should add that I agree with Plantinga, Craig, Swinburne, and most contemporary analytic theists that the "Identity Theory" of God is false.)[37]

The set S1 of logically independent kinds of non-trivial essential properties ascribed by h_1 contains fewer members than the set S2. (It contains infinitely fewer members if "omniscience" designates the transfinitely numerous kinds of knowledge God possesses and "omnipotence" the transfinitely numerous kinds of abilities to act in different ways.) It follows that h_1 has greater a priori attributive simplicity than h_2 and thus, if all other things are equal, has greater prior probability. The point hypothesis is more conservative and more attributively simple than the theistic hypothesis, but the theistic hypothesis exhibits greater symmetry with k. Nothing clearly decisive has emerged from our application of these criteria; there is no defeater for a perfectly rational, finite mind's belief that the prior probabilities of these two hypotheses do not diverge to a significant degree relative to these three criteria.

The Comparative Prior Non-Arbitrariness of the Theistic and Point Hypotheses

Perhaps the issue of prior probabilities could be decisively resolved if we could show, for example, that the theistic hypothesis alone has a high degree of non-arbitrariness and that this is sufficient to make the theistic hypothesis have a significantly greater prior probability than the point hypothesis. It could be that theism is highly non-arbitrary and that the point hypothesis is extremely arbitrary. Is this so?

Swinburne, Unger, and Parfit have all noted that degrees of non-arbitrariness are at least partly determined by maxima and minima.[38] Swinburne uses the word "simplicity" to express the property of non-arbitrariness.[39] He holds that zero and infinity are equally as simple (non-arbitrary). Postulating a universe with zero electrons is equally as non-arbitrary as postulating a universe with an infinite number of electrons (if all other things are equal), and both postulates are less arbitrary than postulating a universe with 874 trillion electrons (if all other things are equal). Zero members of a certain kind and infinite members of a certain kind are less arbitrary numbers of *members of that kind* than some positive, finite number of members of that kind, if all other things are equal.

The fact that *non-arbitrariness* is partly determined by maxima and minima has been noted (under that name) by Parfit and Unger, although they use the maxima criterion in a broader sense than does Swinburne. Parfit and Unger argue that the least arbitrary ontology of concrete objects is one that postulates the maximum of possible concrete objects (all possible worlds exist, in David Lewis's sense) or the minimum of possible concrete objects (there is "nothingness," or, a world containing no concrete objects is actual). This is very close to Swinburne's idea that zero and infinity are equally non-arbitrary (or "simple" as he calls it), except Swinburne's "infinite being" does not refer to all possible worlds but to a being with unlimited knowledge, power, etc., in one world. Other examples of equally non-arbitrary postulates of maxima and minima are postulates that there is a zero-dimensional space (a point) or an infinite-dimensional space (assuming all other things are equal). Cannot we say that God is the *maximal concrete being* (that is able to cause spacetime) in the sense pertinent to perfect theology, namely, in the sense that he has the maximal compossible degrees of the essential properties of being powerful, free, good, knowledgeable, etc., that the metaphysically greatest possible concrete being could possess, and that in this respect theism is a non-arbitrary hypothesis? Certainly. God is "infinite" in the sense of being unlimited in his power, knowledge, goodness, etc. But we also can say that the point is the *minimal concrete being* (that is able to cause spacetime) in the sense that it has the minimal compossible degrees of the essential properties that concrete objects (physical or mental objects) could possess. The point has a zero degree of mentality, a zero degree of physical massiveness, a zero degree of spatiality, a zero degree of temporality, a zero degree of metrication, and so on. (The *minimal* concrete being must be distinguished from the *worst* concrete being, which is a being that has the maximal degrees of evilness, power, knowledge, freedom, etc. This being has maximal degrees of many metaphysically great-making properties, such as omniscience and omnipotence, which enable it to be more evil than any other being, and thus the metaphysically worst being is distinct from the metaphysical minimal being.)[40]

Just as God exhibits "infinity" in the above-explained sense, so the point exhibits "zeroness" in the above-explained sense. In this respect the point hypothesis is a non-arbitrary hypothesis. The point hypothesis and the theistic hypothesis are equally non-arbitrary in this respect and thus have equal prior probability *considering only the maxima/minima aspect of the criterion of non-arbitrariness*. It seems so far, then, that the point and theist hypotheses do not significantly diverge in respect of their prior probabilities with respect to conservativeness, symmetry, simplicity, and non-arbitrariness.

But this statement may need qualification, since the maximum/minimum distinction is only one of the kinds of non-arbitrariness. One hypothesis is less arbitrary than a second hypothesis if (all else being equal) the first hypothesis postulates an entity x whose existence has an explanation and the second hypothesis postulates an entity y whose existence has no explanation. William Craig uses the phrase "explanatorily simpler" to express this second species of non-arbitrariness. Craig writes that, according to my earlier theory, the singularity existing in time for one instant at $t = 0$ "is not explanatorily simpler [less arbitrary] than theism."[41] He writes at more length:

> The sense in which God is unexplained is radically different from the sense in which the initial cosmological singularity is unexplained. Both can be said to be without cause or reason. But when we say that God is uncaused we imply that He is eternal, that He exists timelessly or sempiternally. His being uncaused implies that He exists permanently. But the singularity is uncaused in the sense that it comes into being without any efficient cause. It is impermanent, indeed, vanishingly so. These hypotheses can therefore hardly be said to be on a par with each other. Moreover, God is without a reason for His existence in the sense that His existence is metaphysically necessary. But the singularity's coming to be is without a reason in the sense that, despite its contingency, it lacks any reason for happening.[42]

If the singularity exists timelessly (as I now believe, due to the failure of the B-boundary and G-boundary constructions)[43] and exists necessarily, it is not subject to the criticisms leveled in Craig's passage. Further, Craig is wrong when he says of God and the point that "both can be said to be without cause *or reason*."[44] They are both timeless and uncaused, but the hypotheses h_1 and h_2 also ascribe metaphysically necessary existence. It is a mistake to say with Craig that "God is without a reason for His existence in the sense that His existence is metaphysically necessary."[45] If God exists in every metaphysically possible world, then it belongs to God's essence to exist, since "x's essence includes its existence" means x exists in every metaphysically possible world. Contra Craig, the fact that x's *essence is to exist* is a sufficient reason for x to exist and sufficiently explains why x exists. Just as the answer to the why-question "Why is yellow a color?" is "Because it belongs to the essence of yellow to be a color," so the answer to "Why does God exist?" is "Because it belongs to God's essence to exist." The same holds for the metaphysically necessary point postulated by the point hypothesis (h_1).

However, Craig has given no justification whatsoever for his belief that God's existence is metaphysically necessary. If he has a "metaphysical intuition" about this, this so-called intuition (for all Craig has said) amounts to what Hintikka has called an epistemically valueless "hunch."[46] Another group of "intuiters" could have an epistemically similar "hunch" that God is metaphysically impossible and that the timeless point is metaphysically necessary. If we are to have indefeasibly justified beliefs about the matter, then we would have to argue that the criteria of conservativeness, symmetry, simplicity, and non-arbitrariness provide the theistic and point hypotheses with a significant prior probability conditional upon the proper class of background truths k, and that other criteria, such as predictive success and explanatory power, provide one or the other hypothesis a greater posterior probability conditional upon the observational evidence e. (I think this is the proper avenue to pursue an epistemological theory of how we know metaphysical necessities and possibilities; "modal intuitions" [hunches] are junked in favor of the application of criteria belonging to inductive logic.)

The Posterior Probability of the Point Hypothesis Conditional upon General Relativistic Cosmology

The conclusion of previous parts of this essay is that the theistic and point hypothesis are equally non-arbitrary, that the point hypothesis is more simple and conservative, but that the theist hypothesis is more symmetrical. Given this, it is reasonable to conclude that their prior probabilities are approximately equal or at least not significantly different. The consequence of this more or less approximate equality of h_1's and h_2's prior probabilities is that the contribution of the observational evidence e to the comparative *posterior* probabilities of these two hypotheses will be the overwhelmingly decisive factor in determining which hypothesis deserves a greater degree of rational belief. If $p(h_1/k) \approx p/h_2/k$, then our theism-versus-atheism argument is going to turn on the extent to which $p(h_1/e)$ is greater or less than $p(h_2/e)$.

I think general relativistic big bang cosmology shows that the posterior probability of the point hypothesis is much higher than the posterior probability of the theistic hypothesis, all else being equal. One reason for this is that the *timeless point* I have been discussing has the contingent property of being the *big bang singularity* postulated by contemporary physical cosmology.

The attributively used definite description (in Donnellan's sense of "attributively used") "the metaphysically necessary, timeless, uncaused, simple, independent, and transcendent point-cause of spacetime" has a different sense than the attributively used definite description "the big bang singularity," *but the evidence from physical cosmology shows they have the same referent.* According to general relativistic big bang cosmology, the universe began about 15 billion years ago with a big bang singularity. The big bang singularity is temporally and spatially zero-dimensional. The metric tensor, which is defined on each point in spacetime, is not defined on the big bang singularity, which thereby is not a spacetime point. The metric describes the curvature of spacetime, and since the singularity is an isolated point, it has no curvature; that is to say, the notion of curvature is undefined on the singularity, which is what physicists mean when they say the point has "infinite" curvature. Methods of attaching the singularity to spacetime and defining the metric tensor on the singularity *as the first instant of time*, $t = 0$ (rather than as a metrically undefined timeless point), have run into the problem of being counterexampled. As I have indicated earlier, the two procedures for attaching the singularity as the first instant of time, the B-boundary procedure and the G-boundary procedure, have been shown to be unacceptable definitions of a singularity attached as a first instant of time.[47] But this failure still leaves one able to attach the singularity as an unmetricated spatial point that is topologically attached to certain types of spacetime, most notably, the type of spacetime that general relativists believe we occupy, a Robertson-Walker-Friedmann spacetime. This was first noticed by one of the general relativists who argued that the B-boundary and G-boundary methods fail, Robert Wald. Wald notes that adding an unmetricated singular point to an otherwise metrically well defined spacetime "would allow one to talk in precise terms of a singularity as a 'place' even though the metric is not defined there. However, while this could be done 'by hand' in a few simple cases like the Robertson-Walker or Schwarzschild spacetimes, severe difficulties arise if one tries to give a meaningful general prescription for defining a singular boundary."[48]

John Earman's recent argument that the big bang singularity in no sense "exists" is invalid.[49] He believes that counterexamples to the definition of a general relativistic singularity, counterexamples that consist in possible spacetimes acquiring physically impossible features if an existent singularity is added to them, suffice to show that our universe does not have an existent singularity. However, Earman's conclusion that singularities are not existents, since there is no adequate definition (either the B-boundary definition or the G-boundary definition) that applies to all general relativistic singularities, is a non sequitur. If there is no adequate definition of a game that applies to all games, it does not follow that there are no chess games. There may be no defining essence that is common to all singularities, and "singularity" may not have a univocal meaning. In the case at hand, there can be a big bang singularity in a Robertson-Walker-Friedmann spacetime (which is the spacetime in which we live, according to general relativists) even if there is no adequate definition that applies to all singularities. As I mentioned above, Robert Wald, one of the physicists who showed there is no definition that applies to all singularities, argues that one can nonetheless have a singularity in some cases, one of the cases being our Robertson-Walker-Friedmann spacetime. Since the equations of big bang cosmology predict an initial singularity, the prediction of the singularity requires a realist interpretation if the equations are given a realist interpretation. Physicists correctly note that "the initial singularity is a consequence of the equations of general relativity."[50] A justification for deciding to interpret all of the consequences of the equations of general relativity realistically but this one consequence would be that this consequence has no coherent realist interpretation. But if the Friedmann equations, which general relativists believe describe our spacetime, have an incoherent consequence, how could they even be possibly true, let alone actually true (or highly confirmed)? The singularity has the spatial topology of a point (even though it has no spatial metric and does not exist in time), and it is topologically connected to the metrically well defined spacetime.

I also indicated that the timeless point, by virtue of being essentially attributively simple, need not instantiate any laws, such as the laws of general relativity. The big bang singularity is lawless. As Stephen Hawking writes: "A singularity is a place where the classical concepts of space and time break down as do all known laws of physics because they are formulated on a classical space-time background."[51] The big bang explosion is the effect of the timeless point-cause, and the big bang explosion is the earliest phase of the universe's existence (perhaps the first 10^{-43} seconds). There is a contingent, singular causal relationship between the point and the explosion; the explosion occurs at a temporal interval t, but it is timelessly the case that the point causes the explosion to occur at the temporal interval t.

The timeless point causes spacetime to exist in David Lewis's sense of sufficient cause.[52] Lewis's definition of causation is applicable since it allows for singularist causation and does not require temporal precedence or spatiotemporal contiguity, transfer of energy, or other conditions that are part of other definitions of causality and that preclude the timeless point from being a cause.[53] According to Lewis's definition, c causes e just in case both c and e exist and e would not have existed had c not have existed. (The modality of the subjunctive is a physical rather than a metaphysical or logical modality.) The timeless point c and spacetime's beginning e both exist, and spacetime would not have begun if there were no singular point c. According to the Friedmann equations and Hawking-Penrose singularity theorems that determine the basic physical laws of our universe, spacetime must begin in a singularity, i.e., as an "explosion" of a singular point. Thus, in all physically possible worlds in which c does not exist, e does not exist. (If e exists and c does not, the Hawking-Penrose singularity theorems are violated.) By contrast (and in accordance with Lewis's definition of sufficient causation), if e had not occurred, c would have occurred but would have failed to cause e. In some possible worlds, the point c exists timelessly but does not cause spacetime to begin to exist. It is not governed by any law that implies it causes spacetime if it exists. Spacetime requires a causal point-like singularity to begin to exist, but the timeless point does not need to cause spacetime in order to exist. The point is an unmetricated, timeless, topological "boundary" or "edge" of spacetime (to use these terms in the technical senses they have in general relativity) only in the possible worlds where the point causes spacetime.

Let us consider some objections that are pertinent to my theses that the big bang singularity is a partless point and that the point hypothesis h_1 has the sort of compositional and attributive simplicity I ascribed to it. If the big bang singularity is not the partless point described by the point hypothesis (h_1), then the empirical evidence for big bang cosmology and the big bang singularity is not evidence for the point hypothesis (h_1) I am advocating in this essay.

Robert Deltete states that the big bang singularity is a "complex entity" since "literally everything is concentrated in a geometrical point."[54] If this statement is true, then the big bang singularity is not the timeless point I have been discussing, since the timeless point is partless and thus is not composed of anything (let alone "literally everything"). However, Deltete's statement is necessarily false, since neither Socrates nor Mount Everest nor any other three-dimensional spatial object can occupy a zero-dimensional singularity. These objects exist only in the spacetime that is caused to exist by the singular point.

Deltete also implies that the hypothesis that there is a big bang singularity lacks the compositional and attributive simplicity I attributed to the point hypothesis (h_1); the singularity has "infinite space-time curvature and infinite mass-energy density—surely a complex entity."[55] Thomas Sullivan makes a similar sort of objection: "If the big bang singularity is pointlike in its simplicity, it is nonetheless infinitely dense."[56] I respond that these objections represent a misunderstanding of these concepts, although there is no doubt that the common surface appearance of the way physicists describe the situation lends itself to just this misunderstanding. For example, Michael Berry writes: the "matter and radiation [are] packed into zero initial proper volume; this 'point,' however, includes the whole of space—there is nothing 'outside.' "[57] For another example, Hawking says: "all the matter and energy that was contained in that spherical volume of space will be compressed into a single point, or singularity. . . . [T]he entire observable universe is considered to have started out compressed into such a point. . . . Because of the infinite compression of matter and energy, the curvature of spacetime is infinite at the Friedmann singularities too. Under these circumstances the concepts of [curved, three-dimensional] space and time cease to have any meaning."[58] What does this mean? The singular point has "infinite mass-energy density" in the sense that the measure of its density has zero for its denominator, not in the sense that it has aleph-zero density. Density is the ratio of mass-energy to unit volume, e.g., grams per cubic centimeter. Given the conservation of mass-energy at the singularity, there would be a large number of grams per zero cubic centimeters, since the singularity has zero volume. However, $n/0$ is a mathematically meaningless expression since division by zero is impermissible. The expression "the singularity is infinitely dense" means that the concept of density is inapplicable at the singularity. Likewise "the singularity has infinite curvature" means the concept of curvature is inapplicable, since a point cannot be curved.

The Posterior Probability of the Point Hypothesis
Conditional upon Quantum Gravity Cosmology

Is not my theory of a timeless causal point as outdated as the classical, general relativistic theory of a big bang singularity? If we are talking about empirical confirmation, do we not need to ensure our point-cause hypothesis is consistent with the quantum gravity research program?

Most philosophers believe that the hypothesis of the big bang singularity is inconsistent with quantum gravity cosmologies. However, contra Deltete, Sullivan, Craig, and most other philosophers of physics, quantum cosmologies *do* postulate a big bang singularity. Deltete says that "a key feature of quantum-gravity proposals . . . is that they deny the existence of an initial singularity."[59] *Pace* Deltete, these proposals predict there is a big bang singularity. For example, Barrow and Tipler's quantum gravity cosmology is based on a functional law (a wave function of the universe) that predicts both the existence of a big bang singularity and the explosion of this singularity in a "big bang" that evolves into our present-day universe. There is a singularity at $R = 0$, which means the radius R of the universe is zero (i.e., there exists only a point). One of two quantum laws of nature "tell us what happens to wave packets when they hit (i.e., are mathematically related to) the singularity at $R = 0$. It should be emphasized that in either case, the singularity is a real entity which influences the evolution of the Universe (or more precisely, its wave function) at all times via the boundary conditions at the origin. In the classical universe, the singularity is present only at the end and at the beginning of time, so in a sense the singularity is even more noticeable in quantum cosmology than in classical cosmology."[60] For the reasons I explained above, "the singularity is present at the beginning of time" needs to be interpreted as meaning *the singularity timelessly exists and causes the beginning of time* if Barrow and Tipler's theory is to take into account the failure of the B-boundary and G-boundary constructions. Although the current observational evidence is that time is endless, the phrase "singularity at the end of time" is interpreted as referring to some point other than the point hypothesized by the point hypothesis (h_1). The wave-functional law governing the timeless, causal singularity encodes all the information about the probabilities for the evolution of the universe and explains *why* there is a big bang explosion caused by the singularity.

There is also a big bang singularity in the better-known quantum gravity cosmology developed by James Hartle and Stephen Hawking.[61] In their cosmology, there is a wave function of the universe that gives an unconditional probability "for the occurrence of a given spacetime" as a whole.[62] A probability for the existence of the big bang singularity is obtained from this functional law by means of the derived or more specified wave function.[63] "The wave functions which result from this specification [of the ground state wave function] will not vanish on the singular, zero-volume three-geometries which correspond to the big bang singularity," and thus there is a functional law of nature that implies there is a probability that the singularity explodes in a big bang. (For a given universe, such as the actual universe, "*the* wave function can be finite and nonzero at *the* zero three-geometry," such that the big bang singularity of the single, actual universe does not consist of *many* zero-volume three-geometries.) In this case as well we have functional laws that predict with some degree of probability the existence of a universe, a big bang singularity, and the temporal evolution of the spacetime caused by this singularity.

Quantum gravity does not require us to add attributive complexity to the set of kinds of essential properties ascribed to the point by the point hypothesis (h_1). The reason for this is that (if quantum gravity cosmology is true) the timeless point *contingently* exemplifies the quantum gravity laws in the actual world, and the timeless point's attributive simplicity is defined in terms of the kinds of properties it essentially possesses. If the timeless point instantiates quantum gravity laws ("the wave function of the universe") in the actual world, there are some possible worlds in which it does not instantiate these laws.

As we will see in the next section, these considerations show that quantum gravity cosmology and general relativistic big bang cosmology confirm the point hypothesis to a much higher degree than they confirm the theistic hypothesis (h_2).

The Posterior Probability of the Theistic Hypothesis

First, we shall consider the comparative posterior probability of theism conditional on classical, general relativistic cosmology. Let us see if theism can meet the criteria of posterior probability (predictive success and explanatory power) as well as they are met by the point hypothesis. Consider the point hypothesis and e. If the timeless point caused spacetime to begin to exist, we can predict what sort of state would constitute the beginning state (the first state of some small temporal interval such as 10^{-43} seconds) that would be the effect of this cause. The state that would be the effect of a timeless, partless, attributively simple, and totally lawless cause is a completely unstructured state, i.e., a state of utter chaos or maximal disorder. It is exactly a state of this sort that is found to occur by contemporary big bang cosmology. For example, Hawking expresses the common view when he says that particles were emitted from the singular point in random microstates, which resulted in an overall macrostate state of maximal disorder.[64] This a posteriori scientific discovery constitutes our evidence e. Since the point has no nomological structure or any other structure that could determine or influence some ordered configuration of particles to emerge (e.g., a Garden of Eden), we are left with a chaotic outpouring from the singularity; the singularity "would thus emit all configurations of particles with equal probability."[65] Now this observation statement e corresponds to the *prediction* derivable from the hypothesis that a nomically ungoverned point caused the beginning of spacetime. Numerous observed phenomena, ranging from the cosmic background radiation to the behavior of elementary particles described by the so-called standard model, significantly confirm this prediction of a chaotic singularity. Further, the hypothesis (h_1) *explains* the maximal chaos that obtains at the earliest era of spacetime. The reason that there is maximal disorder is that the hypothesis about the timeless point is compositionally and attributively simple to the extent that it implies the point lacks the structure that could enable its act of singular causation (the initiation of the "big bang explosion," to use the metaphor of big bang cosmologists) to bring about an ordered effect.

But this is not what a perfectly rational, as so far finite mind would *predict* a perfectly good, powerful, and knowledgeable person to cause; the finite, rational mind would predict that spacetime begins in a way that an all-powerful, all-knowing, and good person would begin spacetime, namely, in a highly ordered way. It is perfectly reasonable to expect a very good, wise, and powerful person to begin his creation in a very beautiful and magnificent way that exhibits an admirably high degree of naturally good order. "Complete chaos is just ugly,"[66] and a perfectly rational finite mind would predict that *ugliness* is *not* the very first thing that a good, all-powerful person would want to create. This expectation is so natural and obvious that the belief that the early universe contained the Garden of Eden persisted in Jewish and Christian thought for nearly two thousand years, requiring extensive scientific evidence to be falsified.

This is why the current observational evidence that the beginning of spacetime is a state of maximal chaos falsifies theism. The theistic hypothesis is *predictively unsuccessful* and is *explanatorily valueless*, since "Because God created it" is not an explanatorily informative answer to "Why is the first state of spacetime totally chaotic rather than ordered in a very beautiful and admirably good way?"

This is not the argument I have presented previously.[67] Max Jammer, in his recent book *Einstein and Religion: Physics and Theology*, sums up my earlier argument as follows:

> Smith challenged the theistic interpretation of the Big Bang cosmology not only on the grounds that it has a viable competitor in a nontheistic interpretation, but, more importantly, because, in his view, it is inconsistent with this cosmology. His argument, in brief, runs as follows. According to the Big Bang cosmology, there exists an earliest state, E, of the universe, which, by Hawking's so-called principle of ignorance, does not guarantee to evolve into an animate state. In the theistic interpretation, E is created by an omniscient, omnipotent, and perfectly benevolent God and must therefore evolve into an animate state; for an animate state is better than an inanimate one.[68]

Jammer does not disagree with my argument. Naturally, the above-quoted passage does not include all the details of my earlier argument, such as the requirement that E is an animate state or else E necessarily *or probably* evolves into an animate state. (The detail about probability was also missed by Swinburne in his critique.)[69] Jammer's passage also does not reproduce my explanation of why my use of the premise "an animate state is better than an inanimate one" *cannot* be rebutted by the "there is no best possible world" argument.[70] I will only note here that my comparison of the predictive success of theism versus the point hypothesis does *not* mention whether or not the first state E is an animate state or will (probably or necessarily) evolve into an animate state. Rather, I am here only comparing the point hypothesis's predictive success and explanatory power in predicting and explaining the total lack of *order* of the *caused* first state, and the theistic hypothesis's predictive and explanatory failure with regard to the observational evidence of utter *chaos*. It is *caused order* or *caused chaos*, not the different issue of *caused animinateness* or *uncaused inanimateness*, that my present argument is about.

Theists such as Craig, Swinburne and Robert Deltete (and neoplatonists such as John Leslie) have addressed the general issue of the chaotic nature of spacetime's beginning.[71] They attempt to save theism by replacing the falsified prediction (that spacetime begins to exist in a highly ordered state) that is derived from the conjunction of theism with the auxiliary proposition that *spacetime begins to exist*, with a new prediction that *is not derived from theism and the auxiliary proposition, but is postulated solely for the purpose of making theism consistent with the newly discovered observational data e*. In short, they turn theism into an ad hoc hypothesis, and thereby make it an inductively illogical hypothesis.

Craig offered the most detailed attempt to save theism from the falsifying evidence *e* discovered by general relativistic cosmologists. Instead of predicting the initial stage of spacetime by deriving it from the theistic hypothesis and the auxiliary proposition that spacetime begins to exist, Craig first learns through contemporary cosmology about the nature of this initial stage and then (after this new, falsifying observational evidence is acquired) modifies the theistic hypothesis solely for the purpose of enabling it to predict this newly acquired evidence. Craig redefines perfect being theology so that it now includes the proposition *God delights in fashioning a highly ordered, good, and beautiful universe out of maximal chaos*. Craig writes, "Moreover, what if His goals include, not merely the having of a created order, but the divine pleasure of fashioning a creation [out of disordered 'raw material' God first created]?"[72] Craig seems to commit here a further fallacy: by positing the mere epistemic possibility that God takes pleasure in organizing totally disorganized states, the added assumption cannot be used to derive a predication or explanation of the first state. It is a fallacy in epistemic logic to derive *p is known* from *p is consistent with what is known*. By direct analogy, one cannot derive the prediction that *an ordered, beautiful, and good state such as the Garden of Eden will be the effect of the point* from the assumption that it is epistemically possible that a state such as the Garden of Eden is the effect of the uncaused point. (Moreover, the assumption that these propositions are even epistemically possible remains unjustified.)

The ad hoc modification to theism is even more blatantly demonstrable in Swinburne's work. Swinburne's recent discussion is a modification of his earlier theory in that it is designed solely for the purpose of making his theism consistent with the observational evidence *e* of which he was (apparently) unaware earlier.[73] His earlier theory reads:

> We saw that God has reason, apparently overriding reason, for making, not merely any orderly world (which we have been considering so far) but a beautiful world—*at any rate to the extent to which it lies* OUTSIDE the control of creatures. (And he has reason too, I would suggest, even *in whatever respects* the world does lie *within* the control of creatures, to give them experience of beauty to develop, and perhaps also some *ugliness to annihilate*.) So God has reason to make a basically beautiful world, although also reason to leave some of the beauty or *ugliness of the world within the power of creatures to determine*; but he would seem to have OVERRIDING REASON NOT *to make a basically ugly world* BEYOND THE POWERS OF CREATURES TO IMPROVE.[74]

The "complete chaos" of which the entire world consisted at the big bang explosion, which is "just ugly,"[75] is beyond the power of creatures to improve (unless they have backward causation, which Swinburne denies they do). Thus, the observational evidence *e* directly contradicts Swinburne's original theistic hypothesis, for *e* implies there is *evidence that there is chaos and ugliness beyond the powers of creatures to improve*. But once Swinburne learned that the world initially was in a state of complete chaos, he *changed* his theistic theory to include the thesis that God does have overriding reason to create the early state to be chaotic and ugly; he adopted Craig's ad hoc hypothesis that God delights in ordering chaos (a chaos beyond the control of creatures to improve).

Can middle knowledge save the inductive validity of theism? Craig adds to theism a thesis about middle knowledge designed to make theism consistent with the theistically unexpected observational evidence *e* that turned up. He added the proposition *It is metaphysically necessary that God has the middle knowledge that the beginning of spacetime, in the actual world* W, *would be a state of maximal disorder that would eventually lead to an orderly state of the universe where free, rational, moral agents exist and act.* This is obviously ad hoc. This thesis cannot be derived from the classical creationist hypothesis (from Molina to Suarez to Plantinga and others), but is *an addition to this hypothesis that is made solely for the purpose of making this hypothesis consistent with the newly found observational evidence.* If this is not a purely ad hoc modification to theism, then why did not Molina, Suarez, and other defenders of the middle knowledge theory of divine omniscience derive this prediction from the theistic hypothesis and the auxiliary proposition that spacetime begins to exist? Why could not Craig derive it before he began reading books and articles on physical cosmology?[76]

Returning to the non-ad-hoc point hypothesis (h_1), *quantum gravity cosmology* also supports the prediction of a chaotic first state that is derived a priori from the point hypothesis (h_1) in conjunction with the auxiliary proposition that spacetime begins to exist. The wave function of the universe predicts that there is a big bang singularity, but since the singular point does not have enough structure to determine or constrain its effect to have a certain order, the wave function predicts that a maximally chaotic state will follow from the big bang singularity.[77]

How can the evidence *e* of the nature of spacetime's beginning be *logically sufficient* to falsify the theistic hypothesis (h_2)? Even if Swinburne's and Craig's theories are inductively invalid, cannot the theist maintain that there is an inductively valid version of theism? Specifically, does not the requirement of *total relevant evidence* require that we take into account the existence of the present beauty and orderliness in nature and the existence of free, intelligent, morally capable humans that came into existence billions of years after the beginning of spacetime? The answer is that we *have* taken into account the total relevant evidence for *the prediction of how spacetime would begin*, and the failure of this prediction is sufficient to render the theistic hypothesis false.[78] This can be most clearly demonstrated by exhibiting the logical structure of the theistic and timeless point arguments in the following deductive formats. Regarding the timeless point hypothesis (h_1), we have this argument (A1):

(1) There exists a metaphysically necessary, essentially uncaused, timeless and independent (*"a se"*) point that, if spacetime begins to exists, is the transcendent cause of spacetime's beginning to exist. (Axiom h_1)

In this essay, we derived the conclusion that this axiom has a certain attributive and compositional simplicity that enables the following theorem to be deduced:

(2) The point is structureless and will have an unordered effect if it causes spacetime's beginning to exist. (Theorem T1)
(3) Spacetime begins to exist. (Auxiliary proposition)
(4) Spacetime begins to exist in an unordered way. (Prediction derived from 1–3)
(5) Spacetime begins to exist in an unordered way. (Observational evidence *e*)

Compare argument (A1) with the theistic argument (A2):

(6) There exists the god of perfect being theology that, if spacetime begins to exist, is the transcendent cause of spacetime's beginning to exist. (Axiom h_2)

In this essay, we derived the conclusion that this axiom has a certain attributive complexity that enables the following theorem to be deduced:

(7) God is highly structured in terms of goodness, power, and knowledge and will have a highly ordered effect if he causes spacetime's beginning to exist. (Theorem T2)

(3) Spacetime begins to exist. (Auxiliary proposition)

(8) Spacetime begins to exist in a highly ordered way. (Prediction derived from the conjunction of 6, 7, and 3)

(5) Spacetime begins to exist in an unordered way. (Observational evidence e)

Noting that the observational evidence e falsifies the prediction (8) and thus falsifies the theistic hypothesis (h_2), someone like Craig and Swinburne who wishes to retain theism in the face of the scientific evidence will modify the hypothesis (h_2) *after the fact* for the specific purpose of enabling a prediction of the observational evidence e to be derived. Instead of the prediction of e being derived from the theistic hypothesis and the auxiliary proposition that spacetime begins, we have the reverse situation (A3):

(5) Spacetime begins to exist in an unordered way. (Observational evidence e)

(9) There exists the god of perfect being theology who, given (5), delights in ordering total chaos and, if spacetime begins to exist, is the transcendent cause of spacetime's beginning to exist. (Ad hoc modification of [h_2] that enables it to predict e)

(10) God delights in fashioning order out of original chaos and will have an unordered effect if he causes spacetime's beginning to exist. (Theorem T3)

(3) Spacetime begins to exist. (Auxiliary proposition)

(11) Spacetime begins to exist in an unordered way. (Prediction derived from the conjunction of 5, 9, 10, and 3)

Since the observational evidence statement (5) asserting e is one of the premises from which the prediction (11) of e is derived, the argument is inductively invalid; specifically, it commits the fallacy of being ad hoc. Since the original, non-ad-hoc prediction (8) is falsified by the observational evidence e, the theistic hypothesis (h_2) from which (8) is derived (in conjunction with the relevant premises) is also falsified.[80] We are led to the conclusion that $p(h_2/e \ \& \ k) = 0$ and, on a more metaphysically positive note, that $p(h_1/e \ \& \ k) >> p(h_2/e \ \& \ k)$.

Notes

I am grateful to David Woodruff for extensive, stimulating, and very helpful comments on an earlier draft of this essay. I also thank Dean Zimmerman, for his influential criticisms of an even earlier draft that he offered to me twenty-five thousand feet above the earth.

1. Brian Leftow, *Time and Eternity* (Ithaca: Cornell University Press, 1991).

2. See Alvin Plantinga, *The Nature of Necessity* (Oxford: Clarendon Press, 1974), and Plantinga, "World and Essence," *Philosophical Review* 79 (1970), 466–73.

3. Alvin Plantinga, *Warranted Christian Belief* (New York: Oxford University Press, 2000), 6.

4. I am assuming the theory of time postulated in the standard interpretation of general relativity and quantum cosmology. This is for the purpose of showing how contemporary cosmology, on its standard interpretation, can explain why time exists. A theory based on the theory of time in my "Absolute Simultaneity and the Infinity of Time," in *Questions of Time and Tense*, ed. Robin Le Poidevin (Oxford: Clarendon Press, 1998): 135–83, would be a different project.

5. This earlier theory is articulated in many of my articles, including "Simplicity and Why the Universe Exists," *Philosophy* 72 (1997), 125–32; "Did the Big Bang Have a Cause?" *British Journal for the Philosophy of Science* 44 (1995), 649–68; "Stephen Hawking's Cosmology and Theism," *Analysis* 54 (1994), 236–43; "Can Everything Come to Be without a Cause?" *Dialogue: Canadian Philosophical Review* 33 (1994), 325–35; "Anthropic Coincidences, Evil, and the Disconfirmation of Theism," *Religious Studies* 28 (1992), 347–50; "Atheism, Theism, and Big Bang Cosmology," *Australasian Journal of Philosophy* (1991); "A Natural Explanation of the Existence and Laws of Our Universe," *Australasian Journal of Philosophy* 68 (1990), 22–43; and "The Uncaused Beginning of the Universe," *Philosophy of Science* 55 (1988), 39–57. See also William Lane Craig and Quentin Smith, *Theism, Atheism, and Big Bang Cosmology* (Oxford: Clarendon Press, 1993).

6. For a discussion of the relevant arguments, see my "Problems with John Earman's Attempt to Reconcile Theism with General Relativity," *Erkenntnis* 52 (2000), 1–27.

7. If this is the case, this may suggest to some people that an emotion like Schleiemacher's "feeling of dependence" is appropriately directly upon the only existent transcendent cause of spacetime, the timeless point, and is not appropriately directed upon the hypothetical being postulated by perfect being theology. The theory of this transcendent, creative point is neither monotheism, nor pantheism, nor neoplatonism, nor polytheism, nor animism, but (if one wishes to coin a neologism) *pointism*. Since I argue that theism is probably false, I am not a theist; in this sense I am an atheist. However, qua defender of the theory in this essay, I may also call myself a *pointist*, to coin a second neologism. An atheist is free to appreciate emotionally other intentional objects (in Brentano's sense) of possible feeling-acts, in addition to the point-cause. The atheist's beliefs about the positive nature of reality as a whole, about what does exist, allow her to appreciate emotionally the world-whole, the existence of the universe, presentness, the conjunction of all concrete objects, and perhaps other intentional objects of feeling-acts as well. On this appreciation, see my *The Felt Meanings of the World: A Metaphysics of Feeling* (West Lafayette: Purdue University Press, 1986); "An Analysis of Holiness," *Religious Studies* 24 (1988), 511–27; *Language and Time* (New York: Oxford University Press, 1993); and *Ethical and Religious Thought in Analytic Philosophy of Language* (New Haven: Yale University Press, 1997). Given Bouchard's study of identical twins (Thomas Bouchard, "Whenever the Twain Shall Meet," *Sciences*, September/October 1997, 52–57), from which he plausibly concludes that religiosity and non-religiosity are genetically inherited, and given the steadily increasing encroachment of science upon monotheism, it is my guess that in the distant future such "felt meanings" (the point-cause, the world-whole, etc.) will become the established targets of humankind's religious emotions.

8. See Alvin Plantinga, *Warrant and Proper Function* (New York: Oxford University Press, 1993), 163.

9. Could there be any other sort of atheistic explanatory hypotheses? I think there are many others, such as the three explanatory hypotheses discussed in my "The Reason the Universe Exists Is That It Caused Itself to Exist," *Philosophy* 74 (1999), 579–86; a fourth hypothesis discussed in my "Simplicity and Why the Universe Exists"; a fifth hypothesis discussed in my "A

Defence of a Principle of Sufficient Reason," *Metaphilosophy* 26 (1995), 97–106, and "World Ensemble Explanations," *Pacific Philosophical Quarterly* 67 (1986), 73–86; and a sixth hypothesis discussed in my "A Natural Explanation of the Existence and Laws of Our Universe." Peter Unger's"Reducing Arbitrariness," *Midwest Studies in Philosophy* (1984), involves an explanatory hypothesis that is of interest, namely, that all possible universes (David Lewis's possible worlds) exist. However, this hypothesis presupposes a reductionist, physicalist, nominalist, and tenseless theory of time and can be undermined on this basis. See my *Language and Time*, esp. 242.

10. Jaakko Hintikka, "The Emperor's New Intuitions," *Journal of Philosophy* 96 (1999), 127–47.

11. Paul Moser, *Philosophy after Objectivity* (New York: Oxford University Press, 1993), 8.

12. See W. Marciskwski, *Dictionary of Logic* (The Hague: Nijhoff, 1981), 283–84, for a brief exposition of predicate logic of a transfinite order.

13. See Plantinga, *The Nature of Necessity*, and Plantinga, "World and Essence."

14. Second order predicate logic with identity is first order predicate logic with identity plus the axioms of extensionality and comprehension. The axiom of extensionality is that:

$$(z_1),,,(z_n)\, \Pi\,(z_1 \ldots z_n) \equiv \Phi\,(z_1 \ldots z_n)) \supset \Pi = \Phi$$

Here, Π and Φ are metavariables ranging over predicates, and z_1, etc., are individual variables. "$\equiv$" means material equivalence, and "$=$" means identity (of some sort, e.g., extensional identity). This implies that Π is identical with Φ if everything z is such that it has Π if and only if it has Φ. The axiom of comprehension is that:

$$(E\,\Phi)(z_1) \ldots (z_n)\,(\Phi(z_1 \ldots z_n) \equiv A)$$

This axiom implies that there is a property Φ such that everything z is such that it has Φ if and only if the sentence A is true. A is a sentence implying that everything that satisfies the conditions mentioned in the sentence has the property Φ.

15. See Quentin Smith, "Why Stephen Hawking's Cosmology Precludes a Creator," *Philo* 1 (1998), 75–93, for a discussion.

16. A. Shimony, "Scientific Inference," in *Pittsburgh Studies in the Philosophy of Science*, ed. R. Colodny (Pittsburgh: Pittsburgh University Press, 1970), 92.

17. See George Schlesinger, "Confirmation and Parsimony," in *Induction, Probability, and Confirmation*, ed. G. Maxwell and R. Anderson (Minneapolis: University of Minnesota Press, 1975), 324–42.

18. Derek Parfit, "The Puzzle of Reality: Why Does the Universe Exist?" in *Metaphysics: The Big Questions*, ed. P. van Inwagen and D. Zimmerman (Oxford: Blackwell, 1998), 418–27.

19. To say with Plantinga (*Warrant and Proper Function*, 8) and David Woodruff (private communication) that there are no degrees of belief, but that epistemic probability involves a full belief that a proposition has the probability n of being true, is not to define but use the word "probability." In Plantinga's case, we are left with no satisfactory idea of what a proposition's epistemic probability is, if it is not a degree to which it is believed. In fact, when Plantinga explains the normative component of epistemic probability, he typically characterizes it in such phrases as "the claim that the reasonable or rational degree of confidence, in the judgement in question, is r" (163). "Rational degree of confidence" is left undefined and (as far as I can tell) means rational degree of belief or has no discernible meaning at all.

The other component Plantinga claims belongs to epistemic probability, namely, the objective component, is characterized as the logical probability of a proposition h on an evidence proposition *e* plus propositions such as *simpler theories are more likely to be true than complex ones* (162). This fails because it is circular ("more likely" means more objectively probable, which is the very concept Plantinga is trying to explain). Furthermore, Plantinga's argument against the thesis that probability is degree of belief (8, n. 10) is invalid, since "if I have no idea at all whether the proposition in question is true" it does not follow (*pace* Plantinga) that I believe it to degree 0.5. What follows is that I merely entertain or comprehend the proposition, without any assertoric force (belief of any degree, be it zero or 0.5, etc.) at all. This blocks the contradiction Plantinga tries to deduce from the theory that probability is a degree of belief.

Accordingly, I think that the thesis that there are degrees of belief is defensible and that the definition of epistemic probability in terms of degrees of belief does not suffer the problems confronting Plantinga's theory of epistemic probability.

20. See my various works cited in this essay.

21. Set-theoretic paradoxes arise if we define all truths of mathematical logic in terms of a set. Rather, they must be definable in terms of a *proper class*. For a plausible argument for this claim, see Christopher Menzel, "On Set Theoretic Possible Worlds," *Analysis* 46 (1986), 2.

22. See Saul Kripke, "Naming and Necessity," in *Semantics of Natural Language*, ed. D. Davidson and G. Harmon (Dordrecht: Reidel, 1972), 265.

23. David Kaplan, "Demonstratives," in *Themes from Kaplan*, ed. J. Almog (New York: Oxford University Press, 1989), 508–09.

24. Panayot Butchvarov, *Skepticism in Ethics* (Bloomington: Indiana University Press, 1989), 62–64.

25. See Plantinga, "World and Essence"; Ruth Barcan Marcus, "Essential Attribution," *Journal of Philosophy* 68 (1971), 187–202, and "Discussion of the Paper of Ruth B. Marcus," *Synthese* 14 (1962), 132–43; and Kripke, "Naming and Necessity." For a definition of metaphysical necessity in terms of the semantics for quantified modal logic, see Quentin Smith, "A More Comprehensive History of the New Theory of Reference," in *The New Theory of Reference: Kripke, Marcus, and Its Origins*, ed. James Fetzer and Paul Humphreys (Kluwer Academic Synthese Library Series, 1998), 235–83.

26. Note that Stephen Yablo's "Is Conceivability a Guide to Possibility," *Philosophy and Phenomenological Research* 53 (1993), 1–42, addresses some relevant epistemological issues, but his essay assumes rather than proves that metaphysical "intuitions" (he aptly uses the word "conceiving" rather than "intuiting") have epistemic value, as does George Bealer's insightful essay "The Limits of Scientific Essentialism," in *Philosophical Perspectives*, vol. 1, *Metaphysics*, ed. J. Tomberlin (Atascadero: Ridgeview, 1987). Brian Leftow, *Time and Eternity*, 14–17 does not presuppose this assumption in his outline of an epistemological theory of metaphysical modal claims, and his outline suggests he is on the right track for the development of such an epistemological theory.

27. Alvin Plantinga, "The Probabilistic Argument from Evil," *Philosophical Studies* 35 (1979), 1–53.

28. Alvin Plantinga, *Warrant: The Current Debate* (New York: Oxford University Press, 1993); Plantinga, *Warrant and Proper Function; Plantinga, Warranted Christian Belief*.

29. David Woodruff, private correspondence.

30. Bas Van Fraassen, *Laws and Symmetry* (Oxford: Clarendon Press, 1989), 233–348. See also H. Weyl, *Symmetry* (Princeton: Princeton University Press, 1952); J. Rosen, *Symmetry Discovered* (Cambridge: Cambridge University Press, 1975); and G. E. Martin, *Transformational Geometry* (New York: Springer-Verlag, 1982).

31. Van Fraasen, *Laws and Symmetry*, 233.

32. I am using the terminology of set theory, specifically that found in Michael Potter, *Sets* (New York: Oxford University Press, 1990), since Van Fraassen makes things a little unclear by using words that sometimes have the sense they have in set theory and sometimes have the

sense they have in first order predicate logic with identity. For example, he uses "domain" in the sense of predicate logic (when we talk about quantified variables ranging over a domain of values), but "range" is used to have the set-theoretic meaning of "codomain." (See Van Fraassen, *Laws and Symmetry*, 243.

33. Ibid.

34. Potter, *Sets*, 32. The emphasis of "the graph" is mine.

35. This symmetry argument is one of the (necessary but insufficient) reasons I think the "conceptualist argument for God's existence" is more plausible than the traditional arguments for God's existence, such as the cosmological, teleological, and ontological arguments. See my "The Conceptualist Argument for God's Existence," *Faith and Philosophy* 11 (1994), 38–49.

36. Eliot Sober, *Simplicity* (Oxford: Clarendon Press, 1975).

37. The Identity Theory held by analytic philosophers—namely, William Mann, "Divine Simplicity," *Religious Studies* 18 (1982) 451–71; Eleonore Stump and Norman Kretzmann, "Absolute Simplicity," *Faith and Philosophy* 2 (1985), 353–82; Brian Leftow, "Is God an Abstract Object?" *Noûs* 24 (1990), 594–96, and *Time and Eternity*; William Vallicella, "On Property Self-Exemplification: Rejoinder to Miller," *Faith and Philosophy* 11 (1994), 478–81, and "Divine Simplicity: A New Defense," *Faith and Philosophy* 9 (1992), 508–25; and Barry Miller, *From Existence to God* (London: Routledge, 1992)—implies that God is identical with his essential properties and that each of his essential properties is identical with each of his other essential properties. Perhaps some progress has been made in showing how the proposition *the individual, God, is identical with his essential properties* is not logically incoherent (see especially Vallicella, "Divine Simplicity: A New Defense"), but I have seen no demonstration that the proposition *God's essential properties are identical with each other* is logically coherent. The latter proposition, in fact, is a negation of a theorem of second order predicate logic with identity. This can be briefly illustrated as follows.

Let F be a predicate constant, expressing the degreed property of being powerful. G is a predicate constant, expressing the degreed property of being knowledgeable. Fn is a degree of the property expressed by F, and G_n is a degree of the property expressed by G. Let $F_{n\text{-max}}$ and $G_{n\text{-max}}$ be the highest degrees of F and G or *at least the degrees of* F *and* G *possessed by God*. We can then formulate this argument:

[Note: F ≠ G is read as "*F* is not identical to *G*."]
(1) $(\exists(F \wedge G)) \wedge (F \neq G)$.
(2) $F_n \supset F$.
(3) $G_n \supset G$.
Therefore,
(4) $F_n \neq G_n$
Therefore,
(5) $F_{n\text{-max}} \neq G_{n\text{-max}}$.

Since the Identity Theory implies the negation of (5), it is a negation of a theorem of second order predicate logic with identity.

38. Richard Swinburne, *The Existence of God*, 3d ed. (Oxford: Oxford University Press, 1991); Unger, "Reducing Arbitrariness"; Parfit, "The Puzzle of Reality: Why Does the Universe Exist?"

39. This is demonstrated in my "Swinburne's Explanation of the Universe," *Religious Studies* 34 (1998), 91–102.

40. I argued in "Anthropic Coincidences, Evil, and the Disconfirmation of Theism" that if an omnipotent person created spacetime, it is more likely to be an omnimalevolent being than a perfectly morally good being. (For considerations relevant to this argument, see the post-

Mackie "logical argument from evil" in my *Ethical and Religious Thought in Analytic Philosophy of Language*, 137–57, and the "probabilistic argument from evil natural laws" in my "An Atheological Argument from Evil Natural Laws," *International Journal for the Philosophy of Religion* 29 (1991) 159–74.

41. Craig and Smith, *Theism, Atheism, and Big Bang Cosmology*, 273.

42. Ibid., 272, 273.

43. See my "Problems with John Earman's Attempt to Reconcile Theism with General Relativity."

44. Craig and Smith, *Theism, Atheism, and Big Bang Cosmology*, 272; my emphasis.

45. Ibid.

46. Hintikka, "The Emperor's New Intuitions."

47. See my "Problems with John Earman's Attempt to Reconcile Theism with General Relativity."

48. Robert Wald, *General Relativity* (Chicago: University of Chicago Press, 1984), 213.

49. John Earman, *Bangs, Crunches, Whimpers, and Shrieks* (New York: Oxford University Press, 1995).

50. Michael Berry, *Principles of Cosmology and Gravitation* (Cambridge: Cambridge University Press, 1989), 156.

51. S. W. Hawking, "The Breakdown of Predictability in Gravitational Collapse," *Physical Review* 14 (1976), 2460.

52. David Lewis, "Causation," *Journal of Philosophy* 70 (1973), 556–67.

53. See my "Causation and the Logical Impossibility of a Divine Cause," *Philosophical Topics* 24 (1996), 169–91, and "The Concept of a Cause of the Universe," *Canadian Journal of Philosophy* 23 (1993), 1–23.

54. Robert Deltete, "Simplicity and Why the Universe Exists: A Reply to Quentin Smith," *Philosophy* 73 (1998), 493.

55. Ibid.

56. T. D. Sullivan, "On the Alleged Causeless Beginning of the Universe: A Reply to Quentin Smith," *Dialogue: Canadian Philosophical Review* 33 (1994), 332.

57. Berry, *Principles of Cosmology and Gravitation*, 156.

58. Stephen Hawking, "The Edge of Spacetime," in *The New Physics*, ed. Paul Davies (Cambridge: Cambridge University Press, 1989), 61–69.

59. Deltete, "Simplicity and Why the Universe Exists: A Reply to Quentin Smith," 492.

60. See John Barrow and Frank Tipler, *The Anthropic Cosmological Principle* (New York. Oxford University Press, 1986). These laws are numbered 7.40 and 7.41 in Barrow and Tipler's work.

61. James Hartle and S. W. Hawking, "The Wave Function of the Universe," *Physical Review* D28 (1983), 2960–75.

62. The wave function is equation 2.1, ibid.

63. This equation is numbered 1.11, ibid.

64. Hawking, "The Breakdown of Predictability in Gravitational Collapse."

65. Ibid., 2460.

66. Swinburne, *The Existence of God*, 146.

67. See my "Atheism, Theism, and Big Bang Cosmology"; "A Big Bang Cosmological Argument for God's Nonexistence," *Faith and Philosophy* 9 (1992), 217–37; and *Theism, Atheism and Big Bang Cosmology*, 195–217.

68. Max Jammer, *Einstein and Religion: Physics and Theology* (Princeton: Princeton University Press, 1999), 262.

69. Richard Swinburne, "Review of William Craig's and Quentin Smith's *Theism, Atheism, and Big Bang Cosmology,*" *Philosophical Review* 104 (1995): 337–39.

70. Craig and Smith, *Theism, Atheism, and Big Bang Cosmology*, chs. 7, 9.

71. Craig in Craig and Smith, *Theism, Atheism, and Big Bang Cosmology*; Swinburne in "Review of William Craig's and Quentin Smith's *Theism, Atheism, and Big Bang Cosmology*"; Deltete in "Simplicity and Why the Universe Exists: A Reply to Quentin Smith"; Leslie in "Review of William Craig's and Quentin Smith's *Theism, Atheism, and Big Bang Cosmology*," *Zygon* 31 (1996), 345–49.

72. Craig and Smith, *Theism, Atheism, and Big Bang Cosmology*, 267.

73. Swinburne's most recent discussion is found in "Review of William Craig's and Quentin Smith's *Theism, Atheism, and Big Bang Cosmology*." His earlier discussion is found in *The Existence of God* (1st ed., Oxford: Oxford University Press, 1979), 145–51, and the third edition of this same work (1991), 145–51.

74. Swinburne, *The Existence of God* 1st ed., 150, my emphases and capitalization.

75. Ibid., 146.

76. A separate problem with Craig's argument that I considered is that his (and Swinburne's) concept of God taking aesthetic delight in fashioning order out of chaos is a logically self-contradictory concept, that middle knowledge of the big bang is also a logically incoherent concept, and that the concept of divine causation is logically incoherent. In order to produce an argument logically independent of my above mentioned arguments, I am here granting, for the sake of argument, to the theist her assumption that these concepts are logically coherent. See my "Simplicity and Why the Universe Exists," "Atheism, Theism, and Big Bang Cosmology," "Causation and the Logical Impossibility of a Divine Cause," and "Stephen Hawking's Cosmology and Theism." The mentioned theistic concepts are defended (unsuccessfully, I believe) in Craig and Smith, *Theism, Atheism, and Big Bang Cosmology*; J. McCleland and R. Deltete, "Divine Causation," *Faith and Philosophy* 17 (2000), 1–27; and William Vallicella, "God, Causation, and Occasionalism," *Religious Studies* 35, 3–18.

77. See, for example, J. Halliwell and S. W. Hawking, "The Origin of Structure in the Universe," *Physical Review* D31 (1985), 1777–91.

78. Nonetheless, I have elsewhere addressed "other evidence" or theistic arguments and found them wanting. See the articles of mine cited in this essay.

79. Of course, (h_2) will not be falsified if one rejects science and its auxiliary proposition (3). But by this rejection, one puts oneself beyond the bounds of "natural reason" and is thereby excluded from the intended audience of this essay.

6

The Elimination of Absolute Time by the Special Theory of Relativity

WILLIAM LANE CRAIG

Most physicists and philosophers of science would probably agree with Wolfgang Rindler that with the development of relativity theory Einstein took the step "that would completely destroy the classical concept of time."[1] Many would contend that along with a privileged universal time and absolute simultaneity, temporal becoming and an objective "now" must also go by the board. I believe such judgments to be mistaken and to be predicated upon a deficient understanding of the metaphysical, and particularly theistic, foundations of the classical concept of time, as well as upon a defective epistemological approach to these problems. In order to rediscover those foundations, we must recur to the fountainhead of the classical concept of time: Isaac Newton's great *Philosophiae naturalis principia mathematica*.

Newton's Distinction between Absolute and Relative Time

The *locus classicus* of Newton's exposition of his concepts of time and space is the *Scholium* to his Definitions in the *Principia*.[2] In order to overcome "common prejudices" concerning such quantities as time, space, place, and motion, Newton draws a dichotomy with respect to these quantities between "absolute and relative, true and apparent, mathematical and common." With regard to time he asserts:

> Absolute, true, and mathematical time, of itself, and from its own nature, flows equably without relation to anything external, and by another name is called duration: relative, apparent, and common time is some sensible and external (whether accurate or unequable) measure of duration by the means of motion, which is commonly used instead of true time; such as an hour, a day, a month, a year.[3]

Newton's much misunderstood distinction deserves our thoughtful consideration. The most evident feature of this distinction is the independence of absolute time from the relative measures thereof. Absolute time, or simple duration, exists regardless of the sensible and external measurements which we try, more or less successfully, to make of it. Newtonian time is thus first of all absolute in the sense that time itself is distinct from our measures of time.

But as is well known, Newton also conceived of time as absolute in a more profound sense, namely, he held that time is absolute in the sense that it exists independently of any physical objects whatsoever. Usually, this is interpreted to mean that time would exist even if nothing else existed, that there exists a possible world which is completely empty except for the container of absolute space and the flow of absolute time. But here we must be very careful. Modern secular scholars tend frequently to forget how ardent a theist Newton was and how central a role this theism played in his metaphysical outlook. Noting that Newton considered God to be temporal and therefore time to be everlasting, David Griffin observes that "most commentators have ignored Newton's heterodox theology, and his talk of 'absolute time' has been generally misunderstood to mean that time is not in any sense a relation and hence can exist apart from actual events."[4] In fact, Newton makes quite clear in the *General Scholium* to the *Principia*, which he added in 1713, that absolute time and space are constituted by the divine attributes of eternity and omnipresence:

> He is eternal and infinite . . . ; that is, his duration reaches from eternity to eternity; his presence from infinity to infinity. . . . He is not eternity and infinity, but eternal and infinite; he is not duration or space, but he endures and is present. He endures forever, and is everywhere present; and, by existing always and everywhere, he constitutes duration and space. Since every particle of space is *always*, and every indivisible moment of duration is *everywhere*, certainly the Maker and Lord of all things cannot be *never* and *nowhere*.[5]

Because God is eternal, there exists an everlasting duration, and because He is omnipresent, there exists an infinite space. Absolute time and space are therefore relational in that they are contingent upon the existence of God.

In his treatise *De gravitatione*,[6] Newton declares explicitly that space is *not* in itself absolute (*non absoluta per se*) and therefore not a substance. Rather it is an emanent—or emanative—effect of God (*Dei effectus emanativus*). It is uncreated and coexistent with God and yet ontologically dependent upon Him for its being. God's infinite being has as its consequence infinite time and space, which represent the quantity of His duration and presence. In the neoplatonic tradition the doctrine of emanation is associated with pantheism or panentheism. But, as Newton makes clear, he does not conceive of space and time as in any way aspects of God Himself, but rather, as he says, concomitant effects of God.

It is evident that when Newton speaks of divine eternity, he does not, like scholastic theologians in the Augustinian tradition, mean a state of timelessness, but rather infinite and everlasting temporal duration. In a preliminary draft of the *General Scholium*, Newton had explicitly rejected the conception of God's eternity as an eternal now: "His duration is not a *nunc stans* without duration, nor is his presence nowhere."[7] Far from being atemporal, God's now or present is the present of absolute time. Since God is not "a dwarf-god" located at a place in space,[8] but is omnipresent, every indivisible moment of duration is everywhere, as Newton states in the *General Scholium*. There is thus a worldwide moment which is absolutely present. Newton's temporal theism thus provides the foundation for both absolute simultaneity and absolute becoming. These are features first and foremost of God's time, or metaphysical time, and derivatively of measured, or physical, time.

Now Newton freely grants that although absolute time exists it may well be the case that due to the inaccuracies of our measures the true time is not disclosed to us.[9] What Newton did not realize, nor could he have suspected, is that physical time is not only *relative*, but also *relativistic*, that the approximation of physical time to absolute time depends not merely upon the regularity of one's clock, but also upon its motion. Unless a clock were at absolute rest, it would not accurately register the passage of absolute time. A clock moving relatively to oneself runs slowly. This truth, unknown to Newton, only intimated by Larmor and Lorentz in the concept of "local time," was finally grasped by Einstein.

Where Newton fell short, then, was not in his analysis of absolute or metaphysical time—he had theological grounds for positing such a time—but in his incomplete understanding of physical time. He assumed too readily that an ideal clock would give an accurate measure of time independently of its motion. If confronted with relativistic evidence, Newton would no doubt have welcomed this correction and seen therein no threat at all to his doctrine of absolute time. In short, relativity corrects Newton's concept of physical time, not his concept of absolute time. Of course, it hardly needs to be said that there is a great deal of antipathy in modern physics and philosophy of science toward such metaphysical realities as Newtonian space and time, primarily because they are not physically detectable. But Newton would have been singularly unimpressed with this positivistic equation between physical undetectability and non-existence. The grounds for metaphysical space and time were not physical, but philosophical, or more precisely, theological. Epistemological objections fail to worry Newton because, as Lucas nicely puts it, "he is thinking of an omniscient, omnipresent Deity whose characteristic relation with things and with space is expressed in the imperative mood."[10] Modern physical theories say nothing against the existence of such a God or the metaphysical time constituted, in Newton's thinking, by His eternity. What relativity theory did, in effect, was simply to remove God from the picture and to substitute in His place a finite observer. "Thus," according to Holton, "the *RT* [relativity theory] merely shifted the focus of space-time from the sensorium of Newton's God to the sensorium of Einstein's abstract *Gedanken* experimenter—as it were, the final secularization of physics."[11] But to a man like Newton, who in his *General Scholium* writes, "and thus much concerning God; to discourse of whom from the appearances of things, does certainly belong to Natural Philosophy,"[12] such a secular outlook impedes rather than advances our understanding of the nature of reality. And even if we do not go so far as Newton in including discourse about God in scientific theorizing, still it is clear that if we are prepared to draw metaphysical inferences about the nature of space, time, and spacetime on the basis of physical science, then we must also be ready to entertain theistic metaphysical hypotheses such as Newton deemed relevant.

In this essay I leave aside the question whether Newton was in fact correct in thinking that God's mere existence is a sufficient condition for the existence of time and space. He provides virtually no argument to think that this is the case. Plausibly God could be temporal without being spatial, for a series of mental events alone is sufficient to set up a temporal sequence. Thus, for example, if we imagine God's counting down to the moment of creation: " . . . , 3, 2, 1, *fiat lux!*" then the beginning of the universe would be preceded by a metaphysical time associated with the mental events of counting which would be wholly independent of space. Since God is incorporeal, there is no reason to think that prior to the creation of the universe He would exist spatially even though He were temporal. Nor would His omnipresence seem to entail the existence of metaphysical space prior to His creation of the physical universe, as Newton believed. Newton's conclusion in this regard seems to be a double non sequitur. First, just as "omnitemporal" implies, not "existing throughout infinite time," but "existing at every moment in time that there is" (which is not incompatible with time's having begun and being finite), so "omnipresent" implies, not "existing throughout infinite space," but "existing at every point in space that there is" (which is not incompatible with space's being curved and finite). Second, even if omnipresence implied space's infinitude, it does not follow that infinite space exists for infinite time. Space could have a finite temporal duration and have been created by God who existed in metaphysical time prior to His creation of space. In either case, He would in such worlds be omnipresent, so long as He existed, in some suitable sense,[13] at every point in space that ever exists. Thus, on the orthodox view of God, God's merely thinking discursively is sufficient for the existence of time, but not of space. Whether one holds that God exists temporally or atemporally is apt to hinge crucially on whether one believes time to be dynamic or static, as I have sought to show elsewhere.[14] As a partisan of a dynamic theory of time, I find myself sympathetic to a view of God as temporal, at least since the moment of creation. The question, then, is whether the special theory of relativity (STR) forces one who holds with Newton to divine temporality to abandon belief in the existence of absolute time.

STR's Elimination of Absolute Time

The Positivistic Foundations of STR

The failure of nineteenth-century attempts to detect the earth's motion through the aether, which constituted a relative or physical space at rest with respect to metaphysical space, prompted a crisis in physics which compelled men like Lorentz, Larmor, and Poincaré to revise and then abandon the Galilean transformation equations in favor of the relativistic Lorentz transformations. In so doing, they had already sounded the death knell of Newtonian physics, for they had relativized the sensible measures of metaphysical time and space in a way undreamed of by Newton. But they did so without abandoning the notion that there really is a true time and a true space, even if these remain undetectable to us.

Einstein interrupted this research program with a radically different approach. Foundational to Einstein's approach was his denial of absolute space and his consequent redefinition of time and simultaneity so as to deny their absolute status as well. What Einstein did, in effect, was to shave away Newton's metaphysical time and space, and along with them the aether, thus leaving behind only their sensible measures, so that physical time became the only time there is and physical space the only space there is. Since these are relativized to inertial frames, one ends up with the relativity of simultaneity and of length.

What justification did Einstein have for so radical a move? How did he know that Newton's metaphysical time and space do not exist? The answer, in a word, is positivism. Although one rarely finds this discussed in textbook expositions of the theory or even in discussions of the philosophical foundations of the theory, nevertheless historians of science have demonstrated convincingly that at the philosophical roots of Einstein's theory lies an epistemological positivism of Machian provenance which issues in a verificationist analysis of the concepts of time and space.[15]

Mach's philosophy of science was phenomenalist or sensationalist in character. In experience we are given various sensations, such as colors, sounds, pressures, and so forth, and the aim of scientific theorizing is to construct the simplest possible description of the connections among these sensations.[16] Mach had no use for theoretical entities or even for entities behind the sensations. Statements in theories were meaningful only if they were related directly to sensations. His attitude was militantly "anti-metaphysical," and in his *Die Mechanik in ihrer Entwicklung*, which Einstein studied carefully, Mach declared in the second sentence of his preface that "its intention is an enlightening one, or to put it more bluntly, an anti-metaphysical one."[17]

In line with his phenomenalism, Mach held that "space and time are well-ordered systems of series of sensations" on a par with our sensations of colors, sounds, and smells.[18] He denounced Newton's concepts of absolute time and space:

> Nobody is competent to predicate things about absolute space and absolute motion; they are pure things of thought, pure mental constructs, that cannot be produced in experience. All our principles of mechanics are . . . experimental knowledge concerning the relative positions and motions of bodies. . . . No one is warranted in extending these principles beyond the boundaries of experience. In fact, such an extension is meaningless, as no one possesses the requisite knowledge to make use of it.[19]

Similarly, in his *Wärmelehre* Mach drew applications from his critique of the concept of temperature to Newton's concept of absolute time. Mach thought that the Newtonian concepts of absolute time and space were as misconceived as the concept of an absolute measure of temperature. Just as there is no absolute temperature behind our various conventional measures of our sensation of heat, so no absolute time exists behind the various conventional measures of our sensation of duration.

In 1905, when Einstein published his paper on the electrodynamics of moving bodies, and for several years thereafter, Einstein was a self-confessed pupil of Mach, and the epistemological analysis of space and time given in the opening section of that paper clearly displays this influence. Although Mach came to repudiate relativity theory,[20] and Einstein threw off Mach's phenomenalism for a critical realism, the founder of relativity theory continued to acknowledge Mach's influence on him during his early years. Writing off Mach's rejection of relativity theory to the intransigence of old age, Einstein insisted that "the whole direction of thought of this theory conforms with Mach's."[21] While Mach's positivistic philosophy proved itself unfruitful in positive theory construction, still it served its purpose in eliminating unwanted metaphysical entities such as absolute time and space: "It cannot give birth to anything living, it can only exterminate harmful vermin."[22] Though converted into a "believing rationalist" through his work on gravitation, Einstein conceded that in his earlier work on the special theory he was "coming from skeptical empiricism of somewhat the kind of Mach's."[23] In his later "Autobiographical Notes," Einstein connects his denial of absolute simultaneity with the critical reasoning of Mach and mentions as well the influence of David Hume.[24]

In the 1905 paper itself, the introductory sections are predicated squarely upon positivistic assumptions. Einstein's verificationism comes through most clearly in his operationalist redefinition of key concepts. Newton's distinction between time and the sensible measures thereof is quietly abolished. It is taken for granted that *all* our judgments in which time plays a role must have a physical meaning. Einstein asserts, "Now we must bear carefully in mind that a mathematical description of this kind has no physical meaning unless we are quite clear as to what we will understand by 'time.'"[25] The meaning of "time" is made to depend upon the meaning of "simultaneity," which is defined locally in terms of occurrence at the same local clock reading. When it comes to judgments concerning the simultaneity of distant events, the concern is to find a "practical arrangement" to compare clock times. In order to "define" a common time for spatially separated clocks, we adopt the convention that the time which light takes to travel from A to B equals the time it takes to travel from B to A— a definition which *presupposes* that absolute space does not exist.[26] Thus, time is reduced to physical time (clock readings) and space to physical space (readings of measuring rods), and both of these are relativized to local frames. Simultaneity is defined in terms of clock synchronization via light signals. All of this is done by mere stipulation. Through Einstein's operational definitions of time and space, Mach's positivism triumphs in the special theory of relativity.[27] Reality is reduced to what our measurements read; Newton's metaphysical time and space, which transcend operational definitions, are implied to be mere figments of our imagination.

In Einstein's other early papers on relativity, his verificationist theory of meaning comes even more explicitly to the fore. Concepts which cannot be given empirical content and assertions which cannot be empirically verified in principle are discarded as meaningless.[28] Even subsequent to his development of the general theory of relativity (GTR), Einstein continued to regard absolute space and time as meaningless notions. In 1920, for example, he wrote:

> We thus require a definition of simultaneity such that this definition supplies us with the means by which, in the present case, he can decide by experiment whether both lightning strokes occurred simultaneously. As long as this requirement is not satisfied, I allow myself to be deceived as a physicist (and of course the same applies if I am not a physicist) when I imagine that I am able to attach a meaning to the statement of simultaneity.[29]

For physicist and non-physicist alike the statement that two events occur simultaneously is meaningless unless an operational definition can be given for that concept. Thus, Einstein continued to cling to his rejection of metaphysical time and space.[30]

Einstein's approach struck a responsive chord in the ears of physicists who breathed the atmosphere of positivism that dominated science during the first half of the twentieth century. Under the influence of the verificationist criterion of meaning, physicists and philosophers of space and time openly expressed their abhorrence for what was called "metaphysics."[31] Positivistic philosophers and physicists were thus quick to recognize in STR a kindred spirit and embraced the theory eagerly.[32] For most thinkers it became self-understood that "time" was synonymous with "physical time."[33]

Positivism's Essential Role in STR

What, then, can be said of STR's elimination of metaphysical time and space? The first thing to be noticed is that the positivism which characterized the historical formulation of STR belongs essentially to the philosophical foundations of the theory. The relativity of length depends upon the relativity of simultaneity, which in turn rests upon Einstein's redefinition of simultaneity in terms of clock synchronization by light signals. But that redefinition assumes necessarily that the time which light takes to travel between two relatively stationary observers A and B is the same from A to B as from B to A in a round-trip journey. That assumption presupposes that A and B cannot be at relative rest but both moving in tandem absolutely, or in other words that neither metaphysical space nor a privileged rest frame exists. The only justification for that assumption is that it is empirically impossible to distinguish uniform motion from rest relative to such a frame, and if metaphysical space and absolute motion or rest are undetectable empirically, therefore they do not exist (and may even be said to be meaningless). Such an inference is clearly verificationist and therefore positivistic.

In a clear-sighted analysis of the epistemological foundations of STR, Lawrence Sklar underlines the essential role played by this verificationism: "Certainly the original arguments in favor of the relativistic viewpoint were rife with verificationist presuppositions about meaning, etc. And despite Einstein's later disavowal of the verificationist point of view, no one to my knowledge has provided an adequate account of the foundations of relativity which isn't verificationist in essence."[34] It would be desirable to do so, muses Sklar, but "what I don't know is either how to formulate a coherent underpinning for relativity which isn't verificationist to begin with, or how, once begun, to find a natural stopping point for verificationist claims of under-determination and conventionality."[35]

Untenability and Obsolescence of Positivism

But if positivism belongs essentially to the foundations of STR, the next thing to be noted is that positivism has proved to be completely untenable and is now widely discarded. The untenability of positivism is so universally acknowledged that it will not be necessary to rehearse the objections against it here.[36] Healey observes that "positivism has come under such sustained attack that opposition to it has become almost orthodoxy in the philosophy of science."[37] Positivism provides absolutely no justification for thinking that Newton erred, for example, in holding that God exists in a temporal series which transcends our physical measures of it and which may or may not be accurately registered by them. It matters not a whit whether we finite creatures know what time it is in God's metaphysical time; God knows, and that is enough. Contemporary physics has in any case ignored the constrictions of positivism. When the contemporary student of physics reads the anti-metaphysical polemics of the past generation, he must feel as though he were peering into a different world. For it is now widely recognized that the boundaries of science are impossible to fix with precision, and during the last few decades theoretical physics has become character-ized precisely by its metaphysical, speculative character. In various fields such as quantum mechanics, classical cosmology, and quantum cosmology, debates rage over issues which are overtly metaphysical in character. In a recent essay, "Is Physics at the Threshold of a New Stage of Evolution?" Rompe and Treder echo Planck's question of 1908 and answer in the affirmative: "For several decades physics *'wächst über sich selbst hinaus'* (increases beyond its own limits)."[38] The point is that the positivistic, anti-metaphysical view of physics which dominated the first two-thirds of the twentieth century is simply outmoded in light of contemporary theoretical physics.

Given the failure of positivism, we should insist that an exclusively physical methodology is simply inadequate to deal properly with the problems of time and space.[39] The metaphysician must be given a fair hearing, especially if he is a theist, should he make a distinction between physical time and space (clock and rod meas-urements) and metaphysical time and space (ontological time and space independent of physical measures thereof). STR is a theory about physical time and space and says nothing about the nature of metaphysical time and space. Questions dealing with the latter are philosophical in nature and must be dealt with as such.

All too often physicists' failure to recognize such a distinction has led them into faulty theological inferences. For example, the uncertainty which quantum geometro-dynamics introduces into the cosmic time coordinate prior to the Planck time is ex-ploited by Banks to draw a marvelous metaphysical inference:

> As we enter this regime [prior to the Planck time] the intuitive concept of time loses all meaning. There is no content in the question of what happened before the big bang, not because the universe becomes singular, but because quantum fluctuations invalidate the notion of 'absolute time.'*[40]

> [*Newton, *Philosophiae naturalis principia mathematica* (1687).]

It is not explained, of course, how the indeterminacy of physical time is supposed to invalidate Newton's absolute time, which, based in God's eternity, "ought to be distin-guished from what are only sensible measures thereof."

Sometimes the metaphysical conclusions proclaimed on the basis of the positivis-tic analysis of time can be quite ludicrous. For example, appealing to the invariance of quantum field theories under consecutive reversals of time, charge, and space (TCP invariance), Henryk Mehlberg states:

> If all natural laws are time reversed invariant and no irreversible processes occur in the physical universe, then there is no inherent, intrinsically meaningful difference between past and future—just as there is no such difference between "to the left of" and "to the right of." If this is actually the case, then all mankind's major religions which preach a creation of the universe (by a supernatural agency) and imply, accordingly, a differentia-tion between the past and the future, i.e., an intrinsic difference between both, would have to make an appropriate readjustment of man's major religious and "creationist" creeds and the scientific findings.[41]

This solemn and ridiculous pronouncement clearly rests on the identification of God's time with physical time, a reduction which is positivistic in character.

So I think it is evident that the demise of positivism is not at all to be mourned, but that, on the contrary, its lingering shadow over certain discussions of the concept of time has sometimes resulted in quite unjustified and erroneous metaphysical conclusions. It seems to me that in light of the collapse of positivism a reappraisal of the concept of time is long overdue.

We have thus seen that positivism belongs essentially to the philosophical foundations of STR and that such an epistemological outlook has been justifiably and universally rejected as untenable and obsolete. It is difficult, indeed, to understand how contemporary philosophers and physicists can therefore speak of STR's "forcing" us to abandon the classical concepts of space and time or of its "destruction" of Newtonian absolute time. Lawrence Sklar concludes:

> The original Einstein papers on special relativity are founded, as is well known, on a verificationist critique of earlier theories. . . . Now it might be argued that Einstein's verificationism was a misfortune, to be encountered not with a rejection of special relativity, but with an acceptance of the theory now to be understood on better epistemological grounds. . . .
>
> But I don't think a position of this kind will work in the present case. I can see no way of rejecting the old aether-compensatory theories, originally invoked to explain the Michelson-Morley results, without invoking a verificationist critique of some kind or other. And I know of no way to defend the move to a relativized notion of simultaneity, so essential to special relativity, without first offering a critique, in the same vein as Einstein's, of the pre-relativistic absolutist notion, and then continuing to observe that even the relativistic replacement for this older notion is itself, insofar as it outruns the "hard data" of experiment, infected with a high degree of conventionality.[42]

God and Physical Time

The Independence of God's Time

We have seen that for Newton God's eternity and omnipresence were ontologically foundational for his views of time and space. Unfortunately in our secular age physicists and philosophers of space and time rarely, if ever, give careful consideration to the difference God's existence makes for our conceptions of time and space. Such indifference was characteristic of Einstein himself. Only after 1930 did he begin to refer more frequently in his non-scientific writings to religious questions. But he was, in Holton's words, "quite unconcerned with religious matters during the period of his early scientific publications."[43] Thus, he did not consider the difference theism would make to one's views of time and space.

On the other hand, Poincaré, in a fascinating passage in his essay "La Mesure de temps," does briefly entertain the hypothesis of *une intelligence infinie* and considers the implications of such a hypothesis. Poincaré is reflecting on the problem of temporal succession. In consciousness, the temporal order of mental events is clear. But going outside consciousness, we confront various difficulties. One of these concerns how we can apply one and the same measure of time to events which transpire in "different worlds," that is, to spatially distant events. What does it mean to say that two psychological phenomena in two consciousnesses happen simultaneously? Or what does it mean to say a supernova occurred before Columbus saw the isle of Espanola? "All these affirmations," says Poincaré, "have by themselves no meaning."[44] Then he remarks:

> We should first ask ourselves how one could have had the idea of putting into the same frame so many worlds impenetrable to one another. We should like to represent to ourselves the external universe, and only by so doing could we feel that we understood it. We know we can never attain this representation: our weakness is too great. But at least we desire the ability to conceive an infinite intelligence for which this representation could be possible, a sort of great consciousness which should see all, and which should classify all *in its time*, as we classify, *in our time*, the little we see.
>
> This hypothesis is indeed crude and incomplete, because this supreme intelligence would be only a demigod; infinite in one sense, it would be limited in another, since it would have only an imperfect recollection of the past; it could have no other, since otherwise all recollections would be equally present to it and for it there would be no time. And yet when we speak of time, for all which happens outside of us, do we not unconsciously adopt this hypothesis; do we not put ourselves in the place of this imperfect God; and do not even the atheists put themselves in the place where God would be if he existed?
>
> What I have just said shows us, perhaps, why we have tried to put all physical phenomena into the same frame. But that cannot pass for a definition of simultaneity, since this hypothetical intelligence, even if it existed, would be for us impenetrable. It is therefore necessary to seek something else.[45]

Poincaré here suggests that, in considering the notion of simultaneity, we instinctively put ourselves in the place of God and classify events as past, present, or future according to His time. Poincaré does not deny that such a perspective would disclose to us true relations of simultaneity. But he rejects the hypothesis as yielding a definition of simultaneity because we could not know such relations; such knowledge would remain the exclusive possession of God Himself.

But clearly, Poincaré's misgivings are relevant to a definition of simultaneity only if one is presupposing some sort of verificationist theory of meaning, as he undoubtedly was. The fact remains that God knows the absolute simultaneity of events even if we grope in total darkness. Nor need we be concerned with Poincaré's argument that such an infinite intelligence would be a mere demigod, since it is a non sequitur that a being with perfect recollection of the past cannot be temporal. There is no conceptual difficulty in the idea of a being which knows all true past-tense propositions. That such a being would be temporal is evident from the fact that as events transpire, more and more past-tense propositions become true, so that the content of His knowledge is constantly changing.[46] Hence, it does not follow that if God is temporal, He cannot have perfect recollection of the past.

Poincaré's hypothesis suggests, therefore, that God's present is constitutive of relations of absolute simultaneity.[47] J. M. Findlay was wrong when he said that "the influence which harmonizes and connects all the world-lines is not God, not any featureless, inert, medium, but that living, active interchange called . . . Light, offspring of

Heaven firstborn."[48] On the contrary, the use of light signals to establish clock synchrony is a convention which finite and ignorant creatures have been obliged to adopt, but the living and active God, who knows all, is not so dependent. Inviting us to "imagine a superhuman observer—a god—who is not bound by the limitations of the maximum velocity of light," Milton K. Munitz notes:

> Such an observer could survey in a single instant the entire domain of galaxies that have already come into existence. His survey would not have to depend on the finite velocity of light. It would not betray any restriction in information of the kind that results from the delayed time it takes to bring information about the domain of galaxies to an ordinary human observer situated in the universe, and who is therefore bound by the mechanisms and processes of signal transmission. The entire domain of galaxies would be seen instantaneously by this privileged superhuman observer. His observational survey of all galaxies would yield what Milne calls a "world map."[49]

In God's temporal experience, there would be a moment which is present in metaphysical time, wholly independently of physical clock times. He would know, without any dependence on clock synchronization procedures or any physical operations at all, which events were simultaneously present in metaphysical time. He would know this simply in virtue of His knowing at every such moment the unique set of present-tense propositions true at that moment, without any need of a *sensorium* or physical observation of the universe.

Lorentz-Poincaré Relativity

The question now presses: how does God's metaphysical time relate to our physical time? From what has been said thus far, it seems that God's existence in metaphysical time and His real relation to the world would imply that a Lorentz-Poincaré theory of relativity is correct after all. A theory may be classified as a Lorentz-Poincaré theory just in case it affirms (1) the round-trip vacuum propagation of light is isotropic in a preferred (absolute) reference frame R_o (with speed $c = 1$) and independent of the velocity of the source, and (2) lengths contract and time rates dilate in the customary special relativistic way only for systems in motion with respect to R_o.[50] Such a theory is required in view of divine temporality, for God in the "now" of metaphysical time would know which events in the universe are now being created by Him and are therefore absolutely simultaneous with each other and with His "now." This startling conclusion shows clearly that Newton's theistic hypothesis is not some idle speculation, but has important implications for our understanding of how the world is and for assessment of rival scientific theories.

Despite the widespread aversion to a Lorentz-Poincaré interpretation of relativity theory, such antipathy seems really quite unjustified. Admitted on all sides to be empirically equivalent to the Einsteinian interpretation, the Lorentz-Poincaré interpretation is neither ad hoc nor more complicated than its rival.[51] The relativistic, physical effects it posits are no less real in the Einsteinian version, only there they appear as axiomatic deductions lacking causal explanations.[52] Indeed, its fecundity in opening the question about physical causes seems an important advantage of the Lorentz-Poincaré interpretation.

Of course, one could go on working within the theoretical framework of Einstein's version, being accustomed to so working and thereby retaining the advantage of using a received view of the scientific community, and yet consistently affirm what I have said concerning God, metaphysical time, and physical time simply by eschewing a realistic understanding of Einstein's theory. But if one is interested in being a scientific realist on matters of time and space, then one ought, if one holds God to be in time, to affirm a Lorentz-Poincaré interpretation.

God and Cosmic Time

A final issue now needs to be engaged, and that is whether we have some idea of what measured time coincides with God's metaphysical time, or in other words, what clock time records the true time? The answer to this question will take us from special into general relativity, as we seek to gain a cosmic perspective on time.

Troubled by the non-equivalence of inertial and non-inertial frames, Einstein endeavored in his GTR to enunciate a general principle of relativity which would serve to render physically equivalent all inertial and non-inertial frames alike. In his article "The Foundations of General Relativity Theory" (1915), he boasted that his theory "takes away from space and time the last remnant of physical objectivity."[53] It was, in effect, intended to be the final destruction of Newton's absolute space and time.

In fact, however, Einstein was only partially successful in achieving his aims.[54] He did not succeed in enunciating a tenable general principle of relativity after the pattern of the special principle, nor was he able to show the physical equivalence of all reference frames. He did succeed in drafting a revolutionary and complex theory of gravitation, which has been widely hailed as his greatest intellectual achievement. The so-called general theory of relativity is thus something of a misnomer: it is really a theory of gravitation and not an extension of the special theory of relativity from inertial reference frames to all reference frames.

It might appear, therefore, that GTR has nothing more to contribute to our understanding of time than STR. They differ simply over the presence of curvature in spacetime; if one adds a condition of flatness to GTR, then STR results. But such a conclusion would be hasty, indeed, for GTR serves to introduce into relativity theory a cosmic perspective, enabling one to draft cosmological models of the universe governed by the gravitational field equations of GTR. Within the context of such cosmological models, the issue of time resurfaces dramatically.

Einstein himself proposed the first GTR cosmological model in his paper "Cosmological Considerations on the General Theory of Relativity" in 1917.[55] The model describes a spatially finite universe which possesses at every time t the geometry of the surface of a sphere in three dimensions with a constant radius R. The model is characterized by the static metric $ds^2 = -dt^2 + R^2 [dr^2 + \sin^2 r \, (d\theta^2 + \sin^2\theta d\Phi^2)]$. Time, which is decoupled from space, extends from minus ∞ to plus ∞. Thus, spacetime takes on the form of a four-dimensional analogue to a cylinder, temporal cross-sections of which are the three-spheres. Kanitscheider draws our attention to the sort of time coordinate which shows up in the metric of Einstein's model:

It represents in a certain sense the restoration of the universal time which was destroyed by STR. In the static world there is a global reference frame, relative to which the whole of cosmic matter finds itself at rest. All cosmological parameters are independent of time. In the rest frame of cosmic matter space and time are separated. For fundamental observers at rest, all clocks can be synchronized and a worldwide simultaneity can be defined in this cosmic frame.[56]

Thus, cosmological considerations prompt the conception of a cosmic time which measures the duration of the universe as a whole. Nor is this cosmic time limited to Einstein's static model of the universe. Expansion models, which trace their origin to de Sitter's 1917 model of an empty universe,[57] may also involve a cosmic time. The standard for contemporary expansion models derives from Friedman's 1922 model of an expanding, material universe characterized by ideal homogeneity and isotropy.[58] The nature of the cosmic time which measures the duration of the universe in such models deserves our further scrutiny.

Several features of the cosmic time parameter in Friedman models merit comment. First, although one may slice spacetime into various spatial hypersurfaces wholly arbitrarily, certain spacetimes have natural symmetries that guide the construction of cosmic time.[59] GTR does not itself lay down any formula for dissecting the spacetime manifold of points; it has no inherent "layering." Theoretically, then, one may slice it up at one's whim. Nevertheless, certain models of spacetime, like the Friedman model, have a dynamical, evolving physical geometry, a geometry that is tied to the boundary conditions of homogeneity and isotropy of the cosmological fluid, and in order to ensure a smooth development of this geometry, it will be necessary to construct a time parameter based on a preferred foliation of spacetime. For example, in 1935 H. P. Robertson and A. G. Walker independently showed that a homogeneous and isotropic universe requires that space be possessed of a constant curvature and be characterized by the metric:

$$\frac{dr^2 + r^2(d\theta^2 + sin^2\theta\,d\Phi^2)}{(1 + kr^2/4)^2}$$

In the metric for spacetime, the spatial geometry is dynamic over time:

$$ds^2 = -dt^2 + R^2(t)\frac{dr^2 + r^2(d\theta^2 + sin^2\theta\,d\Phi^2)}{(1 + kr^2/4)^2}$$

In the Robertson-Walker line element, t represents cosmic time, which is detached from space and serves to render space dynamic. The factor $R(t)$ determines that all spatial structures of cosmic proportions, for example, a triangle demarcated by three galactic clusters, will either shrink or stretch through the contraction or expansion of space into a similar smaller or larger triangle. The boundary condition of homogeneity precludes other geometrical changes such as shear, which would preserve the area but not the shape of the triangle. The condition of isotropy further precludes that the triangle should be altered in such a way as to preserve both its area and shape while nonetheless undergoing a rotational change of direction. Thus, in a Friedman universe there are certain natural symmetries related to the dynamic geometry which serve as markers for the foliation of spacetime and the assigning of a cosmic time parameter. Of course, there are other cosmological models which do not involve homogeneity and isotropy and so may involve a different cosmic time or lack such a time altogether.[60] Cosmic time is thus not nomologically necessary, and its actual existence is an empirical question.

Second, cosmic time is fundamentally parameter time and only secondarily coordinate time.[61] Physical time can be related in two quite different ways to the manifold in which motion is represented. If it is part of that manifold, then it functions as a coordinate. If it is external to that manifold, then it functions as a parameter. In Newton's physics time functioned only as a parameter. Motion takes place in absolute space and is parameterized by absolute time. Similarly, in Einstein's original formulation of STR, relativistic time functions only as a parameter. Einstein rejected the existence of absolute space and a fundamental rest frame in favor of a plurality of relatively moving inertial spaces, each of which was characterized by a time parameter which registered the proper time for that inertial frame. There was no absolute parameter time, only separate parameter times assigned to their respective inertial frames. The familiar spacetime formulation of STR used in virtually all contemporary expositions of the theory, according to which time is a coordinate (along with the three spatial coordinates) of an event in spacetime, derives from Minkowski, not Einstein. The spacetime formalism of Minkowski, in which time is part of the manifold in which motion is represented and so functions as a coordinate, was a wonderful aid to the visualization and comprehension of relativity theory; but Newton's theory can also be cast in terms of a spacetime formalism in which time functions as a coordinate of events in spacetime.[62] Both theories admit of either a spacetime formulation (in which spacetime is the manifold) or a space and time formulation (in which the manifold is space[s], and time is a parameter). In the spacetime formulation, time functions as both a coordinate (locating events in the manifold) and as a parameter (recording the lapse of proper time along an observer's inertial trajectory), the chief difference between the two theories being that in STR parameter time loses the universality it possesses in Newtonian spacetime (that is, simultaneity becomes relative).

When it comes to GTR, it is unclear, according to Kroes, whether the theory could be formulated in terms of space and time rather than spacetime. He observes that differences in coordinate time values generally have no direct physical significance in GTR (due to the variable spacetime geometry or gravitational fields which distort the coordinate grids laid on them). But insofar as time functions as a parameter in GTR, it is a more fundamental notion of time because it does possess direct physical significance. Parameter time can serve as a direct measure of the time elapsed between two events. Moreover, parameter time is well suited, according to Kroes, for accommodating the notion of temporal becoming.[63] While there is no intrinsic difference between past and future in coordinate time, there exists such a distinction in parameter time. Thus, the "flow" of time could relate to parameter time. Because parameter time in STR is the proper time of each inertial observer and because no inertial frame is preferred, the "flow" of parameter time is not universal. But insofar as cosmic time plays a role in GTR-based cosmological models, that universality is restored. It is highly significant, then, that cosmic time appears fundamentally as a parameter time in GTR, though it can be used to generate coordinate time as well. As a parameter, it is not part of the spacetime manifold, and it thus measures the duration of the universe in an observer-independent way; that is to say, the lapse of cosmic time is the same for all observers. Moreover, cosmic time supplies a physical time which is well suited to accommodate the philosophical notion of temporal becoming.

Third, cosmic time is intimately related to a class of fundamental observers whose individual hyperplanes of simultaneity mutually combine to align with the hypersurface demarcating the cosmic time.[64] These hypothetical observers are conceived to be moving along with the cosmological fluid so that, although space is expanding and they are therefore mutually receding from each other, each is in fact at rest with respect to space itself. As time goes on and the expansion of space proceeds, each fundamental observer remains in the same place; his spatial coordinates do not change, though his spatial separation from fellow fundamental observers increases. Because of this mutual recession, the class of fundamental observers does not serve to define a global inertial frame, technically speaking, though all of them are at rest. But since each is at rest with respect to space, his hyperplane of simultaneity will coincide locally with the hypersurface of cosmic time. Were he in motion with respect to the cosmological fluid, then his hyperplane of simultaneity would not align with the local hypersurface. But in virtue of being at rest, he can be guaranteed that locally events which he judges to be simultaneous will lie on the hypersurface. This has two important implications: first, that the proper time of each fundamental observer coincides with cosmic time; second, that all the fundamental observers will agree as to what time it is.

It is noteworthy that deviations from this time are purely local effects to be explained due to velocity (STR) or to gravitation (GTR). Thus, on a cosmic scale, we seem to have that universality of time and absolute simultaneity of events which the special theory had denied. Whitrow asserts, "in a universe that is characterized by the existence of a cosmic time, relativity is reduced to a local phenomenon, since this time is world-wide and independent of the observer."[65] Based on a cosmological, rather than a local, perspective, cosmic time seems to restore to us our intuitive notions of universal time and absolute simultaneity which STR denied.

The question, then, becomes an empirical one: does cosmic time exist? The answer to that question comes from the evidence for large-scale homogeneity and isotropy in the universe. In models like Gödel's or Ozsvath and Schücking's, there is posited a worldwide rotation of the homogeneous substratum, so that the isotropy condition of the Friedman model is violated and the proper times of fundamental observers cannot be fitted together into a universal time. However, the observational evidence for cosmic isotropy, particularly for the isotropy of the cosmic microwave background radiation, which has been measured to an accuracy of one part in 100,000, makes it very likely that our actual universe does approximate a Friedman universe. After reviewing the evidence, Martin Rees concludes, "The most remarkable outcome of fifty years of observational cosmology has been the realization that the universe is more isotropic and uniform than the pioneer theorists of the 1920's would ever have suspected."[66] "Consequently, we have strong evidence that the universe as a whole is predominantly homogeneous and isotropic," states Whitrow, "and this conclusion . . . is a strong argument for the existence of cosmic time."[67] In fact, Hawking has shown that the existence of stable causality, that is, the absence of any null or time-like closed causal paths, is a necessary and sufficient condition for the existence of cosmic time.[68] Thus, far from "taking away from space and time the last remnant of physical objectivity," as Einstein thought at first, GTR through its cosmological applications seems to give back what STR had removed.

Now it is my contention that since the inception of the universe and the beginning of physical time, this cosmic time coincides with God's metaphysical time, that is, with Newton's absolute time. It therefore provides the correct measure of God's time and thus registers the true time, in contrast to the multiplicity of local times registered by clocks in motion relative to the cosmological substratum. Already in 1920, on the basis of Einstein and de Sitter's cosmological models, Eddington hinted at a theological interpretation of cosmic time:

> In the first place, absolute space and time are restored for phenomena on a cosmical scale. . . . The world taken as a whole has one direction in which it is not curved; that direction gives a kind of absolute time distinct from space. Relativity is reduced to a local phenomenon; and although this is quite sufficient for the theory hitherto described, we are inclined to look on the limitation rather grudgingly. But we have already urged that the relativity theory is not concerned to deny the possibility of an absolute time, but to deny that it is concerned in any experimental knowledge yet found; and it need not perturb us if the conception of absolute time turns up in a new form in a theory of phenomena on a cosmical scale, as to which no experimental knowledge is yet available. Just as each limited observer has his own particular separation of space and time, so a being co-extensive with the world might well have as special separation of space and time natural to him. It is the time for this being that is here dignified by the title "absolute."[69]

A couple of items in this remarkable paragraph deserve comment. First, Eddington rather charitably interprets STR as positing merely an epistemic limitation on our temporal notions rather than an ontological limitation on time and space. But as friend and foe alike have emphasized,[70] STR requires metaphysical, not merely epistemological, commitments concerning the non-existence of absolute space and time. Otherwise, one winds up with the Lorentz-Poincaré interpretation of the theory, which is, in truth, the position which Eddington is describing. Second, Eddington is quite willing to call cosmic time "absolute" in view of its independence from space, that is to say, its status as a parameter. Relativistic time is, as Lorentz and Poincaré maintained, only a local time, whereas cosmic time, being non-local, is the true time. Third, although in 1920 there was no empirical evidence for cosmic time, within a few short years astronomical evidence confirmed the prediction of the Friedman model of a universal expansion and, hence, of cosmic time. The veil of epistemic limitation had been torn away. Finally, this cosmic time would be the time of an omnipresent being, whose reference frame is the hypersurface of homogeneity itself. Is Eddington recalling here Poincaré's *"intelligence infinie,"* who classified everything according to his universal frame of reference, his "world map," just as finite observers classify events according to their local frames? Cosmic time is not merely the "fusion" of all the proper times recorded by the separate fundamental observers, but, even *more* fundamentally, it is the time which measures the duration of the omnipresent being which coexists with the universe. As the measure of the proper time of the universe, cosmic time also measures the duration of and lapse of time for a temporal being coextensive with the world. For Eddington, it is the time of this being that deserves to be called "absolute."

The theological application is obvious. Given the existence of cosmic time, it is my contention that it represents the correct measure of God's metaphysical time. If the duration of the universe measured in cosmic time is 15 billion years since the singularity, then is not the duration of God's creatorial activity in metaphysical time also 15 billion years? In God's "now" the universe has (present tense) certain specific and unique properties, for example, a certain radius, a certain density, a certain temperature background, and so forth; but in the cosmic "now" it has all the identical properties, and so it is with every successive "now." Is it not obvious that these "nows" coincide and designate one and the same present?

Perhaps we can state this consideration a bit more formally by means of the following proposed principle:

(P) For any constantly and non-recurrently changing universe U and temporal intervals x, y large enough to permit change, if the physical description of U at x is the same as the physical description of U at y, then x and y coincide.

Given that in metaphysical time there is a temporal interval or duration during which a certain physical description of the universe is true and that in cosmic time a similar interval exists, then it follows from P that those intervals of metaphysical and cosmic time coincide. It seems to me, therefore, that cosmic time ought naturally to be regarded as the sensible measure of God's time since the moment of creation.

Such an affirmation will, however, be typically met with passionate disclamations. Any equivalence of cosmic time with Newton's absolute time is vigorously repudiated. Such protestations strike me, however, as being for the most part misconceived. Much of the disagreement seems due simply to the ambiguous term "absolute," compounded by the failure to appreciate the notion of cosmic time as the sensible measure of metaphysical time. For example, it is frequently objected that cosmic time is contingent and therefore cannot be regarded as absolute. Since cosmic time does not exist in all GTR-based models and depends in any case on the existence of hypersurfaces of homogeneity, it cannot be said to record absolute time.

But all that follows from the existence of models lacking a cosmic time is that cosmic time *contingently* coincides with metaphysical time. Our world is characterized by cosmic time, and its absence in other cosmological models is wholly irrelevant to whether it measures God's time in the actual world. In virtue of its coincidence with metaphysical time, it is absolute in the sense that it records the true time in this world. The contingency of cosmic time thus says nothing against its privileged status in this world; in fact, a relationalist can consistently maintain that even metaphysical time exists contingently, for if God had chosen to remain absolutely changeless and never created a world, there would be no events at all and, hence, not even metaphysical time. The existence of both metaphysical and physical, cosmic time would thus be a contingent fact dependent upon God's will.

One of the most intriguing indications that cosmic time does represent the sensible measure of Newtonian absolute time is the surprising demonstration by E. A. Milne and W. H. McCrea that all the results of GTR-based Friedman cosmology can be recovered by Newtonian physics, and in a way that is simpler than Einstein's cumbersome tensor calculus! Milne and McCrea were able to reproduce all the results of big bang cosmology by means of a material universe expanding in empty, classical space through classical time.[71] Comparing relativistic and Newtonian cosmology, Kerszberg observes, "as far as the prediction of the overall history of the universe is concerned, the equivalence seems to be total."[72] This implies, in Bondi's words, that GTR "cannot be expected to explain any major features in any different or better way than Newtonian theory."[73] In particular the concept of cosmic time in GTR-based models corresponds to absolute time in the Newtonian model. Schücking points out that the main asset of the Milne-McCrea formulation was that it gave exactly the same equations for the time development of the universe as the Friedman theory and yet allowed a much simpler derivation.[74] The history of the universe described by the variation of the scale factor $R\,(t)$ in the Robertson-Walker line element is identical in the two theories, even though in the one the scale factor $R\,(t)$ is determined by Einstein's gravitational field equations, while in the other only Newtonian absolute time and Euclidian geometry come into play.[75] All this is not to suggest that Newtonian theory is correct after all; we have already seen how Lorentz was forced to modify Newtonian physics on the local level. But the equivalence of Milne-McCrea Newtonian cosmology with GTR-based Friedman cosmology is a convincing demonstration that cosmic time is, indeed, the physical measure of Newtonian absolute time. Thus, Bondi compares cosmic time with Newton's uniform, omnipresent, and even-flowing time, which enables all observers to synchronize their clocks to a single time.[76] Kerszberg concludes, "On the whole, the equivalence between Newtonian and relativistic cosmology only reinforces the conviction that cosmic time is indeed a necessary ingredient in the formalization of a relativistic cosmology, however alien to general relativity and congenial to Newton's theory the notion of universal synchronization might seem."[77]

In short, then, when one moves from STR into GTR, the application of the latter theory to cosmology yields a cosmic time for our universe which is plausibly regarded as being the measured time which contingently coincides with God's time and therefore registers the true time.

Conclusion

In summary, we have seen that on the basis of God's temporal duration, Newton correctly distinguished between metaphysical time and physical time. Newton's shortcoming lay not in his analysis of metaphysical time, but in his failure to realize that physical time is relativistic. Einstein's STR did nothing to disprove the existence of metaphysical time or absolute simultaneity. Rather his paring away of absolute time was rooted in a positivistic epistemology of Machian provenance, a verificationist philosophy which is philosophically untenable and wholly out of step with contemporary physics and philosophy of science. Moreover, we saw that this positivism belongs essentially to the philosophical foundations of that theory and serves to distinguish it from the Lorentz-Poincaré interpretation of the mathematical core of STR. The almost universally acknowledged failure of positivism permits one to adhere rationally to a doctrine of metaphysical time and objective becoming independent of physical measures. Nothing compels us to adopt Einstein's interpretation of either the mathematics of his theory or of the relevant experimental data.

If God exists in metaphysical time and temporally causes the successive states of the world, then the "now" of His metaphysical time demarcates a three-dimensional slice of spacetime which is equally "now." This universal frame of reference would thus be privileged, so that events which God knows to be present in it are absolutely simultaneous. What the privileged status of such a frame implies is that a Lorentz-Poincaré interpretation of STR is correct. In this frame absolute length, absolute motion, and absolute simultaneity obtain and are known to God, and rods and clocks in motion relative to it undergo intrinsic contraction and retardation.

Finally, we have seen that in order to discover which physical time corresponds with God's metaphysical time, it is necessary to explore the time concept in GTR, which supersedes the restricted concept in STR. GTR, when given a cosmological application, discloses that in models which are causally well behaved, a universal, cosmic time emerges which records the proper time, or duration, of the universe. This cosmic time is plausibly regarded as coincident with metaphysical time since the creation of the world.

Notes

1. W. Rindler, "Einstein's Priority in Recognizing Time Dilation Physically," *American Journal of Physics* 38 (1970), 1112.

2. Isaac Newton, *Sir Isaac Newton's "Mathematical Principles of Natural Philosophy" and his "System of the World,"* tr. Andrew Motte, rev. with an appendix by Florian Cajori, 2 vols. (Los Angeles: University of California Press, 1966), 1: 6. (The critical edition of the *Principia* is Isaac Newton, *Philosophiae naturalis principia mathematica*, 3d ed. [1726], ed. Alexandre Koyré and I. Bernard Cohen, 2 vols. [Cambridge: Harvard University Press, 1972]; for the *Scholium* on time and space, see 1:46.)

3. Newton, *Principles of Natural Philosophy* 1:6.

4. David Ray Griffin, "Introduction: Time and the Fallacy of Misplaced Concreteness," in *Physics and the Ultimate Significance of Time*, ed. David R. Griffin (Albany: State University of New York Press, 1986), 6–7.

5. Newton, *Principles of Natural Philosophy* 2:545.

6. Isaac Newton, "On the Gravity and Equilibrium of Fluids," in *Unpublished Scientific Papers of Isaac Newton*, ed. A. Rupert Hall and Marie Boas Hall (Cambridge: Cambridge University Press, 1962), 132.

7. Cited in J. E. McGuire, "Predicates of Pure Existence: Newton on God's Space and Time," in *Philosophical Perspectives on Newtonian Science*, ed. Phillip Bricker and R.I.G. Hughes (Cambridge: MIT Press, 1990). See also Newton to Des Maizeaux, in *Unpublished Papers*, 357. See also his rejection of God's existing *totum simul* in "Place, Time, and God" (ms. add. 3965, sec. 13, f. 545r-546r), in J. E. McGuire, "Newton on Place, Time, and God: An Unpublished Source," *British Journal for the History of Science* 11 (1978), 121.

8. Newton, "Place, Time, and God," in McGuire, "Newton on Place, Time, and God," p. 123.

9. Newton, *Principles of Natural Philosophy* 1:7–8.

10. J. R. Lucas, *A Treatise on Time and Space* (London: Methuen, 1973), 143.

11. Gerald Holton, "On the Origins of the Special Theory of Relativity," in Holton, *Thematic Origins of Scientific Thought: Kepler to Einstein* (Cambridge: Harvard University Press, 1973), 171.

12. Newton, *Principles of Natural Philosophy* 2:546.

13. See Thomas Aquinas, *Summa contra gentiles* 3.1.68.

14. William Lane Craig, "The Tensed vs. Tenseless Theory of Time: A Watershed for the Conception of Divine Eternity," in *Questions of Time and Tense*, ed. Robin Le Poidevin (Oxford: Clarendon Press, 1998) 221–51.

15. See esp. the writings of Gerald Holton, in particular "Mach, Einstein, and the Search for Reality," in *Ernst Mach: Physicist and Philosopher*, Boston Studies in the Philosophy of Science 6 (Dordrecht: Reidel, 1970), 165–99; "Where Is Reality? The Answers of Einstein," in *Science and Synthesis*, ed. UNESCO (Berlin: Springer-Verlag, 1971), 45–69; and the essays collected in *Thematic Origins of Scientific Thought: Kepler to Einstein* (Cambridge: Harvard University Press, 1973).

16. See Philipp Frank, "The Importance of Ernst Mach's Philosophy of Science for Our Times," [1917], in *Ernst Mach*, 219–34.

17. Ernst Mach, *Die Mechanik in ihrer Entwicklung: Historisch-kritisch dargestellt*, ed. Renate Wahsner and Horst-Heino Borzeszkowski (Berlin: Akademie-Verlag, 1988), 13. (*The Science of Mechanics: A Critical and Historical Account of its Development*, tr. Thomas J. McCormack [La Salle: Open Court, 1960], xxii.)

18. Ibid., 522 (*Science of Mechanics*, 611).

19. Ibid., 252 (*Science of Mechanics*, 280).

20. Or so it has traditionally been believed. According to Brown, Gerion Wolters has shown Mach's rejection of relativity to have been a forgery by his son Ludwig. James Robert Brown, "Einstein's Brand of Verificationism," *International Studies in the Philosophy of Science* 2 (1987), 36.

21. Albert Einstein to Armin Weiner, September 18, 1930, unpublished letter from the Archives of the Burndy Library in Norwalk, Connecticut, cited by Holton, "Where Is Reality?" 55. In his memorial notice "Ernst Mach," Einstein goes so far as to say, "It is not improbable that Mach would have discovered the theory of relativity, if, at the time when his mind was still young and susceptible, the problem of the constancy of the speed of light had been discussed among physicists." A. Einstein, "Ernst Mach," *Physikalische Zeitschrift* 17 (1916), 103, rpt. in Mach, *Mechanik in ihrer Entwicklung*, 683–89.

22. Albert Einstein to Michael Besso, May 13, 1917, in *Correspondance, 1903–1955*, tr. with notes and an introduction by Pierre Speziali (Paris: Hermann, 1979), 68.

23. Albert Einstein to C. Lanczos, January 24, 1938, unpublished letter in the Einstein Archives at Princeton cited in Holton, "Where Is Reality?" 64.

24. Albert Einstein, "Autobiographical Notes," in *Albert Einstein: Philosopher-Scientist*, ed. P. A. Schilpp, Library of Living Philosophers 7 (La Salle: Open Court, 1949), 53. A similar mention is found in Einstein's memorial notice for Mach in 1916: "No one can take it away from the epistemologists that here they paved the way for this development [of Relativity Theory]; for my own part at least I know I have been greatly aided, directly and indirectly, through especially Hume and Mach." Einstein, "Mach," 686; cf. Einstein to Besso, January 8, 1948, in *Correspondance*, 230–31.

25. A. Einstein, "On the Electrodynamics of Moving Bodies," tr. Arthur I. Miller, appendix to Arthur I. Miller, *Albert Einstein's Special Theory of Relativity* (Reading: Addison-Wesley, 1981), 393.

26. A point emphasized by Adolf Grünbaum, *Philosophical Problems of Space and Time*, 2d ed., Boston Studies in the Philosophy of Science 12 (Dordrecht: Reidel, 1973), 712.

27. With admirable bluntness, Heinz Pagels comments, "These definitions, with their appeal to measurement, cut through all the excess philosophical baggage that the ideas of space and time had carried for centuries. The positivist insists that we talk only about what we can know through direct operations like a measurement. Physical reality is defined by actual empirical operations, not by fantasies in our head." Pagels, *The Cosmic Code* (London: Michael Joseph, 1982), 59.

28. See A. Einstein, "Über das Relativitätsprinzip und die aus demselben gezogenen Folgerungen," *Jahrbuch der Radioaktivität und Elektronik* 4 (1907), 417; Einstein, "Über die Entwicklung unserer Anschauungen über das Wesen und die Konstitution der Strahlung," *Physikalische Zeitschrift* 10 (1909), 819; Einstein, "Die Relativitätstheorie," *Vierteljahrsschrift der naturforschenden Gesellschaft in* Zürich 56 (1911), 7–9.

29. Albert Einstein, *Relativity, the Special and the General Theory*, tr. Robert W. Lawson (London: Methuen, 1920), 26. That Einstein was a verificationist outside the realm of physics is also evident from his remarks in an interview with Max Wertheimer that when someone uses the word *hunchback*, "If this concept is to have any clear meaning, there must be some way of finding out whether or not a man has a hunched back. If I would conceive of no possibility of reaching such a decision, the word would have no real meaning for me." Max Wertheimer, *Productive Thinking*, ed. Michael Wertheimer, enlar. ed. (London: Tavistock, 1961), 220.

30. See Albert Einstein, *The Meaning of Relativity*, 6th ed. (1922; rpt. London: Chapman and Hall, 1967), 2. Cf. his "Fundamental Ideas and Problems of the Theory of Relativity," [1923], in *Nobel Lectures, Physics: 1901–1921* (New York: Elsevier, 1967), 479–90, where he lays down a postulate called "the stipulation of meaning," which requires that concepts and distinctions are only admissible to the extent that observable facts can be assigned to them without ambiguity. He considers this postulate to be of "fundamental importance" epistemologically.

31. An instructive piece in this regard is H. Margenau, "Metaphysical Elements in Physics," *Reviews of Modern Physics* 13 (1941) 176–89.

32. Holton, "Search for Reality," 170–71. See, for example, Hans Reichenbach, "The Philosophical Significance of the Theory of Relativity," in Schilpp, *Einstein: Philosopher-Scientist*, 290–91.

33. See John D. Norton, "Philosophy of Space and Time," in *Introduction to the Philosophy of Science*, ed. Merilee Salmon (Englewood Cliffs: Prentice-Hall, 1992), 179.

34. Lawrence Sklar, "Time, Reality, and Relativity," in *Reduction, Time, and Reality*, ed. Richard Healey (Cambridge: Cambridge University Press, 1981), 141.

35. Ibid.

36. See the excellent survey in Frederick Suppe, "The Search for Philosophic Understanding of Scientific Theories," in *The Structure of Scientific Theories*, 2d ed., ed. F. Suppe (Urbana: University of Illinois Press, 1977), 3–118.

37. Richard Healey, "Introduction," in Healey *Reduction, Time, and Reality*, vii.

38. R. Rompe and H.-J. Treder, "Is Physics at the Threshold of a New Stage of Evolution?" in *Quantum Space and Time—The Quest Continues*, ed. A. O. Barut, A. van der Merwe, and J.-P. Vigier, Cambridge Monographs on Physics (Cambridge: Cambridge University Press, 1984), 608.

39. See the sound advice offered by P. J. Zwart, "The Flow of Time," *Synthese* 24 (1972), 134.

40. T. Banks, "*TCP*, Quantum Gravity, the Cosmological Constant, and All That . . . ," *Nuclear Physics B* 249 (1985), 340.

41. Henryk Mehlberg, "Philosophical Aspects of Physical Time," *Monist* 53 (1969), 363.

42. Sklar, "Time, Reality, and Relativity," 132.

43. Holton, "Search for Reality," 198; cf. 188.

44. Henri Poincaré, "The Measure of Time," in *The Foundations of Science*, tr. G. B. Halstead ([Science Press, 1913] rpt. Washington, D.C.: University Press of America, 1982), 228.

45. Ibid., 228–29.

46. If one takes propositions to be tenselessly true or God's knowledge to be non-propositional, it still follows that God's *de se* knowledge is changing. For a discussion, see William Lane Craig, *Divine Foreknowledge and Human Freedom: The Coherence of Theism: Omniscience* (Leiden: Brill, 1990), 8, 71.

47. Cf. Lorentz's illustration in a letter to Einstein in January of 1915 in response to the latter's paper "The Formal Foundations of the General Theory of Relativity." In a passage redolent of the *General Scholium* and *Opticks* of Newton, Lorentz broached considerations whereby "I cross the borderland of physics": "A 'World Spirit' who, not being bound to a specific place, permeated the entire system under consideration or 'in whom' this system existed and who could 'feel' immediately all events would naturally distinguish at once one of the systems *U, U'*, *etc.* above the others" (H. A. Lorentz to A. Einstein, January 1915, Boerhaave Museum, cited in Jozsef Illy, "Einstein Teaches Lorentz, Lorentz Teaches Einstein. Their Collaboration in General Relativity, 1913–1920," *Archive for History of Exact Sciences* 39 [1989], 274). Such a being, says Lorentz, could "directly verify simultaneity."

48. J. M. Findlay, "Time and Eternity," *Review of Metaphysics* 32 (1978–79), 6–7.

49. Milton K. Munitz, *Cosmic Understanding* (Princeton: Princeton University Press, 1986), 157. Kanitscheider proceeds: "The theorist . . . would like to draw up, as Milne put it, a *world map*. On it the state of the world at a specific moment of cosmic time is indicated. All points of space on a hypersurface of space-time are at once grasped and physically described. Such a slice through the happening of events corresponds, of course, to no datum of observation; rather it concerns a theoretical construction. Only a hypothetical, spiritual observer, who could visit all points on the hypersurface without any delay, would be able to achieve such an overview and could confirm the statement that H(*t*) does in fact possess the same value at every place" (Bernulf Kanitscheider, *Kosmologie* [Stuttgart: Philipp Reclam jun., 1984], 193). Kanitscheider explains that we earthbound observers have only a *world picture*, in which distant parts of the world actually belong to earlier moments of cosmic time. Only an omnipresent, cosmic observer, he concludes, who sees the world *sub specie aeternitatis*, can be in the position to draw up a world map. Here the relevance of cosmic time to the theological doctrine of divine eternity becomes explicit.

50. See A.K.A. Maciel and J. Tiomno, "Analysis of Absolute Space-Time Lorentz Theories," *Foundations of Physics* 19 (1989), 507–8.

51. See Martin Ruderfer, "Introduction to Ives' 'Derivation of the Lorentz Transformations,'" *Speculations in Science and Technology* 2 (1979), 243.

52. It is important to realize in comparing these two versions of special relativity that the FitzGerald-Lorentz contraction and clock retardation, which seem to be such stumbling blocks to some for the acceptance of a Lorentz-Poincaré interpretation, are just as much real, physical effects in Einstein's theory as in Lorentz's. Einstein realized right from the start that these effects described in his theory were real, not apparent, and could be shown to be real by various *Gedankenexperimente* (A. Einstein, "Zum Ehrenfestschen Paradoxen," *Physikalische Zeitschrift* 12 [1911], 509–10). Even more engaging thought experiments have been devised to illustrate the point (Dieter Lorentz, "Die Reälität der FitzGerald-Lorentz Kontraction," *Zeitschrift für allgemeine Wissenschaftstheorie* 13, 2 [1982], no. 294–319). See also M. F. Podlaha, "Length Contraction and Time Dilation in the Special Theory of Relativity—Real or Apparent Phenomena?" *Indian Journal of Theoretical Physics* 25 (1975), 74–75.

53. A. Einstein, "The Foundations of General Relativity Theory," in *General Theory of Relativity*, ed. C. W. Kilmister, Selected Readings in Physics (Oxford: Pergamon Press, 1973), 148.

54. See Michael Friedman, *Foundations of Space-Time Theories* (Princeton: Princeton University Press, 1983), 204–15; also Hermann Bondi, "Is 'General Relativity' Necessary for Einstein's Theory of Gravitation?" in *Relativity, Quanta, and Cosmology in the Development of the Scientific Thought of Albert Einstein*, ed. Francesco De Finis, 2 vols. (New York: Johnson Reprint, 1979), 179–86.

55. A. Einstein, "Cosmological Considerations on the General Theory of Relativity," in *The Principle of Relativity*, by Albert Einstein et. al., with notes by A. Sommerfeld, tr. W. Perrett and J. B. Jeffery (rpt. New York: Dover, 1952), 177–88.

56. Kanitscheider, *Kosmologie*, 155. See also G. J. Whitrow, *The Natural Philosophy of Time*, 2d ed. (Oxford: Clarendon Press, 1980), 283–84.

57. Willem de Sitter, "On the Relativity of Inertia," in *Koninglijke Nederlandse Akademie van Wetenschappen Afdeling Wis. en Natuurkundige Wetenschappen, Proceedings of the Section of Science* 19 (1917), 1217–25.

58. A. Friedman, "Über die Krümmung des Raumes," *Zeitschrift für Physik* 10 (1922), 377–86.

59. See Charles W. Misner, Kip S. Thorne, and John Archibald Wheeler, *Gravitation* (San Francisco: Freeman, 1973), 713–14; Kanitscheider, *Kosmologie*, 182–97.

60. Kurt Gödel, "A Remark about the Relationship between Relativity Theory and Idealistic Philosophy," in Schilpp, *Einstein: Philosopher-Scientist*, 557–62.

61. See Peter Kroes, *Time: Its Structure and Role in Physical Theories*, Synthese Library 179 (Dordrecht: Reidel, 1985), 60–96.

62. Such is the formulation of Friedman, *Space-Time Theories*, of all the theories he discusses, including Newtonian space-time (71–124).

63. See Kroes, *Time*, 96.

64. See S. J. Prokhovnik, *Light in Einstein's Universe* (Dordrecht: Reidel, 1985), chs. 4, 5, 6.

65. Whitrow, *Natural Philosophy of Time*, 371; cf. 302. Kanitscheider explains:

With the parameter t we can so order all slices through space-time (the homogeneous hypersurfaces) that an unequivocal earlier/later relation can be set up worldwide. Within such a slice $t = t_0$ (in a three-space) the material quantities p and ρ, as well as the physical geometry, are everywhere the same. Isotropy moreover implies that a particle of the cosmological fluid traces a worldline that orthogonally intersects the hypersurface of homogeneity. One recognizes that there is here again a privileged reference frame; to an observer at rest relative to the substratum, who swims along with the fluid, the universe has a simple form in material structure and space-time geometry. The particular form of the motion of matter in this class of models suggests the utilization of a comoving coordinate system, in which a worldwide, absolute simultaneity is defined. This is, however, no contradiction to the STR, since here the universe itself, with its limited possibility of movement, serves as an instrument of synchronization. The special relativistic time dilation, which we are acquainted with through local experiments, still holds as before for clocks moving relatively to the substratum. Nevertheless, the proper times of all observers who are at rest with respect to the flowing (expanding or contracting) substratum can be harmoniously fitted into a cosmic time (Kanitscheider, *Kosmologie*, 186–87).

66. Martin J. Rees, "The Size and Shape of the Universe," in *Some Strangeness in the Proportion*, ed. Harry Woolf (Reading: Addison-Wesley, 1980), 293.

67. Whitrow, *Natural Philosophy of Time*, 307.

68. S. W. Hawking, "The Existence of Cosmic Time Functions," *Proceedings of the Royal Society of London A* 308 (1968), 433–35.

69. Arthur Eddington, *Space, Time, and Gravitation*, Cambridge Science Classics (Cambridge: Cambridge University Press, 1920, rpt. 1987), 168.

70. Grünbaum, *Space and Time*, 368; Richard Swinburne, *Space and Time*, 2d ed. (London: Macmillan, 1981), 201.

71. E. A. Milne, *Relativity, Gravitation, and World Structure* (Oxford: Clarendon Press, 1935); Milne, "A Newtonian Expanding Universe," *Quarterly Journal of Mathematics* 5 (1934), 64–72; W. H. McCrea, "On the Significance of Newtonian Cosmology," *Astronomical Journal* 60 (1955), 271–74.

72. Pierre Kerszberg, "On the Alleged Equivalence between Newtonian and Relativistic Cosmology," *British Journal for the Philosophy* of Science 38 (1987), 349.

73. H. Bondi, *Cosmology*, 2d ed. (Cambridge: Cambridge University Press, 1960), 89.

74. E. L. Schücking, "Newtonian Cosmology," *Texas Quarterly* 10 (1967), 274.

75. Bondi, *Cosmology*, 105; Kerszberg, "Equivalence," 349.

76. Bondi, *Cosmology*, 70–71.

77. Kerszberg, "Equivalence," 376.

Part Three

THE NATURE OF
DIVINE KNOWLEDGE

7

Timelessness out of Mind

On the Alleged Incoherence of Divine Timelessness

EDWARD R. WIERENGA

According to an ancient strand in Christian thought, God has a unique perspective on all of history: he sees everything that ever happens all at once. Here is one statement of that idea:

> When we attribute foreknowledge to God, we mean that all things always were, and perpetually remain, under his eyes, so that to his knowledge there is nothing future or past, but all things are present. And they are present in such a way that he not only conceives them through ideas, as we have before us those things which our minds remember, but he truly looks upon them and discerns them as things placed before him. And this foreknowledge is extended throughout the universe to every creature.[1]

This passage is from John Calvin, who is perhaps less well known for attributing this perspective to God than are his more prominent predecessors, Augustine, Boethius, and Aquinas. In this tradition, God's unique perspective is taken as a key component of his special *mode of existence*, eternity or timelessness. In Boethius's famous phrase, "eternity . . . is the complete possession all at once of illimitable life."[2]

The opposing view is that God is not eternal, but *everlasting*; he is not timeless, but *in time*. In recent years it seems to have reached the status of a new orthodoxy among philosophers of religion.[3] Nevertheless, I am not persuaded that the objections in the literature to the doctrine of divine timelessness or the reasons *in favor* of divine temporality are especially convincing. In fact, the main considerations advanced in favor of divine temporality, it seems to me, are *objections* to divine eternity. The latter fall into two categories. The first appeals to claims about required changes in what God knows. The second appeals to claims about divine action in the world.

Knowledge, Change, and Indexicals

The first objection to divine eternity notes that what we know changes as time goes by. As things change, we acquire new knowledge, and some of the things we believed become false, so they would no longer count as knowledge if we persisted in believing them. Now if God is omniscient, he knows everything that we know. More precisely, what any of us knows at a given time must be a (proper) subset of what God knows at that time. Since some of the things we know to be true at certain times we know to be false at other times, what God knows must similarly vary over time; and that could not happen if he were outside of time.[4]

This informal statement of the argument covers up some substantive and typically undefended assumptions.[5] One is that in at least some cases when what we know changes, when we add to what we know, some propositions we formerly knew become false. How could it be otherwise? After all, the set of propositions I knew yesterday included the proposition I then expressed by

(1) It is sunny today.

whereas the set of propositions I know today includes the proposition I express today by

(2) It is not sunny today.[6]

Well, it is surely true that sentences like these containing temporally indexical elements such as tenses or terms like "now" or "yesterday" can express true propositions on some occasions of use and false ones on other occasions. But what is not obvious— at least not to me—is that such sentences as (1) and (2) express propositions that themselves vary in truth value over time. For all I can tell, (1) expressed a certain true proposition yesterday and if used today it would express a *different* false proposition. Perhaps the truth that (1) expressed yesterday is still true. In that case, the union of the set of propositions I knew yesterday and the set of propositions I know today is consistent, and perhaps, also, God knows them all from an atemporal perspective.[7]

Of course, it is one thing to make this logical point, and it is another thing to give a plausible account of the objects of our knowledge and belief according to which temporal indexicals do function in this way. It is well known, for example, that the proposition that (1) expressed yesterday is not the same as the proposition expressed by

(3) It is, was, or will be sunny on March 2, 1999.

For I could have known yesterday the proposition then expressed by (1) without knowing the date. More strikingly, someone could know the proposition expressed by (3) at another time without knowing what I knew yesterday when it was then *present to* me that it was then sunny.

In *The Nature of God* I defended an account according to which sentences like (1) express at a given time a proposition involving the *haecceity* or individual essence of that time. On this account, we have knowledge *de praesenti* when we grasp a proposition involving the haecceity of the present time. As a matter of fact, we never grasp such propositions at other times, but there is no obstacle in principle to God grasping all such propositions. Whether that gives him knowledge *de praesenti* depends on whether he grasps them at their time or whether he grasps them at other times or from an eternal perspective. Accordingly, that God knows the propositions we know when we have knowledge *de praesenti* does not settle the question of whether he is in time or out of time. What would settle that question is whether he knows such propositions *at their times* or not—but nothing about the argument we are considering gives us an answer to that question. I concede, of course, that the idea that moments of time each have their own individual essences is a little hard to believe. But I think that this account is technically adequate. And it nevertheless remains the case that someone who wants to use the argument from temporal indexicals against God's eternality needs to provide an alternative account of the objects of our temporal knowledge and belief.

It might seem obvious that there is a readily available alternative account. It is the claim that many propositions are *perspectival*.[8] A proposition can be true at one time and false at another. More generally, a proposition can be true at one *index*, consisting of a person and a time (and perhaps a place and a world), and false at another. Consider the proposition

(4) I am sitting.

On the present proposal, this proposition, as it happens, is true at the index of <Wierenga, 3:00 P.M. EST on March 2, 1999>. But that very proposition, (4), is false at the index of <Wierenga, 4:30 P.M. PST on April 9, 1999>.

If propositions are thus perspectival, we should distinguish *believing that a proposition is true at an index* from *believing at an index that a proposition is true*. An example of the former is believing

(5) *I am sitting* is true at <Wierenga, 3:00 P.M. EST on March 2, 1999>.

An example of the latter is believing (4) *at the index* <Wierenga, 3:00 P.M. EST on March 2, 1999>. Anyone can have the former belief; only someone actually at the index in question can have the latter belief.[9]

The informal argument with which we began included the claim that if God is omniscient, he knows everything that any of us knows. That assumption ought to be challenged. Hardly anyone accepts the parallel claim for omnipotence, that if God is omnipotent he can do anything that any of us can do.[10] Why should we accept it for omniscience? In particular, if I know (4) at the index <Wierenga, 3:00 P.M. EST on March 2, 1999>, God should not have *that* knowledge, that is, he should not know (4) *at that index*, for he could only do that by being me, which, of course, is impossible for anyone but me. So if some propositions are perspectival, a more sensible account of omniscience would be something like

(6) x is omniscient if and only if for any proposition p and perspective $<S, t>$ (i) if p is true at $<S, t>$ then x knows that p is true at $<S, t>$, and (ii) if x is at $<S, t>$ and p is true at $<S, t>$ then at $<S, t>$ x knows that p.

On this account it will follow that an omniscient being is in time only on the assumption that it is at some temporal perspective. In particular, it will follow that *God* is not eternal, given that he is omniscient, only on the further assumption that he is at some temporal perspective. Merely noting that the knowledge of those of us who are in time changes as time goes by does not establish anything about God's perspective or mode of existence. Moreover, if we could show that God is at some temporal perspective, it would follow straightaway that he is in time, without any excursus through omniscience.

I conclude that the attempt to argue against divine timelessness by appeal to the claim that our knowledge changes over time is unpersuasive. The issues are clear, it seems to me: what needs to be added to the argument is a convincing account of the objects of knowledge and belief, one according to which God's own knowledge changes over time.

Divine Action and Temporality

The second kind of objection to divine eternity appeals to God's activity. It holds that if God is an agent, if he creates or redeems, for example, then he performs actions which occur in time, and that is something he could not do if he were timeless.

Aquinas has a reply to this objection. He holds that God's action in eternity could have effects that occur in time:

> Nor, if the action of the first agent is eternal, does it follow that His effect is eternal. . . . Now, an effect follows from the intellect and the will according to the determination of the intellect and the command of the will. Moreover, just as the intellect determines every other condition of the thing made, so does it prescribe the time of its making, for art determines not only that this thing is to be such and such, but that it is to be at this particular time, even as a physician determines that a dose of medicine is to be drunk at such and such a particular time, so that, if his act of will were of itself sufficient to produce the effect, the effect would follow anew from his previous decision, without any new action on his part. Nothing, therefore, prevents our saying that God's action existed from all eternity, whereas its effect was not present from eternity, but existed at that time when, from all eternity, He ordained it.[11]

Critics have not been content with this view. Wolterstorff claims, for example, that "in the case of certain of God's actions the temporality of the event that God acts on infects his own action with temporality."[12] Ironically, however, the actions Wolterstorff cites in support of this claim are God's acts of knowing what we express by tensed sentences. God "knows what is happening in our history, what has happened, and what will happen. Hence, some of God's actions are themselves temporal events."[13] So this development of the argument from divine action just appeals once more to the argument from omniscience, which I have already claimed to be inconclusive. Another critic of Aquinas's perspective is Stephen Davis. His primary complaint is that it requires that we have a "usable concept" of atemporal causation, which he thinks we do not.[14] What more is required? Is it somehow deficient or mistaken to hold with Aquinas that God's eternal action has as effects various events that occur in time? Exactly what is wrong with that suggestion? Without taking the time to survey other recent attempts to object to divine eternal action, let me merely record my impression that they tend to assert that *something* is wrong with this picture, without saying precisely what it is.

In this context, Richard Swinburne's recent work on God and time[15] can be seen as an attempt to add the missing details, to show from principles about the nature of causation and time that no agent can be eternal. I turn then, in the remainder of this essay, to examine Swinburne's claims.

Swinburne's Principles about Time

In a characteristically principled way Richard Swinburne attempts first to uncover some fundamental or metaphysical principles about time before applying them to the problem of the relation of God and time.[16] In fact, Swinburne presents and defends four such principles. Two of them, however, are introduced as part of an effort to make Swinburne's preferred view that God is in time palatable, despite having the consequence that God is "time's prisoner," or, as I shall put it, that time waits for no one, not even God. So I shall not discuss those principles. The remaining two he brings to bear on the doctrine of divine timelessness, claiming that they can show that "the 'timeless' view is incoherent."[17]

Swinburne states his first principle as follows: "everything that happens, every event, that is—including the mere existence of a substance with its properties—happens over a period of time and never at an instant of time, or is analyzable in terms of things happening over periods of time."[18] Swinburne then claims that "the most natural reading of the tradition [that God exists at a single "moment"] seems to me to read 'moment' as 'instant', and in that case the doctrine is in conflict with the first principle. . . . A state of affairs must last for a period of time; it cannot occur at an instant. God cannot be omnipotent or omniscient just at an instant."[19]

To evaluate this objection, we will need to look more closely at both the principle in question and the way by which Swinburne attempts to derive a conflict between the principle and the doctrine of divine timelessness. For the principle to apply to a *state of affairs*, such as God's being omniscient, it must be stated in a way that applies not merely to *events* or to *what happens*, despite Swinburne's summarizing it as "First Principle: Events Happen at Periods."[20] And, indeed, in his defense of it, it is clear that Swinburne intends something more general. For, immediately after formulating the principle in the way I quoted it above, Swinburne goes on to defend a slightly different thesis:

> In general, our ascription of properties to objects is ascription to them over periods of time—things are green or wet or weigh 10 lb. for periods of time. And normally when we do ascribe properties to objects at instants, our doing so is to be read as ascribing them to objects for periods which include the instant. To say that the object is green at 2 P.M. is to say that it is green for some period which includes 2 P.M.

This suggests that the thesis Swinburne intends as his first principle can be expressed as:

(P$_1$) For every object x, property P, and interval or instant t, if x has P throughout or at t, then t is an interval.[21]

In other words, if a thing ever has a property, then it has it for an interval of time.

It would be tempting to put Swinburne's thesis as the claim that nothing ever has a
property for merely an instant, but that would not be what he means. For he quite literally asserts that things do not possess properties *at* instants at all. An apparent attribution of *being green* to an object at an instant t is to be understood or analyzed as the attribution of *being green* to the object throughout an arbitrary interval that contains t. A
thing can be green throughout a period of time, but not at an instant. Similarly, to cite
another example Swinburne develops at some length, moving objects do not literally
possess an instantaneous velocity at an instant. Rather, instantaneous velocity at an instant t is to be understood as the limit of the average velocity over intervals that end or
begin at t. More precisely, an object has an instantaneous velocity of 10 ft./sec. at 2:00
P.M. if and only if

$$\underset{t \to t_2}{Lim} \frac{s_2 - s}{t_2 - t} \to 10, \text{ for } t < t_2 \text{ and} \qquad \underset{t \to t_2}{Lim} \frac{s - s_2}{t - t_2} \to 10, \text{ for } t > t_2,$$

where t_2 = 2:00 P.M., s_2 is the distance in feet covered by the object at t_2 since some arbitrary origin, s is the distance in feet covered at t since the origin, and time is measured in seconds.[22]

I find Swinburne's defense of (P$_1$) to be unconvincing. For one thing, even if it cannot happen that an object is, say, green, for *merely* an instant, I do not see why it could
not be green for every instant included in any interval during which it is green. But, in
the second place, from the fact that some apparent attributions of a property at an instant can be translated into talk of property possession over intervals, it does not follow that all such ascriptions can be similarly paraphrased away. Indeed, Swinburne's
own example of instantaneous velocity seems to provide the ingredients of a coun-
terexample.

Consider Swinburne's moving object during the time around 2:00 P.M. when it is in
motion. Since it is in motion, at each instant it is in a different location. Thus, for some
place P and instant t, *being wholly at P* is a property the object has just at t. Moreover,
it does not seem possible to reduce talk of being at a place at an instant in favor of
some circumlocution about occupying a bigger region throughout an interval of time,
for the object never fully occupies any region larger than it is itself. It never fully occupies the *path* that it travels, for example, but only a part of that path at each instant
it is in motion. Furthermore, we can now see why Swinburne's example of the reduction of instantaneous velocity to the limits of average velocities over intervals not
only suggests this objection but seems committed to it. The average velocities to
which Swinburne appeals are the ratios of distance traveled to intervals of times. But
what is the distance traveled by an object if not the length of the path it took from *the
position it occupied* at the beginning of the interval to *the position it occupied* at the
end of the interval? So it looks as though some properties can be had by objects only
for an instant.

I just claimed that it does not seem possible to reduce talk of being at a place at an instant in favor of some circumlocution; Swinburne thinks otherwise. He suggests (in correspondence) that "the analysis (for the object in motion) consists in more and more of it lying within the region as we approach the instant from beforehand, and less and less of it lying within the region as we get further away from [it]."[23] Suppose our moving object is a cup, and let R be the cup-sized region that, as I see it, the cup occupies at some instant t. Swinburne's proposal, then, is that the claim that the cup has the property of *being located at R* at t can be analyzed in terms of the cup's properties throughout intervals of time surrounding t. More precisely, at the instants before t, the closer they are to t, the greater is the proportion of the cup that is then within or overlapping R. And at the instants after t, the later they are after t, the less is the proportion of the cup that is then within or overlapping R. But I do not see how this eliminates all reference to possession of properties *at instants*. For how could the proposed analysis be understood without involving some such claims as the following? There are instants t_1 and t_2 earlier than t such that t_2 is closer to t than t_1 and such that a greater part of the cup is within R at t_2 than is within R at t_1. But then it looks like the cup will have such properties as *being 50 percent within R* or *being 75 percent within R* at instants. So the proposed analysis seems to require that the cup have at least some properties at instants and thus provides no support for the claim that such reference can always be analyzed away.

So far I have been arguing against Swinburne's principle

(P_1) For every object x, property P, and interval or instant t, if x has P throughout or at t, then t is an interval.

Now it is time to ask how he derives

(7) God is not eternal

from it. Well, strictly, what Swinburne deduces is

(8) God is not omniscient for just an instant.

Now (8) follows from (P_1) with the help of

(9) There is an interval or instant t such that God is omniscient at t.

From this it follows that God is omniscient throughout an interval, and hence not at an instant. And, of course, if God is omniscient throughout an interval of time, then he is *in* time and thus not eternal.

I think that the defender of divine eternity has two replies to this argument. The first is to deny premise (9): God is omniscient *in eternity* and not in time; so there is no interval of time nor instant of time such that, strictly speaking, God is omniscient *then*. The second is to note that (7) does not follow from (8). There are three categories: instants of time, intervals of time, and eternity.[24] The first two are kinds of time; the third is instead a "mode of existence" which includes a certain perspective on time. That God is not omniscient either for just an instant of time or for a temporal interval leaves it entirely open that he is omniscient in eternity. I see no way of making Swinburne's first objection more compelling.

Swinburne's remaining argument appeals to what he calls a "causal theory of time." According to Swinburne, "a period of time is future if it is logically possible that an agent can now causally affect what happens then; and a period of time is past if it is logically possible that an agent acting then could have causally affected what happens now."[25] Swinburne explicitly puts his claims here by reference to what we are able to think, that is, by reference to our conceptual scheme. For example, he says that "the concepts of past and future cannot be connected to the rest of our conceptual scheme unless we understand the past as the logically contingent that is causally unaffectible. Unless we suppose that, any grasp we might have on the concepts would be utterly mysterious and irrelevant to anything else."[26] My own jaundiced reaction to such a "Kantian" claim about, as we might put it, a "necessary precondition" of our experience of the passage of time is to embrace the skepticism it invites, to wonder what time is really like apart from our experience of it. Fortunately, we can avoid both the complexities of conceptual schemes and their relation to the world as well as the difficult project of filling in the details of Swinburne's principle, for his objection to divine timelessness appeals not to the principle itself, but to some claims he makes in support of it. Swinburne writes that the doctrine of divine timelessness "remains open to a conclusive objection from principle 3 [the causal theory of time]: if God causes the beginning or continuing existence of the world, and perhaps interferes in its operation from time to time, his acting must be prior to the effects that his action causes."[27] Since the causal theory of time does not explicitly say that causes must precede their effects, we should look at Swinburne's reasons for that claim.

Those reasons are included in the following paragraph:

Causation in a circle is not logically possible. If A causes B, B cannot cause A (or cause anything which by a longer circle causes A). For what causes what is logically contingent—'anything can produce anything', wrote Hume. Let us put the point in this way: a sufficiently powerful being could, it is logically possible, alter the laws of nature in such a way that some event had, instead of its normal effect at a certain time, one incompatible with that normal effect. So if causation in a circle were logically possible and A caused B and B caused A, a sufficiently powerful being at the moment of B's occurrence could have altered the laws of nature so that B caused not-A; in which case A would have (indirectly) caused A not to occur—which is absurd. So since manifestly the future is causally affectible, the past is not. It follows that backward causation is impossible—causes cannot be later than their effects. It follows too that simultaneous causation is impossible. For if simultaneous causation were possible and A caused B simultaneously, and B caused C simultaneously, then, by Hume's principle cited earlier, it would be logically possible that B could have had, instead of its normal effect, not-A. That logically impossible conjunction of causal sequences is, given Hume's principle, only rendered impossible if we suppose simultaneous causation itself to be impossible. Hence, given that causes and effects are events, which last for periods of time, any effect (which has a beginning) must begin at an instant later than its cause begins; and any effect (which has an end) must end at an instant later than its cause ends.[28]

So Swinburne gives two applications of what he calls Hume's principle, one for the conclusion that causes cannot be later than their effects, and the other for the conclusion that causes cannot be simultaneous with their effects. That leaves only the remaining possibility, that causes *precede* their effects. At this level of exposition, it seems clear that there are two ways for the defender of divine timelessness to escape the objection. The first is to note that, as Swinburne himself indicates, his argument presupposes that causes are *events*, and, thus, whatever it establishes applies only to event-causation. But God is an *agent*-cause, and agents—in contrast to their actions—are neither before nor after the effects they cause. I myself am sympathetic to this reply, but since the medieval defenders of divine eternity sometimes speak of God's eternal "action" or of God as "pure act," I shall not insist upon it. The second obvious reply is to note that Swinburne's assumption that there are just three possibilities for the relation of a cause to its effect—prior to, simultaneous with, and later than—ignores an important alternative, namely, that a cause is *eternal* while its effect is *temporal*. Just as in his first objection, Swinburne assumes that if God is omniscient that is *in time*, either at an instant or throughout a temporal duration—without admitting the alternative that God is eternally omniscient—so in this case, too, he assumes that the only way a cause can be related to its effect is *temporally*. Both assumptions thus fail to take seriously the idea of eternality as a distinct mode of existence. I am sympathetic to this second reply, as well. Nevertheless, I propose in the remainder of this essay to examine more closely Swinburne's argument that a cause cannot be simultaneous with its effect (and by unstated extension, his parallel argument that a cause must precede its effect).

Hume's principle, in unrestricted form, is the claim that anything can cause anything, more formally:

(10) For any events A and B, $\Diamond$(A causes B).

I say that this is the principle in "unrestricted" form, since surely some restrictions ought to be placed on it, if it is to have a chance of being true. For one thing, presumably no event can cause itself, so no instance of (10) instantiated onto a single event is true. Thus, at the very least, (10) should be revised to:

(10') For any events A and B such that $A \neq B$, $\Diamond$(A causes B).

As we saw, Swinburne holds that "if simultaneous causation were possible and A caused B simultaneously, and B caused C simultaneously, then, by Hume's principle cited earlier, it would be logically possible that B could have had, instead of its normal effect, not-A." Thus he seems to deduce from (10') both

(11) $\Diamond$(A causes B) and
(12) $\Diamond$(B causes not-A)

and then concludes from them that

(13) $\Diamond$(A causes B, and B causes not-A).

Swinburne then reasons that this "logically impossible conjunction of causal sequences is, given Hume's principle, only rendered impossible if we suppose simultaneous causation itself to be impossible." But surely there is a simpler and more obvious way to block (13); it is to note that it fails to follow from (11) and (12). Possibility is not closed under conjunction.[29] This is a point that should be insisted upon, apart from issues of temporal priority in causation. For other instances of "Hume's principle" are

(11) $\Diamond$(A causes B) and
(14) $\Diamond$(A causes not-B)

But we should not be tempted to infer

(15) $\Diamond$(A causes B, and A causes not-B).

Indeed, we can see this without raising the question of the temporal relation between the events in question.

In conclusion, I have looked at two recent proposals of Richard Swinburne's, construed as attempts to fill in the details of the objection to divine eternity from facts about divine agency. I have argued that these attempts do not succeed. I conclude, therefore, that it is premature to put divine timelessness out of mind.

Notes

I am grateful to the editors of this volume and to the organizers of the 1999 Pacific Regional Meeting of the Society of Christian Philosophers for encouraging me to present this paper at that conference, as well as to the participants who offered helpful suggestions. I am also indebted to Greg Ganssle and, especially, to Richard Swinburne for their written comments on an earlier draft. Despite the fact that I persist in disagreeing with Swinburne over some points, trying to address his comments in the limited time I had resulted in what I take to be numerous improvements in the essay.

    1. John Calvin, *Institutes of the Christian Religion*, 3.20.5.
    2. Boethius, *The Consolation of Philosophy* 5.6. For a recent sympathetic discussion, see Eleonore Stump and Norman Kretzmann, "Eternity," *Journal of Philosophy* 78 (1981), 429–58.
    3. See Nicholas Wolterstorff, "God Everlasting," in *God and the Good: Essays in Honor of Henry Stob*, ed. C. Orlebeke and L. Smedes (Grand Rapids: Eerdmans, 1975), rpt. in *Contemporary Philosophy of Religion*, ed. S. Cahn and D. Shatz (New York: Oxford University Press, 1982), 77–89, and Stephen Davis, *Logic and the Nature of God* (Grand Rapids: Eerdmans, 1983), esp. chs. 1–2.
    4. An influential version of this argument was presented by Norman Kretzmann in "Omniscience and Immutability," *Journal of Philosophy* 63 (1966): 409–21. It was earlier defended by Franz Brentano, *Philosophische Untersuchungen zu Raum, Zeit, und Kontinuum*, ed. Stephan Korner and Roderick M. Chisholm (Hamburg: Felix Meiner Verlag, 1976), 105. More recent defenders, in addition to Wolterstorff and Davis, include Arthur Prior, "The Formalities of Omniscience," *Philosophy* 37 (1962), 114–29; Anthony Kenny, *The God of the Philosophers* (Oxford: Oxford University Press, 1979); and Patrick Grim, "Against Omniscience: The Case from Essential Indexicals," *Noûs* 19 (1985), 151–80. Critics include Hector-Neri Castañeda, "Omniscience and Indexical Reference," *Journal of Philosophy* 64 (1967), 203–10; Nelson Pike, *God and Timelessness* (London: Routledge and Kegan Paul, 1970); Richard Swinburne,

The Coherence of Theism (Oxford: Oxford University Press, 1977); and Stump and Kretzmann, "Eternity."

5. I have argued in some detail against versions of this argument elsewhere. See Edward Wierenga, "Omniscience and Knowledge *de se et de Praesenti*," in *Philosophical Analysis: A Defense by Example*, ed. D. F. Austin (Dordrecht: Reidel, 1988), 251–58, and Wierenga, *The Nature of God* (Ithaca and London: Cornell University Press, 1989), ch. 6. Here I want merely to sketch two alternative lines of criticism.

6. I write this during a blizzard in Rochester, New York, in March!

7. Cf. Aquinas: "Words denoting different times are applied to God, because His eternity includes all times, and not as if He Himself were altered through present, past and future," *Summa theologiae* 1.10.2. ad 4.

8. I borrow this term from Ernest Sosa, "Consciousness of the Self and of the Present," in *Agent, Language, and the Structure of the World*, ed. J. Tomberlin (Indianapolis: Hackett, 1983), 131–43. The account I present derives from David Kaplan, "Demonstratives" (with "Afterthoughts") in *Themes from Kaplan*, ed. Joseph Almog, John Perry, and Howard Wettstein (New York: Oxford University Press, 1989), 481–613, with an assist from Richard Feldman, "On Saying Different Things," *Philosophical Studies* 38 (1980), 79–84.

9. This account has a nice application to the problem of first-person reference or of de se belief that has been prominent in the literature. If I am sitting at 3:00 P.M. on March 2, 1999, am aware that I am sitting, but suffer from amnesia or don't know what day it is, I will not then believe (5). Nevertheless I do believe (4) at the index <Wierenga, 3:00 P.M. EST on March 2, 1999>.

10. The exceptions include Descartes and Earl Conee. For the latter, see "The Possibility of Power beyond Possibility," *Philosophical Perspectives*, vol. 5, *Philosophy of Religion, 1991*, ed. James Tomberlin (Atascadero: Ridgeview, 1991), 447–73.

11. *Summa contra gentiles* 2.35.3.

12. Wolterstorff, "God Everlasting," 93.

13. Ibid.

14. I am here simplifying Davis's objection. See Davis, *Logic and the Nature of God*, ch. 1. I have discussed his claims in greater detail in *The Nature of God*, 196–98.

15. Richard Swinburne, "God and Time," in *Reasoned Faith*, ed. Eleonore Stump (Ithaca and London: Cornell University Press, 1993), 204–22, and Swinburne, *The Christian God* (Oxford: Oxford University Press, 1994).

16. In "God and Time" this is the explicit order of presentation. In *The Christian God* the discussion of time is found in ch. 4 in part 1 (on metaphysics), whereas the application of this topic to God is found in ch. 6 of part 2 (on theology).

17. *The Christian God*, 139. Cf. "God and Time," 206.

18. *The Christian God*, 72. The parallel formulation in "God and Time" is somewhat less helpful to Swinburne's cause. There he writes that "everything that happens *in time* [emphasis added] happens over a period of time and never at an instant of time—everything, that is, apart from anything analyzable in terms of things happening over periods of times" (206). The inclusion of "in time" makes it uncertain that the principle can really be applied, as Swinburne intends, to God's being omnipotent (216) without *assuming* that God is in time.

19. *The Christian God*, 139. Cf. "God and Time," 216. Swinburne concedes that the objection does not succeed if eternity is not an instant. But he holds that his second objection, to be discussed below, succeeds in any case. As the objection is presented, it might not be clear that it a version of the argument from divine *action*, and, indeed, it is somewhat more general. But Swinburne could just as well have used *God's creating the world* instead of *God's being omniscient* as his example. And given that his first principle is supposed to apply to actions, he is committed to holding that actions cannot occur at just an instant.

20. *The Christian God*, 73.

21. I ignore the task of extending (P_1) to sequences of individuals and *n*-adic relations.

22. *The Christian God*, 73.

23. Richard Swinburne, personal communication, August 23, 1999.

24. Swinburne (in correspondence) denies that there are three such alternatives. He notes that Stump and Kretzmann in their classic paper "Eternity" consider just two ways of understanding eternity, namely, as instantaneous or as extended. Their terms are "of infinite duration" and "illimitable in the way in which a point or an instant may be said to be illimitable" (see 432). They are thus asking about possible understandings of eternity, conceived, nevertheless, as an *alternative* both to the *temporally* extended and the *temporally* instantaneous.

25. *The Christian God*, 81; cf. "God and Time," 211.

26. *The Christian God*, 85–86; cf. "God and Time," 214.

27. "God and Time," 216; cf. *The Christian God*, 139–40. Swinburne adds (in both places), "Similarly, his [God's] awareness of events in the world must be later than those events." I shall ignore this last contention, however, since the suggestion that God's awareness of events in time is due to their affecting him causally is contrary to classical Christian thought and raises, in addition, the exceedingly difficult issue of the source of God's knowledge.

28. *The Christian God*, 82; cf. "God and Time," 212, 214.

29. Swinburne, of course, knows that possibility is not closed under conjunction. In correspondence he claims that I have misinterpreted his argument. It should be taken instead as arguing from (11') A causes B, and (12')~◊((A causes B) and (B causes not-A)), to (13')~◊(B causes C), where C is simultaneous with A. But this inference is invalid, too. So we still are not required to prohibit simultaneous causation in order to prevent Hume's principle from leading to a contradiction.

8

Direct Awareness and God's Experience of a Temporal Now

GREGORY E. GANSSLE

Many philosophers have argued that if God is outside time, we can preserve both God's foreknowledge of the future and genuine libertarian free will. Boethius was the first major thinker to apply God's atemporality to the problem of God's knowledge of future free actions. He certainly was not the last. Anselm, Aquinas, and a host of others have followed. This tradition is so strong that William Hasker thinks that no doctrine of divine timelessness can be considered adequate unless it solves this problem. He writes:

> An acceptable doctrine of timelessness must provide a solution to the problem of free will and foreknowledge. It is true that not all theologians who have espoused timelessness have put the doctrine to this use, and I am not claiming that this problem was the main reason for the adoption of the theory of timelessness. But Boethius, Anselm and Aquinas are the central figures of the eternalist tradition, and the fact that all three of them used the doctrine to solve the free will problem justifies my claim that a doctrine that could not be so used would not be faithful to their intentions. Furthermore, this stipulation has significant philosophical advantages in that it places constraints on the doctrine of timelessness that will be of considerable assistance as we seek to develop the best possible formulation.[1]

I am not sure that Hasker's reasons support this requirement, though that is a subject for another essay. In any case, it can safely be said that the topic of divine knowledge of future free acts has dominated the discussion of God's knowledge, especially as far as God's relation to time is concerned. I want to point out, however, that there are other important issues linking God's knowledge with his relation to time. The issue I want to discuss is the *mode* of God's knowledge, that is, how God knows what he knows.

In discussions of God's knowledge, it is generally assumed that God necessarily knows everything that can be known and that God cannot be mistaken (i.e., that God is necessarily omniscient and infallible). It is also generally assumed that God's knowledge involves beliefs. Human knowledge is thought to require belief, and this understanding of knowledge is often carried over into construals of divine knowledge.

William Alston has recently argued against this assumption. According to Alston, not only does God not need beliefs, but God's knowledge does not involve beliefs at all.[2] After considering several ways to support the thesis that divine knowledge is not of the form "true belief + . . . ," Alston defends the position that there is "another construal of divine knowledge that is superior to any true belief + . . . construal."[3] This construal is that God's knowledge of a fact consists in direct awareness of the fact in question. Alston calls this an intuitive conception of knowledge or knowledge by direct awareness.[4] Alston's position is that when God knows any fact, the fact itself is *immediately* present to God.[5] There is no divine mental representation of the fact by means of which God knows it. Therefore, his knowledge is not constituted (or partly constituted) by beliefs.

A further clarification of the idea of knowledge by immediate awareness is in order. There are, in fact, three grades of immediacy.[6] The basic distinction is between immediate awareness of an object and mediate awareness. One is *immediately aware* of an object if there is no other object of awareness through which one is aware of the first. In contrast, one has *mediate awareness* of an object if one's awareness of it is through one's awareness of some other object. An example of mediate awareness which Alston discusses is seeing a table on television.[7] The table is the object of my perception, but I see it through my perception of the television set. I perceive the television set itself directly.

The further distinction Alston makes is between *mediated immediacy* and *absolute immediacy*. Ordinary visual perception, on the assumption of direct realism, is an example of the former. When I see a table directly, there is no other object of vision through which I see the table. My perception of the table is mediated, however. It is mediated by my conscious state. My conscious state is not identical with the table, but my perception of the table is mediated by it. I am aware of my conscious state but not as the object of my visual perception.

In the case of absolute immediate awareness, my awareness of an object is not mediated by anything distinct from the object itself, even my conscious state. In human beings, perhaps only our awareness of our own conscious states is absolutely immediate. If this is the case, when I am aware that I feel tired, there is no other conscious state (apart from that of feeling tired) involved in my awareness.

God's direct intuitive awareness of facts in the world is taken to be absolutely immediate. His knowledge is not mediated by any other objects of awareness nor by anything other than the facts themselves, even his own mental states. Rather than give a comprehensive defense of this view, in the next section, I shall suggest two reasons to hold that it is the right way to think about divine knowledge.[8] For the rest of the essay, I will explore the implications of this view for God's relation to time.

Reasons to Think of Divine Knowledge as Direct Awareness

Why should we not ascribe beliefs to God? First, none of the reasons for which we ascribe beliefs to ourselves apply to God. Beliefs, in God's mental life, are superfluous. A second reason to hold that God knows by direct awareness is simply that it is a better mode of knowledge. Alston points this out:

> The basic point is that the intuitive conception represents the fullest and most perfect realization of the cognitive ideal. We reject the intuitive account for human knowledge, not because we suppose ourselves to have something better, but because it represents too high an aspiration for our condition. If we could be continuously directly aware of every fact of which we have knowledge, that would be splendid; but we must settle for something more modest. Immediate awareness of facts is the highest form of knowledge just because it is a direct and foolproof way of mirroring the reality to be known. There is no potentially distorting medium in the way, no possible unreliable witnesses, no fallible signs or indications. The fact known is "bodily" present in the knowledge. The state of knowledge is constituted by the presence of the fact known. This is the ideal way of "registering" a fact and assimilating it into the subject's system of cognition and action guidance. Hence this is the best way to think of God's knowledge. Since God is absolutely perfect, cognitively as well as otherwise, His knowledge will be of this most perfect form.[9]

We do not attribute direct awareness to God because we are afraid that beliefs might infect his knowledge with fallibility. On the contrary, absolute immediacy in knowledge is the cognitive ideal. Direct awareness is a greater mode of knowledge than knowledge by way of belief because it grants God's cognitions the most metaphysical independence. By way of analogy, God's independence of the universe is an indication that he is metaphysically greater. The fact is that he does not depend on the universe but it depends on him. This metaphysical independence provides grounds for the claim that God is metaphysically greater than the universe.

God's knowledge, involving absolute immediate awareness, is independent of propositions and mental representations. Thus his knowledge is metaphysically greater than it would be if it required these things. One reason, then, that it is better to think of God's knowledge as direct awareness is simply because it does not require propositions or any other medium by which God knows facts. The facts themselves are present in God's cognition. Hence, direct awareness is the greater mode of knowledge.

We see that there is some reason to hold that God knows what he knows by direct awareness. I want to argue that if this is how God knows what he knows, God must be atemporal.[10] The argument I will develop turns on the claim that knowledge by direct awareness *cannot span time*. If it cannot, God can know by direct awareness only those facts which persist simultaneously with his act of knowing. If God knows *every* fact by direct awareness, then, he must be atemporal.

Of course, the question of whether God's direct awareness of facts can span time only arises if God is in time. If God is atemporal, there is no temporal duration between his act of awareness and any object of his awareness. There is no need for a time-spanning relation. An atemporal God can know all facts (past, present, and future) by direct awareness. In what follows I shall assume that God is *temporal*, and I shall investigate what it would be for God to have his experiences sequentially.

God's Experience of a Temporal Now

My reasons for thinking that direct awareness cannot span time involve the nature of God's experience of the temporal now. If God is in time, he must experience a temporal now somewhat as we do. What is his experience of the temporal now?

Thomas Nagel, in an influential essay, pointed out that extrapolating from our own experience will not give us much insight into the inner life of a bat.[11] He does not conclude that we are totally ignorant of what it is like to be another being, however. Nagel writes:

> There is a sense in which phenomenological facts are perfectly objective: one person can know or say of another what the quality of the other's experience is. They are subjective, however, in the sense that even this objective ascription of experience is possible only for someone sufficiently similar to the object of ascription to be able to adopt his point of view—to understand the ascription in the first person as well as the third, so to speak. The more different from oneself the other experiencer is, the less success one can expect with this enterprise.[12]

Nagel claims that sufficient similarity between subjects will make it possible for one to know what it is like to be the other. Obviously what it is like to be God is very different than what it is like to be a human being. It is impossible to have much confidence in knowing what God's *total* experience is like. There are, however, *some* aspects of being God that are such that I can grasp what they are like from my own experience. This will not give me complete understanding, but I can know something of what it is like to be God. For example, I have a sense of what it is to love someone sacrificially. My own experience as a parent gives me a basis for grasping, to some degree, what it must be like for God to love us. To the degree that I share some experiential feature with God, I can know a little of what it is like to be God in that respect. To be sure, the extent of my parental love, even on a good day, is nowhere near the magnitude of God's love. But it is similar in kind to his love.

I share another feature of God's experience if God is in time: his temporal experience. If God is temporal, part of what it is like to be God is to experience things temporally. I can grasp this aspect of divine experience because I experience things temporally as well. This is not to say that I can know exhaustively what it is like for God to experience things temporally, but I do have some sense of what God's experience is like. By investigating the temporal experience of human beings, we can come to some understanding of what divine temporal experience is like.

Furthermore, unlike the experience of loving sacrificially, to experience temporal things sequentially does not admit of degrees. Either one's experiences are sequential or they are not. This can be the basis for a degree of confidence that I can know what it is like to be God in this very limited arena. Both God and I experience temporal things sequentially. It is true that the nature of God's experience is not constituted solely by his relation to time. His experiences are also constituted by his divine nature. His omnipotence, omniscience, moral perfection, and spiritual nature all contribute to the way he experiences the world. These are features of his experience which are not shared by human beings.

What is it for a human being to experience a temporal now? In what ways does our temporality determine our experience? To answer these questions, we need to search out the ways in which our relation to what is temporally present is different than our relation to what is past or future. The fact that we have an experience of the now will make it the case that we stand in certain relations to the present in which we do not stand to other temporal locations. Part of an adequate construal of our experience of the temporal now will involve our cognitive experience. My knowledge of the present differs from my knowledge of the past or the future. This difference is not only in the extent of my knowledge, it is also a difference in the mode of my knowledge.

If I can be directly aware of anything at all, I am directly aware of my own present mental states. Suppose that I am hungry and that I am directly aware of my hunger. My direct awareness of my present hunger is a case of absolute immediate awareness. My awareness is *immediate* in that I am not aware of my hunger in virtue of being aware of some other object. It is *absolute* immediacy because my awareness is not mediated by anything other than the mental state itself. My direct awareness of my present hunger is constituted by the presence of my hunger to my consciousness.

Being aware of the hunger I felt two hours ago is different. I must remember that hunger. Memory of my past hunger is a case of *mediated* immediacy. I do not know my hunger in virtue of some other *object* of awareness, but my knowledge of it is mediated by at least three items. First, it is mediated by my conscious state. This conscious state is not identical with the conscious state of my hunger. Second, there must be some causal chain between the fact remembered and the conscious act of remembering.[13] My memory is mediated by this causal chain. In addition to this, there is some kind of memory storage in the brain. My awareness of the past fact is mediated also by this storage and retrieval mechanism.

Memory, of course, is a time-spanning cognitive relation. As in sense perception, it is the presence of the causal chain between the object known and the act of knowing that allows human memory to span time. Knowledge by direct awareness of facts is taken to be absolute immediate awareness. There is no causal chain or any other factor which mediates direct awareness. The mediating factors in human memory, and in sense perception, indicate that these are not analogous to direct awareness of facts.

So it seems that my experience of the temporal now is grounded, at least in part, by my absolute immediate awareness of my present mental states. There is a phenomenal difference between my awareness of my own present mental states and my memory of my past mental states (or of past facts). This difference constitutes (or partly constitutes) my experience of the now.

It is not possible to argue from this claim about human experience to the conclusion that God's experience of a temporal now must involve an analogous difference between his cognition of present facts and his cognition of past facts. There are two reasons for caution here. First, some of the other things we know about God show that his cognitive awareness is markedly unlike ours. For example, he does not need a storage and retrieval mechanism for any of his knowledge. The extent of his cognitive abilities is such that he can entertain all of the things he knows at once. Perhaps these differences make God's experience of the now sufficiently disanalogous to our own to undermine this argument.

The second reason is that it might be circular to assume that God (even if God is in time) *remembers* the past. If a causal chain between the fact remembered and the act of remembering is required in order for any cognitive activity to count as memory, no act of memory is an act of absolute immediate awareness. If God's knowledge of the past is through direct awareness, God does not *remember* the past at all. Rather, God has absolute immediate awareness of past facts without memory. To assume that God's knowledge of the past is by way of *memory* then is to argue in a circle.

If God's direct awareness of facts can span time, the mode of his cognitive experience of the present is identical to the mode of his experience of the past or future. But if God experiences a temporal now, *something* about God's experience must be different from moment to moment. On the assumption that direct awareness *can* span time, this difference cannot involve the mode of his knowledge. It must be in something else. In the next section, I consider whether God's experience of the temporal now can be constituted by something other than his cognitive relation to what is present. The most salient option is his ability to perform direct actions on the present but not on the past or future.

Direct Action and the Temporal Now

If God's experience of the temporal now does not involve a difference in his *cognitive* experience from moment to moment, it must be grounded in some other difference. Another candidate is that God's experience of the temporal now could be constituted by a difference in his ability to act. It may be that God's ability to bring about the present is different than his ability to bring about the past or future. He can act directly only on the present, but he brings about the future only indirectly.[14] If God can act directly only on the present, perhaps this temporal limitation constitutes his experience of the temporal now.

Can I bring about the past or future directly? It is true that I can bring about the future. I can act so that certain events will occur in the future. When I do anything that makes a difference to the future, I do so in virtue of bringing about some present fact. In other words, I indirectly act on the future through directly acting on facts which persist at the time of my action. For example, I may now bring it about that I will get no work done today by deciding (now) to take a nap rather than to get to work. My bringing about the future in which I get nothing done is accomplished indirectly.

The difference between an indirect action and a direct action can be summarized as follows. An action is direct (or basic) if and only if the agent performs the action without performing any other action as a means to it. It is not that the action is performed without the performance of any other action at all. It is that no other action was a means to its performance. All other actions are indirect. For example, I pull a rope in order to ring a bell. The ringing of the bell is an indirect action. Is the pulling of the rope a direct action? This depends upon whether there are other actions that I perform in order to pull the rope. I cannot pull the rope without moving my hands and arms. So the pulling of the rope is not a direct action either. Thomas Tracy explains this: "Returning to an example already used, if the cook is to call people to dinner, he may have to ring a bell. If he is to ring the bell, he may have to pull a rope. And if he is to pull the rope, he will have to move his hands and arms in certain ways. This regress can only come to an end in an action that he undertakes without having to do anything else in order to act as he intends. This will be a basic action."[15] The basic actions I perform can make a difference only to facts which persist at the time of my action. In fact, I can perform basic actions only on a limited range of present facts. It may be that none of my basic actions take place outside my own body. I can act directly to move my limbs or change facial expressions or mouth words. Actions such as asking a question or hitting a softball are indirect. I perform these only in virtue of performing some basic actions.

The fact that I can act directly only on currently persisting facts is a distinction between my relation to the present and my relation to other times. Could it be the case that God's experience of a temporal now consists in his directly acting only on the present but indirectly acting on the future?

Let us assume that God's direct action *cannot* span time.[16] It does not follow that this is sufficient to constitute his experience of the temporal now. One reason is that his ability to act directly is not an experience he has. To be sure, God *knows* that he can act directly only on the present. So God experiences this limitation. His experience of this limitation, however, is not a direct experience of the world. It is God experiencing his own nature.

It is well known that Thomas Aquinas held that God knows the world through his knowledge of his own essence. If he thought that God was temporal, he might claim that God's experience of the temporal now could be constituted solely by God's knowledge of his ability to act directly only on the present. For example, God is directly aware of the fact of George Washington's presidency being past. He knows it is past, however, through his knowledge that he no longer can act directly on Washington's presidency.

Aquinas's position will not solve this difficulty because, for Aquinas, God's experience of the now would not be a case of *direct* awareness. He would experience now as now in virtue of his knowledge of his own ability to act directly on this temporal location. God's experiential knowledge of the now would then be knowledge in virtue of his knowledge of his own nature. God might know some facts by direct awareness, but many facts he would know only indirectly.

Direct Awareness Cannot Span Time: The General Argument

We have seen that God's ability to act directly only on the present is not sufficient to constitute his experience of the temporal now. I will now return to the claim that God's experience of the temporal now would be constituted by a difference in the mode of his knowledge of the present compared with the mode of his knowledge of other times. To this end, I will present a *general* argument that if God is in time, he cannot know all facts by direct awareness. In the next section I will discuss the argument with reference to the major theories of the nature of the now. Here is the argument:

1. God is temporal. [Assumption]
2. If God is temporal, God's experience of temporal facts is a sequential experience. [Premise]
3. Therefore God's experience of temporal facts is a sequential experience. [1, 2]

4. At any given time, God knows all the facts that can be known at that time. [Premise]
5. God's sequential experience of temporal facts involves his cognitive experience of those facts. [Premise]
6. God's cognitive experience of present facts is different than his cognitive experience of past or future facts. [3, 5]
7. The difference in God's cognitive experience of a past or future fact and his experience of a present fact will involve a difference either in the extent of his knowledge or in the mode of his knowledge of those facts. [Premise][17]
8. God's knowledge of a past or future fact is no different in *extent* than his knowledge of present facts. [4]
9. Therefore, the *mode* of God's knowledge of past and future facts is different than the mode of his knowledge of present facts. [7, 8]
10. The mode of God's knowledge of facts is either through believing true propositions that correspond to those facts or by having direct awareness of the facts themselves. [Premise]
11. Therefore, if God is temporal, he does not know all facts by direct awareness. [1–10][18]

I begin with the assumption that God is temporal. I aim to show that if this assumption is true, then God does not know all facts by direct awareness. My proof, then, is a conditional proof. Statement [2] is part of what most philosophers mean when they claim that God is temporal. It may be that there are ways in which God could be temporal without his experiencing temporal facts sequentially.[19] For example, God's existence could be temporally located but his experience of all temporal facts could be in one, spread out now. No one who holds this view will take my argument as presenting an objection to her position. Most philosophers who argue that God is temporal, however, do not take this view. They hold that God's experience of temporal reality is sequential. Given [1] and [2], God's experience of temporal facts is a sequential experience.

Statement [4] is part of the claim that God is omniscient. He knows everything that can be known. Statement [5] claims that God's experience of temporal facts (and the temporal now) will involve his knowledge of those facts. It may be possible for me to have experiences without having knowledge of the facts relevant to the experience. For example, I may be depressed about my research without knowing that I am depressed. I may not introspect about my feelings at all. In this case I can experience the depression without knowing that I am doing so or why. In God's case this kind of situation is impossible. God is always cognitively aware of every fact. God cannot experience a temporally present fact without knowing all of the facts relevant to it. If an event is now occurring, God's experience of the temporal now will involve his knowledge of that event occurring. So God's experience of the temporal now is at least partly constituted by his knowledge of facts.

Statement [6] further amplifies what it means to claim that God is temporal. From [3] we learn that some facts are past (relative to his experience), some are present, and some are future. Statement [6] points out that this means that his experience of facts that persist at temporal locations other than now will be different than his experience of those that persist now. To experience a temporal now is (at least) to experience what is happening now in a manner qualitatively different than the manner in which one experiences what is past or what is future.

Statement [7] indicates that this difference will either be in the extent of God's knowledge or in the mode of his knowledge. Since there can be no difference in the extent of God's knowledge [8], the difference must be in the mode of his knowledge [9]. Statement [10] indicates that there are two contenders for the mode of God's knowledge of a fact. Either God knows the fact through believing a true proposition that corresponds to the fact or God has direct awareness of the fact in question. If the mode of God's knowledge of the present is different than the mode of God's knowledge of other times, God cannot know all facts by the same mode. That is, God cannot know all facts by direct awareness. If God is temporal, then, God cannot know all facts by direct awareness. By contraposition, if God does know all facts by direct awareness, he must be atemporal.

While God's experience of a temporal now might not be exhausted by his awareness of present facts, it seems that his temporal experience is at least partly constituted by his direct awareness of those facts. In other words, part of what it means for God to experience a temporal now is to have direct awareness of facts which occur now, but only indirect awareness of facts (or mediated awareness of facts) that occur at other times.

God's Experience of a Temporal Now and the A and B Theories of Time

As note 17 above indicates, one item was left out of our consideration of this argument. Let us return to [7]. This statement claims that God's experience of the temporal now involves a difference either in the mode of his knowledge or in the extent of his knowledge. It turns out that this claim does not exhaust the possibilities. It could be that there is a difference in the *objects* of his knowledge at different times. There may be something about present facts that, simply in virtue of their presentness, makes them different than past or future facts. Present facts, some hold, have the property of "persisting now" while past or future facts do not. If there are such properties, perhaps God's experience of the temporal now could be constituted by his experience of those facts with the property of presentness.

Pursuing this option involves an investigation into the different theories of time. What the now is believed to consist in will vary depending on the theory of time one holds. There are two basic theories of time. These are the A-theory (or tensed theory) and the B-theory (or tenseless theory).[20] The fundamental commitment of the A-theory of time is that there is a privileged temporal location. This privileged location is the present. Temporal items (events and some facts and objects) have their temporal determinations relative to the present. Events are past, present, or future. A-theorists claim that the privileged status of the present is an objective feature of temporal reality. Therefore, the temporal determination of any event relative to the present is an objective feature of that event. This objective feature of the event is a property that the event gains or loses. The event of my finishing this essay is now future. That is, it is future as I write and rewrite this sentence. Eventually it will be present. Finally it will be past. It will continue to become further and further past. The temporal location of the event changes with respect to its relation to the privileged present.

B-theorists reject this objective privileged position. While it is true on B-theories that some temporal items are now present, the most fundamental features of temporal objects are marked out relative to all other temporal items. For example, my finishing this essay is later than my typing this sentence. It is earlier than the sun burning out (I assert with moderate confidence), and it is simultaneous with other events. These relative locations do not change. My typing this sentence-token is earlier than my completing the essay. These will never change their temporal order. The relative temporal location of events remains fixed.[21]

A-theorists do not deny that events have a fixed temporal order. B-theorists do not deny that we experience events as future and then present and then past. So on both theories any temporal event will have both A-properties (e.g., the event occurred in the past) and B-properties (e.g., the event occurred on January 20, 1961). The disagreement is about which features of time (or of events and facts in time) are more fundamental. The A-theorist holds that it is the pastness or presentness or futureness of an event that is fundamental. What is most fundamental on the B-theory is the relative order of events. The present is not privileged.

There are two ways B-theorists analyze A-properties. The classical B-theorist reduces statements attributing A-properties to events (call them A-statements) to statements attributing only B-relations. When a classical B-theorist reports, "It is now raining," she is claiming that the event of it raining is simultaneous with her utterance. The basic temporal determinations do not consist in past, present, and future. They are before, simultaneous, and after. "The rain is past" is understood as "The rain occurred prior to this utterance."

The "new B-theorist"[22] does not claim to reduce A-statements to B-statements (or A-properties to B-relations). Rather he claims that the word "now" in "it is now raining" does not ascribe a property at all. The word "now" in the sentence refers to a time directly. It refers to the time the sentence is uttered. These times do not have A-properties. They stand in B-relations to all other times. So when I say, "It is now raining," I am referring to the time of the utterance of my sentence and claiming that it is raining at that time. I am not ascribing a property such as "occurring now" to the event of raining. In the "new B-theory" as well as in the classical B-theory, there is an elimination of A-determinations (past, present, and future) in favor of B-determinations (earlier, simultaneous with, later than).

The A-theorist rejects both of these attempts to eliminate A-determinations. When we assert the sentence "It is now raining," we are claiming more than the fact that it is raining at time x, that is, the time of the utterance of the sentence. Not only is the rain simultaneous with the utterance, it is happening *now*.

In the remainder of this essay, I will examine the relevance of the different theories of time to my argument. I will conclude that if God knows all facts by direct awareness, his experience of the temporal now cannot be constituted by his knowledge of which facts have the A-property of persisting now, even if there are such properties. We will find that in the end, the distinction between the A and the B theories will not be relevant to the cogency of my argument.

Before I deal with God's experience of the now on the A-theory, I shall discuss what his experience would amount to on the B-theory. If the B-theory is true, A-determinations (past, present, and future) are eliminated in favor of B-determinations (earlier than, simultaneous with, and later than). A claim such as "My cup is now on the table" may be analyzed as "My cup's being on the table is simultaneous with this utterance (or mental state)." Or it may be analyzed as "My cup is on the table at t_1," where t_1 is the time the sentence is thought or uttered. So the temporal now is analyzed in terms of simultaneity with other facts or events which have the same temporal location.

On the old B-theory, if God is temporal, his B-analysis of the temporal now will involve simultaneity with his own present mental states. For God, the thought "Greg's cup is now on the table" is analyzed as "Greg's cup's being on the table persists simultaneously with this thought." The claim "Greg's cup was on the table" is analyzed as "Greg's cup's being on the table *persisted before* this thought."

A difficulty will emerge when we consider how God picks out his own present mental states. Assume that God knows *all* facts by absolute immediate awareness (i.e., assume that direct awareness spans time). His knowledge of his past mental states is no less complete than his knowledge of his own present mental states. Moreover, he knows his past mental states in the same way (with absolute immediate awareness) that he knows his present mental states. His past mental states are cognitively present to his consciousness in exactly the same way that his present mental states are cognitively present.

In order for God to differentiate facts that persist simultaneously with his present mental state from those that persist simultaneously with his past mental state, he must be able to tell which of his mental states occurs in the present and which has already occurred. But which of his thoughts occurs now? If God's knowledge of all of his own mental states is by direct awareness, all of his mental states are cognitively present to his consciousness now. If this is the case, there is no way for him to distinguish between present and past mental states. There is then no way for him to know which facts are persisting simultaneously with his present mental states. In short, God cannot locate facts or events in time. Such location presupposes an ability to locate temporally one's own mental states. Granted the three assumptions we are making in this paragraph (the B-theory is true, God is temporal, and God knows all facts by direct awareness), God cannot have this ability.

On the new B-theory, God's situation is no better. His analysis of "Greg's cup is now on the table" is "Greg's cup is on the table at *this* time," where "*this* time" refers directly to the time the sentence is uttered or thought. He does not, however, have any way to discern whether *this* time or *some other* time is now.

Now suppose that the A-theory is true. In this case the presentness, pastness, or futureness of facts is not analyzed in terms of B-determinations. Temporal facts simply have the property of persisting at some A-determination. On the A-theory it is the *object* of God's knowledge that is different from moment to moment. Take the fact of my cup's being on the table. This fact has two properties (among others). First, it has the property of persisting at 10:30 A.M. on April 10, 1999. We might call this a B-property, the property of having a certain B-determination. The fact will never lose this property. It also has the property of persisting *now*. This is the A-property of the fact. The fact will soon lose this property. On the A-theory, these properties are not reducible to one another. The A-determination of every temporal fact is an objective property of that fact. In fact, the A-property is more fundamental than the B-property.

If God has direct awareness of all facts, he has direct awareness of the A-determinations of all facts.

Since the A-determination of a fact or an event is a property of the fact or event, we might say that a fact and its A-determination together constitute a *higher order* fact. If there is a fact in which my cup is on the table, there is a higher order fact in which my cup is on the table *now*. It is a fact consisting in a *fact* having a certain property. If I place the cup on the table now, the *event* of my placing the cup on the table has the property of occurring now. This is a higher-order fact—a fact involving the *event* and its A-determination.

Alternately, we could say that my cup being on the table is a fact-*type*. As such it is repeatable. My cup being on the table *now* is a fact-*token* of that type. So a sentence of the form "Greg's cup is now on the table" reports a fact-token. The fact-token is not repeatable even though the sentence can be uttered truly at various times.

So God does not need to pick out his own present mental states in order to know that my cup is on the table now. He is directly aware of the (higher order) fact involving the first order fact (my cup's being on the table) and the property the fact has, of persisting now.

At first glance it seems that the A-theory will dispose of all of the problems of God's experience of a temporal now. God reads the simple property of "persisting now" off of the fact. So the difference in God's knowledge of the present and his knowledge of the past and future is not in the extent or in the mode of his knowledge. It is in the *content* of his knowledge. The facts that are present have the property of persisting now. The past or future facts have different A-properties. God can differentiate the present from other times and experience the temporal now even if his direct awareness spans time. So God's experience of the temporal now is constituted by his direct awareness of which facts have the property of occurring now.

The A-theory, however, cannot deliver such an easy escape. Consider the situation as follows. The following two facts are taken from the career of my coffee cup and persist sequentially. First my cup is on the shelf; later it is on the table. Suppose that the second of these persists now. My cup used to be on the shelf, but now it is on the table. On the A-theory, this second fact, my cup's being on the table, has the property of persisting now. This constitutes the higher order fact—the fact of my cup being *now* on the table. What are we to say about the past fact, my cup being on the shelf yesterday? We may say that the past fact *had* the property of persisting in the present or *has* the property of persisting in the past. On this view, the higher order fact (my cup's being on the shelf in the past) is a fact which now persists.

How many higher order facts are there that involve my cup's location? More than the one that now persists. Among the other higher order facts that there are is the fact of my cup's being on the shelf now. This higher order fact *exists*, but it does not now persist. My cup is not now on the shelf. This higher order fact *used to* persist, however. Yesterday, the fact of my cup's being on the shelf *was* present though it is not present any longer. It *did* have the property of persisting now (though it does not have this property any longer). The fact lost this property when the cup was removed from the shelf. Every temporal fact (including every higher order fact) gains and loses these kinds of A-properties.

If God's direct awareness spans time, his direct awareness is not limited to facts that now persist. Not only does God now have direct awareness of my cup's being on the table (the fact which now persists), he now has direct awareness of my cup's being on the shelf. This fact persisted yesterday.

Which higher order facts involving my cup's position does God know by direct awareness? Well, all of them. If his direct awareness spans time, he is directly aware of the world as it was yesterday. This means he is also directly aware of the *higher order* facts that persisted yesterday. One of these higher order facts consisted in the fact of my cup's being on the shelf having the property of *persisting now*.

So God is directly aware of the following two higher order facts. The first is *my cup's being on the table now*. This fact persists now. The second higher order fact is *my cup's being on the shelf now*. This higher order fact persisted yesterday. How does God know which of these facts persists now? If we say that he reads the simple property of persisting now off of the higher order facts, we wind up in a vicious regress.

We do not want to say that "persisting now" is reduced to "simultaneous with this mental state." First, to make such a reduction is to abandon the A-theory. Second, as we saw earlier, he would have no way to determine which of his mental states is now persisting. At any given time he has direct awareness of all of his mental states (past, present, and future). Furthermore, for each of his mental states, no matter when they occurred, God has direct awareness of the higher order fact of that mental state persisting now.[23]

If the A-theory is true, the best attempt to find a difference between God's direct awareness of what is happening now and his awareness of what happened at some time in the past will be to find it in the objects of his knowledge. A fact that now has the simple property of being temporally present in the first case does not have the property in the second. Right now God is directly aware of both of these cases. The difficult question is, how does he know which case obtains now? In short, there is nothing in his cognitive capabilities to pick out a unique, privileged temporal location.

If God's direct awareness can span time, it seems that the A-determinations drop out of his cognition altogether. God can know the B-determinations of facts and events, but he cannot locate a fact or an event in the A-series. This is not to say that the A-theory is false. It does imply that, if the A-theory is true, there are many facts that God cannot know by direct awareness.

Another way to look at these issues is that if direct awareness can span time, God's awareness of the past will be a little like time travel. What I mean is the following. If we could travel back to the year 1492, we would experience the events of 1492 as they were happening. The object of our direct visual perception would be the state of the world (or of part of the world) *as it was in 1492*.[24] The event of Columbus launching his ships, as far as our vantage point goes, would be occurring now. Suppose God is now directly aware of where my cup was yesterday. His awareness will take as its object the state of the world (or part of the world) *as it was yesterday*. But my cup was on the shelf yesterday. The higher order fact of *my cup being now on the shelf* persisted yesterday. This higher order fact will be present to God's consciousness today. It is as if God is now present yesterday and he takes in the state of my cup then. When God has direct awareness of the position my cup enjoyed yesterday, what is present to his consciousness is my cup being located on the shelf. The object of his cognition is not my cup *having been* located on the shelf *in the past*.

The similarity to time travel is further complicated by the fact that God has direct awareness of facts at every temporal location.[25] So it is not as if God's knowledge is like traveling in time to one specific temporal location. It is more like God is traveling to every temporal location simultaneously. God's direct awareness of every fact at every temporal location means that his access to every temporal location is exactly like his access to every other. God experiences the facts of 1927 in exactly the same way as he does the facts of 1999. Apart from their B-determinations, there does not seem to be any temporal difference between them as far as God's experience is concerned.

So right now, God has present to his consciousness the fact that my cup is now on the shelf and the fact that my cup is now on my table. Although these facts persist sequentially, God cannot locate them in time. He can know, to be sure, which of these facts occurs before the other and which occurs on April 10, 1999. What he cannot know is which of them is occurring now.

The A-theory of time does not provide a way to allow God to be in time and have direct awareness of all facts (past, present, and future). So whether the A-theory or the B-theory is true, if God's direct awareness can span time, God cannot experience a temporal now.

Two objections have been raised to my account.[26] First, if presentism is true, then there are no past facts (at least, in my sense of the word "fact"). Another way to express this idea is that the only past facts there are consist in true propositions that correspond to states of affairs that no longer obtain. The states of affairs that no longer obtain do not exist. The propositions exist, and God could have direct awareness of these true propositions. Any awareness God has of the past will be of this type. This account gives us the three items we are after. We could hold that direct awareness is not a time-spanning relation, God knows all past facts by direct awareness, and he could experience a temporal now. His temporal now would be constituted by his awareness of the present by his direct awareness of states of affairs and his awareness of the past by his direct awareness of propositions.

I do not think this objection succeeds, because I do not think God's knowledge of the past, in this case, would count as direct awareness. God's access to the concrete events and states of affairs of the past would be *through* or, at least, *mediated by* his direct awareness of certain abstract objects that correspond to those events. The object of God's knowledge of a past event is the event itself. God's knowledge of the proposition would be a means to this knowledge of the event. On the presentist story we are discussing, God has direct awareness of the abstract object but only indirect or mediated awareness of the concrete event. So if we want to explore the implications of God having direct awareness of all facts, we cannot hold that his knowledge of past facts is knowledge of propositions.[27]

The second objection is that there is a better way to construe higher order past facts than the way I construe them and that on this better construal my account will not succeed. I talked about my cup being on the table now as a higher order fact. My cup being on the shelf yesterday is a past higher order fact. We could say either that my cup *had* the property of *being on the shelf now* or that it *has* the property of *having been on the shelf in the past.* I went on to discuss the issue by talking in the former terms. My cup *had* the property of *being on the shelf now*.

The objection is that if we think of this fact in the latter way instead, we will see that my account will not succeed. If the past higher order fact is that my cup *has* the property of *having been on the shelf in the past*, then the A-theory can provide a solution to my argument. God can know all higher order facts and still sort them out in terms of which of them are happening now. Some higher order facts are past and some are present. God's direct awareness of the past fact takes as its object my cup's having been on the shelf in the past. God's awareness of the present fact takes as its object my cup being on the table now. God can read the A-properties directly off of these facts and locate himself in the present accordingly. God can, on this view, experience a temporal now.

I think that this objection fails to grasp what is involved in direct awareness of a past fact. When God directly knows a fact, the fact itself is present to God. It is present as it persists (or as it happens if it is an event). This point is why I liken direct awareness of past facts and events to time travel. God's awareness (if it can span time) takes as its object the world as it existed at that time. If God's direct awareness of the career of my coffee cup can span time, then his knowledge of the past fact that my cup was on the shelf yesterday takes as its object my cup being on the shelf as it happened. As this event happened, it was present. God's knowledge of the fact is as the fact happened.

What about the fact that my cup being on the shelf has the property of being past? Well, God knows this as well, but his knowledge of this fact will not help him locate himself in the now. Consider God's direct awareness of the world as it was yesterday. Among those facts is the fact of my cup being on the table today. Yesterday this fact was future. Today it is present. So God's direct awareness of all facts involves his awareness of my cup being on the shelf as future, as present, and as past.

So again, if God's direct awareness of facts can span time, God cannot experience a temporal now. If God cannot experience a temporal now, my argument succeeds. So the A-theory does not provide a way for a temporal God to have direct awareness of all facts (past, present, and future).

Rather than embracing this surprising conclusion, it is more reasonable to reject the assumption that direct awareness can span time. There are two ways this claim can be rejected. First, we can hold that God is temporal but that he only knows temporally present facts by direct awareness.[28] On this view, we can grasp how God knows the A-properties of facts and how God can experience a temporal now. At any given time God knows all facts. Only some facts, however, are known by direct awareness. These are the facts that are now occurring. God knows all past and future facts by some other mode of knowledge. Perhaps his knowledge of past and future facts is through belief in propositions that correspond to the facts. His knowledge of present facts could be through direct awareness. His experience of the temporal now is constituted partly by the difference in the mode of his knowledge.

The second way we can reject the view that direct awareness can span time is to hold that God is atemporal. In this case, he can have direct awareness of all facts regardless of their temporal locations. Since there are some reasons to think that God knows everything by direct awareness, this strengthens the case for divine atemporality.

Many philosophers, I must concede, will prefer the former approach to the latter. One reason I think this option will be more popular is that most philosophers have thought a good deal more about God's relation to time than they have about the mode of God's knowledge. Changing our minds about the mode of God's knowledge involves a smaller adjustment to our views than revising our position about whether God is in time.

As more work is done about the mode of God's knowledge, more philosophers will become convinced that God's knowledge is in virtue of direct awareness of facts. In turn, more philosophers will adust their views about God's relation to time. More will become convinced that God is atemporal. I have shown that we have good reason to believe that direct awareness cannot span time. As we have seen, this argument goes through whether the B-theory or the A-theory is true. So if God is temporal, he can know by direct awareness only those facts which now persist. If he knows *all* facts (past, present, and future) by direct awareness, he must be atemporal.

Notes

I would like to thank Sam Levey, Sandra Visser, David Woodruff, and William Alston for help on earlier versions of this chapter. I would also like to thank Ed Wierenga, Dean Zimmerman, Andrew Cortens, and Sandra Visser for comments and discussion on a near ancestor of the final version.

1. William Hasker, *God, Time, and Knowledge* (Ithaca: Cornell University Press, 1989), 146.

2. William P. Alston, "Does God Have Beliefs?" in Alston, *Divine Nature and Human Language: Essays in Philosophical Theology* (Ithaca: Cornell University Press, 1989), 178–93.

3. Ibid., 187.

4. For more on this, see ibid.

5. By "a fact" I do not mean a true proposition. Rather, I mean an object having a property or standing in some relation. On this account, some facts, such as my cup's being red, are concrete and temporal. Some philosophers prefer to call this an event. I will continue to use the term "fact" in keeping with Alston's use of "fact."

6. Alston discusses these three grades in "The Perception of God," *Philosophical Topics* 16 (Fall 1988); 23–52, and in *Perceiving God: The Epistemology of Religious Experience* (Ithaca: Cornell University Press, 1991), 20–28.

7. Alston, "Perception of God," 30.

8. Alston develops both of these reasons in "Does God Have Beliefs?"

9. Ibid., 190.

10. For earlier discussion of this argument, see my "Atemporality and the Mode of Divine Knowledge," *International Journal for the Philosophy of Religion* 34 (1993), 171–80, and "Leftow on Direct Awareness and Atemporality," *Sophia* 34, no. 2 (1995), 30–37.

11. Thomas Nagel, "What Is It Like to Be a Bat?" *Philosophical Review* 83 (1974), 435–50.

12. Ibid., 442.

13. See C. B. Martin and Max Deutscher, "Remembering," *Philosophical Review* 75 (1966), 161–96.

14. This line of reasoning was suggested by Bill Alston.

15. Thomas F. Tracy, *God, Action, and Embodiment* (Grand Rapids: Eerdmans, 1984), 89.

16. Of course, if God's direct action *can* span time, then my main point goes through more easily. God's experience of the temporal now cannot be grounded in his ability to act directly only on the present.

17. A third alternative is that the difference may be in the object of God's experience. Some facts have the simple property of persisting now, and others do not. This alternative is specific to the A-theory of time and will be discussed in the next section.

18. I would like to thank Ed Wierenga for detailed comments on this argument.

19. Dean Zimmerman pointed this position out to me.

20. For an exceptionally clear explanation of the A and B theories of time, see Samuel Levey, "Remarks on Time," unpublished paper. For a discussion of the classical B-theory and the response by A-theorists, see the introduction to sec. 2 of Richard M. Gale, ed., *The Philosophy of Time* (London: Macmillan, 1968), 65–86, and the first three papers in Robin Le Poidevin and Murray MacBeath, eds., *Philosophy of Time* (Oxford: Oxford University Press, 1993). For the distinction between the old and the new B-theories, see Nathan Oaklander and Quentin Smith, eds., *The New Theory of Time* (New Haven: Yale University Press, 1994), and Quentin Smith, *Language and Time* (New York: Oxford University Press, 1993).

21. This is, of course, assuming we remain in the same reference frame. An event which is earlier than another event in one frame of reference may be simultaneous with it in another. The temporal order of events in any single reference frame does not change.

22. See Oaklander and Smith, *The New Theory of Time.*

23. Actually, God has direct awareness of all of the higher order facts involving first order facts, events, and his own mental states. For example, for any of his thoughts, he is aware of his thinking the thought persisting in the future, persisting in the present, and persisting in the past. These are different higher order facts involving his thinking but, at any given time, God has direct awareness of all of them.

24. This is allowing that there is a slight temporal gap in cases of direct sensory perception due to the time it takes the light to travel from the object to the eyes.

25. This point was brought out in discussion by Sandra Visser.

26. These objections were raised by Dean Zimmerman and vigorously discussed by Dean, Andrew Cortens, and Sandra Visser.

27. It may be that the position that God has direct awareness of all facts is incompatible with presentism. I think I have shown that a temporal God cannot have direct awareness of all facts whether or not presentism is the case. If God is atemporal, much of the motivation for presentism is undermined. It is another question whether presentism rules out an atemporal God. Many philosophers, including several represented in this anthology, think so.

28. This is Bill Hasker's view. See Hasker, "Yes, God Has Beliefs!" *Religious Studies* 24 (1988) 385–94, Hasker, *God, Time, and Knowledge,* ch. 9, and Hasker, "The Absence of a Timeless God," ch. 9 in this volume.

9

The Absence of a Timeless God

WILLIAM HASKER

That God is eternal is a common confession of believers in the biblical God. But how the divine eternity is to be understood is very much in question. The predominant theological tradition, deriving from Augustine and Boethius, has understood eternity as timelessness, so that the contrast between time and eternity is the contrast between changeable reality and absolute changelessness. But there is a minority tradition—which among contemporaries is perhaps no longer a minority—that understands eternity as everlastingness, so that the contrast is rather between that which is temporally bounded, having a distinct beginning and perhaps also an ending, and that which is boundless, without beginning or end.[1]

The burden of the present essay is that a certain way of understanding divine timelessness is in the end incoherent. The incoherence arises, however, only if one holds also that the biblical God is also *present* to his creation in a unique and intimate fashion. In order to avoid the incoherence, one must acknowledge that God is *not* thus present but is rather absent from the world. It is controversial whether this consequence should be accepted. If one finds it unacceptable, one should conclude that the timeless God is "absent" in yet another sense—that there is no timeless God, that the Creator, Sustainer, and Redeemer of the universe is the God who is everlasting.

The essay proceeds in several stages. First, there is a brief exposition of divine timelessness, emphasizing the particular aspects of the doctrine that are crucial for the present discussion. Then the argument is presented to show that a timeless God cannot be present—in particular, that a timeless God cannot have "immediate knowledge" of the created world. This is followed by a discussion of several different attempts, by adherents of timelessness, to show that the argument fails and that a timeless God can indeed be present in the sense that the argument denies. In the course of responding to these objections, we shall consider additional reasons why the aspects of the doctrine of timelessness that generate the problem are essential to that doctrine and cannot well be abandoned while retaining timelessness itself.

The Doctrine of Divine Timelessness

The classic definition of divine timelessness was given by Boethius: "Eternity therefore is the complete possession all at once of illimitable life."[2] Also of note is the following quotation from Augustine:

> Nor dost Thou by time, precede time: else shouldest Thou not precede all times. But Thou precedest all things past, by the sublimity of an ever-present eternity; and surpassest all future because they are future, and when they come, they shall be past; but Thou art the Same, and Thy years fail not. . . . Thy years are one day; and Thy day is not daily, but To-day, seeing Thy To-day gives not place unto to-morrow, for neither doth it replace yesterday. Thy To-day, is Eternity.[3]

The central idea is stunningly simple: whereas we temporal creatures experience our lives spread out in time, moment by moment, the eternal God experiences the whole of time *all at once*, so that nothing of the world's life is "past and gone," and nothing of it is "yet to come"; rather, all is enjoyed at once in the divine Eternal Present.

Such thoughts, while intuitively appealing, raise a great many questions and call out for a more systematic exposition. No modern rendition of the doctrine of timelessness is uncontroversial, but the two that are most frequently cited are credited to Eleonore Stump and Norman Kretzmann and to Brian Leftow.[4] It has been questioned whether a God that is timeless in the sense of the doctrine can be a *living* God, and whether he can be an agent in the world or can know what transpires in the temporal world. The expositions cited make a good case that a timeless God can do all of these things, and while the matter remains controversial we shall assume for present purposes that the replies to these objections are successful.

One aspect of the traditional doctrine deserves special emphasis here. According to Anselm it is improper, strictly speaking, to assign any location in the temporal continuum to God: "You were not, therefore, yesterday, nor will you be tomorrow, but yesterday and today and tomorrow you *are*. Indeed you exist neither yesterday nor today nor tomorrow but are absolutely outside all time."[5] This implies that while God knows temporal realities, his knowledge of them is not in time, and while God performs actions that have temporal consequences, the acts themselves are not temporal. We shall refer to this principle of Anselm's, which holds that God neither exists, nor acts, nor knows in time, as "Anselm's Barrier." The point is well summarized by Delmas Lewis:

> Thus God, if eternal, bears no temporal relations to any object or event whatever. It cannot be said that God exists *now*, for this would assign him a position in the temporal series, which he cannot have. Strictly speaking, then, it cannot be said that God *did* exist in the past or *will* exist in the future, because he does not exist pastly or futurely: he simply exists in the timeless mode of existence peculiar to an eternal thing.[6]

It needs to be said, however, that in spite of this Anselm did hold that God is in a certain sense present to temporal realities, and they to him. How this is so, is something we shall be exploring in due course.

Another feature which characterizes many versions of the doctrine of divine timelessness is adherence to *libertarian free will*. This adherence is not universal, of course, but it has characterized many in the eternalist tradition and is clearly the majority view among contemporary proponents of timelessness. It is well known that Boethius introduced a solution to the problem of foreknowledge and free will based on timelessness: God does not *fore*know temporal events, but *knows* them in the Eternal Present, and this, it is claimed, creates no more problems for free will than does our own knowledge of events which occur in our temporal present. It may be that divine timelessness has seldom been adopted merely as a solution to the foreknowledge problem. Nevertheless, timelessness would clearly lose a good deal of its appeal for many if it did not lend itself to a solution of this problem.

There is another doctrine which, like libertarian freedom, is not strictly a part of the doctrine of timelessness but is nevertheless associated with it in the thought of many contemporaries. This is the teaching that God in eternity has *immediate knowledge* of everything that transpires in time. This view has been forcefully stated by William Alston in his article "Does God Have Beliefs?" In support of a negative answer to this question, Alston points out that the analysis of knowledge as justified true belief (+ . . .), usually taken as a given by contemporary philosophers, stands in contrast with a historical tradition in which knowledge is understood as *immediate awareness*, which is quite a different psychological state than belief. On this traditional view, "Knowledge is not a state that could be just what it is intrinsically without the actual existence of the object; it has no intrinsic character over and above the presence of that object to consciousness. . . . Whereas belief that *p* is, by its very nature, a state that can be just what it is whether or not there is any such fact that *p*."[7] Alston recognizes that this account will cover at most only a small fraction of human knowledge. It is difficult, in fact, to find any convincing examples of such knowledge, other than knowledge of one's own present psychological states. He says, "We reject the intuitive account for human knowledge, not because we suppose ourselves to have something better, but because it represents too high an aspiration for our condition."[8] But it is precisely the ideal character of intuitive knowledge which, while it renders such knowledge for the most part humanly unattainable, also recommends this as the best and most adequate conception of divine knowledge:

> Immediate awareness of facts is the highest form of knowledge just because it is a direct and foolproof way of mirroring the reality to be known. There is no potentially distorting medium in the way, no possibly unreliable witnesses, no fallible signs or indications. The fact known is "bodily" present in the knowledge. The state of knowledge is constituted by the presence of the fact known. This is the ideal way of "registering" a fact and assimilating it into the subject's system of cognition and action guidance. Hence this is the best way to think of God's knowledge. Since God is absolutely perfect, cognitively as well as otherwise, His knowledge will be of this most perfect form.[9]

Recent experience has shown that many philosophers find Alston's conception appealing and wish to incorporate it into their own views of divine knowledge. However, there is in the medieval tradition a contrary view, one which, so to speak, minimizes rather than maximizes the intimacy of God's cognitive contact with his creation. This preference is supported by the traditional doctrine of divine impassibility, which rejects any dependence of God on creatures such as would be involved in his having creaturely states of affairs as literal components of his cognitive states. According to Thomas Aquinas, for example, "He sees himself through His essence; and He sees other things not in themselves, but in Himself: inasmuch as His essence contains the similitude of things other than Himself."[10] He also says, "Now those things which are other than God are understood by God, inasmuch as the essence of God contains their images as above explained."[11] Yet again, "Now the species of the divine intellect, which is God's essence, suffices to manifest all things."[12] On any reasonable reading, it would seem that Aquinas is speaking here of some sort of *inner representation* of temporal things in the divine intellect rather than of a literal immediate presence of temporal things to God.[13] The thinking behind such a view is nicely summarized by Anthony Kenny: "The Psalmist asked, 'Is the inventor of the ear unable to hear? The creator of the eye unable to see?' These rhetorical questions have been answered by Christian theologians with a firm, 'Yes, he is unable.'"[14] It is the main burden of this essay that supporters of divine timelessness may be forced, willy-nilly, to embrace this Thomistic conception of divine knowledge rather than Alston's.[15]

The Objection: Timeless Intuitive Knowledge Is Incoherent

The time has now come to present the basic argument of this essay, to the effect that the conception of divine intuitive timeless knowledge of temporal realities is incoherent. Previously I have stated the argument as follows:

> Just how is it . . . that temporal events are directly present to God? Temporal events exist in time as the medium of temporal succession, so it would seem that a being which experiences them directly must itself exist in time and experience temporal succession—but of course, this is just what a timeless being cannot do. What the tradition has said about this is that temporal beings *also* exist in eternity and *as such* are present to God. But how is *this* possible? In God's timeless eternity, *nothing* exists in temporal succession, so how can temporal events and processes, whose very essence involves temporal succession, exist *there*? If they do so exist, does that mean we are mistaken in thinking them essentially temporal?
>
> The same argument can be put in a slightly different way. Let us assume that some temporal reality is literally immediately present to a timeless God. But of course temporal realities are different from moment to moment, whereas a timeless God *cannot* experience things differently at different moments; in the life of such a being, there *are no* different moments. So we may ask, *which* momentary aspect or "temporal cross-section" of the temporal entity is present to God? The answer, of course, must be that *all* of the temporal aspects of the entity are present—*literally* present—to God, not successively but *simultaneously*. But for an entity to have a number of apparently temporally successive aspects present simultaneously is precisely what it is for that entity to be timeless rather than temporal. So if an apparently temporal entity is literally immediately present to a timeless God, that entity *really* is timeless rather than temporal.[16]

It will be convenient to have the argument before us in a formalized version, as follows:[17]

1. If God is directly aware of a thing, that thing is metaphysically present to God. (Premise)
2. If God knows temporal beings, God knows all of their temporal stages. (Premise)
3. If God is directly aware of temporal beings, all of their temporal stages are metaphysically present to God. (From 1–2)
4. If the temporal stages of a temporal being are metaphysically present to God, they are present either sequentially or simultaneously. (Premise)
5. If God is timeless, nothing is present to God sequentially. (Premise)
6. If God is timeless and is directly aware of temporal beings, all their temporal stages are simultaneously metaphysically present to God. (From 3–5)
7. If the temporal stages of a temporal being are simultaneously metaphysically present to God, those stages exist simultaneously. (Premise)
8. The temporal stages of a temporal being do not exist simultaneously. (Premise)
9. If God is timeless, God is not directly aware of temporal beings. (From 6–8)

The expression "metaphysically present" may call for a bit of explanation. By this is simply meant that the thing in question is literally present, in its own proper being, as opposed to being merely "epistemically present." If we recall in vivid detail the last moments we spent with a loved one who is now far away, that person may be epistemically present to us but is certainly not metaphysically present, as she would be if she were sitting across the room from us.

This argument, of course, by no means settles the matter; instead, it provides a basis for further discussion. In the next three sections, we shall see how three leading proponents of timelessness respond to the argument and attempt to defeat it.

Leftow's Reply

Brian Leftow attributes to me the following argument:[18]

1. God is immediately aware of temporal facts.
2. For all x, if x is immediately aware of temporal facts, these are really present to x's awareness.
3. For all x, if temporal facts are really present to x's awareness, x is temporal.
4. Therefore God is temporal.

Leftow then proceeds to suggest a number of different interpretations of premise (2), and he argues in the case of each such interpretation either that the premise thus interpreted is unreasonably strong or else that it can be satisfied by a timeless God and the conclusion does not follow. The details of these different readings need not concern us, however. What is important is that Leftow understands me as arguing that God must have the sort of "direct realist" perception of temporal entities that we human beings have of ordinary physical goings-on. Thus, he suggests that

2a. For all x, if x is immediately aware of temporal facts, these facts obtain at the same time that x is aware of them

is not always true of human sense perception, because of the time lags involved in the latter. (This is particularly evident, of course, in the case of our perception of stars that may be millions of light-years away.) Unfortunately, Leftow considers only the argument as presented in *God, Time, and Knowledge* and does not refer to Alston's and my articles. If he had consulted those articles he would have realized (as is evident above) that ordinary human perception *does not* qualify as "immediate awareness" in the sense that is pertinent to our discussion.[19] In view of this, his arguments simply are not relevant to the case I was trying to make.

For further light on these matters, we can do no better than turn to the first chapter of Alston's *Perceiving God*, in which he distinguishes three grades of immediacy as follows:

(A) Absolute immediacy. One is aware of X but not through anything else, even a state of consciousness.

(B) Mediated immediacy (direct perception). One is aware of X through a state of consciousness that is distinguishable from X, and can be made an object of absolutely immediate awareness, but is not perceived.

(C) Mediate perception. One is aware of X through the awareness of another object of perception.[20]

To illustrate the concept of mediate perception, Alston suggests that "we can distinguish directly seeing someone from seeing her in a mirror or on television"; in the latter sort of case, we perceive the person by perceiving something else, namely, the mirror or the television set.[21] In ordinary (direct) sense perception, on the other hand, there is nothing else we perceive in order to perceive the object of the perception; that is what makes it direct. Nevertheless, this is still not the highest degree of immediacy. Ganssle makes the point nicely:

> When I see a table directly, there is no other *object* of vision through which I see the table. My perception of the table is mediated, however. It is mediated through my conscious state. My conscious state is not identical with the table but my perception of the table is mediated by it. I am aware of my conscious state but not as the object of my visual perception.
>
> In the case of absolute immediate awareness, my awareness of an object is not mediated by anything distinct from the object, even my conscious state. In human beings, perhaps only our awareness of our own conscious states is absolutely immediate. When I am aware that I feel tired, there is no other conscious state (apart from that of feeling tired) involved in my awareness.[22]

The claim that divine knowledge consists in intuitive awareness means, as Ganssle rightly says, that "God's direct intuitive awareness of facts must be absolutely immediate. This is because God will have the greatest mode of knowledge possible. Absolute immediacy is a 'greater' type of direct awareness than mediated immediacy."[23] But, one might ask, why is this so? Why must we think of God's knowledge as absolutely immediate? Why should we not be content to attribute to God knowledge which is "direct" in the sense in which ordinary sense perception is direct, as Leftow's discussion might suggest?

I do not think we should place primary emphasis here on the infallibility, the freedom from possible error, of absolute immediacy. After all, any mode of knowledge attributed to God will be said to be infallible. So infallibility is not a strong argument for any particular view of God's awareness of things, unless good reasons can be given why God would be fallible were he to lack this most favored type of awareness. I do not think the prospects for showing this are bright, so we must look elsewhere to argue for the "greatness" of absolute immediate awareness.

It seems to me there is a strong case for regarding directness or immediacy *in itself* as a ground of cognitive excellence. To whatever extent cognition is "indirect," there is something separating the knower from the known, something that (at least potentially) keeps the knower from apprehending the object fully in its true nature. Clearly this is the case with human sense perception; the limitations involved may be limitations we happily accept, but limitations they are nonetheless. We can hardly help but regard phenomenal color and sound as genuine properties of external objects, in spite of what science tells us about the matter. We are completely lacking in faculties that would enable us to directly apprehend the true nature of physical reality at the molecular, atomic, and subatomic levels. To be sure, direct apprehension of such matters would be of little use to us in everyday life; no doubt we should be thankful to Providence and/or evolution for equipping us with the kinds of faculties we possess. Nevertheless, there is an incompleteness here and even a certain distortion (though doubtless a benign distortion) which we should hesitate to attribute to the divine knower of all. In the case of God, we should ask: why should we suppose God would lack immediate awareness of the "mechanism" which mediates his perceptions? Why should we assume that anything at all is needed to mediate to God the awareness of the world he has created? It seems to me, then, that it is the attribution to God of anything less than absolute immediacy in his knowledge of creatures that requires justification.

Stump and Kretzmann's Reply

Eleonore Stump and Norman Kretzmann reply to my argument in their essay "Eternity, Awareness, and Action." This topic is only one of a number of objections to their views addressed there, but several things they say are pertinent. For one thing, they correct the impression, which I had mistakenly formed, that they would agree with the view of divine knowledge as representationalist rather than intuitive. And they modify their definition of "ET-simultaneity" in order to forestall such an impression.[24]

They also challenge me, in effect, with the parallel to my conclusion

9. If God is timeless, God is not directly aware of temporal beings

with regard to space, namely,

9'. If God is non-spatial, God is not directly aware of spatial beings.

Neither I nor any traditional theist, they say, could accept 9', but if we do not accept 9' we cannot reasonably accept 9 either.[25] This conclusion, however, is much too hasty.

For one thing, a traditional theist might very well accept 9'. Such a theist might hold, as I understand Aquinas to have held, that God's knowledge of creatures is not a matter of direct awareness at all. Or she might accept 9' but hold that God is not non-spatial in the same sense in which he is non-temporal. God is not spatially bounded or spatially divisible, of course, nor is he essentially spatial, all of which distinguishes him sharply from ordinary spatial things. But it might be true all the same that, as suggested by the traditional doctrine of divine omnipresence,[26] God is present in space in such a way as to make direct awareness of spatial beings possible.

For that matter, Stump and Kretzmann give no compelling reason why it would be unreasonable to accept 9 but reject 9'. I have, after all, given an *argument* in support of 9, and until they have shown that an equally strong argument (based on premises I accept or should accept) can be marshaled for 9', the mere fact that 9' is the analogue of 9 with respect to space is hardly compelling. This challenge, then, is not one that need give us pause.

It is not clear, from Stump and Kretzmann's discussion, which premise of my argument they would reject. This could hardly be expected of them, since the formalized argument was not available to them when they wrote their essay. One might reasonably ask of them, however, some kind of explanation of how it *is* possible, in their view, for an eternal God to be directly aware of temporal realities. They address this issue, among others, through a story they tell. The story concerns a one-dimensional world, Aleph, and a human being, Monica, who is aware of Aleph and its inhabitants and has established communication with one of them, called Nabal.[27] In a charming dialogue they show the difficulty Nabal has, operating within the constraints of his one-dimensional world, in understanding Monica's explanation of her three-dimensional existence. Many of the things she says seem to him flatly impossible. Nevertheless, we who read the story can see that everything she is saying is strictly coherent and readily intelligible. The message, then, is clear: what seems incomprehensible, and indeed impossible, to us temporal beings is nothing of the sort from the standpoint of the higher dimensionality inhabited by the Eternal Being, and it is short-sighted of us not to acknowledge this fact.

Stump and Kretzmann's story is both lucid and enjoyable, but it is not without its weaknesses. We must remember, of course, that Stump and Kretzmann, who tell us the story, are themselves "Alephians" in the wider context. And many of us have severe doubts as to whether the Being in question has communicated to us that he is timeless rather than temporal! But there is one disanalogy that effectively disqualifies the story from providing any sort of insight into the relationship between eternity and time. *Monica in the story fully shares in the single dimension that measures Nabal's existence.* The single linear dimension of the world Aleph is only one of the three dimensions of her world, to be sure, but it *is* a dimension of her world, and there is nothing in the story that even suggests any sort of problem concerning her access to Nabal's linear spatiality. But on the doctrine of timelessness, *God does not share in the temporal dimension of the created world*—to suppose that he does is to breach Anselm's Barrier. It is, of course, precisely this that creates the problem, and there is nothing analogous to it in the story of Nabal and Monica. The question of how it is possible for an eternal God to be directly aware of temporal realities remains without an answer.

Alston's Reply

The direct target of my argument, both in "Yes, God Has Beliefs!" and in the book session (see note 17) on *Divine Nature and Human Language*, was William Alston. It is not surprising, then, that Alston has replied to it in a more concerted and detailed fashion than either Leftow or Stump and Kretzmann. This reply was contained both in his response at the book session and in some correspondence we engaged in subsequently, and I shall take the liberty of relying on these unpublished materials in setting out his position. In his "Response to Critics" Alston raises questions about several of the premises of the formal argument. The best way to understand his objection to the argument, however, is to see him as denying

7. If the temporal stages of a temporal being are simultaneously metaphysically present to God, those stages exist simultaneously.

Alston holds, on the contrary, that "there is no reason to suppose that God cannot non-sequentially be directly aware of something that is itself temporally successive." Now, this is initially puzzling, given that the mode of the divine direct awareness is what Alston described in his essay "Does God Have Beliefs?" Recall his assertion there that "knowledge . . . has no intrinsic character over and above the presence of that object to consciousness." And in case we might wonder whether this is "presence" in the full, metaphysical sense, we have also his statement that "the fact known is 'bodily' present in the knowledge. The state of knowledge is constituted by the presence of the fact known." But then how can it be that the temporal stages of a temporal being are simultaneously metaphysically present to God, and yet those stages do not exist simultaneously?

An intriguing answer to this question emerged in the course of our correspondence on the matter. The key to Alston's view lies in his conception of what it takes for a subject (S) to be directly aware of a fact (X). He wrote, "As I see it, S's direct awareness of X is a relational fact, an irreducibly relational fact, one involving both S and X as relata. This fact 'stretches over' both relata, as one might say. This is what renders intuitive knowledge infallible. If one intuitively knows that p, one stands in the appropriate relation (direct awareness of) to the fact that p. If there were no such fact, one would, naturally, not stand in any such relation to it." Alston further states that, since he takes the concept of direct awareness as basic and unanalyzable, he considers it to be "up for grabs, conceptually speaking, what it takes for one or another subject to be directly aware of something."[28] In our subsequent correspondence, Alston adhered resolutely to his contention that direct awareness is unanalyzable and that, in view of this, one cannot derive from the notion of direct awareness any conclusions as to what else must be the case in order for direct awareness to be possible. For instance: I pointed out that even if direct awareness does not *consist of* any other facts it may nevertheless *entail* other facts, such as that the subject is conscious and non-comatose at the time. My thought was, of course, that if direct awareness can entail *these* facts then it might have other entailments as well, including some which might provide support for my argument. Alston agreed that for a subject to be directly aware entails that the subject is conscious. "But," he wrote, "that is not a different (concrete) state; it is simply a determinable fact, of which, in this case, SAF [S's being immediately aware of F] is the determinate."[29] He rejected my contention that SAF must involve some intrinsic state of S, in the sense in which "intrinsic" is contrasted with "relational." He wrote,

> Awareness . . . seems clearly to "make a difference" to the subject of that awareness. If I am aware of a book on the shelf, then I am *different* in some significant way from what I would be if I were not so aware. And you, along with many other thinkers, take it that this implies that I have some non-relational property I wouldn't have otherwise. But this is where we part company. I don't see why the way in which I am different by virtue of being aware of X can't be *just that I stand in that relation*. Why isn't that something that "makes a difference to the way I am"?[30]

At this point it becomes possible to see more clearly just what Alston's attitude is toward the formal argument presented above. He can assent to

(1) If God is directly aware of a thing, that thing is metaphysically present to God,

if what this means is simply that the thing God is aware of is one of the relata in the direct awareness relation. But this, in his view, does not license any further inference concerning the way in which God and the item in question are present to each other—for instance, that God and the things he is aware of must all be "simultaneously present," whether in time or in eternity. Given this understanding of direct awareness, Alston can very well deny

(7) If the temporal stages of a temporal being are simultaneously metaphysically present to God, those stages exist simultaneously,

and, along with it, the conclusion of my argument.

At this point, our discussion ground to a halt—inconclusively, as is so often the case with such discussions. I must confess that I could not see then, nor can I see now, how direct awareness can be a relational fact that does not imply any intrinsic, nonrelational fact about the subject. But my failure to comprehend this is not an argument against it, and with no additional arguments forthcoming, there was no way for the discussion to make further progress.

Now, however, I think it may be possible to find a way forward. And I suggest we begin with Alston's contention that it is conceptually possible (whether or not it is metaphysically possible) that a temporal God should be directly aware of past and future facts.[31] Greg Ganssle, a student of Alston's, has produced an intriguing argument on this topic.[32] Suppose, as Alston thinks possible, that his model of divine knowledge as immediate awareness can be applied to a God who is temporal. We then have the following assumptions:

1. God is temporal, so that there is one moment that is present for God.
2. God knows all facts, past, present, and future, by immediate awareness.
3. God's knowledge consists entirely of his immediate awareness of all facts.

From these assumptions it can be deduced that

4. God does not know which moment is present.

Why is this so? Let t_1, t_2, and t_3 be three moments of time, such that t_1 is past, t_2 present, and t_3 future. In what does God's knowledge that t_2 is present consist? God is immediately aware of all the facts concerning each of t_1, t_2, and t_3; so far, there is no difference between them. So something more has to be added to our description of the situation, in virtue of which God knows that it is t_2 that is present rather than t_1 or t_3. A natural thought is that there is some special property—call it "Nowness"—that belongs to t_2 in virtue of its being present. And God, being immediately aware of this property of Nowness, thereby knows that it is t_2 that is present and not t_1 or t_3.

Such a conclusion would be hasty. To be sure, it is quite true that t_2, and t_2 alone, possesses the property of Nowness at t_2. But it is equally true that t_1 possesses the property of Nowness *at* t_1, and t_3 possesses the property of Nowness at t_3. And God, who always enjoys immediate awareness of all the facts concerning each of these moments, is fully aware that each moment possesses Nowness in its own time. So symmetry is restored, and there is still nothing special about t_2 in virtue of which God could be said to know that t_2 is present *now*.

One may be tempted, at this point, to say something like "But it is t_2, and t_2 alone, that *really* possesses the property of Nowness *now*." Quite so. But of course, at t_1 it is t_1, and t_1 alone, that "really possesses the property of Nowness now." And similarly with t_3. Once again, symmetry is restored. And it is obvious that additional moves along the same line will get no further. Whatever property is ascribed to the present moment, each other moment will enjoy that same property in its own time, and God, being at all times immediately aware of all the properties of all moments, will not thereby have any way to distinguish the moment that is "presently present" from all the others that *have been* or *will be* present. God still doesn't know what time it is.

What conclusion should be drawn from this argument? The conclusion Ganssle wants to draw is that a temporal God can be immediately aware only of present facts. I have a great deal of sympathy with this conclusion, but it is not forced by the argument. This is because there is another way of avoiding the conclusion that God does not know which moment is present; namely, by relaxing the requirement of premise (3), which states that God's knowledge consists *entirely* of immediate awareness. Suppose that, in addition to his immediate awareness of all facts, God *judges* at t_2 that t_2 is now present. To be sure, it will likewise be true that at t_1 God *judges* that t_1 is now present, and that God judges at t_3 that t_3 is now present. And God at t_2 will be immediately aware of the fact that he makes these judgments at t_1 and t_3. But over and above these immediate awarenesses, God *actually judges* at t_2 that t_2 is now present, and he does *not* make this judgment at t_2 about t_1 or t_3. So it is by God's making this judgment that t_2 is distinguished from t_1 and t_3, and in making it God knows which moment is present.

I conclude, then, that Ganssle's argument does not quite accomplish what he intended, which was to show that a temporal God cannot have immediate awareness of past and future facts.[33] It does show, however, that, contrary to Alston's assertion, Alston's model of divine knowledge as consisting entirely of intuitive awareness cannot be applied to a temporal God. And that is no mean achievement!

Is it possible to go further, and establish directly that a temporal God cannot be immediately aware of past and future facts? I do have an argument to offer for this, but I cannot be sure that it will convince Alston or readers who may be inclined to agree with Alston. As so often happens, I can only lay out my argument and hope for the best. I once wrote about the intuitive knowledge of a temporal God as follows:

> Suppose, then, that God does experience temporal succession. Now we are free to suppose that temporal things *really are* immediately present to God. . . . To that extent, then, the intuitive theory of knowledge comes into its own.
>
> But not completely. Temporal entities may indeed be immediately, "bodily" present in God's awareness. But they can only be so present *at the times when they exist to be present!* But of course, God's knowledge of such realities cannot be so limited. It follows, then, that there *is* a requirement for an inner mental representation on God's part, to enable him to know what has passed away or (perhaps) what is yet to come.[34]

The reasoning here is straightforward: temporal entities can be immediately present in God's awareness only when they exist; past and future entities do not at present exist; therefore, past and future entities are not immediately present in God's awareness. The argument is clearly valid, but in order to make my argument convincing I must make the case that, in order for temporal entities to be the objects of immediate awareness by a temporal God, it is not enough for them to exist *at some time or other*. Rather, they must exist *now*.

Look at it this way. An event can ground the truth of propositions in the present so long as it exists tenselessly;[35] the mode of its existence as past, present, or future is not relevant, except as specified by the particular proposition in question. But in order to exert causal influence in the present, the event must exist *now*. So ask yourself: which of these two situations—grounding the truth of a proposition, or exerting causal influence—is more closely similar to the event's existing "bodily" as part of God's present cognitive state?

The point can be developed further. We accept that past events can exert causal influence in the present, given that this influence is mediated by an appropriate causal chain. They cannot, however, be causally affected by what happens in the present. Future events, on the other hand, cannot affect what is going on now, but they can be causally affected by events in the present—again, when this influence is mediated by an appropriate causal chain. Now as we "shorten" the causal chain in each case, we bring the past and future events closer; eventually, we bring them into the "immediate past" and the "immediate future." If the causal chains connecting these events to the present disappear entirely, then in order to have either causes or effects in the present they must themselves *be* temporally present—they must not only exist, but exist *now*.

But now, suppose we proclaim that divine cognition is a matter of "absolutely immediate" awareness of its objects—that the objects are, as Alston has said, "bodily present" in the knowledge. What then? Are we now to say that existence in the present is no longer required of the objects—that existence *at some time or other* is sufficient? Are we to conclude that when the ultimate grade of immediacy is reached these objects can be "bodily present" in God's present knowledge even though they ceased to exist long ago, or will never come into existence until some remote future time? And why would we say something as bizarre as that? Surely, God's immediate awareness of temporal events is awareness of them *as actually occurring*, not of them as *having occurred* or as *going to occur*. (That would be more like a "ghostly presence" than a "bodily presence"!)

More could be said along these lines, but it is time to bring this part of our discussion to a close. Readers who are inclined to be receptive to my ideas are probably already convinced, whereas those who are determined to resist would continue to do so whatever more might be said. In any case, it is time to return to the main theme of this essay. These last few pages may have seemed a diversion, pursuing the notion of intuitive knowledge by a temporal God when our proper subject is the intuitive knowledge of a timeless God. But if you have been convinced by Ganssle and me that a temporal God cannot have intuitive knowledge of facts at times other than the present, a fairly direct refutation of Alston's main position becomes available.

Assume that there is a timeless God who has immediate awareness of all objects and events in time. Now take an event, E, and a time at which E occurs, say our old friend t_2, and ask yourself this question: given that God is immediately aware of E, *when* does this immediate awareness of E occur? The only possible answer is that it occurs at t_2. (Recall Alston's remark that the relational fact " 'stretches over' both relata.") One might be tempted to say that the act of awareness occurs in eternity, and it is only its *object*, E, that exists at t_2. But this is ruled out by Alston's insistence that the relational fact is basic and unanalyzable, an insistence that is incompatible with the notion that the fact can be divided into parts, one existing at one time and another at another. What we must say, rather, is that the relation exists *both* in eternity and at t_2; it stretches over the ontological space between them. But this conclusion is a momentous one. We have now been forced to assign to one of God's cognitive acts a location on the temporal continuum: Anselm's Barrier has been breached.[36]

Here is another question: *what else* is God aware of at t_2, in addition to E? Here again, only one answer is possible: Everything. It is out of the question that the timeless God knows one thing at one time and another thing at another time. On the contrary, he knows at all times whatever he knows at any time. If we say this, however, we have in effect sacrificed the advantage that was supposed to attach to divine timelessness with regard to the problem of foreknowledge and free will. That advantage, it will be remembered, came because God's timeless knowledge does not exist in the *past*, and therefore cannot be used to ground the premise of an argument based on the "necessity of the past." But on the view now being considered, God's knowledge *does* exist in the past, and the Boethian solution to the foreknowledge problem must be rejected.

But there is more. On the view being considered, God is immediately acquainted at t_2 with X, which occurs at t_1, and with Y, which occurs at t_3, as well as with E. Or so it would seem. But *at t_2 X and Y do not exist to be known*. Or rather, to speak more moderately, they exist only tenselessly—which is to say, they exist only in the mode of *having once existed*, or of *going someday to exist*. But such objects are not, cannot be, the relata in a relation of direct awareness. That relation may, as Alston suggests, be able to span ontological gaps of various kinds. But one gap we cannot ask it to span is the gap between existence and non-existence—or rather, between existence and no-longer-existence, or existence and not-yet-existence.

The argument of the last three paragraphs can be summarized as follows:

1. If God has timeless immediate awareness of temporal objects, that awareness occurs at the time when those temporal objects exist.
2. At all times God is aware of everything that he is aware of at any time. Therefore,
3. If God has timeless immediate awareness of temporal objects, God has this awareness at times when the objects do not yet exist or no longer exist. But,
4. God does not have immediate awareness of temporal objects at times when those objects do not exist. Therefore,
5. God does not have timeless immediate awareness of temporal objects.

Unless some way can be found to avoid this argument, the prospects for timeless divine immediate awareness are grim.

A Medieval Solution

For an eternalist who has been stymied by the argument so far, it is still too soon to capitulate. Help is available; indeed it has been available for a long time.[37] The objection to Alston's view of divine intuitive knowledge, both for a temporal God and for a timeless God, is that the objects of that knowledge exist to be known only at a particular time, whereas "immediate awareness" requires their actual existence whenever the awareness occurs. But is it so clear that they do *not* exist except for a brief duration? Anselm thought not; he wrote:

> For within eternity a thing has no past or future but only a present; yet, without inconsistency, in the dimension of time this thing was and will be. . . . However, although within eternity there is only a present, nonetheless it is not the temporal present, as is ours, but is an eternal present in which the whole of time is contained. For, indeed, just as present time encompasses every place and whatever is in any place, so in the eternal present the whole of time is encompassed at once, as well as whatever occurs at any time. . . . For eternity has its own "simultaneity" wherein exist all things that occur at the same time and place and that occur at different times and places.[38]

As Delmas Lewis points out, this passage is decidedly metaphysical in tone and clearly asserts the real, objective existence of time and its contents in the eternal present. Note in particular the analogy Anselm develops: just as items existing at many different *places* coexist in the same *time,* so items from many different *times* coexist in the one *eternity*. In order for the analogy to work, it must be the case that, just as items in different parts of space are on a par with each other with regard to existence, so items from past, present, and future must be on a part with regard to existence. The real existence of past and future events (though not, of course, their existence *in the temporal present*) is strongly affirmed.

Lewis gives evidence that the same view occurs both in Boethius and in Aquinas.[39] Such a view immediately resolves the problem posed in the previous section. The first premise,

1. If God has timeless immediate awareness of temporal objects, that awareness occurs at the time when those temporal objects exist,

is seen to be dubious because it assumes that temporal objects exist only for a brief period. *In time*, to be sure, their existence is so limited, but they also possess an existence in eternity that knows no temporal bounds. And step (4) of the argument,

4. God does not have immediate awareness of temporal objects at times when those objects do not exist,

is simply false, for though there are indeed times during which the objects do not *temporally* exist, those same objects exist in eternity and are thereby available for God's immediate knowledge. And finally, this view enables the eternalist to defeat our initial argument by rejecting premise (8):

8. The temporal stages of a temporal being do not exist simultaneously.

For while the various stages do not exist simultaneously *in time*, it is also true, as Anselm says, that eternity has its own simultaneity, and in eternity all temporal things whatsoever coexist and are available for God's knowledge.

There is yet another benefit that can be derived from "Anselm's Solution," as we may call it: it permits Anselm's Barrier, which forbids the assigning of temporal location to God and God's acts, to be repaired and put back in place. On Alston's view, the Barrier was breached because the divine intuitive awareness of temporal realities had to "stretch over" the gulf between eternity and time, thus assigning a temporal location to the act of awareness. But now we see that the temporal realities are available to God *in eternity*, and there is no need of a relatum in time for the awareness relation. And this is a major gain for the theory of timelessness.

It seems, then, that divine timelessness has nicely survived the challenges that it has encountered. But like other solutions to philosophical problems, this one comes with a price tag—and the price is not cheap. For one thing, there is a sort of metaphysical extravagance involved in the idea that all the familiar things and events of everyday life do not really pass away, as we seem to see them do, but instead persist eternally—that they do so *quite literally*, and not merely as "thoughts in the mind of God." It is one thing to attribute timeless existence to God himself—not that such an attribution can be lightly made, but God is in any case so far beyond us that we may well hesitate to set limits to what could be true of him. But that the chalk-stub that I wore down on the chalk-board and eventually threw away—that this chalk-stub *literally exists in eternity,* and indeed still exists at *every one* of the innumerable temporal stages of its existence—this is a mind-boggling thought, and one might well wonder whether eternal existence is not being dispensed a bit too freely.

Anselm's Solution also causes a certain strategic embarrassment for the friends of timelessness. In virtually any exposition of the doctrine, one will find early on some disparaging remarks about the evanescence of temporal existence; these remarks are intended to motivate the recognition of the need to attribute to God a superior, eternal mode of existence. According to Boethius, for example, "There is nothing placed in time which can embrace the whole extent of its life equally. It does not yet grasp tomorrow, and it has already lost yesterday. Even in today's life you do not live more than in the moving and transitory moment."[40] For a contemporary example, take the following from Stump and Kretzmann:

> The existence of a typical existent temporal entity, such as a human being, is spread over years of the past, through the present, and into years of the future; but the past is not, the future is not, and the present must be understood as no time at all, a durationless instant, a mere point at which the past is continuous with the future. Such radically evanescent existence cannot be the foundation of existence.[41]

But from Anselm's Solution we learn that the existence of temporal things is misdescribed in these passages. Far from being "radically evanescent," the existence of my chalk-stub is as enduring as that of the Andromeda galaxy. Boethius's "moving and transitory moment" possesses an existence as eternal as that of God himself. The motivationally important contrast between temporal beings and the Eternal Being has been undercut. To be sure, it could still be said that temporal beings like ourselves are *not aware* of their own eternal existence—but this is not what Boethius, or Stump and Kretzmann, are saying, and it is doubtful that their words would be equally effective, were the Anselmian doctrine put in place of what they actually do say. But if Anselm's Solution is going to be invoked to save timelessness from logical collapse, the friends of timelessness need to be true to that solution in the rhetoric they use to commend their doctrine.

The metaphysics of Anselm's Solution causes yet other difficulties. Specifically, it is fatal to libertarian free will. This is doubly ironic because Anselm, like Boethius before him, was concerned to preserve free will and saw in divine timelessness a means of doing so. But whatever benefits the doctrine of timelessness might otherwise have had on that score are negated by Anselm's Solution. That solution destroys libertarian freedom by negating the existence of "alternative possibilities" to the actions that are taken. Remember that the future events of the world, including your and my future actions, *always exist* in the timeless eternity of God. In Anselm's words:

> I am not saying that my action tomorrow at no time exists; I am merely denying that it exists today, even though it always exists in eternity. And when we deny that something which is past or future in the temporal order is past or future in eternity, we do not maintain that that which is past or future does not in any way exist in eternity; instead, we are simply saying that what exists there unceasingly in its eternal-present mode does not exist there in the past or future mode.[42]

In that eternity, nothing can be changed and nothing will be changed. There is no more possibility that I will act differently than the action which exists, in all its concrete actuality, in the divine eternity—there is no more, indeed there is less, possibility that this will happen than that I will fly to the moon tomorrow.

I do not expect that this conclusion will be readily accepted. Why, it will be asked, does the fact that my actions are already present in the divine eternity entail that those acts are causally determined? The answer is that it does not. But causal determination is not the issue. Causal determinism is inimical to freedom because it eliminates alternative possibilities for the action that is taken. But alternative possibilities can be eliminated in other ways as well, not least by the fact that the act to be done already exists—and exists, let us recall, in its full concrete particularity—in eternity.

We will also be told, no doubt, of the dreaded Frankfurt Counterexamples, which show that, libertarians or not, we must be prepared to give up the principle of alternative possibilities. These counterexamples have my vote as being the most overrated philosophical objection of recent times. The argument cannot be spelled out here, so let me just state that these counterexamples fail entirely to refute the principle of alternative possibilities as this principle is employed by libertarians.[43]

Finally, we will be reminded that divine foreknowledge is thought to be a problem for free will because the divine knowledge (or belief) exists in the *past*—but divine timelessness, by removing God's knowledge from the past, also removes the problem. But once again, this misconceives the problem. Divine knowledge existing in the past is problematic for free will because the past is now fixed, and beyond anyone's power to make it otherwise. But as Marilyn Adams has observed, "if the necessity of the past stems from its ontological determinateness it would seem that timeless determinateness is just as problematic as past determinateness."[44] Previously I pointed out that divine timelessness can be reconciled with libertarian freedom only if the following proposition is true: *there are things that God timelessly believes which are such that it is in my power, now, to bring it about that God does not timelessly believe those things*.[45] Given Anselm's Solution, we may add another necessary condition: *there are future actions of my own which timelessly exist in the divine eternity which are such that it is in my power, now, to bring about that those actions do not exist in eternity*. Does anyone seriously believe that these requirements are satisfied?

Another Objection

The final objection to be considered against divine timelessness is independent of those considered so far, though some of our previous discussion may be helpful in motivating it. It does not depend on immediate awareness as the mode of divine knowledge, nor on the espousal of libertarian free will. It has the additional benefit that the assumptions it makes about the nature of time are strictly minimal. I believe that this objection, if successful, is decisive against all versions of divine timelessness. But the difficulty is perhaps somewhat subtle, and it has certainly proved easy to overlook. I myself, in earlier writings, mistakenly dismissed the objection as ineffective. So this section serves the purpose, among others, of the confession and purging of old errors.

Recall once again Ganssle's objection to Alston's theory of divine intuitive knowledge as applied to a temporal God. It was shown that God, having immediate awareness of all facts concerning all moments of time, has nothing whereby to distinguish the present moment, the one that is actually occurring, from others. God does not know what time it is. What is needed to break the impasse is that God's awareness should contain some additional feature—my suggestion was a judgment that "such-and-such a moment is now present"—that would serve to pick out the present moment and distinguish it from others.

Next, try the thought experiment of making the same assumptions about divine immediate awareness, with the subject of this awareness a timeless God. Now what is required in order for God to be able to identify the present moment? A very little reflection shows that no answer is possible. For any feature of God's mental life which served to pick out the present moment would have to alter from moment to moment—at one time, the feature picked out the moment in which George Washington crossed the Delaware River, while more recently it picked out the time of President Clinton's 1999 State of the Union address. But in eternity *nothing* can alter; everything is eternally the same. It simply is not possible, then, that a timeless God should know what time it is, or what is happening now. This much is absolutely clear, and there should be no dispute about it. Where the dispute will begin is about the significance of this undeniable fact.

It was stated that the objection makes only minimal assumptions about the nature of time. It could, however, be avoided if someone were to hold that our experience of the passage of time is wholly illusory—that there simply is no such thing as a present moment. But in spite of Parmenides, such a view seems simply unintelligible. To deny that I experience sequence and change in my experience is entirely on a par with denying my own existence, and neither of these views can be commended as lying on the path of wisdom. Even if all the physical, "objective" facts in the world, facts that we designate as past, present, and future—even if all such facts are ontologically exactly on a par and neither come into being nor pass away, there remains the fact that *I experience* these facts in a certain order, an order that involves succession and change. If this is denied, the denial (which will of necessity involve succession and change) is self-refuting.[46]

An eternal God cannot identify the present moment, cannot know what is happening right now. (On the "minimalist" view described in the previous paragraph, God cannot know what *I am experiencing* right now.) This much is clear; the question that must be answered is whether this amounts to real, substantive ignorance on God's part, ignorance which is incompatible with the perfect knowledge we wish to attribute to God. One philosopher who has answered this question in the affirmative is Arthur Prior, who wrote:

> For example, God could not, on the view I am considering, know that the 1960 final examinations at Manchester are now over; for this isn't something that he or anyone could know timelessly, because it just isn't true timelessly. It's true now, but it wasn't true a year ago (I write this on 29th August 1960) and so far as I can see all that can be said on this subject timelessly is that the finishing-date of the 1960 final examinations is an earlier one than 29th August, and this is *not* the thing we know when we know that those examinations are over. I cannot think of any better way of showing this than one I've used before, namely, the argument that what we know when we know that the 1960 final examinations are over can't be just a timeless relation between dates because this isn't the thing we're *pleased* about when we're pleased that the examinations are over.[47]

In contrast with this, I argued that this does *not* amount to substantive ignorance on God's part. The arguments I used now seem to me to contain a mixture of truth and error. I wrote, quite correctly, that "It is not of course a question of its being 29th August *for God*, but of whether God can know the thing that Prior knows, when Prior knows it is the 29th of August." In order to answer this, we must consider the nature of Prior's own knowledge:

On 28th August he does not yet know that "It is now 29th August," for this is not yet true. Nor does he know this on 30th August, for it is then no longer true. Does it follow that there is some item of knowledge that Prior has on the 29th but lacks on the 28th and 30th? This does not seem very plausible. When Prior said, on 28th August, "Tomorrow is 29th August," or when he said, on 30th August, "Yesterday was 29th August," it seems reasonable to suppose that he expressed thereby the *same item of knowledge* that he expressed on the 29th with "It is now 29th August."

I then went on to suggest that God could express this same item of knowledge by saying (or timelessly affirming), "When Prior says, 'It is now 29th August,' and . . . [assume other information added so as to identify the occasion uniquely], it is *then* 29th August."[48]

Now, God could certainly affirm such a proposition as this one. Would God thereby express the same item of knowledge as is possessed by Prior when he says, "It is now 29th August"? It seems reasonable to agree that this is so, *if* we concur that the same item of knowledge is also expressed by Prior himself when he said, on the 28th, "Tomorrow is 29th August." We would then have a situation in which the same temporal fact is described in different ways from different temporal or eternal perspectives; the expression is different, but the substantive item of knowledge remains constant.

But *does* Prior know the same thing on the 28th and the 30th that he knows on the 29th? It now seems clear to me that he does not. To be sure, from a certain standpoint the difference in information-content is minimal. Any normal person who knew on the 28th that "tomorrow is 29th August" would, barring exceptional circumstances, also know on the 29th that "today is 29th August" and on the 30th that "yesterday was 29th August." Nevertheless, Prior knows something perfectly definite and concrete on the 29th that he does not know on the 28th or the 30th. He knows that the world's history, and especially his own personal history, have reached a certain point, a point marked on the calendar by the date 29th August, and perhaps more significantly by the fact that the examinations are now over. It is this knowledge that enables Prior to take advantage of opportunities, and respond to challenges, that may be unique to that particular day. The world's having reached that particular stage is a perfectly definite and concrete fact. That this fact cannot be expressed from the standpoint of a timeless eternity reveals the inherent limitations of such a standpoint; it does not cast doubt on the reality and significance of the fact itself.

This assessment is confirmed in an interesting way by a passage in Stump and Kretzmann's article "Eternity, Awareness, and Action." They ask us to

imagine two parallel horizontal lines, the upper one representing eternity and the lower, time; and let presentness be represented by light. Then from a temporal viewpoint the temporal present is represented by a dot of light moving steadily along the lower line, which is in this way lighted successively, while the eternal present is represented by the upper line's being entirely lighted at once. . . . On the other hand, . . . from the eternal being's point of view the entire time line is lighted at once. From an eternal viewpoint, every present time is present, co-occurrent with the infinite whole of the eternal present.[49]

This picture illustrates in an elegant fashion the eternalist conception of the relation between time and eternity. And it seems altogether fitting that there should be "more light" from the eternal standpoint than is visible from the temporal standpoint. But the picture also illustrates the point made in the argument given above: on the time-line, there is a single point that is *now*, the actual present, the point which the world's history has reached. This fact, however, is necessarily invisible from the eternal perspective. There are facts that are well known to human beings of which the eternal God knows nothing.[50]

One might think that, providing the argument given here succeeds, all theists would agree in rejecting divine timelessness. Brian Leftow, however, argues that this need not be so:

> If two claims conflict, one should drop the claim with less backing. The friends of MTOA [the metaphysical timelessness-omniscience argument] evidently think that "God is timeless" has less to back it than "God is omniscient" does. The late-classical and medieval philosophers who developed and defended the doctrine of God's eternity might not agree. These writers took this doctrine to be a consequence of a well-supported overarching theory of God's perfection. So if faced by the inconsistency MTOA alleges, these philosophers might not reject divine timelessness. They might instead reject the claim that an omniscient being knows all truths or facts . . . or simply drop the claim that God is omniscient.[51]

Personally, I would be very surprised if any contemporary theistic philosopher were to deliberately and knowingly adopt the sort of position suggested (but not adopted) by Leftow.[52] But it is rash to speculate about what one's colleagues may or may not do; instead, I must commend the issue to my readers for their own consideration and decision.[53]

Summary and Conclusions

We began by setting out briefly the doctrine of divine timelessness, with its companion doctrines of libertarian free will and divine intuitive knowledge. We then presented the argument that divine timeless intuitive knowledge is incoherent. We saw that neither Leftow nor Stump and Kretzmann have effective answers to the argument. Alston, on the other hand, initially seemed able to block the argument by his contention that the immediate awareness relation is basic and unanalyzable. But this view led to our locating the divine act of immediate awareness on the temporal continuum, which in turn created the paradox that God is immediately aware of temporal realities at times when they do not exist to be the objects of his awareness. Anselm avoids this by holding that temporal objects and events literally coexist with God in eternity. But this leads to still further difficulties; in particular, it has devastating consequences for libertarian free will.

All of these objections depend on the assumption that God has intuitive knowledge of the world; they can be avoided by accepting the Thomistic representationalist model of divine knowledge. A further objection, however, cannot be avoided in this way. It was shown that God, because he is timeless, cannot have knowledge of present-tense facts; he cannot know what is happening now. It was argued that this is a significant cognitive deficiency on God's part, one that arguably is inconsistent with the divine perfection. The fact that temporal facts are "invisible" from a timeless perspective in no way calls into question the genuineness of such facts; rather, it reveals an inherent limitation of that perspective.

I believe these considerations add up to a compelling case for rejecting the doctrine of timelessness. It is with considerable relief—indeed, with a powerful sense of liberation—that we turn from the labyrinth of timelessness to the biblical conception of a God who has freely created our spatiotemporal world and involves himself actively in its history. God calls things into existence, he orders and arranges them, he speaks to his rational creatures and involves himself intimately in their lives. He issues promises and commands and suffers grief when the promises are spurned and the commandments broken. He frames a plan for the redemption of his broken world and executes that plan at great cost to himself. He places before us his children the goal of a Kingdom that shall have no end.

Why, one might ask, would a timeless God have created a world that is so deeply historical? We have not merely the constant, repetitive cycles that might well be, as Plato surmised, a "moving image of eternity." The cycles exist, but overlying them is the theme of a unique, unrepeatable historical process—a process, in the case of human beings, that is fraught with sin and tragedy, but one that all the same is guided to its ultimate goal by a wisdom that is able to overcome all obstacles. God pleads, promises, cajoles, rejoices at the sheep that returns safely to the fold, and thunders judgment at those who cause a little child to lose her way. The ontological aloofness so prized by Parmenides, Plato, and Plotinus is altogether lacking from the biblical picture of God.

The climax of the story, of course, is the incarnation of God in Jesus Christ. This event is astonishing on any reading, but taken together with the doctrine of timelessness it comes close to being incoherent. On that account, *the eternal divine Logos is not aware of the events of "his" incarnate Life as they occur!* All of human history finds its focus in that incarnate Life—but for a timeless knower, the distinction of "before" and "after" the Messiah, so crucial for all the writers of the New Testament, has no significance whatsoever. On the Anselmian view the crucifixion, the siege of Troy, the betrayal by Judas, the day of Pentecost, and the Nazi holocaust *are all occurring now* in the eternity of God; nothing new ever happens, and nothing old, however worthy of being forgotten, is left behind. This, I submit, is profoundly inconsistent with the thoroughly temporal and historical outlook that permeates the biblical text. We may well be thankful that the biblical story has served as a corrective, and has prevented many who embraced timelessness from suffering the distortion of the life of faith that could have resulted from the doctrine. Surely, however, the time has now come for a decisive break from a doctrine that has in it so much of pagan speculation and so little that is biblical and Christian. There are signs, indeed, that such a break has already begun.

Notes

My thanks to William Alston, William Craig, Greg Ganssle, Del Kiernan-Lewis, and Brian Leftow for helpful comments on an earlier version of this essay.

1. There is a third view, which seems to have gained some ground recently, which holds that God is timeless "prior to creation" and temporal thereafter. This view has been termed "accidental temporalism" by Thomas Senor and "an Ockhamistic model of divine eternity" by William Craig. (Neither of them explicitly adopts the view; see Senor, "Divine Temporality and Creation *ex Nihilo*," *Faith and Philosophy* 10, no. 1 [January 1993], 87–89, and Craig, "Divine Timelessness and Necessary Existence," *International Philosophical Quarterly* 37, no. 2 [June 1997], 223.) The idea is roughly this: "prior to creation," God is absolutely unchanging and therefore (contingently) timeless; in the absence of all change, there are no events and therefore no time. With the act of creation God initiates time and the flow of events, and thereafter he participates in the temporal process. This view deserves careful consideration, which I hope to provide on another occasion. But on the topics covered in this essay it does not differ from the view that God is temporally everlasting, so it will not receive separate discussion here.

2. Boethius, *The Consolation of Philosophy* 5. 6, in *The Theological Treatises and the Consolation of Philosophy*, ed. H. F. Stewart et al. (Cambridge: Harvard University Press, 1973).

3. *The Confessions of St. Augustine*, tr. Edward B. Pusey (New York: Random House, 1949), bk. 11, pp. 252–53.

4. Eleonore Stump and Norman Kretzmann, "Eternity," *Journal of Philosophy* 78 (1981), 429–58; Stump and Kretzmann, "Eternity, Awareness, and Action," *Faith and Philosophy* 9, no. 4 (October 1992), 463–82; Brian Leftow, *Time and Eternity* (Ithaca: Cornell University Press, 1989). Occasional references are also made here to my article "Concerning the Intelligibility of 'God Is Timeless,'" *New Scholasticism* 57 (1983), 170–95, and to ch. 8 of *God, Time, and Knowledge* (Ithaca: Cornell University Press, 1989). Both of these selections defend the intelligibility of divine timelessness, but not necessarily its truth.

5. *St. Anselm's Proslogion*, tr. M. J. Charlesworth (Notre Dame: University of Notre Dame Press, 1965), 141.

6. Delmas Lewis (now Kiernan-Lewis), "Eternity, Time, and Tenselessness," *Faith and Philosophy* 5, no. 1 (January 1988), 75.

7. William P. Alston, "Does God Have Beliefs?" *Religious Studies* 22 (1986), 287–306; quotation, 295. This article is reprinted, in a somewhat abbreviated and otherwise altered form, in Alston, *Divine Nature and Human Language* (Ithaca: Cornell University Press, 1989).

8. Ibid., 297.

9. Ibid., 297–98.

10. *Summa theologiae* 1a.14.6.

11. Ibid., reply obj. 2.

12. Ibid. 1a.24.14.

13. Admittedly, there are also in Aquinas passages which suggest a direct, quasi-perceptual sort of awareness of creatures on God's part. Eleonore Stump and Norman Kretzmann, in their essay "God's Knowledge and Its Causal Efficacy" (in *The Rationality of Belief and the Plurality of Faith*, ed. Thomas D. Senor [Ithaca: Cornell University Press, 1995], 94–124), argue that it is this latter conception which best expresses Aquinas's considered view, and that passages such as those cited above can be interpreted to harmonize with it. My inclination, for what it is worth, is to agree rather with Alfred J. Freddoso, who asserts, "St. Thomas never intends to suggest that God is a passive recipient of information about the created world. To the contrary, in many places he states quite unambiguously that the created world is known by God just as an artifact is known by the artisan who has fashioned it; and in equally many places he explicitly denies that created things are a cause of God's knowledge of them" (introduction to Molina, *On Divine Foreknowledge: Part 4 of the Concordia*, tr. with introduction by Alfred J. Freddoso [Ithaca: Cornell University Press, 1988], 7–8). It should be stated, however, that nothing in the substantive conclusions of this essay depends on this question of interpretation.

14. Anthony Kenny, *The God of the Philosophers* (Oxford: Oxford University Press, 1979), 29.

15. In the version of "Does God Have Beliefs?" contained in *Divine Nature and Human Language*, Alston says, "I suggest that we might make progress in getting some sense of what nonpropositional divine knowledge might be like, by switching from the Thomistic view that God knows the world through knowing His own essence to the idea that God directly intuits the world" (181). This sentence is not present in the original version of the article.

16. "Yes, God Has Beliefs!" *Religious Studies* 24 (1988), 385–94; quotation, 389. A similar argument is developed in my *God, Time, and Knowledge*, 162–70. Delmas Lewis reached similar conclusions in his paper "Eternity, Time, and Tenselessness," *Faith and Philosophy* 5, no. 1 (January 1988); our conclusions were arrived at quite independently.

17. This version of the argument occurs in "Eternity and William Alston," presented at a book session on Alston's *Divine Nature and Human Language* at the American Philosophical Association, Pacific Division, in 1991.

18. See Brian Leftow, "Timelessness and Divine Experience," *Sophia* 30 (1991), 43–53. Leftow's version is based on Hasker, *God, Time, and Knowledge*, 169, 194.

19. This point is correctly noted by Gregory E. Ganssle, "Leftow on Direct Awareness and Atemporality," *Sophia* 34, no. 2 (1995), 30–37.

20. William P. Alston, *Perceiving God: The Epistemology of Religious Experience* (Ithaca: Cornell University Press, 1991), 21–22.

21. Ibid., 21.

22. Ganssle, "Leftow on Direct Awareness and Atemporality," 34–35.

23. Ibid., 35.

24. Stump and Kretzmann, "Eternity, Awareness, and Action," 475–78.

25. Ibid., 476.

26. "Omnipresence is an attribute of God, the infinite and first cause of all, who is actually present in all existing places and things" ("Omnipotence," *The New Catholic Encyclopedia*).

27. Stump and Kretzmann, "Eternity, Awareness, and Action," 471–73.

28. Quotations are from a letter dated April 9, 1991.

29. Letter of May 14, 1991.

30. Letter of May 29, 1991 (emphasis in original).

31. This is affirmed in the letter of May 2, 1991. And compare the following from Alston, "Does God Have Beliefs?" 297: "He could be aware of all facts at every moment, or aware of all facts timelessly if that is the mode of his existence."

32. See Gregory Eugene Ganssle, "Atemporality and the Mode of Divine Knowledge," Ph.D. diss., Syracuse University, 1995, ch. 5. A less developed form of the argument may be found in Ganssle, "Atemporality and the Mode of Divine Knowledge," *International Journal for the Philosophy of Religion* 34 (1993), 171–80.

33. Ganssle, however, says that "it seems that God would have to know which moment is present in order to make the judgment. So God can, at t_2, judge that is present only if God knows at t_2 that t_2 is present" (private communication). Now in my argument, as given above, I simply assume that God makes this judgment. If, however, as Ganssle claims, God's knowledge that t_2 is present must be logically prior to his judgment that this is so, then my objection to his argument fails, and the argument itself may succeed—a result which I would welcome.

34. Hasker, "Yes, God Has Beliefs!" 391.

35. I take it that "exists (tenselessly)" is equivalent to "existed, or exists now, or will exist"; thus "tenseless existence" is purely a semantic notion with no metaphysical implications.

36. As we might expect, Alston wishes to avoid this conclusion. He writes, "You say that on my view 'the relation exists *both* in eternity and at t_2.' And I suppose that is right, assuming one tries to locate relations. But I don't take that to imply that the *knowledge* in question exists at

both places. The knowledge in question is God's knowledge of an event, and that is located where God is. . . . Intuitive knowledge, as I construe it, necessarily involves consciousness. And even though the consciousness involved is essentially *of* something else, rather than being a self-enclosed state, still only one of the relata has that consciousness. And that is where the knowledge the subject has by virtue of being that relatum in this relationship is located" (private correspondence). Alston recognizes, however, that in order to take this line he must give up his claim that "the fact known is 'bodily' present in the knowledge." It seems to me that this amounts to a major alteration of Alston's original doctrine of divine intuitive knowledge. On the present account, we have an object existing in time, but no divine knowledge or consciousness of that object in time; in eternity, on the other hand, there is consciousness and knowledge, but no object. It is difficult to see how, on this account, the relational fact (viz., immediate awareness) is basic and unanalyzable, as Alston insists that it is.

37. In this section I am heavily indebted to Lewis, "Eternity, Time, and Tenselessness."

38. *The Harmony of the Foreknowledge, the Predestination, and the Grace of God with Free Choice,* ch. 5, in ed. and tr. *Anselm of Canterbury,* ed. and tr. Jasper Hopkins and Herbert Richardson 4 vols. (New York: Edwin Mellen, 1974–76), 2:189.

39. The French Thomist Reginald Garrigou-La Grange says, "According to Thomists and many other theologians . . . future things are eternally present in God not only objectively and intentionally, but physically and really." *The One God: A Commentary on the First Part of St. Thomas's Theological Summa* (St. Louis: Herder, 1936), 456; quoted by Lewis, 85, n. 21.

40. Boethius, *The Consolation of Philosophy* 5.6.

41. Stump and Kretzmann, "Eternity," 444.

42. Anselm, *The Harmony of the Foreknowledge,* 190.

43. For a detailed counterrefutation, see ch. 4 of my *The Emergent Self* (Ithaca: Cornell University Press, 1999).

44. Marilyn Adams, *William Ockham* (Notre Dame: University of Notre Dame Press, 1987), 1135.

45. Hasker, *God, Time, and Knowledge,* 176.

46. Compare the following from Peter Geach: "Even if a man's impressions as to which realities are past, present, and future are illusory, the fact that he has in that case different and uncombinable illusions shows that at least his illusions are really successive—that they are not all present together, but now one illusion is present and now another. . . . But in that case temporal succession itself cannot be an illusion, since the so-called illusion of successiveness is already a real succession of experience; just as misery cannot be an illusion, because to be under the illusion of misery would be real misery" (Geach, *God and the Soul* [London: Routledge and Kegan Paul, 1969], 92).

47. A. N. Prior, "The Formalities of Omniscience," in Prior, *Papers on Time and Tense* (Oxford: Oxford University Press, 1968), 29.

48. Quotations are from Hasker, *God, Time, and Knowledge,* 160–61.

49. Stump and Kretzmann, "Eternity, Awareness, and Action," 475.

50. Some remarks of Brian Leftow's are illuminating in this connection: "The reason a timeless God does not know the essentially tensed fact that (T) is that in His framework of reference, eternity, *this is not a fact at all.* (T), again, is the claim that a proper subset S of the set of temporal events, consisting of a, b, c, etc., now has present-actuality. In eternity this claim is false" (Leftow, *Time and Eternity,* 333). The issue, however, is not whether the events in S have present-actuality (in a way that other events do not have it) *in eternity*; clearly they do not. The difficulty is that these events do have present-actuality *in time,* but the fact that this is so is one of which a timeless being can take no cognizance.

51. Ibid., 321.

52. Leftow himself considers MTOA to be unsuccessful; so far as I can tell, the reasons he gives have no bearing on the argument as presented here. See ibid., 327–35.

53. But is my own view not subject to a similar challenge? I have endorsed the following definition of omniscience:

> God is omniscient $=_{df}$ It is impossible that God should at any time believe what is false, or fail to know any true proposition such that his knowing that proposition at that time is logically possible (*God, Time, and Knowledge,* 187).

Modifying the definition to fit the doctrine of timelessness, we have:

> God is omniscient $=_{df}$ It is impossible that God should believe what is false, or fail to know any true proposition such that his knowing that proposition timelessly is logically possible.

Now, it has been argued here that it is logically impossible for a timeless God to know such present-tense propositions as "It is now 29th August." But if so, God's failure to know such propositions does not count against his being omniscient according to the definition. One might reply that, whatever may be the case according to a certain definition, God is *cognitively imperfect* if he does not know present-tense propositions. But of course, my position has been challenged on the ground that God is cognitively imperfect if he does not know with certainty truths about the contingent future. My response is that truths about the contingent future are inherently unknowable, whereas present-tense propositions are well known to all of us ordinary humans. But the final decision about such matters must in the end be a matter of judgment.

Part Four

GOD'S RELATION
TO THE WORLD

10

The Problem of Dialogue

PAUL HELM

"Calvinists," says William Hasker, "seem not to devote a great deal of theological reflection to the topic of divine-human dialogue."[1] In fact, non-Calvinists seem not to either, though William Alston has begin the good work with his "Divine-Human Dialogue and the Nature of God."[2] It is the aim of this essay to take up Alston's baton, though not to attempt to wear his colors.[3] The chief aim of what follows is to show that the very idea of dialogue with God, on various alternative and widely held views about the nature of God, whether Calvinist or non-Calvinist, is somewhat problematic, more problematic, perhaps, than Alston reveals.

As Alston points out, there are a number of reasons why dialogue matters.[4] One reason that it matters for those in the Judeo-Christian tradition is that it has a central place in the Bible; in prayer, for example, and in the scriptural accounts of God's relation with Israel. It is fundamental to our understanding of certain parts of the Bible; the book of Jonah, for example, and the redemption of Israel from Egypt, and the death of Hezekiah. In these parts of the Bible, as in others, it is integral to what happens that God holds a conversation with some human being, either directly or through some appointed intermediary. He says things to which his interlocutor replies, to which he in turn replies, and so on. The drama of the passages largely consists in the unfolding of these conversations, together with their implications.

What exactly *is* dialogue? As Alston understands it, there is a dialogue when two people are in conversation and there is mutual openness. What the necessary and sufficient conditions of such mutual openness are is not clear, but one important necessary condition is something like the following; when, say, A asks B a question A must not have programmed B's answer to that question. "A and B are not in genuine communication if A is exercising an ability to determine B's moves in accordance with A's intentions. It is this intentional effective control of one participant by the other that I am claiming to rule out as genuine communication."[5] Alston cites cases of ventriloquism, a computer programmed to make replies, and hypnotism as being cases where this necessary condition is not met.

What challenges are there to this view of dialogue as applied to God and man? Prima facie, there are three: from divine omniscience, from omnidetermination, and from timelessness. The cases of ventriloquism, computer programming, and hypnotism are sufficient to make it clear to Alston that omnidetermination, the view that God has "decided every detail of His creation, including all the putatively free choices and actions of human beings,"[6] and dialogue, genuine dialogue, are incompatible. So there cannot be genuine dialogue if one of the dialogue partners is an omnideterminer.[7]

What according to Alston does *not* rule out genuine dialogue is A's knowledge of B's response before speaking to him, for there may be genuine dialogue between partners one of whom is omniscient. With regard to infallible foreknowledge of the sort that we may suppose God has, Alston says that "we could learn to live with divine foreknowledge if we had to."[8] That is, our awareness of God's infallible foreknowledge would not undermine genuine dialogue, if we were to suppose ourselves to be in dialogue with God. As we shall see, however, it turns out to be the fact of omniscience which does present difficulties to genuine dialogue.

With regard to timelessness, Alston wishes to say that the timelessness of God confers an advantage over the idea of God in time maintaining the idea of divine-human dialogue. This claim is somewhat paradoxical in view of the fact that very many philosophers have claimed the precise opposite, that genuine human-divine dialogue requires that God is in time.[9] Alston claims that one advantage of supposing that God is timeless is that it removes the idea of God knowing "in advance" what his interlocutors will utter, and therefore ameliorates the strain that omniscience places on the mutuality that is essential to dialogue.[10] Infallible knowledge in advance *would* compromise the mutuality that is an essential condition of genuine dialogue.[11] But because divine omniscience is timeless omniscience, it does not qualify the mutuality between the partners that is necessary for the creation of genuine dialogue. It is this claim that I shall principally be concerned with in what follows.

Let us look at two proposed solutions to *the problem of dialogue,* as I shall call it. I shall argue that Alston's solution is no more or less appropriate for omnidetermination than it is for omniscience, while the second, a Swinburnian solution, is satisfactory in preserving divine human dialogue but at the cost of an "attenuated" sense of divine omniscience. I shall end by proposing a third solution in which dialogue is compatible with unattenuated divine omniscience (whether timeless or not) and also with what Alston calls divine omnidetermination.

Alston's Solution

Alston explores the conditions that are necessary for genuine dialogue between God and humankind to take place. As we have noted, what in particular interests him is whether dialogue is essentially temporal in character and hence out of bounds for the God of classical theism, who is both timeless and omniscient. Alston concludes that it is not.[12] A timeless, omniscient God can be a dialogue partner. He can perform acts, including conversational acts, and he can even make replies in time, as part of a genuine dialogue, provided that such a God is not omnidetermining.

In parentheses, there is reason to think that Alston's characterization of God as an omnideterminer would not be sufficiently nuanced for Aquinas and the others whom he cites as omnideterminers. I fancy that they would distinguish between decreeing and determining, between those events God wills to permit and those which he actually brings about. There are action-types which God can decree but not determine, if by determine one means causally effect; e.g., acts done out of an evil intention; whereas God can and may determine "all holy desires, all good counsels and all just works"[13] by causally effecting them. God is a timeless omnideterminer if he, from all eternity, causally determines every event including every secondary cause; he is a timeless partial determiner if in addition to those acts which he determines there is at least one act which, though he foreordains, he does not causally determine.

I shall argue that Alston has not made out a convincing case that divine-human dialogue is possible on the assumption that divine omniscience is timeless while not possible on the assumption of omnidetermination such as he attributed to Aquinas. His case fails because his argument does not discriminate sufficiently between dialogue with God as a timeless omnideterminer and dialogue with God as a timeless partial determiner.[14] I shall go on to argue that it is, in fact, divine omniscience, whether timeless or temporal, which qualifies the sort of dialogue that Alston envisages, if anything does. Determination, whether omnidetermination or partial determination, adds nothing significant. If timeless omniscience and timeless omnidetermination are in the same boat as regards dialogue, then a fortiori timeless omnidecreeing is in that boat as well.

First, then, let us consider Alston's claim that timelessness removes the difficulty over knowledge "in advance," and so removes one significant constraint on mutual openness. Conversational dialogue obviously entails the possibility of making a reply to whatever has been said. Can a timeless God say things in time, and make a reply to what has been said to him in time? An obvious objection is that if God is timeless he cannot reply to some speech-event in time, for replies must necessarily occur later than what is replied to. Or so it may seem. But Alston argues that it is a contingent feature of replies that they occur later than that to which they are replies. Something would equally well be a reply if it were contemporary with that to which it was a reply. While I do not think that Alston's solution to this objection is totally convincing, there are other ways of overcoming this particular difficulty.

Let us take as our example of dialogue the story of Hezekiah's sickness and recovery.[15] The Lord tells Hezekiah that he will die and then, in answer to a prayer from Hezekiah about this, promises his recovery. Here is a case not simply of God changing his mind, but of him changing his mind having implied that he will not change his mind. What are we to make of this? Can this be made consistent with what the Bible elsewhere says about God's immutability and steadfastness? If God is steadfast, how could God's first utterance, that Hezekiah will not recover, be sincere? For only if Hezekiah believes it to be sincere could it cause Hezekiah to pray for his own recovery. If God were simply *making as if* to bring about the death of Hezekiah, while all the while not intending it, and Hezekiah knew this, then there would be no reason for anyone, including Hezekiah himself, to pray for his recovery. And if Hezekiah was correct to believe this, then would not God be guilty of deception? But if God is sincere in what he says, does he not really change his mind when Hezekiah prays? And if he does change his mind, then is not God changeful, and so not timelessly omniscient?

Perhaps an answer to at least some of these questions can be gained if we ask: could the entire incident of Hezekiah and his recovery be encompassed within one indivisible divine intention, or must we resort to a temporal series of intentions formed as God reacts to successive circumstances?[16] There is reason to believe that we *can* talk about one indivisible intention, along the following lines.

The prophet's utterance "Hezekiah will not recover" can be understood as occurring within a framework of conditions or promises, and as having, under certain circumstances, the force of a warning or a threat. In understanding the utterance in this way, we may find help from an analogy. Under certain circumstances, the sentence of a judge in a court of law may be an appealable sentence: where, say, a court of appeal exists and leave to appeal against the sentence is granted. If the judge says to the convicted man, "You will serve ten years," he is sentencing him to a certain term of punishment. But in circumstances which are appealable, the convicted man will serve his full term only if any appeal that he may make against his sentence is unsuccessful. The judge's sentence, like the Lord's pronouncement about Hezekiah, may seem from its grammatical features to be final and unconditional. Yet its place within a particular legal framework—say, within a covenantal framework—makes it tacitly conditional, liable to be overturned through appeal. Given the framework of divine promises to answer prayer, the divinely authorized utterance "Hezekiah will not recover" may be regarded as tacitly conditional in character. In terms of the analogy that we have been using, God is both the sentencing judge and the appeal judge. So what God intends, the one unchanging intention, might be (rather cumbersomely) expressed as "that Hezekiah will recover from sickness having expressly indicated that Hezekiah will die if his recovery is not requested, knowing that as a matter of fact his recovery will be requested."

Provided we are prepared to place God's various utterances to Hezekiah (and any similar utterances) within a covenantal framework, then the language of change and variability applied to God can be rendered consistent with his unchangeableness, the unchangeableness of his covenantal promises. This approach is surely congenial with the biblical picture of God's relations with Israel and with wider humanity. What God says to Hezekiah is sincerely intended, but it is not irrevocable if Hezekiah prays for some other outcome, a prayer warranted by a covenantal framework such as that suggested.[17]

Let us suppose, then, that as far as the nature of dialogue is concerned, there is nothing odd about the notion of a timeless reply to an utterance in time. Could a timeless deity make such a reply? Alston divides this question into two.[18] The first question is: could an omnidetermining timeless deity, a God who decides every detail of his creation, reply to a question from Moses, say? And the second question is: could a timeless deity who is omniscient but not omnidetermining do so?

In answer to the first question Alston says that God's utterance could be expressed as a reply to Hezekiah, but not as a piece of genuine dialogue; for a genuine dialogue requires that the one who is replied to "stands over against" God as something independent of his will, something introduced into the situation by the initiative of another, something to which he has to adjust his conduct, something that requires a special ad hoc "response" on his part.[19] If it is sufficient for genuine dialogue that what Alston calls the *uttered as a reply* condition is present, this condition must include the requirement that what is responded to is, to some degree, independent of the utterer's will.[20]

What of the second case? Could a timeless, omniscient God, but a God who nevertheless does not decide every detail of his creation, enter into genuine dialogue? Alston claims that he could. Given that the divine response to a free human action could be simultaneous with that action, there is no bar to the awareness of each and every free act, along with the responses thereto, occupying the one eternal "now."[21]

Despite our earlier reservations, let us suppose that Alston is correct in this claim about simultaneity. Let us suppose that divine responses can be exactly simultaneous with free human requests uttered in time; that is, ET-simultaneous with those requests.[22] I shall argue that it seems that such a God, a timeless, omniscient, partly determining God, can no more or less fully enter into dialogue than a timeless omnidetermining God can. If omnidetermination rules out true dialogue, then the case of a timeless, omniscient, but not omnidetermining God rules this out as well. In attempting to argue for this conclusion, I shall make what I hope is a reasonable assumption, that the human participant in such dialogue as we are envisaging understands something of what it is for God to be timeless and omniscient, and believes that his divine interlocutor is both.

If what Alston says about timelessness and the possibility of dialogue is correct, then, assuming divine omniscience, to every piece of human dialogue with God there timelessly exists a specification of the divine reply. To every request made to God there timelessly exists in the mind of God both a specification of that request and a specification of the reply to be made to it; specifications in the form of belief in their respective propositional contents or of a direct apprehension of the relevant states of affairs. The reply does not exist *as a reply* until it is uttered, but the specification of the reply exists timelessly. So what the timeless omniscient deity does in entering into dialogue is not to formulate a reply upon receiving the request from his dialogue-partner but to utter in time what is timelessly prepared as a reply. He does not formulate a response upon being addressed; he simply makes available his timelessly ready response at the appropriate time.

In a situation in which the human participant in dialogue with God believes that God is timeless and omniscient, the human participant is entitled to believe that the specification of the proposition that he is about to conceive and to utter exists timelessly in the mind of God. God, being timelessly omniscient, knows the content of every human utterance past, present, and future. If God is timelessly omniscient, then he knows the content of what a human interlocutor is about to say, and of his own reply to what is to be said. So let us suppose that the human interlocutor is entitled to believe that such a specification timelessly exists in the mind of God. If he is entitled to believe this about the specification in the mind of God of one of his, the interlocutor's, future utterances, then presumably he is entitled to believe it about specifications in the divine mind of every such future utterance. If so, dialogue in such divine-human cases differs in fundamental respects from dialogue in human-human cases, for in the

212 God and Time

latter no one infallibly knows the content of the specification of the dialogue in advance. So I argue that a situation in which one of the partners A in dialogue has a timeless specification of the content of any utterance of his partner B in dialogue, and B knows this (though he may not himself yet know the content), fundamentally alters the character of any dialogue that may occur between A and B.

If I know what you are going to reply to my request, suppose as the result of possessing some telepathic power, and you know that I possess this power, then the usual point of such dialogue, to elicit information or consent, say, is lost or at least badly skewed. For I already have the information telling me whether or not you will consent. I have this information as a result of having been appropriately causally affected, via my telepathic powers, by certain brain states of you, my dialogue partner, brain states which are themselves causally sufficient for you saying such and such in dialogue with me.

Suppose that the person follows through the logical consequence of believing that there is such a timeless omniscient God, and does believe that specifications both of his request and of God's reply timelessly exist, known to God. We may suppose that such a person does not know what the specification of either the request or the reply is, but he justifiably believes that there is one. Then the fact that God knows this specification, and that his dialogue partner believes that there is such a specification, means that they each believe something which is not a normal condition of dialogue between people, on Alston's understanding of dialogue. For it is a normal condition of human dialogue, of its mutual "openness" between A and B, that not only does A not know what B will say until B formulates and utters his thought, but also that B does not believe that there exists a specification of what he will say known, as yet, to A alone before B enters into dialogue with A. If there were to be such a belief, and particularly if there were such a belief which is justified, then the mutual openness of the dialogue would be compromised. We are familiar, it is true, with cases where A knows B so well that he is able to anticipate how he will react. But, as Alston points out, such knowledge is highly fallible and incomplete.[23] If one supposed a human being with abnormal powers, such that he infallibly knew in advance what his interlocutor would say, then clearly Alston's conditions for dialogue would not be met.

So dialogue in the divine-human case contains the important feature that, in virtue of divine timeless omniscience, together with the assumption that the human interlocutor believes that God is timelessly omniscient, the human partner in the dialogue believes that God timelessly possesses a specification of both the request and of the reply. And this is sufficient to upset the mutuality which Alston seeks to preserve in divine-human dialogue.[24] For in virtue of his omniscience God timelessly possesses a specification of the request and of his reply to it, but his human interlocutor does not and cannot possess any such specification. Because the necessary mutuality is not present, the dialogue cannot be truly "open" dialogue, and so cannot be true dialogue at all, and so cannot serve to alleviate the strain that omniscience may be thought to place upon mutuality.[25]

In such circumstances the point of dialogue becomes unclear. Perhaps in entering into such dialogue, God wishes to put his human conversation partner through the motions, and certainly his partner will go through the motions, since his brain states are such that, other things being equal, they are causally sufficient for him making certain utterances. Perhaps there is value in doing so, as there is value in practicing drills of certain kinds. But whatever the rationale for dialogue, it is certain that God does not need it to take place in order to inform himself of the intentions of his human dialogue partner, for he is timelessly informed of these.

But is this argument not, in effect, the old objection about God knowing "in advance," the argument which Alston meets by postulating God's timeless existence? I do not think so, for even if God is timeless (and omniscient) the specification of the human interlocutor's response will nevertheless exist in the divine mind. It may be granted that if what is known by God is known timelessly it cannot be *already* known, or known *in advance* by God.[26] But this does not quite meet the point. For any item of the timeless omniscient participant's uttered dialogue has a timeless specification as its logically necessary and sufficient condition. It is God's timeless knowledge of his interlocutor's request and of his answer to that request which logically entails what he will utter as a reply to him, which is not to say that such knowledge causes the reply. (But is it not the truth of what God knows, and not the fact that he knows it, that is doing the work here? Again, no, because truth that is unknown does not constrain dialogue in any way.) The partner in dialogue is surely entitled to believe that God has such a specification in his mind. Moreover, because (as we are assuming) he does believe that God is both timeless and omniscient, he does in fact believe that God has the specification.

Whether or not this means that the reply is known by God *in advance* or *already* is neither here nor there. For the fact is that the human participant in the dialogue is entitled to believe that his forthcoming utterance is timelessly known to God and a fortiori that God knows it but does not come to know it as a result of him uttering it. (If he is not entitled to believe this, then what does God's timeless omniscience mean?) A corresponding belief such as this is not normally present in human dialogue; were it to be generally present it would, in Alston's view, radically change the character of that dialogue, for it would severely compromise its characteristic openness, its mutuality. Hence it would seem that timeless omniscience compromises openness, at least if the human interlocutor believes that God is omniscient.

However, even if the above argument *were* the old objection about God knowing in advance, this objection is capable of being given a stouter defense, I believe, than Alston allows for, even granted God's timelessness. It may be granted that God is not in time and though what he knows is dated, his knowledge is not.[27] Nevertheless, if God is capable of disclosing in time what he timelessly knows (as we are assuming he is), then what he timelessly knows he could have disclosed at any time. For instance, God could have uttered yesterday what he timelessly knows about tomorrow. Or he could have caused it to be written down on a scroll and deposited in a desert cave, say.[28]

Had he done so, the deposited scroll would have provided some veridical trace yesterday of God's timeless knowledge of tomorrow, and (had the inscription been made available, by being discovered by a shepherd boy playing in the cave, say) what God timelessly knows about tomorrow could have been known by some knower in time. And so under these circumstances what God timelessly knows can also be known in advance of the occurrence of what he timelessly knows. Whether this does or does not imply that God knows in advance what Hezekiah will do is an issue we need not further debate;[29] what is clear is that God could provide a specification of what Hezekiah will say in advance, and (for all we know to the contrary) he may have provided such a specification. Suppose that Joe is praying and suddenly begins to believe that God could have written the specification of their conversation on a scroll which is in a yet-to-be-discovered cave in the Middle East. Will not Joe think, and justifiably so, in the light of his new belief, that he is no longer involved in genuine dialogue with God, as Alston understands this?

So even if, as Alston argues, "a timeless God can be all-at-once simultaneous with every temporal state of affairs" and so "we can see that there is no logical impossibility in God's creating the world, 'hearing' Moses ask a question, and answering that question, all in the same timeless *now*,"[30] "dialogue" is going to contain an important condition that it does not have in what Alston regards as the standard human cases of dialogue.

One possible response to these arguments is to accept the consequence that in the case of dialogue between a timeless, omniscient, but not omnidetermining God and a human being who is to some degree independent of God's will, "dialogue" is somewhat stretched in meaning. But then if this is granted, and there can nevertheless be "dialogue" between a timeless omniscient God and a human interlocutor, why is it not possible to suppose that there can be "dialogue" (in this sense, or some similar stretched sense) between an omnidetermining timeless God and a human interlocutor? This would not be possible, of course, if divine omnidetermination is a case of ventriloquism, hypnotism, or computer programming; but then none of that noble company of omnideterminers cited by Alston (Augustine, Aquinas, Luther, and Calvin)[31] believed for one moment that ventriloquism or hypnotism was an adequate analogy of the relation between an omnidetermining (or omnidecreeing) God and his creation; nor, one suspects, would they have been any more attracted by the idea of computer programming. The point is: if "dialogue" is stretched in the case of a conversation between a timeless God and an individual in time, why may it not be more stretched in the case of an omnideterminer? Is not the difference between the two cases a difference of degree, raising no issue of principle?

Alston would reject the suggestion that "dialogue" might be stretched in meaning to embrace omnidetermination because in the omnidetermining case God "is not confronted with something to which He has to fashion a response,"[32] and this seems to be plausible. But it is no less plausible as a comment on omniscience per se. An omniscient God is not confronted with something to which he has to fashion a response. He timelessly knows what he is "confronted" with and timelessly "fashions" a response. The quotation marks indicate how stretched the notion of dialogue then becomes. What this reply may show, however, is not that dialogue of any kind is impossible between an omniscient omnidetermining God and a human interlocutor, but that no such dialogue can be fully mutual or symmetrical in character. But this cannot be a crucial objection, since as we have seen dialogue between parties one of whom is omniscient but not omnidetermining cannot be symmetrical either. If asymmetrical dialogue, dialogue thus stretched in meaning, is nevertheless true dialogue, and dialogue between partners one of whom is timelessly omniscient is dialogue stretched, but not to breaking point, why does it stretch to breaking point if one of the interlocutors is a timeless omnideterminer?

One of the things that this examination of Alston's argument may appear to suggest is that the meaning of "dialogue" in divine-human dialogue, whether God is supposed to be either timeless or temporal, provided that he is omniscient, differs in meaning, or is a different sort of dialogue, from what Alston supposes to be the meaning of "normal" interhuman dialogue. This is because such a God, timeless or not, is at least omniscient, and in normal human dialogue neither partner is omniscient.

But matters are not quite as straightforward as such a contrast between the "normal" and the "abnormal" suggests. For even granted the "normal" case of dialogue between human beings, if it is supposed that that dialogue is also known to God, even though he is not a participant in it, then the outcome of that dialogue is known to God, if God knows the future. The perfect mutuality of dialogue may be constrained not only by one of the partners controlling the dialogue, or by one of the partners knowing in advance the outcome of the dialogue, but by anyone, such as a spectator of the dialogue, knowing its outcome in advance, given that at least one of the partners believes this. Such belief is a constraint upon the symmetrical openness of dialogue, in that the dialogue cannot be perfectly open if its outcome is known even by a spectator. Dialogue would have lost some of the conditions of "normal" mutuality. We shall return to this point in the final part of the essay.

So what significantly constrains or controls the dialogue is at least one partner believing that the outcome is known either by himself or by the other partner in dialogue or by some spectator who could, in principle, broadcast what he knows. For then genuine openness is compromised. So perfectly mutual dialogue in the Alston sense appears to require not only two independent participants, neither of whom wholly controls the responses of the other, but also two independent participants, neither of whom knows in advance the decisions of the other and neither of whom believes that anyone else knows the outcome in advance. If the outcome is known—by one partner, or by God, or by someone else—then each partner is entitled to believe that the outcome is known, and what Alston regards as perfectly open dialogue disappears.

I conclude that Alston has not shown that dialogue between a timeless omniscient God and an independent human being is possible, while dialogue between an omnidetermining God and a human being is impossible. In other words, he is not warranted in concluding that "a timeless omniscient God can enter into genuine dialogue with human beings. But God has achieved this capacity by forgoing the complete determination of His creation."[33]

So we can say, by way of preliminary conclusion, that the mutuality of dialogue is qualified by the presence of omniscience. Mutuality may be more qualified by omnidetermination (or it may not), but it is certainly significantly qualified by omniscience, and omnidetermination, while qualifying it, may not rule it out.

Swinburne's Solution

Let us attempt to take matters a stage further by considering divine-human dialogue in a case in which God is in time. In *The Coherence of Theism*, Richard Swinburne holds that God, though omniscient, does not know the truth about those future states that are not physically necessitated by anything in the past.[34] This, a "Modified Account of Omniscience,"[35] does not depend upon the claims that such future states do not yet have a truth-value, but upon God's own choice to forfeit the knowledge of such truth, a choice made in the interests of preserving his own freedom and of granting freedom to others.[36] God is omniscient but only in an "attenuated" sense.

Let us suppose that Swinburne's is the correct account of the matter, that our understanding of divine omniscience ought indeed to be modified in these ways. And let us also suppose a dialogue between a person and this Swinburnian God (S-God). These individuals know that how their dialogue will eventuate has a truth-value, but they also know that in the interests of preserving their freedom S-God has decided not to know this truth beforehand.

So what the person in dialogue with S-God knows, as the two enter upon their dialogue, is that there now exists a true specification of the outcome of the dialogue, and of each of its phases, a specification that S-God could know were he so to choose, though were he so to choose then his own autonomy and human autonomy would vanish.[37] This fact provides a sufficient reason for God never so to choose. So neither the person concerned nor S-God with whom he is in dialogue in fact knows what this true specification is. But does not this knowledge, the knowledge that there could be such knowledge, also acts as a constraint upon their dialogue? For if the person knows that there exists a specification of the outcome of his dialogue with S-God, and of each step of the dialogue, how can the interaction between the two be genuinely open?

To this there is the following objection: that so long as each of the participants in the dialogue is ignorant of the specification of the outcome of the dialogue, neither is constrained in his action by the mere knowledge that there is such a specification. For how could such knowledge constrain? Such knowledge permits many outcomes, many outcomes are epistemically possible, and a fortiori it does not rule out planning, striving for, or working toward some particular outcome through dialogue.

So in the interests of preserving dialogue it is necessary to distinguish here between logical and epistemic possibility. If in this situation anything frees the participants from constraint it is their belief in the possibility of a range of outcomes; that for all they know when they enter into dialogue either a or b or c is the outcome of their dialogue, while the logical or metaphysical truth, on Swinburnian grounds, is that there is only one outcome, which S-God could know had he not freely forfeited that knowledge in the interests of preserving our own and others' autonomy.

This seems to me to be a satisfactory solution, but it is not the only possible solution. I shall propose a solution that does not depend on Swinburne's view of divine omniscience.

An Alternative Solution

I have argued that if one preserves the essentials of dialogue in the case where one partner is timelessly omniscient (in a non-attenuated sense), then one may do so also where one of the partners is a timeless omnideterminer. And we have just seen how a Swinburnian might preserve the mutuality of dialogue by postulating divine omniscience in an attenuated sense. If so, then our conclusion so far appears to entail that what preserves the genuineness of dialogue, if anything does, is what is epistemically possible for those in dialogue. But if such epistemic possibility is sufficient for the retention of the genuineness of the dialogue in a Swinburnian world, then it is also sufficient for its retention in the world envisaged by Alston. More to the point, it is also sufficient for genuine human dialogue with God if we suppose what few theists have in fact supposed, that God is an omniscient omnideterminer, provided such omnidetermination leaves intact a range of epistemic possibilities for the human partner (the one controlled) sufficient for free participation in the dialogue, whatever that range of possibilities needs to be. Certain states of affairs rule out epistemic possibility. For example, the determination of the omnideterminer could not be exercised by the physical compulsion or felt psychological constraint of the determined, for the presence of such compulsion or constraint would signal a reduction in the opportunities for choice and would correspondingly reduce the epistemic possibilities. And the stronger the compulsion or constraint, the fewer the epistemic possibilities. If I am being compelled to do X (and I know that I am being compelled) then not doing X cannot be among my epistemic possibilities.

To this line of argument there is one obvious retort: that if one of the partners in the dialogue controls the outcome of the dialogue, then the fact that the one controlled has certain beliefs about alternative possible outcomes simply means that he suffers certain illusions, in particular the illusion of freedom in dialogue when there is no such freedom. Control is, after all, control; and if one partner in the dialogue is controlled by the other, then he is not free to do whatever he wants, but only to do what he is controlled to do.

Perhaps so. Perhaps knowledge of epistemic possibilities of a certain range is not sufficient to ensure true freedom. But if this is a difficulty for a view of freedom in dialogue that presupposes omnidetermining power in one of the partners, then, by parity of reasoning, it would appear to be a difficulty if merely the infallible omniscience of one of the partners is presupposed. For since the omniscient partner, God, knows the determinate outcome of the dialogue, the decisions of the human partner cannot be perfectly open even though that partner may entertain a range of epistemic possibilities in the situation.

But does this conclusion matter as far as the reality of dialogue is concerned? Does it matter to the human partner in dialogue if she knows or believes that her divine partner knows in advance the answer to, say, her request? Does it matter if she knows or believes that her divine partner has determined in advance both the request and its answer even though she does not know what that determination is? Not necessarily.

Take, as an analogy, the following situation: John calls Jeremy, his lawyer, to ask a question about the case. In the circumstances Jeremy's previous advice was such that John had no real alternative but to call him. When John calls, Jeremy is not available. But (somewhat unusually for lawyers, you may think) Jeremy has already anticipated John's request, and the answer to what he knew John would ask is in the post. Is there a reason to think that in this situation John will call off the dialogue and will not bother to open the letter to find out the answer, giving as his reason that Jeremy knew what he was going to ask before he did so, and therefore that Jeremy's reply is "present in its causes" in the unopened letter?

Would it matter to Hezekiah if he believes before he prays that God has determined some particular outcome regarding his death? Suppose that Hezekiah believes that God has determined that he will die at a given, precise date in the future, and has not disclosed the date to Hezekiah. Does this circumstance spoil the reality of

Hezekiah's dialogue with God? For perhaps (for all Hezekiah knows to the contrary) God has decided that he will do whatever he has decided to do in answer to Hezekiah's prayer.

The reality of dialogue may be accounted for in terms of mutual metaphysical openness of the sort that Alston seeks to clarify. Certainly this is a sufficient condition for dialogue, but one that may not be readily achievable. But is it a necessary condition? As we have already noted, it does not seem to be an appropriate model in those divine-human cases in which God has infallible knowledge of the future. The partners are not "on the same level," and one of the partners has knowledge (infallible knowledge) that is superior to that possessed by the other partner, even if he is not an omni-determiner. And in any case, given that God is timeless, he cannot adjust his beliefs in the face of any request from his partner in dialogue.

Mutual openness of the sort that Alston specifies may be sufficient for genuine dialogue. But I have argued that mere ignorance of what one's dialogue partner will do, even if what he will do is fixed, together with a strong interest in knowing what he will do, is also sufficient for dialogue. Genuine dialogue may occur when one of the partners in dialogue needs to know what the other partner already knows, including what the other partner already knows that the first partner will do, knowledge which can only be disclosed by that partner or his agent. Provided, that is, the partner is willing to disclose his knowledge.

So I conclude that Alston has not shown that mutual open dialogue is possible between a timeless omniscient God and a human partner, but that this does not rule out divine-human dialogue of some kind or other under a wide variety of theological suppositions.

Notes

1. William Hasker, "Providence and Evil," *Religious Studies* 28 (1992), 91–105. 94.

2. William P. Alston, "Divine-Human Dialogue and the Nature of God," in Alston, *Divine Nature and Human Language* (Ithaca: Cornell University Press, 1989), 144–61.

3. In another article, "God in Dialogue," in *Interpreting the Bible*, ed. A.N.S. Lane (Leicester: Apollos, 1997), I have argued that the biblical language of dialogue between God and mankind is to be plausibly thought of as a case of divine accommodation.

4. Alston, "Divine-Human Dialogue," 145–46.

5. Ibid., 148.

6. Ibid., 147–48.

7. Alston assumes, as I shall, that the idea of God speaking or talking is unproblematic.

8. Alston, "Divine-Human Dialogue," 152.

9. For example, Vincent Brummer, *What Are We Doing When We Pray?* (London: SCM Press, 1984); Brummer, *Speaking of a Personal God* (Cambridge: Cambridge University Press, 1977); and Keith Ward, *Rational Theology and the Creativity of God* (Oxford: Blackwell, 1982).

10. Alston, "Divine-Human Dialogue," 152.

11. Ibid.

12. Ibid., 153–54.

13. *Anglican Book of Common Prayer*, Second Collect at Evening Prayer.

14. With an eye to such discrimination it may be more accurate to characterize Aquinas and the others as thinking of God as an omnidecreer. But to avoid undue complexity we shall go along with Alston's usage.

15. Isaiah 38.

16. The following paragraphs are closely related to Paul Helm, "Omnipotence and Change," *Philosophy* 51 (1976), 454–61.

17. See ibid. for further details and Thomas V. Morris, *Anselmian Explorations* (Ithaca: Cornell University Press, 1987), 89, for another suggestion.

18. Alston, "Divine-Human Dialogue," 157.

19. Ibid., 158.

20. Ibid.

21. Ibid., 159.

22. For the idea of ET-simultaneity, see Eleonore Stump and Norman Kretzmann, "Eternity," *Journal of Philosophy* 78 (1981), 429–58.

23. Alston, "Divine-Human Dialogue," 151.

24. Ibid., 153.

25. Ibid., 152.

26. Ibid.

27. Ibid.

28. For a discussion of some of the issues raised by prophecy, see Edward Wierenga, "Prophecy, Freedom, and the Necessity of the Past," in *Philosophical Perspectives*, vol. 5., *Philosophy of Religion, 1991*, ed. James E. Tomberlin (Atascadero: Ridgeview, 1991), and Eleonore Stump and Norman Kretzmann, "Prophecy, Past Truth, and Eternity," ibid.

29. Alston, "Divine-Human Dialogue," 160 n. 21.

30. Ibid., 160.

31. Ibid., 148.

32. Ibid., 158.

33. Ibid., 160.

34. Richard Swinburne, *The Coherence of Theism* (Oxford: Clarendon Press, 1977), 175.

35. Ibid., 172.

36. Ibid., 176.

37. Ibid., 175–76.

11

Incarnation, Timelessness, and Leibniz's Law Problems

The Issue at Hand

According to classical Christian theology, God exists atemporally. Orthodox Christology insists that Jesus Christ is numerically identical with God the Son, the Second Person of the Trinity. This identity statement, however, when taken in conjunction with other claims a traditional Christian wants to make, can be seen to provide a prima facie powerful argument against the doctrine of atemporality. Stated very briefly, the argument runs like this:

1. Jesus Christ was the bearer of temporal properties.
2. No bearer of temporal properties is atemporal.
3. Jesus Christ = God the Son (a divine person).
4. God the Son is not atemporal.

Now Christian theology does not want to identify one member of the Trinity with any other, much less with them all. So the atemporality of the Godhead does not obviously follow from (4). It does follow, however, that there exists a temporal divine being and, a fortiori, atemporality is not essential for divinity; each of these consequences would be resisted by the standard defender of divine timelessness.

It rarely behooves one to be too dogmatic in asserting theological conclusions, so I conclude only that the above argument is prima facie sound and that it provides the theological temporalist with the upper hand in his dispute with the atemporalist.

My purpose in this essay is not to rehash an argument that I have presented more fully elsewhere.[1] Rather, I am interested in defending an argument like that above from an objection that I have heard voiced by the three most able defenders of atemporalism, viz., Eleonore Stump, Norman Kretzmann, and Brian Leftow.

The reply to the argument that the Incarnation rules out timelessness that will concern us runs as follows: well, sure, you can generate a problem with combining atemporality and incarnation, but why is that at all interesting? Everyone knows that there is a whole set of such so-called Leibniz's Law problems. These logical difficulties are generated as follows: since Jesus Christ is fully human, and property P is essential to humanity, he exemplifies property P. So if he is identical to God the Son, then according to Leibniz's Law, the latter must exemplify P, too; but necessarily, no divine being can exemplify P, so the identity claim must be false. For the property-term-placeholder P, one may substitute "being limited in knowledge," "being limited in power," "being morally corruptible," "existing contingently," etc. Now, to be sure, one problem instance involves the attribute of temporality; but so what? If you are a Christian who also believes in the Law of Noncontradiction, then you had better believe that there is a way of working out such problems; and if you find a solution for all of these other Leibniz's Law difficulties, you will find one for the temporality/atemporality problem, too. So there is no better reason for thinking that the Incarnation shows that the Son is temporal than there is for thinking that it shows that the Son is limited in knowledge and power.[2]

It is this objection that I want to examine critically in this essay. I hope to show that, the above line of reasoning notwithstanding, the doctrine of the Incarnation does pose a special, if not unique, problem for the doctrine of timelessness.

A Preliminary Distinction

In order to show that the doctrine of timelessness raises particularly thorny problems with respect to the Incarnation, I will have to distinguish two kinds of properties. I begin by marking this dichotomy.

The distinction that I have in mind is epistemological rather than metaphysical. That is, it divides properties according to the access that we have to their instances rather than according to their essences. First, consider what I will call an "observable property." As one might think, this is a property that one can come to know to be exemplified by an object just in virtue of observing that object. Hence, color, relative size (within rather generous parameters), shape, texture, etc., are examples of such properties. Now of course, I am being far too simplistic here, at least far too simplistic for certain purposes. For there is a fact about the current color and texture of my heart but, fortunately for me, that is not an observable property at this time. However, I propose not to bother tidying up this very loose notion of observable property. For while I acknowledge that it is quite rough, it is adequate for our purposes.[3]

As one might expect, I wish to contrast observable properties with "unobservable properties." An unobservable property is a property the exemplification of which cannot be known by simple observation. Clear examples of such properties are being combustible, being well liked by the president, and being the sort of organism brought about by random genetic mutation. Since my characterization of observable properties is loose, my description of unobservable properties is as well. One point to note, however, is that whether a property is observable or unobservable is relative to the attributes of the cognizer or the class of cognizers and to the conditions of observation.

The color of medium-sized physical objects is, in the right circumstances, an observable property of that object if one is a human being with a properly functioning visual system. However, to those who lack such a system, color might well be an unobservable property. It will make matters more manageable if I do not always have to acknowledge explicitly the cognizer and context relativity of this distinction; so unless I say otherwise, assume that the class of cognizers is that of properly functioning human beings, and that the conditions of observation are optimal for observing the property in question.

Why Ours Is Not Simply Another Leibniz's Law Problem

Armed with this distinction, let's return to our primary problem. Orthodox Christology demands that we identify Jesus of Nazareth with God the Son, the Second Person of the Trinity. But which properties are we constrained by orthodoxy to impute to the Incarnate God? Well, clearly if he is to be God we shall have to ascribe to him all of those properties that are kind-essential for divinity. So, inter alia, we shall have to say that he is omnipotent, Creator of all that exists other than himself, and omnibenevolent; I assume that no being who lacks these properties can count as divine.[4] And we must also ascribe to him those properties which are kind-essential for humanity. Which properties are those? That is rather hard to say. Thomas Morris and Richard Swinburne have argued that it is not at all clear in precisely what the human kind-essence consists.[5] If we knew the essence of humanity, the job of checking for the logical consistency of the doctrine of the Incarnation would be straightforward. But since there is no known univocal answer to what is essential for being human, things are anything but simple.

Nevertheless we are not completely at a loss on this issue. Although it is, perhaps, easier to see what is not a part of the human kind essence rather than what is: it may or may not be necessarily true that each human is embodied at every moment that he or she exists; however, no one would seriously maintain that being disembodied is essential for humanity. Even if, necessarily, humans have stages during which we are disembodied, *being disembodied* (i.e., at every moment of one's existence) is not a part of the human kind-essence. Similarly, even the Christian who accepts the doctrine of total depravity will not claim that *being totally depraved* is essential for being human. For this would preclude the logical possibility of an individual's ceasing to be sinful and with it the Christian commitment to the eventual completion of the sanctification process.[6] Indeed, the example of total depravity illustrates a key point: a property may be extremely common without being essential.

Furthermore, our ignorance does not preclude our ascribing certain particular human properties to Christ. Because he was in many respects a rather ordinary man, there are a whole host of properties that he shared with his fellow first-century Jews; so we must ascribe to him those accidental features of the time and place of the Incarnation. The Gospels are another source of data concerning Christ's human properties. One need not think that a Christian has to hold that Jesus did everything that he is portrayed as doing in the Scriptures; but surely the traditional believer will take seriously the account of Christ in the Gospels and reject only that which there is strong reason to reject.

Now among those properties that Christ exemplifies, some will be observable and some will be unobservable. Presumably, his divine attributes will fall into the second classification. Peter, for example, could not just look at Jesus and observe that he was the omnipotent Ground of All Being. However, many of the accidental features of Jesus would have been observable. For example, Peter could see that Jesus had dark hair, that he wore a robe and sandals, and that he broke bread with his hands. In fact, there are properties that are clearly not kind-essential for humanity but that we can nevertheless be sure that Jesus had. The most obvious of these are that Jesus had a body with certain particular characteristics, that his primary mode of transportation was walking, and that there was a particular temporal ordering to what he did. Any of Christ's properties that was observable to the disciples is surely a property that we must be willing to ascribe to him.

Now when we add these observable properties to the divine properties, we get a pretty robust description of God Incarnate. He is a male human being who was physically very much like other men of his time and place, who nevertheless was the omnibenevolent, omnipotent Creator of all that is other than himself. We have here what appears to be a coherent description; at least it involves no obvious contradiction. However, if we add other attributes that are sometimes thought kind-essential for humanity, things change rather quickly. For example, if we think that every human must be limited in power and morally fallible, and we thus add this to our description of Christ, the inconsistency of the resulting description is overdetermined. However, as Morris and Swinburne have pointed out, it is hard to see why a Christian should feel constrained to make these claims about the human kind-essence. Surely a normal or typical human is limited in power and knowledge, but that is not an indefeasible reason to think it necessary that nothing could be human without being so limited.

At this point one might worry that the view thus far sketched would allow that every human being is only accidentally not divine. That is, if the human kind essence does not preclude omnipotence or any other divine-kind attributes, then it might look as though we may each be possibly divine, that for each of us there is a possible world in which we are God. But surely that is too much to swallow and completely contrary to what Christianity teaches about human beings. Fortunately, the view I am interested in defending is not saddled with this consequence. In addition to our human natures or kind-essences, we each also have individual essences. Our kind-essences are shared by all humans, but our individual essences are unique. A property is a part of the individual essence of a being if that being could not continue to exist if it ceased to have that property. One's individual essence is the set of all such properties for the given individual. Thus, one can insist both that there is no inconsistency in claiming that *some being* might have all the kind-essential attributes of divinity and humanity while at the same time denying that every individual who is a human is only contingently so. For it could be that the standard human's individual essence includes his or her being created and limited in power and wisdom. So one who defends the coherence of the Incarnation has only to claim that, possibly, there is an individual who is human (i.e., who instantiates the human kind-essence) and whose individual nature contains the kind-essential properties of divinity.

Let's return to the main lines of argument: the point here is that once we recognize that it is not obvious that limits to power and goodness are a part of the human kind-essence, then we can see that there is substantial room to maneuver in face of the standard Leibniz's Law problems. One has those difficulties only if one already accepts a robust philosophical anthropology that there is no particularly good reason to adopt. The Christian only has a serious problem if there is a clash between a human property that one is *compelled* to ascribe to Christ and a kind-essential property of divinity. If that happens, one is in a serious Christological bind.

Now from what we know about Jesus in the Gospels, it is clear that he had the observable properties listed above (i.e., he had a body with certain particular features, walking was his primary mode of transportation, and he did certain things before he did others, etc.); these properties can be ascribed to Christ without making *any* important anthropological assumptions other than that he was human. Were we to have had the good fortune of being original disciples, we could simply "read off" such properties from Christ's physical appearance and his actions. And as we have seen, these properties are consistent with the properties of divinity that we have been considering. But what if we add to the list of kind-essential properties for divinity "atemporality"? Now we get a description of a person with a human body whose actions (both the acts and their consequences) are temporally ordered but who is nevertheless timeless. I say "both the acts and their consequences" because the Scriptures portray Jesus Christ as not simply a person who *brings about effects* that are in time, but as a *person who is in* time; so if we add atemporality to this portrait, we get a sketch that no one could possibly satisfy. Therefore, I contend that this account of the Incarnation is incoherent.

The general point, then, can be put as follows: unless you begin your Christological investigation with a certain, rather strong philosophical anthropology, there is no good reason to think that there are irresolvable Leibniz's Law problems concerning such divine kind-essential properties as omnipotence, necessary existence, and omnibenevolence. None of these properties is obviously inconsistent with one's being human since none of them entails the denial of any observable human property. However, were timelessness thought to be kind-essential for divinity, things would be rather different. For traditional Christology insists that Christ had a body of flesh and blood. But every embodied human exemplifies observable, temporal properties. So if Christ is embodied, he exemplifies observable, temporal properties; and if he has such properties he is not timeless. So if one insists that atemporality is necessary for divinity, it will be very hard to assert that Christ was divine without committing oneself to a contradiction. And once again the key point is that one can generate such a contradiction without making any significant anthropological claims whatsoever.

An Objection

We must now consider a very important objection that would seem to seriously undermine the argument of this essay. Although superficially this appears to be two, mostly unrelated, problems we will be able to see presently that there is a uniting thread. Here is the problem: okay, so your position is not completely without merit. Certain of the kind-essential features of divinity (e.g., omnipotence, omnibenevolence, and necessary existence) are consistent with Christ's observable properties; and atemporality would seem not to share this desirable trait. However, you have spoken as though this problem is unique to timelessness. But it is not. Surely, e.g., incorporeality is kind-essential for divinity, but it is also apparently inconsistent with the observable properties of Christ. So your main thesis, i.e., that timelessness is in conflict with the Incarnation in a way all other attributes are not, is mistaken.[7] Besides, the situation is not nearly as bad as you make it sound. For there is a long tradition that recognizes that the attributes of deity are had by Jesus Christ *qua divinity* while the typical observable properties are had *qua humanity*. Now to be sure, more needs to be said about this; but here we have the seeds of a reply to all Leibniz's Law objections.

There are two discernible parts to this objection. The first is aimed at my claim that the Incarnation poses a special problem for the doctrine of timelessness. It is alleged that even if the Morris/Swinburne line defuses the problem for many of the divine properties, there are others that are recalcitrant; i.e., there are observable properties of Christ that are apparently inconsistent with characteristics traditionally attributed to God. So my claim that the timelessness problem is unique is incorrect.

The second part of the above objection is more general. The claim is that I have exaggerated how bad these Leibniz's Law problems are and that we do have a good idea of how to go about solving them; apparently inconsistent properties can be had by Christ so long as they are attributed to him qua different natures. So Christ qua God is omnipotent but Christ qua human is not. This move (call it the "qua-move"), perhaps with a few added bells and whistles, will solve all the traditional Leibniz's Law problems. So there is no special worry regarding atemporality.

Let's take these problems in turn.

On the Uniqueness of the Atemporality Problem

It is clear that there is something right and important about this objection. There are other attributes that would seem to follow from the observable properties of Christ that, prima facie, cause problems for the traditional understanding of the Incarnation.

How serious this objection is will depend on two things: the number of allegedly divine kind-essential properties that are inconsistent with Christ's observable properties and the significance of those properties. If there is massive conflict or if the conflict is with what we might call "core" (alleged) divine properties, then we shall have to hope for some solution to the Leibniz's Law problems that is radically different from the Morris/Swinburne line sketched above. However, if the number of apparently inconsistent properties is small and if, for each troublesome pair, either the alleged divine or alleged human property is sufficiently negotiable (i.e., not central), then the Morris/Swinburne line looks promising indeed and the above objection to the argument for the temporality of God based on the Incarnation is not troubling.

One final prefatory note. One who adopts the Morris/Swinburne line and gives up atemporality (and perhaps other allegedly divine properties) will be bucking a certain tradition, there are no two ways about it. There are deep and important issues of philosophical and theological methodology here that we will discuss briefly later in the essay.

Which alleged divine properties seem to directly conflict with observable properties of Christ? Incorporeality is an example. Christ's having a body means that he has an observable property (i.e., being embodied) that is inconsistent with the doctrine of incorporeality (and with that of aspatiality as well). Are there other attributes normally ascribed to God by traditional theology that are inconsistent with observable properties?

One might think that Christ's being born of Mary (a property he was observed to have by at least Mary) is inconsistent with his being necessarily existent or even preexistent. As plausible as this sounds, I believe it can reasonably be resisted. For in order for this to be a worrisome pair of properties, there would have to be a fairly direct logical relation between "being born" and not existing necessarily or being preexistent. Now if "X is born at t" implied that "X did not exist prior to t," then we would have a real problem. But of course the former does not imply the latter. Not only is there not a relation of logical necessity between the two, but most of the true substitution instances of the first are cases in which the appropriate substitution instances of the second are false. Surely the being who leaves the birth canal at t existed in the canal at t_{-1}.[8]

Are there other attributes, traditionally ascribed to God, that conflict with the observable properties of Christ? Perhaps, but I fail to see what they are. What we are looking for here are properties (or their immediate logical consequences) that were directly observable by any first-century resident of Palestine. Being embodied implies being "in" space and time, but from what I can see not much else.

There is a second sort of problem case that might be thought relevant here. Jesus is often portrayed in the Gospels as showing standard human emotions (e.g., sorrow and anger). Having these emotions is inconsistent with the attribute of impassibility, so that would seem to be another attribute in jeopardy.[9] Similarly, Jesus claimed that only the Father knows the date of the Second Coming, which in the context of his utterance strongly suggests that Christ took himself to lack such knowledge. These sorts of difficulties might be classified as conflicts between observable properties and traditional divine properties, because while the complements of the divine properties are not entailed by observable properties the latter nevertheless provide relatively direct warrant or justification for the attribution of properties inconsistent with the properties of impassibility and omniscience. For example, Christ's having the property of wearing a facial expression generally associated with anger while overturning tables and casting the money changers out of the Temple is pretty good prima facie evidence of genuine anger; still, it is by no means conclusive. These facial and behavioral properties do not *entail* anger. Similarly, Christ's apparent claim of ignorance regarding the timing of the Second Coming does not entail a lack of omniscience, although it might be seen as pretty good evidence for it.[10]

Problems of this second sort are, perhaps, more in number but are almost certainly less in impact. For they provide only prima facie evidence of incompatibility; the philosophical theologian has options for defeating the alleged incompatibility. These options range from reinterpreting the troublesome biblical passages, to denying their accuracy, to giving alternative accounts of the divine properties in question (e.g., one can claim that omniscience does not require constant access to the information contained in the omniscient mind, and one can take a behaviorist view of the divine mental life in order to save impassibility as, e.g., Anselm does). Now back to the more straightforward problem concerning incorporeality and impassibility. Does my position force me to accept the corporeality and passibility of Christ? Yes, I believe so. Does that mean I must accept the corporeality and passibility of God? Well, yes and no. Inasmuch as I accept the truth of the Incarnational identity claim "Jesus Christ is God the Son" as well as the corporeality and passibility of Christ, I must accept the corporeality and passibility of God the Son. That does not mean, however, I must accept the corporeality and passibility of the Godhead (i.e., of the Trinity), and still less that I must accept that the Father or Spirit is corporeal and passable.

If I do accept that Christ was divine and yet corporeal and passable, then I must accept that incorporeality and impassibility are not kind-essential for divinity. As I mentioned above, this is not to affirm that either the Father or the Spirit is corporeal or passable. Further, it is instructive to see that one can hold all of the above and still maintain that the Godhead is naturally incorporeal and impassable, i.e., that incorporeality and impassibility are what I have elsewhere called *"ceteris paribus"* properties of divinity.[11] P is *ceteris paribus* property for kind k if and only if property instances of k will have P if other things are equal, or in normal or standard circumstances. So, e.g., water has the *ceteris paribus* property of boiling at 212 degrees Fahrenheit. However, if water has salt added or is being heated at a high altitude, or if the laws of nature were different in certain ways, then this property is not exemplified. So while water has the property of boiling at 212 degrees F. naturally, as it were, it does not have this property essentially (although it does have the *ceteris paribus* property essentially).

The traditional Christian who holds both the corporeality and passibility of Jesus Christ and hence of God the Son (at least during his earthly ministry) can nevertheless maintain that a divine being is "naturally" (though not essentially) incorporeal and impassable. It is only when a divine Person takes on a second nature or in some other way alters himself that incorporeality and impassibility are set aside.[12] The account of divinity is unchanged except that what is essential for being divine are not, say, the properties of simple omniscience, incorporeality, etc., but is instead the second order property of having the *ceteris paribus* properties of omniscience, incorporeality, etc. But if we make this move, one might think: do we not in the end really give up the whole idea of the divine nature? Does it not risk making the notion of "a nature" so malleable as to be no longer profitable to discuss? I think not. For the kind-nature that an entity exemplifies will (partially) determine its *ceteris paribus* properties. It is because water has the essential properties that it does that it has the *ceteris paribus* property of boiling at 212 degrees F. Similarly, it is because of the essence of divinity that any divine being will have the *ceteris paribus* property of omniscience. This way of construing the divine kind-nature makes divinity more closely analogous with kind-natures in general. If we think the essential properties of divinity are omniscience, omnipotence, omnibenevolence, and the like, and that the way we know this is via a priori reflection on the concept of God, then we are seeing the concept of God as much more like a "cluster concept" (like, e.g., *bachelor*) than like a natural (or supernatural) kind-concept. If we see divinity as closely analogous to a natural kind, then we shall think there is a fundamental divine nature not knowable a priori—or at least not by simple reflection on the concept of divinity. Of course, it is perfectly consistent with everything said here that God may choose to reveal himself to us and that we shall learn certain of his important properties that way. Even if they turn out not to be technically *essential* for divinity, that God is *ceteris paribus* omniscient and incorporeal can be important truths for God to reveal to his followers.

In this discussion I have heretofore avoided the question of whether the traditional Christian should hold that divinity includes the properties of impassibility and incorporeality. There is a broad theological tradition, however, even within Christological orthodoxy, that maintains that impassibility should be jettisoned. This is not the place to thrash about in these deep and often turbulent theological waters. For our purposes it is sufficient that we note that these matters are of great controversy and that even many who accept the two-natures view of the Incarnation are not inclined to accept the complete traditional package.

Despite my position that there are ways the friend of divine temporality can mitigate the damage of the objection we have been considering, I want nevertheless to acknowledge that it raises key issues in Christian philosophical theology. The primary issue it brings to light centers on the implications of the Incarnation: to what extent should a Christian allow her Christology to influence her theology? That is, is it theologically permissible to let what she believes about Jesus inform what she believes about God? It is clear, I suppose, that one can go either too far or not far enough on this score. For instance, one who said that Christ's distaste for empty piety did not reflect God's attitude would clearly be denying an important revelation. On the other hand, if I claim that because Jesus wore sandals, God prefers that we all do, I would not deserve to be taken seriously. So we can all agree that while God might be most fully revealed in the life and person of Jesus Christ, there are limits to reading the mind and nature of God from the preferences and actions of Jesus.

But there will be important points of disagreement, too. For example, I am inclined to take the Gospels' portrait of Christ to reveal the depth to which God has compassion for humanity; and by "compassion" I do not mean to say, as does Anselm, only that God acts in compassionate ways. I also intend to assert that God has some analogue of the human emotional state of compassion. But to accept this is to reject the traditional doctrine of impassibility. Now one fully persuaded of the classical picture in its entirety will insist that the Gospels can be consistently read behavioristically. Or perhaps she will say that the compassion and suffering of Christ are to be predicated "qua humanity" only. This then leads us to the second part of the above objection. The objector's second claim is that as long as, e.g., incorporeality or impassibility is had qua divinity and its logically complementary property is had qua humanity, then the person identified as Jesus Christ and God the Son (for simplicity's sake, we will hereafter refer to him as the Redeemer) can consistently possess them both.

The defender of the qua-move is claiming that the traditional divine properties are held by the Redeemer only qua God. But precisely what is it that is being claimed? It seems that there are three ways of spelling out the details of the qua-move, i.e., of what are known as reduplicative sentences. In the next section, I will have a look at each of these three possibilities and argue that two of them simply cannot do the job of avoiding the Leibniz's Law problems that motivate their adoption. The third is apparently able to solve such problems, but adopting it requires accepting an account of properties that is motivated solely by the desire to avoid Leibniz's Law problems and as such is simply an ad hoc adjustment that creates as many problems as it solves.

The Three Ways

Although the qua-move is somewhat familiar, let's take a moment to rehearse it. Suppose someone claims that Christian theology is logically inconsistent because it asserts or entails

A. Jesus Christ was omnipotent

and

B. Jesus Christ was not omnipotent.

The friend of the qua-move will say that both A and B are ambiguous and that the only readings of them that the orthodox believer is committed to are expressed by the following reduplicative sentences (i.e., sentences that ascribe a property qua God or qua humanity):

A*. Qua God, Jesus Christ was omnipotent.
B*. Qua human, Jesus Christ was not omnipotent.[13]

Unlike A and B, the propositions expressed by A* and B* are not straightforwardly inconsistent. So, apparently, the qua-move works to dispel the prima facie contradictions in traditional Christology.

Things are not so clear-cut, however. While it is plain that A* and B* are not explicitly inconsistent, it is by no means obvious how they are to be understood and whether there is a way of understanding them that will do the job of undercutting claims of logical inconsistency. There are, I believe, three ways that one might understand reduplicative sentences. The first, and most straightforward, reading is "In virtue of being N, S is F." Thus, understood this way, if one says, "Qua God, Jesus Christ was omnipotent," one is saying that it is in virtue of his deity (or his divine nature) that Christ was omnipotent. This interpretation has the twofold advantage of being clear and intuitive in addition to being uncontroversial within the Christian tradition. Everyone will say that Christ has his divine properties in virtue of his divine nature and his human properties in virtue of his human nature.

The difficulty with this interpretation of qua-sentences for the purpose of solving Leibniz's Law problems is that it does not solve them, for the "F-entailment" still goes through. This is easy to see: sentences of the form "In virtue of N, S is F" entail sentences of the form "S is F." So "In virtue of being divine, Christ is omnipotent" entails "Christ is omnipotent"; and "In virtue of being human, Christ is not omnipotent" entails "Christ is not omnipotent." We are right back where we started. Hence, understanding reduplicative sentences like this will not help defend orthodoxy because in the end we will still be left with *simpliciter* properties and the contradictions they promote.

A second way of understanding reduplicative sentences is to take the qua-clause to be imbedded in the grammatical subject of the sentence. We can make this clear by appropriately placing hyphens. "Qua N, S is F" becomes "S-qua-N is F." Applying this to our example, we get "Christ-qua-God is omnipotent" and "Christ-qua-human is not omnipotent." The properties of omnipotence and non-omnipotence are predicated *simpliciter*, but contradiction is avoided because the properties are predicated of different subjects, i.e., of Christ-qua-God and Christ-qua-human. So while it is true that the relevant property is attributed *simpliciter*, this interpretation of qua-sentences still manages to block the inference from "Qua N, S is F" to "S is F," because the subjects are not identical.

Herein lies the difficulty. If one is to claim that in the Incarnation there are two subjects of predication one will be in effect adopting the heresy of Nestorianism. For this interpretation avoids the logical problems of the Incarnation by predicating the incompossible properties of different subjects. It is not the single person, the Redeemer, who bears these properties, but rather the divine nature bears the divine properties and the human nature bears the human properties. So the bearers of the divine and human properties are at best the two respective natures; this is Nestorianism pure and simple.

I will discuss one final way of interpreting reduplicative sentences and hence the qua-move; this "third way" has the considerable virtue of avoiding each of the pitfalls that do in the other possibilities. On this rendering, "Qua N, S is F" is to be understood as "S is F-qua-N." That is, the qua-clause gets packed into the predication in such a way as to form a single, non-compositional, simple property. The F-entailment is blocked here because the properties being ascribed bear no non-trivial logical relation to each other. The problem with the first reading was that the properties being ascribed were logical complements; this fact was thinly masked by the fact the ascriptions were made to the subject via the respective natures. In contrast, the properties "incorporeal-qua-God" and "corporeal-qua-human" are, despite appearances, non-composite properties that are not logically complementary. Hence, the F-entailment is blocked. And because reference to the natures is embedded in the property being ascribed rather than in the subject, there is a single subject of predication, and so Nestorianism is avoided.

Looked at slightly more technically, the proposal we are considering is the following: the Redeemer has at least two very distinct sets of properties, each set consisting of members that are ordered pairs. The first member of each pair in one set is divinity; the second member of each pair is some particular divine property (e.g., omnipotence). In the second set, the first member of each ordered pair is humanity (or human nature), and the second member is some quality necessarily exemplified by anything that has that nature.[14]

So far, so good. However, this view also generates serious problems. Recall that it is not sufficient that the Redeemer have the relevant hyphenated property and that that property fail to entail the relevant *simpliciter* property, i.e., that the F-entailment is blocked; it must also be the case that the Redeemer not have either the divine or the human property *simpliciter*. That is, suppose that "qua-subtraction" is a bad inference rule and that the way to understand reduplicative sentences is as the third way suggests. It does not follow from this that the problem is solved. For even if we accept that the Redeemer has the encapsulated properties of, e.g., omnipotent-qua-God and limited-in-power-qua-human, there is still the question of whether he has the property of omnipotence *simpliciter*. If he does (presumably because of his divinity), then we shall also need to know if his humanity requires that he is limited in power. If the answer to both is affirmative, then we are right back where we started. On the other hand, if the answer to one (either one) is yes and the answer to the other is no, then we have no need of the qua-move after all since we are not, even prima facie, attributing incompossible properties to the Redeemer.

Therefore, the third way on its own accomplishes nothing. In order for the third rendering of reduplicative sentences to provide a solution to these Leibniz's Law problems, it shall have to block any ascription of the traditional attributes to the Redeemer; furthermore, it shall have to block the limitation properties typically thought to be essential to humanity. What this comes down to, I believe, is that if it is to be helpful at all, the third way shall have to be accompanied by a denial of a version of the Law of the Excluded Middle. The particular version of this law that is relevant here says that for every property and every object, either that object has that property or it lacks it.

So my claim is that for the third reading to reduplicative sentences to be potentially helpful in solving Leibniz's Law problems, its proponent will have to ensure that neither the *simpliciter* divine properties nor the *simpliciter* limitation properties are ascribed to the Redeemer. Perhaps the most natural way to do this is to deny the Law of the Excluded Middle for properties. For suppose it is not false: then no matter how we interpret the reduplicative sentences, it must be that either the Redeemer has the property of, say, omnipotence or he lacks it. Now we have been assuming the Law of Noncontradiction for properties, so it will follow that the "or" is exclusive. Similarly, he will either have or lack the human limitation properties. If he has both omnipotence and the limitation properties, we are back where we started. But if he lacks omnipotence, then it is impossible for him to be God. And if he is omnipotent and lacks human limitations regarding power, then we have our original questions about his humanity.[15] So the friends of the third way will have to supplement their reading of reduplicative sentences in order for it to even begin to help with Leibniz's Law problems. One such supplement is the denial of the Law of the Excluded Middle for properties.

There is, however, one way of attempting to save the third rendering and its potential ability to solve the Leibniz's Law problems without denying the Law of the Excluded Middle for properties. One might claim that there just are no such properties as omnipotence *simpliciter*, omniscience *simpliciter*, and all the rest. Nominalism about the traditional divine properties would eliminate the need for denying the relevant version of the Law of the Excluded Middle, there being no such properties to begin with.

Is there any way of motivating divine property nominalism that is not hopelessly ad hoc? Maybe. Perhaps each of the divine properties is so completely embedded in the divine essence that it is necessarily, indissolubly related to it. Such a view might be thought to have attractive theological implications. First and most obviously, it would seem to provide a certain kind of unity to the divine nature. Rather than thinking of divinity as a collection of otherwise diverse properties, this proposal has omnipotence, omniscience, and the like as inseparably united with the divine nature and as not logically capable of instantiation apart from it. Secondly, it is also thought to be theologically odious to think of the "omni" properties as possibly instantiated by any being but that than which none greater is possible, i.e., God. Now strictly speaking, one can consistently hold that, e.g., omnipotence *simpliciter* is both a genuine property and yet is such that, necessarily, it can be instantiated only by God. However, if there is no such *simpliciter* property, if God's power is so entangled in the divine nature as to be inseparable from it, then there simply, and obviously, is no possibility of there existing a non-divine omnipotent being. Finally, the proponent of divine property nominalism can refer to the distinction between concepts and properties as a means of adding some plausibility to her position. She can claim that although we do have concepts of omnipotence, omniscience, omnibenevolence, and all the rest that seem to be (or indeed "are") conceptually independent of divinity, that does not tend to show that there are properties that are metaphysically independent of divinity.

We have distinguished two versions of the third way: one adds a denial of the Law of the Excluded Middle to the hyphenated, non-compositional property understanding of the qua-move; the other adds nominalism regarding traditionally understood theological properties. For the purpose of evaluating their ability to solve Leibniz's Law problems, however, we can treat them as one, since they have in common their reading of reduplicative sentences and their denial of *simpliciter* properties' application to God.

Despite its initial attractiveness, however, the third way brings with it its own set of problems. First, it requires a change in the way the divine nature is frequently construed. It has become common to cash out the divine nature by reference to the "omniproperties." Thus, to be divine is to be omnipotent, omniscient, omnibenevolent, and the like.[16] Now the natural way to understand this proposal regarding the divine nature has these properties as *simpliciter* properties. However, if that is right, then the Redeemer (and each other member of the Trinity) will fail to be divine, since he will lack simple omnipotence.

There is an obvious way of trying to avoid these charges. One might take these considerations to show that our account of divinity needs to be altered. Rather than requiring, say, omniscience for divinity, one should require omniscience-qua-God. This is a property that the Redeemer (and the other members of the Trinity, one would suppose) has on the present proposal. But to think that this alteration fixes things is to misunderstand the matter, for the resultant account is blatantly circular. For we have an account of the nature of God that consists of the properties of omnipotence-qua-God, omniscience-qua-God, etc. Having the properties necessary and sufficient for divinity make reference to "God" is to render the account viciously circular. A second problem with this solution is that even if it manages to avoid paradigm-case Leibniz's Law problems, there are other parallel problems that it does not address at all. For example, as we are understanding it now, the qua-move asserts that the Incarnation does not involve attributing contradictory properties to an individual, because the property of, say, being omnipotent-qua-God is a simple property which does not include the property of being omnipotent. So we can consistently say of the Redeemer that he was omnipotent in his divine nature and not omnipotent in his human nature, since it does not follow from these attributions that he had the property of omnipotence and lacked the property of omnipotence. The third way claims that this entailment is blocked because either the Law of the Excluded Middle for properties does not apply or there is no such property as simple omnipotence. So the Redeemer has the property of being omnipotent-qua-God. What does his humanity require? One possibility is that it requires that he have the property of being only-finitely-powerful-qua-humanity, where this property too is encapsulated, and so the inference that the Redeemer is only finitely powerful is blocked. This is, I think, the best that the defender of third way could hope for.

So what is the parallel problem that I alluded to in the above paragraph? Take any action that is clearly out of the range of standard human powers but would seem clearly performable by a divine being. Suppose the action is parting the Red Sea. Now we can ask whether or not the Redeemer can perform that action, whether he has the ability to do such a thing. If he can perform it, then his range of powers is clearly not within the standard range of human powers. And even if he possesses the insulated property of being limited-in-power-qua-humanity, the fact is that there are not the limitations on the Redeemer's actions that there are on the rest of us—at least, whatever limitations there might be are not nearly as severe as the limitations on us. Then again, if we say that he cannot perform the action, then it would seem that his range of action falls short of that required for divinity even if he has the hyphenated property of omnipotence-qua-divinity.

The point here can be expanded beyond the issue of the Redeemer's ability to perform a single miraculous action. Even if we grant that either the Redeemer neither has nor lacks omnipotence or that there is no property of omnipotence *simpliciter*, and we grant that the Redeemer has all his divine properties in an encapsulated way, one would still think that it would have to be true that, with respect to any broad range of action, either the Redeemer could perform those actions or he could not. Now suppose that we are considering the concept (rather than the property) of omnipotence, and suppose our account is in terms of a maximal set of powers any being could possess. Call that set of powers (whatever set it turns out to be) "PG." Now does the Redeemer possess all those powers that comprise PG? If he does, then his range of powers goes far beyond those of standard, limited humans (this is, of course, no surprise). If he does not possess those powers, then one might wonder how he could be even "omnipotent-qua-divine," or at any rate how he could possess enough power for divinity. Similarly, let's call the set of powers possessed by human beings in virtue of their humanity "PH."Now we can ask if the Redeemer's set of powers is significantly greater than PH. If it is significantly greater, then we are again faced with the question of how such a being could legitimately be one of us (particularly when one realizes that this is only one of many key differences between us and the Redeemer; there are similar differences in knowledge, goodness, contingency/necessity, etc.). If it is not, then the Redeemer lacks PG, and the questions about how such a being could be divine pop back up. In short, we find ourselves not substantially better off than we were before the qua-move was employed. So the third way, together with either a denial of the Law of the Excluded Middle for properties or omniproperty nominalism, fails as a means of resolving the logical puzzles of the Incarnation.

Conclusion

Let's take stock. This essay began with the claim that the Incarnation causes trouble for the doctrine of divine atemporality. We then looked at an objection of sorts to the argument presented; the objection stated that the problem at hand was just one of many similar Leibniz's Law problems and that once a solution was found to one, a solution would be found to all. The qua-move was thought to be a model for a solution of the right sort. However, close examination has revealed that the qua-move is unlikely to be helpful as a means of resolving any of our Incarnational difficulties. So we are once again left with the argument that the Incarnation would seem to be inconsistent with timelessness for the Godhead.

Yet it can be objected that if we accept divine temporality, then the very same line of reasoning should convince us that God is also corporeal and spatial. In this essay, I have argued that the traditional Christian can acknowledge that the Redeemer was indeed corporeal and spatial during his earthly ministry, and perhaps from thenceforth, without saying anything terribly unorthodox. For while she cannot consistently say that divinity requires incorporeality and aspatiality, she can claim that these are *ceteris paribus* properties of divinity. And of course, there are two other divine persons, Partakers in the Triune Life, who are not in any respect corporeal. However, if one holds that Christ no longer has a human body, one can certainly claim that the present-tense proposition "God is corporeal" is false since there is no divine person who has a body.

I am concerned in this essay to argue for only two points. First, it will not do for the advocate of atemporality to dismiss the charge that her view is inconsistent with the orthodox understanding of the Incarnation. For there are ways of handling the standard Leibniz's Law problems that cannot be pressed into service to dispel the apparent inconsistency between the doctrines of timelessness and the Incarnation. The second conclusion is that there is at present some reason to doubt the utility of the qua-move as a means of solving Christological problems. Perhaps there is some way of understanding the property ascription qua natures that can be pressed into service here, but the three clearest possibilities are in the end unhelpful.

Notes

Thanks to Laura Garcia for discussion and to David Woodruff for written comments on an earlier version of this essay.

1. Thomas D. Senor, "Incarnation and Timelessness," *Faith and Philosophy*, 7, no.2 (April 1990), 149–64.

2. Brian Leftow offers an argument similar to this in the introduction to his book *Time and Eternity* (Ithaca: Cornell University Press, 1990). Leftow credits Eleonore Stump with having suggested it to him. I also heard this argument from Norman Kretzmann in response to a question at the conference "The God Who Acts in History," held at UCLA, March 31, 1990.

3. As we have described them so far, it is not clear whether properties that can be only observed via instruments count as observable. I do not think that for our purposes it matters. As long as we have a concept clear enough to be usable in many ordinary cases, we have a concept clear enough for our purposes.

4. In this essay, I will write as though the standard theistic attributes of omnipotence, omniscience, omnibenevolence, and the like constitute the kind-essence of divinity. I do have serious reservations about this, but laying them aside will cause no problems here. For a discussion of my reservations, see my article "God, Supernatural Kinds, and the Incarnation," *Religious Studies* 27 (1992) 353–70.

5. Thomas V. Morris, *The Logic of God Incarnate* (Ithaca: Cornell University Press, 1986); Richard Swinburne, first in "Could God Become Man?" in *The Philosophy in Christianity* (Cambridge: Cambridge University Press, 1989), 53–70, then in *The Christian God* (London: Oxford University Press, 1994).

6. It would, of course, cause yet another Leibniz's Law problem for the Incarnation, for surely no divine being can be depraved.

7. Thanks to Laura Garcia for reminding me of this objection.

8. Now one might think that "X's being conceived at *t*" entails that "X begins to exist at *t*," and hence that if Jesus were "conceived by the Holy Spirit" we would have a Leibniz's Law problem here (since, being God the Son, Jesus must also be said to be pre-existent and necessarily existent). I am relegating this discussion to a footnote since this is not a case of a conflict between an observable property and alleged divine properties. Nevertheless, I think that the Morris/Swinburne line has an answer here as well, although it is admittedly not as smooth as the answer to the previous problem. One can maintain that conception is the first moment of existence for a typical human (if indeed it is; this is, of course, a very controversial assumption) but that it is not kind-essential for being human. Furthermore, as we have seen, we can distinguish between kind and individual essences and claim that for a standard human being the property of, say, beginning to exist at conception is a part of his or her individual essence.

9. Although "impassibility" has many meanings, I intend to understand "God is impassable" as "God is without an inner emotional life." For a good discussion of the many meanings of "impassable," see Richard E. Creel, *Divine Impassibility: An Essay in Philosophical Theology* (Cambridge: Cambridge University Press, 1986).

10. One can see that Christ's apparent claim does not entail a lack of omniscience by noting that Christ's being reported to have made that claim does not entail that he actually made it. I am making only a minimal assumption about the way the Christian theologian needs to take biblical data. Note that the problems the Incarnation creates for timelessness and incorporeality depend only on the claim that Jesus Christ, a human being, was God Incarnate; it matters not whether the Gospels' accounts of his life and ministry are generally accurate.

11. Senor, "God, Supernatural Kinds, and the Incarnation."

12. Clearly, one who adopts this view will reject a traditional reading of the attribute of immutability since taking on a nature is a paradigm of intrinsic change.

13. This is precisely the line taken (or at least suggested) by Eleonore Stump and Norman Kretzmann in sec. 5 of their important paper "Eternity," *Journal of Philosophy* 78 (1981), 429–58.

14. It is not clear whether these sets exhaust all of the Redeemer's properties or whether there is a third set of simpliciter properties. For example, it is not clear whether the property "having knowledge" is an attribute of the Redeemer's or whether the relevant attributes are "having-knowledge-qua-God" or "having-knowledge-qua-man."

15. Recall that the qua-move is made for the purpose of showing how the apparently contradictory properties of, e.g., omnipotence and non-omnipotence, can be had by a single individual. If, however, one is not committed to the truth of sentences like "The Redeemer is omnipotent" and "The Redeemer is non-omnipotent," then the whole motivation for the qua-move is shot, at least as far as I can see.

16. This is a rather weak account by contemporary (and medieval) standards. It is frequently maintained that to be God involves having the omniproperties essentially. In what follows, I will assume only the weaker understanding of divinity; but it should be noted that any problems that we encounter with the weaker notion and its compossibility with human nature will be at least as significant as what we would encounter with the stronger notion.

12

On the Incarnation of a Timeless God

DOUGLAS K. BLOUNT

While a number of objections to the doctrine of divine timelessness have been aimed at atemporalists in general, I discuss in this essay an objection to that doctrine aimed not at atemporalists in general but rather at *Christian* atemporalists.[1] In so doing, I examine two recent versions of this objection, arguing that they fail and offer a suggestion as to how one can affirm both Christian orthodoxy and the doctrine of divine timelessness without thereby contradicting oneself.[2]

The Objection from the Incarnation

Arguably, the doctrine which more than any other sets Christianity apart from other types of theism is the doctrine of the Incarnation, according to which Jesus Christ is God.[3] About this doctrine, Thomas Morris writes, "The traditional doctrine of the Incarnation has as its central affirmation the claim that Jesus of Nazareth was one and the same person as God the Son, the Second Person of the divine Trinity. In the case of Jesus, the tradition tells us, we are faced with one person in two natures—divine and human."[4] And, at least since the Council of Chalcedon in 451, orthodox Christians (or, at least, such Christians in the West) have taken this to mean that, while Jesus is consubstantial with God the Father in his divinity and with us in his humanity, his divine and human natures are neither changed, confused, divided, nor separated.[5] Indeed, rather than being obliterated, the differences between those natures remain intact. As the council's Definition of the Faith stresses, Christian orthodoxy insists that equal emphasis be placed on both the Incarnate Son's unity and his duality. And, while the emphasis on unity comes via the insistence that Jesus is exactly one person, the emphasis on duality comes via the emphatic affirmation that he possesses two wholly distinct—though united—natures. With respect to this latter emphasis, J. N. D. Kelly writes, "So, side by side with the unity, the Definition states that, as incarnate, the Word exists 'in two natures', *each complete and each retaining its distinctive properties and operation unimpaired in the union.*"[6] Here two points deserve mention: first, while Jesus Christ is God the Son, he is God the Son Incarnate; second, as the *Incarnate* Son, he possesses two natures each of which retains its distinctive character. This last point features prominently in the discussion which follows.

Now, according to Nelson Pike, "it could hardly escape notice that the doctrine of God's timelessness does not square well with the standard Christian belief that God once assumed finite, human form (the doctrine of the incarnation)."[7] That the doctrines of divine timelessness and the Incarnation are at odds seems to follow from the apparent fact that Jesus existed in time.[8] In discussing the apparent tension between these two doctrines, Pike acknowledges that the doctrine of the Incarnation is regarded by Christian theologians in general as a paradox. In fact, he states, "The claim that God assumed finite and temporal form is not *supposed* to fit well with other things that Christians believe about the nature of God."[9] So, having raised the question of whether the two doctrines are compatible, Pike puts it aside, declining to discuss it further.

More recently, however, Thomas Senor has taken up the task of answering this question. In so doing, he concludes that a consequence of the doctrine of the Incarnation is that God the Son is not timeless. He presents two arguments in support of this conclusion, the first of which he calls [A]. [A] goes as follows.

(1) Jesus Christ read in the synagogue (at the start of His ministry) before He carried His cross.
(2) So, temporal predicates apply to Jesus Christ.
(3) Jesus Christ = God the Son.[10]
(4) So, temporal predicates apply to God the Son.
(5) Temporal predicates don't apply to timeless beings.
(6) So, God the Son isn't timeless.[11]

While (1) follows from an apparently straightforward reading of the biblical narratives of Jesus' life, (3) is intended simply to affirm the central claim of the doctrine of the Incarnation—namely, that Jesus Christ and God the Son are one and the same person. Statement (5), Senor tells us, is a conceptual truth.[12] Statement (2) follows from (1), (4) from (2) and (3). Statements (4) and (5) jointly entail (6). So, from an apparently straightforward reading of Scripture, a claim central to Christian orthodoxy, and a conceptual truth, Senor argues that God the Son is not timeless. In so arguing, he presents Christian atemporalists with a significant challenge.

Fortunately for such atemporalists, however, a response to that challenge is not far to seek. For, apparently anticipating such concerns as those underlying [A], Eleonore Stump and Norman Kretzmann appeal to Jesus' dual nature to undergird their contention that God's being timeless is consistent with the Son's being incarnate. In a passage worth quoting in full, they state:

One of the explicitly intended consequences of the doctrine of the dual nature is that any statement predicating something of Christ is ambiguous unless it contains a phrase specifying one or the other or both of his two natures. That is, the proposition

(7) Christ died.

is ambiguous among these three readings:

(7)(a) Christ with respect to his divine nature (or *qua* God) died.
(7)(b) Christ with respect to his human nature (or *qua* man) died.
(7)(c) Christ with respect to his divine and human natures (or *qua* both God and man) died.

From the standpoint of orthodox Christianity (7)(a) and (7)(c) are false, and (7)(b) is true. (7)(b) is not to be interpreted as denying that God died, however—such a denial forms the basis of at least one Christian heresy—but to deny that God, the second person of the Trinity, died with respect to his divine nature. Such an account is loaded with at least apparent paradox, and it is not part of our purpose here even to sketch an analysis of it; but, whatever its internal difficulties may be, the doctrine of the dual nature provides *prima facie* grounds for denying the incompatibility of God's eternality and God's becoming man.[13]

Now, according to this line of thought, [A] needs to be reformulated to take account of Jesus' dual nature. So reformulated (and rechristened [A']), its first three premises go as follows.

(1') Jesus Christ qua man read in the synagogue before Jesus Christ qua man carried his cross.
(2') So temporal predicates apply to Jesus Christ qua man.
(3') Jesus Christ qua God = God the Son.[14]

But, as Senor states, "nothing interesting follows" from (2') and (3').[15] So, as he himself recognizes, such a defense of the prima facie compatibility of the two doctrines under consideration merits serious attention.

On Senor's view, however, such a defense fails. To see this, he invites us to consider John, "an American citizen and father of an infant."[16] Few would find either

(8) John qua American citizen has the duty to vote

or

(9) John qua father has the duty to change his child's diaper

difficult to understand. "Roughly," Senor tells us, "these statements mean that *in virtue of* John's having a certain property (being a citizen or being a father), he has a certain duty (to vote or to change a diaper)."[17] While Senor thinks that (8) and (9) are true, he also thinks that both

(10) John qua citizen has the duty to change his child's diaper

and

    (11) John qua father has the duty to vote

are false because it is not *in virtue of* being a citizen that John is obligated to change his child's diaper and it is not *in virtue of* being a father that John is obligated to vote. "Nevertheless," he claims, "it is important to see that 'John qua citizen has the duty to vote,' entails that 'John (*simpliciter*) has the duty to vote,' since if it is true that John, in virtue of being a citizen, has the duty to vote, then it is true that John has the duty to vote."[18] Given such considerations, Senor asks, "Why should we think that sentences predicating things of Christ are any different?"[19] In other words, if Jesus qua man is not timeless, why does it not follow that Jesus (*simpliciter*) is not timeless?

    Now, as far as I can see, Senor's interpretation of statements of the form "S qua P has D" simply is not plausible as an interpretation of the statements about Jesus relevant to the issue at hand. For, when one claims that

    (1') Jesus Christ qua man read in the synagogue before Jesus Christ qua man
          carried his cross,

one typically does not mean to be claiming that

    (1") Jesus Christ *in virtue of* being human read in the synagogue before Jesus
          Christ *in virtue of* being human carried his cross.

So, even if Senor shows that "S qua P has D" entails "S (*simpliciter*) has D" in cases where it ought to be read as "S has D *in virtue of* possessing P," this turns out to be irrelevant. For, however one interprets statements of the form "Jesus qua man has D," it seems that one ought not interpret them—or, more precisely, those of them to which Senor appeals—as "Jesus has D *in virtue of* being human."

    And, while this suffices to show the inadequacy of Senor's rejoinder to Stump and Kretzmann, much remains to be said on the matter. For there seem to be cases of "S qua P has D" which do not entail "S (*simpliciter*) has D" (or, at least, which do not entail "it is not the case that S (*simpliciter*) has ~D").[20] To see this, consider the Notre Dame football team, which, despite playing quite well defensively, played quite poorly offensively in its last game. Letting *t* be the period of time during which that game was played, it seems in such a case that both

    (12) The Fightin' Irish qua defensive team played well during *t*

and

    (13) The Fightin' Irish qua offensive team did not play well during *t*

are true. But what are we to infer from (12) and (13) concerning the Fightin' Irish (*simpliciter*)? Well, from (12), one might be tempted to infer that

(14) The Fightin' Irish (*simpliciter*) played well during *t*.

But, if one legitimately infers (14) from (12), why cannot one legitimately infer from (13) that

(15) The Fightin' Irish (*simpliciter*) did not play well during *t?*

And, *if* (i) (12) and (13) are consistent, (ii) (14) follows from (12), and (iii) (15) follows from (13), *then* one cannot infer from (14) that

(16) It is not the case that the Fightin' Irish (*simpliciter*) did not play well during *t*.

Of course, (12) and (13) certainly seem to be consistent. So it follows that *either* (14) and (15) do not follow from (12) and (13), respectively, *or* (14) does not entail that (15) is false (and vice versa).[21] So *either* some cases of "S qua P has D" do not entail "S (*simpliciter*) has D" or some cases of "S (*simpliciter*) has D" do not entail "it is not the case that S (*simpliciter*) has ~D" Thus, since Senor offers no reason for thinking that such cases do not include either "Jesus qua man has D" or "Jesus (*simpliciter*) has D," his rejoinder to Stump and Kretzmann fails.[22]

Of course, that his rejoinder to Stump and Kretzmann fails does not mean that the move they make in response to the concerns which underlie [A]—the move Senor calls the "qua-move"—succeeds. No doubt their defense would be bolstered by a positive account of how a timeless God could be incarnate. In the next section, I offer a suggestion intended to help make sense of the Incarnation of a timeless God. Before doing so, however, I first argue that, even if the qua-move fails, there remain compelling reasons to think [A] unsuccessful, and then respond to Senor's second argument against the consistency of the doctrines of divine timelessness and the Incarnation.

With respect to [A], it is important to notice that, whatever problems the Incarnation poses for atemporalists, it poses them for temporalists as well. For, as Brian Leftow suggests, reconciling God's timelessness with the Incarnation is no more difficult than reconciling God's omnipotence, omniscience, omnipresence, or spacelessness with the Incarnation.[23] So, for instance, one can envisage an argument for the incompatibility of the doctrines of divine omnipresence and the Incarnation which parallels [A]. Such an argument—which, for the sake of convenience, I shall refer to as [A*]—might go as follows.

(17) For some place *p*, Jesus Christ went to *p*.
(18) So, for some place *p* and time *t*, "Jesus is at *p*" is not true at *t*.
(19) Jesus Christ = God the Son.
(20) So, for some place *p* and time *t*, "God the Son is at *p*" is not true at *t*.
(21) For every person *S*, time *t*, and place *p*, if "*S* is omnipresent" is true at *t*, then "*S* is at *p*" is true at *t*.
(22) So, for some time *t*, "God the Son is omnipresent" is not true at *t*.

In support of (17), one could appeal to any of a number of biblical texts describing Christ's travels.[24] If *t* refers to a time just prior to Jesus' going to a place *p*, then from the assumption that one cannot go to a place where one already is it follows that Jesus is not at *p* at *t*. Statement (18) follows from this apparent fact. Statement (19) is (3) of [A]. If [A]'s (4) follows from its (2) and (3), then by parity of reasoning (20) surely follows from (18) and (19). I take (21) simply to be a conceptual truth, comparable to [A]'s (5).

To avoid the force of [A*], one might invoke the doctrine of divine spacelessness and argue that, strictly speaking, (21) is false because omnipresent beings are spaceless. But, of course, such a move will not work. For, as Senor himself acknowledges, one can formulate a similar argument for the incompatibility of the doctrines of divine spacelessness and the Incarnation. Here he offers the following, which he calls [A''], as an example of such an argument.

(23) Jesus Christ is in Nazareth and not in Jerusalem.
(24) So, local predicates apply to Jesus Christ.
(25) Jesus Christ = God the Son.
(26) So, local predicates apply to God the Son.
(27) Local predicates don't apply to spaceless beings.
(28) So, God the Son isn't spaceless.[25]

In responding to [A''], Senor concedes that in becoming incarnate the Son ceased to be spaceless. Moreover, he does so precisely because he thinks it inconsistent to maintain both that [A] succeeds and that [A''] fails. And, while I do not know how he would respond to [A*], it is difficult to see how one who accepts (21) could conclude that [A''] succeeds but [A*] fails. For this reason, it seems likely that Senor would respond to [A*] by conceding that in becoming incarnate the Son ceased to be omnipresent.

Now he seems to me to be correct about the connection between [A] and [A'']. It is difficult to see how one consistently could hold that the former but not the latter is persuasive. So also I find it difficult to see how one consistently could hold that [A] succeeds but [A*] fails. And, while Senor is correct about the connection between [A] and arguments such as [A''], his response to such arguments seems ill considered. To see this, consider the remarks of Athanasius of Alexandria, who writes:

> For [the Savior] was not, as might be imagined, circumscribed in the body, nor, while present in the body, was he absent elsewhere; nor, while he moved the body, was the universe left void of his working and providence; but, thing most marvelous, Word as he was, so far from being contained by anything, he rather contained all things himself; and just as while present in the whole of creation, he is at once distinct in being from the universe, and present in all things by his own power—giving order to all things, and over all and in all revealing his own providence, and giving life to each thing and all things, including the whole without being included, but being in his own Father alone wholly and in every respect—thus, even while present in a human body and himself quickening it, he was, without inconsistency, quickening the universe as well, and was in every process of nature, and was outside the whole, and while known from the body by his works, he was none the less manifest from the working of the universe as well.[26]

So, on Athanasius's view, in becoming incarnate, the Son did not cease to be omnipresent. And, as indicated above in the discussion of the Council of Chalcedon,

Athanasius is not alone in this regard. Indeed, at least since that council, Christian orthodoxy has maintained not only that Jesus Christ possesses two natures but also that
each of those natures retains its distinctive properties. Thus, on the apparently uncontroversial assumption that omnipresence is constitutive of deity, the claim that, in becoming incarnate, the Son ceases to be omnipresent departs from Christian orthodoxy.
So, even if the claim that the Incarnate Son is not spaceless can be countenanced, the
claim that he is not omnipresent cannot be. Or, at least, not by those who wish to remain within the parameters of Christian orthodoxy established at Chalcedon.[27]

Moreover, one can envisage arguments similar to [A*] being mustered for the incompatibility of the doctrine of the Incarnation with, say, the doctrines of divine omnipotence and divine omniscience. Thus, the problems which arise from the doctrine
of the Incarnation for atemporalists arise also for temporalists. Or, at least, so it seems.
In this case, however, atemporalists have no more reason to respond to [A] by abandoning God's timelessness than temporalists have to respond to arguments such as
[A*] and [A"] by abandoning God's omnipotence, omniscience, omnipresence, or
spacelessness. And, in light of the central role played by omnipotence, omniscience,
omnipresence, and spacelessness within the theistic tradition, it seems more reasonable for Christian theists to conclude that arguments such as [A*] and [A"] fail than to
abandon those divine attributes. But, if Christian temporalists can reasonably affirm
God's omnipotence, omniscience, omnipresence, and spacelessness despite such arguments, I see no reason for thinking that Christian atemporalists cannot reasonably
affirm the doctrine of divine timelessness despite arguments such as [A]. So, rather
than concluding with Senor that [A] succeeds, I think that atemporalists ought simply
to hold their ground and insist that it fails.

At the risk of overkill, I want to conclude this discussion of [A]—or, perhaps, of
Senor's defense of [A]—simply by considering the following arguments. Following
his interpretation of "S qua P has D," one can conclude from

(29) Jesus Christ qua man exists contingently

that

(30) Jesus Christ (*simpliciter*) exists contingently.

And, given (30), one can construct an argument similar to [A] as follows.

(30) Jesus Christ (*simpliciter*) exists contingently.
(31) Jesus Christ = God the Son.
(32) So, God the Son exists contingently.
(33) So, God the Son does not exist necessarily.

Now, given the parameters placed on Christian orthodoxy at Chalcedon, (33) is
clearly unacceptable. In fact, even if one disregards those parameters, (33) is not acceptable. For, if (33) is true, the Son turns out—whatever else one says about the Incarnation—not to be divine. This follows from the fact that, if God the Son exists contingently, it is necessarily true that, if he exists, he exists contingently. So, even if the

Son had never become incarnate, it would follow from Senor's defense of [A] that the Son does not exist necessarily (and, hence, is not divine). Or, at least, so it follows if (29) is true. And, given the traditional Christian belief that the Son could have refrained from becoming incarnate, it seems hard to quibble with (29). For this reason, *all* theists-or, at least, all *Christian* theists—ought to insist that [A] fails.

From biblical affirmations that the Son "became flesh" and "took on" the form of a servant,[28] Senor develops a second argument for the incompatibility of the doctrines of divine timelessness and the Incarnation. This argument, which he calls [B], goes as follows.

(34) God the Son eternally (and essentially) has His Divine nature.
(35) The human (accidental) nature of God the Son is assumed (or "taken on").
(36) X's assuming (or "taking on") a nature involves a change in X's intrinsic properties.
(37) So, the assumption of the human nature brings about a change in the intrinsic (though non-essential) properties of God the Son.
(38) So, the Son is mutable.
(39) Mutability entails temporal duration.
(40) So, the Son is not timeless.[29]

The Son's assuming a human nature requires his being temporal because assuming a nature requires changing and changing requires being temporal. Or, at least, so says [B]. Here the critical premise is (36). For, of course, changing *does* require being temporal. So, if the Son's assuming a human nature requires him to change, he is not timeless. Thus, if assuming a nature requires changing, it follows that the Son is not timeless.

But *does* assuming a nature require changing? Here Senor writes:

> Is there any such reading of what it is to 'take on' or 'assume' a nature (or anything else, for that matter) that is compatible with immutability? Typically, when one 'takes on' something (such as a new attitude or job), one brings it about that one has something which one previously lacked. That is to say, in run-of-the-mill cases, if a person 'takes on' X, she changes in at least one of her intrinsic properties. The question presently before us is whether one's taking on X entails that in virtue of assuming X, one has changed. It certainly sounds to my ear as if the entailment holds. I can't see how, if the Second Person of the Trinity is perfectly immutable (and atemporal), He could 'take on' anything. What He has, He has; what He has not, He has not.[30]

That the Son has whatever properties he has and lacks whatever properties he lacks is certainly beyond dispute. Even so, as far as I can see, this does not preclude the Son from having a nature accidental to himself. Of course, if by "S assumes a nature X" one just *means* "S at one time lacks X and then at a later time possesses X," no timeless being could assume a nature. I should think, however, that the traditional language about the Son's assuming a nature is intended not to make a claim about what is true at two different times *t* and *t** (namely, that at *t* the Son lacked a human nature but at *t** the Son possessed such a nature). Rather, such language is intended to emphasize the fact that, while the Son possesses a human nature, such a nature is accidental to him (and, perhaps, that he has it voluntarily).[31] So, in the sense of "assume" relevant to the

Incarnation, it seems that assuming a nature does not require changing. For it to be true that the Son assumes a nature, it is enough that he possess a nature accidental to himself. And, moreover, there seems to be no reason for thinking that a timeless being could not possess a nature accidental to itself.[32] So, pace Senor, that the Son assumes a human nature does not entail that the Son changes. Thus, like [A], [B] fails.

Timelessness and the Two-Minds Christology

As mentioned, the responses to [A] and [B] given there certainly would be strengthened by a positive account of how a timeless God could be incarnate. In what remains of this essay, I hope to suggest that atemporalists have available to them just such an account. As the title of this section implies, I have in mind here an account of the Incarnation known as the two-minds view. On that account, the Incarnation involves "a duality of consciousness or mentality . . . introduced into the divine life of God the Son."[33] In fleshing this out, Thomas Morris—perhaps the most eloquent of the two-minds view's recent advocates—states that

> in the case of God Incarnate we must recognize something like two distinct minds or systems of mentality. There is first what we can call the eternal mind of God the Son, with its distinctively divine consciousness, whatever that might be like, encompassing the full scope of omniscience, empowered by the resources of omnipotence, and present in power and knowledge throughout the entirety of creation. And in addition to this divine mind, there is the distinctly earthly mind with its consciousness that came into existence and developed with the human birth and growth of Christ's earthly form of existence.[34]

In becoming incarnate, then, God the Son assumed not only a human body but also a human mind. Moreover, the Incarnate Son's divine and human minds stand in what Morris describes as "an asymmetrical accessing relation" to one another so that, while the former enjoys complete access to the latter, the latter does not enjoy such access to the former.[35] Or, at least, so says the two-minds view.

So, while the Incarnate Son's divine mind is omniscient, it does not follow that his human mind—lacking, as it does, complete access to the contents of his divine mind—is also omniscient. And, insofar as it allows one to maintain that the Incarnate Son's divine mind is omniscient but his human mind is not, the two-minds view seems to me to allow one to make good sense of such pairs of claims as "Jesus qua man lacks knowledge" and "Jesus qua God lacks no knowledge." Moreover, on such a view, it appears to make perfectly good sense to say *both* that Jesus qua man lacks knowledge *and* that Jesus (*simpliciter*) lacks no knowledge. But, as things go here for omniscience, so they go for other divine attributes such as omnipotence, omnipresence, and spacelessness. What is more, insofar as its advocates can maintain plausibly that the Incarnate Son's human mind has genuine limitations, such a view also has the obvious advantage of allowing them to treat the biblical narratives of Jesus' life straightforwardly. When such Incarnational narratives seem to indicate that he either developed intellectually or experienced real limitations, advocates of the two-minds view can take such passages at face value and maintain that Jesus in fact did develop intellectually or experience limitations. And, as Morris indicates, this alone gives us significant reason to take such a view seriously.

Here one might object that, since the kenotic view also allows its advocates to take the Incarnational narratives straightforwardly, the fact that the two-minds view allows this does not warrant preferring it over the kenotic view.[36] Of course, even if this were true, it nonetheless might be that other reasons exist for preferring the two-minds view over the kenotic view. But it certainly is not obvious that, with respect to taking the Incarnational narratives seriously, the two views are on equal footing. For, by stipulating that in becoming incarnate God the Son gives up, say, omniscience, the kenotic view appears to violate the parameters of orthodoxy set at Chalcedon. And, while advocates of such a view might be able to avoid this unwelcome consequence by stipulating that, rather than *being omniscient*, the divine nature includes some such property as *being omniscient unless giving it up*, such a maneuver seems unsatisfying at best and ad hoc at worst. Still, since my purpose in this section is to suggest both that the two-minds view merits serious consideration and that, with the help of such a view, Christian atemporalists can account for the Incarnation of a timeless God, I shall put aside questions about the adequacy of the kenotic view.

Whatever the virtues (or vices) of the kenotic view, the two-minds view fits well with two other claims to which the Christian tradition seems to commit its adherents. First, according to the Definition of the Faith affirmed at Chalcedon, Jesus possesses a "rational soul."[37] I take this affirmation to commit the council to the view that Jesus possesses a human soul. Indeed, since the Definition clearly affirms that he is fully human, it follows from it and the assumption that being fully human involves possessing a distinctively human soul that Jesus possesses such a soul. Second, according to the Council of Constantinople, Jesus possesses two wills—one divine, one human.[38] That Jesus possesses both a human soul and a human will implies that he possesses in addition to a divine mind a distinctively human mind. Of course, it is hard to resist the temptation to infer from this that Christian orthodoxy demands the two-minds view. Hard, but not impossible. For one might maintain that a human mind is simply a mind which attains at least a certain minimum level of excellence and happens to be embodied in a human body. In such a case, one could maintain that, once it becomes embodied in a human body, the divine mind of the Son *becomes* a human mind. Thus, one could maintain that, while Jesus has both a divine and a human mind, those minds are not numerically distinct. Such a position might suggest itself to those Christians who think that minds individuate persons and thus that, if Jesus is one person with two natures, he must have one mind with two natures. Still, since I believe neither that minds individuate persons nor that this sort of position is as much in keeping with the spirit of Chalcedon as is the two-minds view, I find it less plausible than that view. So, given that the two-minds view of the Incarnation seems to me to comport extraordinarily well with Christian orthodoxy, I conclude that it deserves serious consideration.

In addition to those advantages in virtue of which it deserves such consideration, the two-minds view seems to provide its advocates with at least a rudimentary account of how a timeless being could be incarnate. For, given such a view, one could claim that Jesus' divine mind is timeless but that his human mind is temporal. Such a claim puts flesh on the bones of the claim of Stump, Kretzmann, and other atemporalists that, while Jesus qua man is temporal, Jesus qua God is timeless. So, just as one can employ the two-minds view to defend the claim that the Son's being incarnate need not preclude his being omniscient (or omnipotent, or omnipresent), one also can employ it to defend the claim that his being incarnate need not preclude his being timeless. Thus, at least on the face of it, the two-minds view provides atemporalists with resources sufficient for responding plausibly to the objection to divine timelessness which arises from the Incarnation.

Notes

For helpful comments on earlier versions of this essay, I am indebted to D. Jeffrey Bingham, Thomas P. Flint, Gregory Ganssle, James Leo Garrett, George Klein, and Glenn Kreider.

1. By "doctrine of divine timelessness," I mean that doctrine according to which

(DT) For every time *t*, while *God exists* is true at *t*, it is not the case that God exists at *t*,

where "God" is taken to be a title-phrase referring to the greatest possible being. (Those familiar with Nelson Pike's *God and Timelessness* [New York: Schocken, 1970] will recognize the notion of a title-phrase as having been borrowed from the second chapter of that work.) I shall refer to those theists who endorse the doctrine of divine timelessness as "atemporalists" and to those who deny it as "temporalists." Elsewhere I argue for a more complicated account of the central atemporalist claim, but (DT) is sufficient for my purposes here. For that more complicated account, see my "An Essay on Divine Presence" (Ph.D. diss., University of Notre Dame, 1997), 59–75; for a detailed discussion of the more prominent objections to the doctrine of divine timelessness which appear in the recent literature on God and time, including the objection from its alleged religious inadequacy, see ibid., 81–172.

2. Here I assume that Christian orthodoxy itself is consistent so that, in affirming it, one is not thereby contradicting oneself. Of course, if it were *not* consistent, neither the atemporalist nor temporalist could consistently affirm *both* her position *and* Christian orthodoxy (though this would not count against her position).

3. Perhaps the only other doctrine which can challenge it in this regard is that of the Trinity.

4. Thomas V. Morris, *The Logic of God Incarnate* (Ithaca: Cornell University Press, 1986), 13.

5. For the Definition of the Faith affirmed by the Council of Chalcedon, see Richard A. Norris Jr., ed. and tr., *The Christological Controversy* (Philadelphia: Fortress Press, 1980), 155–59; for the Greek text of the most significant paragraph of that affirmation, see the Symbol of Chalcedon in Philip Schaff, ed., *The Creeds of Christendom*, vol. 2, *The Greek and Latin Creeds*, 6th ed. (rpt. Grand Rapids,: Baker Book House, 1990), 62–63. My own understanding of the Council of Chalcedon and the controversy which led to it has been informed significantly by J. N. D. Kelly, *Early Christian Doctrines* (New York: Harper and Row, 1960), 280–343, as well as G. W. H. Lampe, "Christian Theology in the Patristic Period," in *A History of Christian Doctrine*, ed. Hubert Cunliffe-Jones (Philadelphia: Fortress Press, 1978), 121–48. I also am indebted to D. Jeffrey Bingham for helpful discussion of the Chalcedonian Definition.

6. Kelly, *Early Christian Doctrines*, 341 (emphases added).

7. Pike, *God and Timelessness*, 172.

8. Cf. ibid.: "As a man, of course, God had both temporal extension and temporal location."

9. Ibid., 173.

10. Here, and in what follows, "=" stands for "is identical to." So "Jesus Christ = God the Son" should be read as "Jesus Christ is identical to God the Son."

11. Thomas D. Senor, "Incarnation and Timelessness," *Faith and Philosophy* 7 (1990), 150. My (1), (2), (3), (4), (5), and (6) are (P1), (C1), (P2), (C2), (P3), and (C3), respectively, of [A].

12. Ibid., 151. In a note, Senor acknowledges that, as it stands, (5) is less than perspicuous. So, for the sake of clarity and precision, he suggests that it be understood as the claim that "no positive, strictly temporal predicates apply to timeless beings" (162).

13. Eleonore Stump and Norman Kretzmann, "Eternity," in *The Concept of God*, ed. Thomas V. Morris, (New York: Oxford University Press, 1987), 245–46. My (7), (7)(a), (7)(b), and (7)(c) are their (14), (14)(a), (14)(b), and (14)(c), respectively.

14. Senor, "Incarnation and Timelessness," 152. My (1'), (2'), and (3') are (P1), (C1), and (P2), respectively, of [A'].

15. Ibid.

16. Ibid.

17. Ibid., 152–53.

18. Ibid., 153.

19. Ibid.

20. Here ~D refers to the complement of D.

21. Since I take it as obvious that there are no non-arbitrary grounds for claiming that, while (12) entails (14), (13) fails to entail (15) (or vice versa), I regard as untenable a response which involves such a claim.

22. I have not shown—and have not *attempted* to show—that cases of "S qua P has D" (or "S (*simpliciter*) has D") in which "Jesus" replaces "S" resemble those in which "the Fightin' Irish" replaces it. Does this undermine my claim to have shown that Senor's rejoinder to Stump and Kretzmann fails? (I am indebted to Gregory Ganssle for raising this question.) Well, in making that rejoinder, Senor argues that "Jesus qua man has D" entails "Jesus (*simpliciter*) has D." His argument amounts to pointing out that some cases of "S qua P has D" entail "S (*simpliciter*) has D." (As seen above, the case on which this argument relies is "John qua citizen has a duty to vote.") Now it seems that either (12) and (13) are cases of "S qua P has D" which do not entail "S (*simpliciter*) has D" or (14) and (15) are cases of "S (*simpliciter*) has D" which do *not* entail "it is not the case that S (*simpliciter*) has ~D." So, even if some cases of "S qua P has D" entail "S (*simpliciter*) has D" and some cases of "S (*simpliciter*) has D" entail "it is not the case that S (*simpliciter*) has ~D," not all such cases have such entailments. In order for Senor's rejoinder to succeed, then, he must show not only that some cases of "S qua P has D" entail "S (*simpliciter*) has D" but also that such cases include those in which "Jesus" replaces "S" and that "Jesus (*simpliciter*) has D" entails "it is not the case that Jesus (*simpliciter*) has ~D." But, as far as I can see, he fails to show either of these things. Hence, I conclude that his rejoinder to Stump and Kretzmann fails.

23. Brian Leftow, *Time and Eternity* (Ithaca: Cornell University Press, 1991), 19.

24. For a particular text, I suggest, say, John 4:3: "he left Judea and started back to Galilee" (NRSV).

25. Senor, "Incarnation and Timelessness," 155. My (23), (24), (25), (26), (27), and (28) are (P1), (C1), (P2), (C2), (P3), and (C3), respectively, of [A''].

26. Athanasius, "On the Incarnation of the Word," tr. Archibald Robertson, in *Christology of the Later Fathers*, ed. Edward R. Hardy (Philadelphia: Westminster Press, 1954), 70–71. Immediately following the passage quoted above, Athanasius contrasts the Incarnate Son with other men, who are bound to their bodies: "Now, the Word of God in his man's nature was not like that; for he was not bound to his body, but was rather himself wielding it, so that he was not only in it, but was actually in everything, and while external to the universe, abode in his Father only. And this was the wonderful thing that he was at once walking as man, and as the Word was quickening all things, and as the Son was dwelling with his Father."

27. But why wish to remain within those parameters? If Christian orthodoxy insists that the Incarnate Son is omnipresent, why not simply reject such orthodoxy? Since such questions deserve more attention than I can give them here, I shall content myself with noting that there *do* seem to me to be compelling reasons for wishing to remain within the parameters of Christian orthodoxy. Still, regardless of whether one agrees with me on this, Senor cannot save [A] by abandoning such orthodoxy. For not only does his defense of (3)—which, of course, plays a crucial role in [A]—amount simply to pointing out that one who denied it "would no longer be orthodox" (Senor, "Incarnation and Timelessness," 151), but he takes the upshot of [A] to be that one cannot be *both* an atemporalist *and* an orthodox Christian: "I therefore conclude that if one is committed to an orthodox Christology, one shall have to reject . . . the doctrine of timelessness" (161). Obviously, one who defends [A] by rejecting Christian orthodoxy cannot legitimately conclude that [A] shows the doctrine of divine timelessness to be inconsistent with such orthodoxy.

28. Cf. John 1:14, Philippians 2:5–7.

29. Senor, "Incarnation and Timelessness," 157. My (34), (35), (36), (37), (38), (39), and (40) are (P1), (P2), (P3), (C1), (C2), (P4), and (C3), respectively, of [B].

30. Ibid., 158–59.

31. Perhaps one's assuming a nature entails not only one's possessing a nature accidental to oneself but also one's possessing such a nature voluntarily. Since, so far as I can see, such a complication has no bearing on the issue at hand, I shall not pursue the matter.

32. Cf. Stump and Kretzmann, "Eternity," 246: "The divine nature of the second person of the Trinity, like the divine nature of either of the other persons of the Trinity, cannot become temporal; nor could the second person at some time acquire a human nature he does not eternally have. Instead, the second person eternally has two natures."

33. Thomas V. Morris, "The Metaphysics of God Incarnate," in *Trinity, Incarnation, and Atonement: Philosophical and Theological Essays*, ed. Ronald J. Feenstra and Cornelius Plantinga Jr. (Notre Dame: University of Notre Dame Press, 1989), 121. See also Morris, *The Logic of God Incarnate*, 102–7. In conversation, Morris has indicated that he thinks that his view of the Incarnation *is* consistent with the doctrine of divine timelessness.

34. Morris, "The Metaphysics of God Incarnate," 121.

35. Cf. ibid., 121–22: "the human mind [of Christ] was contained by but did not itself contain the divine mind, or, to portray it from the other side, the divine mind contained, but was not contained by, the human mind." While Morris takes the claim that the Incarnate Son's divine and human minds stand in an asymmetrical accessing relation to one another to be a necessary feature of the two-minds account of the Incarnation, he explicitly denies that such a claim suffices for such an account. Cf. 125–27.

36. By "kenotic view," I mean the view of the Incarnation according to which, in becoming incarnate, God the Son gave up (or "emptied himself" of) certain divine attributes. For an interesting defense of the kenotic view which responds to Morris, see Ronald J. Feenstra, "Reconsidering Kenotic Christology," in 33 Feenstra and Plantinga, *Trinity, Incarnation, and Atonement*, 128–52.

37. See Norris, *The Christological Controversy*, 159.

38. For background on the controversy which led to the Council of Constantinople, see Lampe, "Christian Theology in the Patristic Period," 141–46.

Index